D1751554

Employment Policy in Transition

Springer
*Berlin
Heidelberg
New York
Barcelona
Hong Kong
London
Milan
Paris
Singapore
Tokyo*

Regina T. Riphahn · Dennis J. Snower
Klaus F. Zimmermann (Editors)

Employment Policy in Transition

The Lessons of German Integration
for the Labor Market

With 32 Figures

Springer

Priv.-Doz. Regina T. Riphahn, Ph.D.
University of Munich
Ludwigstraße 28 RG
80539 Munich
Germany
E-mail: regina.riphahn@selapo.vwl.uni-muenchen.de

Professor Dennis J. Snower
Department of Economics
Birkbeck College
University of London
7–15 Gresse Street
London W1P 2LL
United Kingdom
E-mail: dsnower@economics.bbk.ac.uk

Professor Dr. Klaus F. Zimmermann
Institute for the Study of Labor (IZA)
Schaumburg-Lippe-Straße 7–9
53113 Bonn
Germany
E-mail: zimmermann@iza.org

ISBN 3-540-41166-6 Springer-Verlag Berlin Heidelberg New York

Cataloging-in-Publication Data applied for
Die Deutsche Bibliothek – CIP-Einheitsaufnahme
Employment Policy in Transition. The Lessons of German Integration for the Labor Market / Riphahn, Regina T.; Snower, Dennis J.; Zimmermann, Klaus F. (eds.). – Berlin; Heidelberg; New York; Barcelona; Hong Kong; London; Milan; Paris; Singapore; Tokyo: Springer, 2001
ISBN 3-540-41166-6

This work is subject to copyright. All rights are reserved, whether the whole or part of the material is concerned, specifically the rights of translation, reprinting, reuse of illustrations, recitation, broadcasting, reproduction on microfilm or in any other way, and storage in data banks. Duplication of this publication or parts thereof is permitted only under the provisions of the German Copyright Law of September 9, 1965, in its current version, and permission for use must always be obtained from Springer-Verlag. Violations are liable for prosecution under the German Copyright Law.

Springer-Verlag Berlin Heidelberg New York
a member of BertelsmannSpringer Science+Business Media GmbH

© Springer-Verlag Berlin · Heidelberg 2001
Printed in Germany

The use of general descriptive names, registered names, trademarks, etc. in this publication does not imply, even in the absence of a specific statement, that such names are exempt from the relevant protective laws and regulations and therefore free for general use.

Hardcover-Design: Erich Kirchner, Heidelberg

SPIN 10733689   42/2202-5 4 3 2 1 0 – Printed on acid-free paper

Table of contents

Employment Policy in Transition: The Lessons of German Integration for the Labor Market 1

    1. REGINA T. RIPHAHN – DENNIS J. SNOWER – KLAUS F. ZIMMERMANN
       Introduction 1

    2. HOLGER BONIN – KLAUS F. ZIMMERMANN
       The Post-Unification German Labor Market 8

I. Analysis of the German Labor Market Problem 31

    1. MICHAEL BURDA – MICHAEL FUNKE
       Wages and Structural Adjustment in the New German States 31

    2. KARL-HEINZ PAQUÉ
       East/West-Wage Rigidity in United Germany 52

    3. AXEL H. BÖRSCH-SUPAN – PETER SCHMIDT
       Early Retirement in East and West Germany 83

    4. THOMAS HINZ – ROLF ZIEGLER
       Employment Effects of Newly Founded Businesses in East Germany 103

    5. JOHANNES SCHWARZE – GERT G. WAGNER
       Earning Dynamics in the East German Transition Process 125

II. Policy Options 140

    1. DAVID BEGG – RICHARD PORTES
       Eastern Germany Since Unification: Wage Subsidies Remain a Better Way 140

    2. HENNING KLODT
       Economic Efficiency and Social Acceptance of Wage Subsidies 154

    3. DENNIS J. SNOWER
       Revenue-Sharing Subsidies as Employment Policy: Reducing the Cost of Stimulating East German Employment 172

4. GERHARD ILLING
   Investment Wages and Capital Market Imperfections 192

5. MARTIN EICHLER – MICHAEL LECHNER
   Public Sector Sponsored Continuous Vocational Training in East
   Germany: Institutional Arrangements, Participants, and Results of
   Empirical Evaluations 208

6. HARTMUT LEHMANN
   Active Labor Market Policies in Central Europe:
   First Lessons 254

Indices

1. Authors Index 294
2. Subject Index 300

Employment Policy in Transition: The Lessons of German Integration for the Labor Market

1. Introduction

Regina T. Riphahn, University of Munich; IZA, Bonn, and CEPR, London

Dennis J. Snower, Birkbeck College, London; IZA, Bonn, and CEPR, London

Klaus F. Zimmermann, Bonn University; IZA, Bonn; DIW, Berlin, and CEPR, London

The Gift of the Century

The unification of Germany has been described as "the gift of the century." Dramatic political developments in the former Soviet Union and the disintegration of the Communist economic bloc provided Germans with a historic opportunity to reunite. The opportunity arrived so suddenly and unexpectedly that, to many Germans at the time, it seemed like a colossal, unaccountable gift.

So far, this gift has cost the German government far more than DM 1 trillion, and ten years after the unification we're still counting. For West Germans, this bill has meant higher taxes and higher interest rates, as well as years of economic dislocation. It has been estimated that the transfers from West to East Germany amount to a massive 5% of West German GDP. For East Germans, the cost has been high unemployment, financial collapse of many enterprises, lagging productivity and ongoing economic dependency. At the time of writing, unemployment in East Germany lies at around 19%, more than twice the rate in West Germany. If one looks beyond the official statistics and includes the people who have had to retire, who work less than they would like, and participate in job creation and training schemes, the East German unemployment rate may easily be three times as high as the West German one.

German unification has, in short, turned out to be a far more costly and lengthy process than most Germans had expected. The importance of this transition experience extends far beyond Germany's borders. There is a widespread perception that East Germany faced particularly favourable conditions in moving from communism to capitalism. Other economies undergoing such change – in Europe, Asia, and Africa – have not had the good fortune of massive financial support from a major industrial power. Thus, some have argued that if the German transition process turns out to be long and difficult, then the other transition economies are likely to face far greater problems. If the East Germans are discouraged by their lagging productivity and deficient employment opportunities, their counterparts elsewhere are likely to remain far more discouraged. On the other hand, other commentators have maintained, that the massive financial support from West Germany, far from easing the transition process, actually lengthened and complicated it. The best way of embracing capitalism, on this line of argument, is for people to be thrown back on their own resources and left free to swim or sink in the free market system.

On this account, the analysis of the German employment experience is not just of interest in its own right. It may also shed light on the opportunities and dangers inherent in labor market transitions elsewhere, and may indicate how the strengths and weaknesses of German employment policies could be used to formulate guidelines for the transformation of other economies.

What Has Gone Wrong?

The disenchantment with the transition process is palpable throughout Germany, in both the West and East. What has gone wrong? There are two particularly popular answers to this question – and both, we shall argue, are at least partially misguided.

The first is that the gargantuan cost of German unification is the inevitable by-product of the German insistence on economic equality. The demand for equality is part of the German constitution. Article 106 of the Basic Law requires that "uniformity of living standards in the federal territory be ensured." Given this objective, unification had to raise living standards in East Germany to West German levels within a short span of time. Understandably, however, it was impossible to raise average productivity in East Germany to the West German standard within an equally short period. The rebuilding of the Eastern infrastructure, the wholesale relocation of employees to productive pursuits, and the transformation of legal, administrative, and economic institutions – all these invariably take time. Thus, in the process of transition, wages in East Germany had to exceed productivity, and unproductive people had to be re-educated, retrained, or retired. Such a process is unavoidably costly.

The alternative to this costly but incredible transition, it is alleged, is the "American model" of wage flexibility, large disparities in income, relatively low transfers, and few social safety nets. This model yields low unemployment, but at the expense of job insecurity and economic inequality. However this model is unacceptable to the vast majority of Germans. According to this view, policy makers need to choose between equity and efficiency, between unemployment and working poverty, between equality and productivity. There is a trade-off between these pairs of goals and – so the story goes – Germany has chosen its preferred position on this trade-off.

The second answer to "What has gone wrong?" is "Nothing much." According to this view, the economic turn-around – the *Wende* of 1989-90 – was the beginning of a massive readjustment in which extraordinary achievements have taken place within a remarkably short period of time. The starting point of the reassessment process, it will be recalled, was extremely unfavourable. The stock of physical capital inherited from the GDR was largely worn out and obsolete. The *Treuhandanstalt* – the trust body that privatised and sold the GDR state assets – witnessed the total collapse of their value, from an initial conservative estimate of DM 600 billion to a negative value of about DM 200 billion. Furthermore, the GDR's links to the other Eastern block markets became worthless as well, since these markets vanished with the collapse of communism.

A decade has passed since the Berlin Wall came down, but the economic landscape in East Germany has been utterly transformed. West German laws of crime, property, and contract cover the entire nation, and the systems of national administration are functioning smoothly. Inefficient state enterprises of the former GDR have been broken up, sold off, and privatised. Massive in-vestment in the infrastructure of the new Lander has taken place – housing has been revitalised, road systems built, telecommunication networks erected, and so on. The growth rate of the unified Germany is now that inside the range typical of mature industrialised economies. This economic progress has been attained without creating large economic inequalities. East German living standards have risen dramatically since the communist days.

In this light, the German economic miracle lives on. To have expected more within the available time, the argument runs, is manifestly unrealistic.

The Approach of this Book

This book takes issue with both of these positions. While it agrees with the second approach that the unification process has brought about a broad array of impressive achievements, it denies that little more could have been done. On the contrary, its broad message is that - regardless of the progress that has been made in raising living standards, rebuilding infrastructure, and reorganising business enterprise – the transition process has been a dismal failure in the labor market. In particular, the transition has failed to promote employment, sustain active labor force participation, and suppress unemployment. Our general thesis is that these deficiencies are not the inevitable outcome of equalizing wages in the face of unequal productivities. Rather, the deficiencies are the outcome of policies that have amplified, instead of reduced, labor market inefficiencies, and that have redistributed incomes in an unnecessarily wasteful way.

While it agrees with the first approach that economic equality is a legitimate objective for the transition process, it denies that the only feasible alternative is what we have dubbed the "American model." We maintain that it is wrong to think that policy makers are confronted by an immovable trade-off between equity and efficiency, and that the "American model" emphasizes efficiency while the German one concentrates on equity. Instead we argue that there exist a variety of policy options that shift this trade-off. In fact, policies that promote efficiency in the labor market transition process frequently promote equity at the same time, and vice versa.

The reason is that inefficient policies often increase unemployment and reduce labor force participation They thereby create important inequalities in the labor market – the inequality between those who have the opportunity to work and those who don't, those who can improve their living standards through their own efforts and those who cannot. These inequalities give rise to a sense of helplessness and dependency which needlessly prolongs the transition process. As long as unemployment in East Germany remains substantially higher than in West Germany, and as long as people in the East have fewer incentives to acquire skills and to become so productive than their counterparts in the West, there will be a need for the West to subsidize the East. As long as these disparities continue, Germany will remain mired in a costly transition process. The only way to find the light at the end of the tunnel is to adopt employment policies that equalize incomes by equalizing people's employment opportunities and their productivities. This is the approach pursued in this book.

Specifically, the book has two aims: (i) it seeks to provide an analysis of the strengths and weaknesses of the German labor market in transition, and (ii) on that basis, to examine a wide range of policies that could have made the transition process less painful. This analysis is meant to be much more than a *post mortem*. As the still high unemployment rates and low productivity rates in East Germany indicate, the German labor market transition is far from over after ten years of unification. How long it will last, and how costly it will be, depends significantly on what employment policies will be implemented. This book is meant to provide some guidance on the available policy options and their likely effectiveness.

The book accepts the objectives of German economic policy – particularly those concerning the equalization of living standards – predetermined, and inquires whether these objectives could be met more effectively than they have been thus far. The book also takes the political and historic setting for granted. We do not question the terms on which German unification took place. We note that currency union at a 1:1 exchange rate, together with West German unions' ability to establish substantial wage equalization between East and West, made many East German employees unprofitable. On this account, millions of East Germans lost their jobs. Furthermore, we note that the productivity differential between East and West continues. All this we take as given. And on this basis, we inquire how to achieve the predetermined policy objectives in an effective manner.

For this purpose we analyse the existing market failures in the German labor market and identify employment policies that are designed to overcome these failures. We consider a wide variety of promising policies – wage subsidies, qualifications vouchers, revenue-sharing subsidies, investment wages, benefit transfers, pension reform, wage flexibility, infrastructure investment, training schemes, and more – and we examine the strengths and weakness of each. The resulting picture is meant to provide an overview of the available policy portfolio and a discussion of the issue guiding the resulting policy choices.

Organisation of the Book

The book is organised as follows. A first chapter by Bonin and Zimmermann studies the labor market development in East Germany in the decade after unification. The large increase in unemployment has been moderated by substantial active labor market policies. However, most of these measures have had no substantial impact on re-employment. Due to hidden unemployment, actual unemployment has been 40 percent higher than registered unemployment even in 1999. The employment structure has not yet adjusted to the West, especially the service sector is less developed. However, the importance of too high union wages has been overevaluated. Effective wages are much closer to productivity than union wages. Eastern effective wages are 75% of the Western level, while productivity in the East is 60% of the Western level in 1997. It is not so much the wage level, but the slow adjustment of employment structure, infrastructure and investment that is responsible for the employment crisis. The crisis, however, is also a consequence of institutional constraints: measured total hours worked divided by the number of persons available to the labor market is not much different in Eastern Germany than in the West.

After this round-up, the first part of the book looks at the dimensions of the East German labor market problem in greater detail. First, Burda and Funke evaluate the impacts of the wage explosion in East Germany in the first period after unification on structural change and the accumulation of human capital. One conclusion is that the permanent increase in wages devaluated the value of capital and thus was followed by a period of low investment and declining employment. Burda and Funke also show that the high wage strategy could be insufficient to induce enough investment in human capital to be self-sustainable. In the long-term, the wage explosion may not only cause high unemployment, but also leave a poorly skilled labor force in the east. In his contribution, Paqué analyses what caused the attempts at rapid wage equalization between East and West Germany. It is maintained that there were no substantial normative reasons to argue in favour of wage equalization. It seems that the main driving force of the collective bargaining behaviour has been the union philosophy of 'equal pay for equal work', that is deep-rooted in Germany and was soon applied even under the somewhat extreme circumstances of unification. The work of Börsch-Supan and Schmidt uses an option value model to analyze the early retirement patterns in East and West Germany past unification. Retirement behaviour is influenced by strong incentives to early retirement set by the pension system. Strikingly, conditional on the different incentives in the two parts of the two regions, the response to these incentives has been very similar in East and West Germany. The creation of new firms represents an important aspect of the economic restructuring in East Germany. The chapter by Hinz and Ziegler investigates the employment dynamics of firms newly established under the conditions of economic transformation. They show that the job growth in newly created enterprises was not enough to compensate for the job destruction in privatised former state firms. Firms with access to the capital market fared remarkably better than firms without, and the occupational history of founders strongly affected entrepreneurial success. Thus, it seems, that the human capital acquired in the GDR was not totally devaluated under the conditions of the market economy. The final chapter in the first part again takes a closer look at the earnings dynamics in the transition process. Schwarze and Wagner estimate to what degree the wage structure in East Germany has become responsive to the qualification of employees. They observe that wage differentiation has been used by employers reallocating workers in the now market-oriented economy. As earnings reacted more dynamically in newly established firms who mostly employ younger workers, this generally positive development has had problematic social implications for older workers.

The second part of the book deals with the policy options which could be implemented given the labor market problems in East Germany. First, Begg and Portes advocate the adoption of a universal, temporary wage subsidy in Eastern Germany. Since significant productivity differentials between east and west are in existence even now, the case for wage subsidies remains compelling. Klodt agrees that wage subsidies instead of investment subsidies would have been the better way for solving the East German unemployment problem. It seems that the main driving force for not introducing wage subsidization schemes has been their low social acceptance. Snower takes a somewhat different view in favouring revenue- or profit-sharing subsidies over wage subsidies. One advantage of such a system could be the significant lower social and budgetary costs associated with these subsidies, since wage subsidies are associated with higher wages and revenue- or profit-sharing subsidies are not. In the next chapter, Illing favours a combination of a switch to investment wages at the time of privatization and government subsidies. If a wage cut is not feasible, this proposal could be a way both to introduce more flexibility in the labor market and to let Eastern workers take part in the rents of the firms.

The chapter by Eichler und Lechner investigates the effects of subsidised training courses on labor market outcome, such as earnings, employment status and career prospects in Germany. Their general finding is that no positive effects of training courses could be observed, although some evidence suggests that over a longer time horizon positive returns to training measures might exist. In the final chapter in the second part of the book, Lehmann looks at the effects of active labor market policy in the economies of Central and Eastern Europe by giving an extensive overview over the institutional rules and regulations as well as over the major empirical findings regarding the effects of active labor market policies. The author emphasises the role of such policies especially in transition economies since core groups of the labor force are affected by unemployment and, therefore, such policies may play a special role.

August 2000

2. The Post-Unification German Labor Market

Holger Bonin, IZA, Bonn

Klaus F. Zimmermann, Bonn University; IZA, Bonn; DIW, Berlin, and CEPR, London

1. Introduction

Even a decade after the unification of the two German states, Germany is struggling with the integration of the former eastern command economy into the West German social market-led economy. As the economic catching up process slowed down in recent years, expectations that the economic transformation could be completed fast and smoothly, fuelled by many political leaders, were disproved as overly optimistic. Instead, the impression is rising that it will still take a considerable amount of time until the East German states will become the flourishing landscapes (*blühende Landschaften*) once promised by the former German chancellor Helmut Kohl.

The Economic, Monetary and Social Union between East and West Germany, which was established on July 1, 1990, uncovered the structural weaknesses of the run-down East German economy. The sudden exposure to competition from West Germany and from abroad, together with a breakdown of traditional export markets, destroyed the economic viability of large parts of the East German capital stock and caused an unprecedented increase in effective unemployment. Immediately after unification, a complete collapse of productivity and employment in East Germany was avoided only with substantial financial transfers from the West.

The deep recession during the first year after the economic union was succeeded by a period of continuous economic growth, which started, however, from a very low level of economic activity. In 1991, GDP per capita in East Germany amounted to less than one third of the western level. Restructuring and privatization of the East German economy, which were fostered through massive investment incentives, and the renewal of public infrastructure initially supported rapid economic expansion. Until 1994, annual growth rates in East Germany reached up to 10 percent.

Since then, economic progress has turned much less substantial. In recent years, annual growth merely ranged between 2 and 3 percent. The catching up of the eastern economy, it seems, has come almost to a standstill. Although the eastern capital stock improved significantly, productivity has not reached up to two thirds of the western level. Private absorption, which is financed through public transfers to a large extent, continues to exceed domestic product by about one third, imposing sizeable pressure on government budgets.

One of the most striking features of the eastern economy after ten years of unification is the persistence of very high levels of unemployment. The restructuring and modernization of the East German command economy had a dramatic impact on employment and labor utilization. Since unification, the number of regularly employed in East Germany declined by almost 40 percent. By the end of 1999, registered unemployment was still exceeding 19 percent of the labor force, compared to a rate of less than 10 percent in the West German states. Considered the rather poor recent performance of the eastern economy, a significant employment upswing seems unlikely in the medium-term future.

The issues to be discussed are what caused the emergence and persistence of unemployment in East Germany, and whether there are promising policy instruments to reduce what appears to many as an intolerably high number of displaced workers. This paper contributes to these issues by monitoring the development of the East German labor market after unification. Section 2 summarizes the main trends in both unemployment and employment in East Germany during the past decade, and describes how labor market policy responded to emerging unemployment. Section 3 surveys the available evidence regarding the success of active labor market policies. Section 4 explores to what extent the adjustment process in the East to West German standards is completed. To conclude, Section 5 debates whether labor market convergence is really an adequate goal for East Germany.

2. The East German Labor Market Since Unification

The process of transforming the eastern command economy necessarily affected the level of employment negatively. The artificial full employment policy of the GDR that gave a constitutional right to work and employment made state-owned companies and public administration overstaffed, compared to western standards. The monetary union at parity forced the eastern economy into competition with the world market at a high real exchange rate, which according to one early estimate (Akerlof et al. (1991)) left only 8 percent of the East German workforce employed in enterprises whose revenue was able to cover operating costs.

Due to the serious shortage of economically viable jobs, unemployment in East Germany increased sharply in the first two years after unification. The number of registered unemployed was rising from 83 thousand in the second quarter of 1990 to almost 1.2 million persons in 1992. As is displayed in Figure 1, the official unemployment rate (based on the civil dependent labor force), reporting 1.1 percent before economic unification, soon approached 15 percent.

Figure 1 Official German Unemployment Rates, Period 1991 - 1999

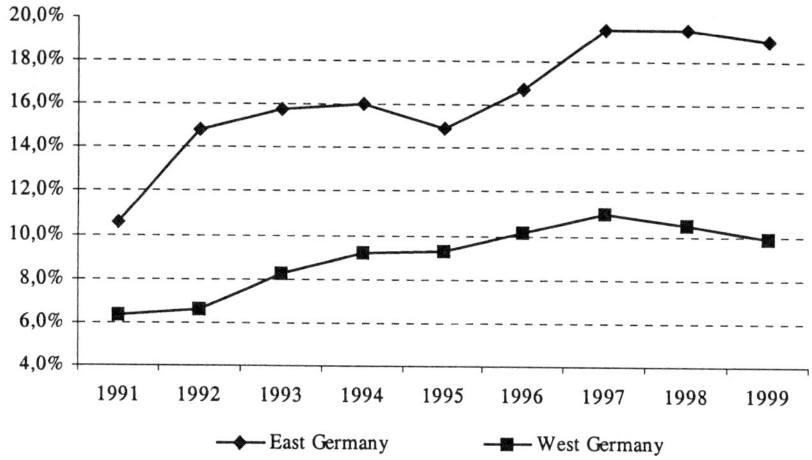

Source: *Amtliche Nachrichten der Bundesanstalt für Arbeit,* various issues.

During the period from 1992 to 1994, as the eastern economy entered into the recovery phase of the output J-curve, the contraction of employment slowed down. By the year 1995, the number of registered unemployed declined to about 1 million persons. However, when the German economy as a whole entered into a recession, the unemployment rate in the East, following the West German pattern, rose further to 19.5 percent in 1997.

The recent economic upswing, which brought down the West German unemployment rate below the mark of 10 percent, has not significantly relieved the eastern labor market so far: The ongoing rectification of structural distortions due to the transformation process, notably the contraction of an inflated construction sector, is reducing employment opportunities further (Brenke/ Schmidt (1999)). In 2000, the number of registered unemployed is likely to persist above 1.3 million, which is about 19 percent of the labor force.

Inspection of officially published unemployment figures only vaguely covers the actual size of the employment problem in East Germany. As a reaction to the unparalleled level of worker displacement, government authorities established extensive work creation measures. Figure 2 gives an impression of the number of effective unemployed who are hidden through labor market policies.

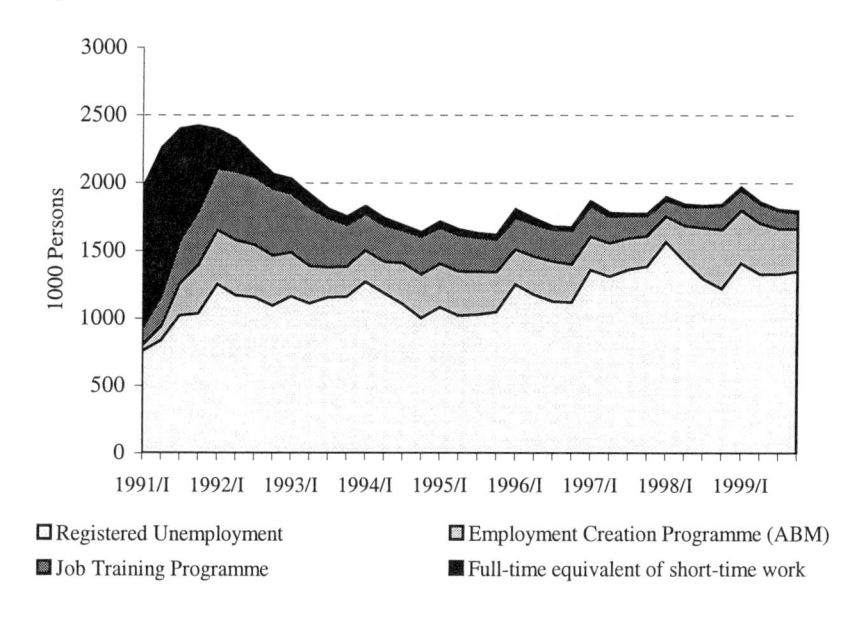

Figure 2 The Structure of Unemployment in East Germany, Period 1991 - 1999

□ Registered Unemployment   □ Employment Creation Programme (ABM)
▨ Job Training Programme   ■ Full-time equivalent of short-time work

Source: *Sachverständigenrat,* Yearly Report, various issues.

In the last quarter of 1991 when the employment crisis reached its peak about 2.4 million persons were effectively without employment. At that time, almost 30 percent of the eastern labor force was registered unemployed, engaged in short-time work or in training and employment creation programs.[1] This rate fell to 22.3 percent due to the recovery of production during the period between 1992 and 1995. Since then, however, the real level of unemployment in East Germany has been increasing again and approached 1.9 million persons by the end of 1999. Thus effective joblessness is still more than 40 percent higher than registered unemployment.

This calculation of effective unemployment ignores east-west labor migration and commuters. Seeking employment in the West was a frequent response to the economic uncertainties and worsening eastern labor market conditions in the aftermath of unification (Wagner (1992)). In fact, there was a widespread fear that East Germans immigrating westward could overflood their West German

---

[1] The full-time equivalent of short-time work is calculated using information on the distribution of actual hours worked. Participation in training programs does not necessarily cover full-time education. As a consequence, the figure may overstate the level of hidden unemployment.

countrymen, which enforced rapid economic integration of East Germany. Between 1989 and 1991, 400,000 East Germans (net) of working age migrated to the West. An additional 200,000 employable persons had left the East German states by the end of 1994 when net migration between East and West turned almost into balance.

Moreover, a considerable number of East Germans is prepared to travel long distances to avoid unemployment. Already in 1991, about 290,000 workers (net) were commuting to the West. The number of commuters rose further to more than 350,000 when unemployment peaked in 1992 and thereafter has only gradually declined. Commuting and out-migration hence could reduce current labor supply in East Germany by about 1 million persons. Had commuters and labor emigrants stayed in the eastern labor market, it seems not unlikely that an equivalent size of workers would have been unemployed additionally. Re-evaluating effective joblessness on the base of this argument, the real East German unemployment rate peaked at 37.1 percent in 1992 and was still as high as 33 percent in 1999.

The quotas of effective unemployment would be even higher accounting for the number of early pensioners who were driven out of the labor force by tight labor market conditions and government incentives for early retirement. A vast majority of workers between age 55 and 65 (the normal retirement age) who lost their jobs did not return to employment, but entered pre-retirement schemes (DIW et al. (1999, p. 11). Until the end of 1992, labor market authorities financially supported early retirement of workers older than age 55. At the peak in 1993, some 893,000 former workers were paid one of the different types of early retirement settlements (*Vorruhestandsgeld, Altersübergangsgeld*). Although early retirement programs ran out in 1995, the working-age labor force was still relieved from close to 300,000 early pensioners during the year 1999.

A different way of illustrating the size of the unemployment problem in East Germany is to compare the present size of truly employed people to the size of employment at the end of 1989. At the beginning of the transformation, 9.89 million people were gainfully employed in the GDR. This number was reduced to 6.06 million in 1998. Subtracting the full-time equivalent of short-time work, the number of participants in employment creation programs and persons in further education results in 5.75 million persons who were effectively employed. This is only 58 percent of the size of employment at the time when the socialist system collapsed. Roughly speaking, every second worker has not regained a job in East Germany even after ten years of economic transformation.

As noted above, the formidable level of unemployment, which was a traumatic experience for many East Germans, enforced the introduction of labor market and social policy measures in order to avoid social tensions and out-migration. For the most part, the conventional labor market tools of the Federal Labor Office, the *Bundesanstalt für Arbeit*, were extended to the East. However, to some degree they were applied in a different manner.

As is evident from Figure 2, the focus of the labor market instruments employed changed over time. In the first period after unification when creation of fresh employment was expected to start before long, policy aimed at stretching out the unavoidable reduction of obsolete jobs. The *Treuhandanstalt*, the central privatization agency founded to privatize the state-owned enterprises, frequently negotiated job guarantees with private investors (at the expense of privatization profits), which ensured at least temporary job stability. The most important labor market instrument was the support of short-time workers under more favorable conditions than in the West.[2] Until the end of 1991, the Federal Employment Office heavily subsidized workers who frequently were producing nothing. At the peak in the first half of 1991, there were about 2 million short-term workers; the subsidized loss of working hours was equivalent to 1.1 million full-time jobs.

When most of the short-term workers became unemployed soon after, the emphasis of labor market policy shifted to employment creation programs, so-called *Arbeitsbeschaffungsmaßnahmen* (ABM), and government training schemes. Although the eastern labor force was seen to exhibit a comparatively high level of formal qualification attainment,[3] western-style retraining was expected to improve the speed of labor market integration of East German workers. Chambers of commerce or private training companies were providing education and training under the monitoring of the Federal Labor Office.

Almost 500,000 unemployed persons participated in such training schemes during 1992. In the following years, training activities were gradually reduced, as the qualification demand was declining and the reputation of education programs to promote re-employment was coming into doubt. In 1999, only 138,000 persons took part in training activities. The share of the unemployed involved in training programs had almost converged on the western level.

In contrast, publicly financed work creation, intended to avoid qualification loss during periods of unemployment, has stayed a popular policy instrument to reduce registered unemployment in East Germany. In 1999, 18.9 percent of the unemployed benefited from the public creation of work, compared to only 2.7 percent in the West. The size of ABM participation (351,000) was again almost as high as in the peak year 1992 (388,000).

The rapid expansion of ABM in the eastern states was achieved through generous subsidies (covering all personnel and non-personnel costs) and a less rigid targeting of job creation measures, which are typically directed at the hard-

---

[2] In Germany, labor market authorities usually support short-term work to bridge a temporary decline in demand or production.

[3] The proportion of persons entering the labor market with an occupational credential was much higher in the East than in the West. Furthermore, a much higher proportion participated and completed apprenticeships and vocational training (Lange/Pugh (1998)).

to-place unemployed in the West. During the first years of the transformation, the Federal Labor Office subsidized a large number of *Beschäftigungsgesellschaften* (employment companies) that were mostly set up from non-viable parts of *Treuhand* firms to provide training and jobs. At present, most workers involved in ABM are employed by specific firms to engage in public works that do not (or should not) compete with private enterprise. These firms pay tariff or comparable wages which are subsidized between 80 and 100 percent by the Federal Labor Office (Brinkmann/Gottsleben (1994)).[4]

As an innovative instrument of publicly financed job creation in East Germany, specific wage subsidies (*Lohnkostenzuschüsse Ost*) were introduced in 1993. In contrast to the conventional job creation programs, coverage of the subsidies was limited to the amount of the average unemployment benefit. Since 1997, also private enterprise has become eligible to this new type of wage subsidies, which might turn a useful instrument to promote reintegration into the first labor market.

At present, while the level of unemployment seems to be stabilizing on a stubbornly high level, the structure of employment in the East continues to differ significantly from that in the West. Table 1 shows how the structure of gainful employment across sectors has been developing after the unification. In 1991, there were some marked differences between the large aggregates agriculture (including forestry and fishing), the government sector, the producing sector, trade and transportation, and services. As the economically backward GDR had maintained the structure of an advanced industrial society, similar to that of West Germany in the mid-1960s (Grünert/Lutz (1995)), the employment share of the first three sectors was larger, that of the last two smaller than in the West.[5]

---

[4] Wages of ABM participants initially even exceeded market wages in some regions. As a consequence, in 1993, the average hours of work in job creation programs was reduced, in order to avoid disincentives for market employment.

[5] Analysis of employment shares gives a somewhat awkward impression of the actual economic weight of the manufacturing sector in eastern economy. In terms of gross product, the producing sector accounted for more than 50 percent in the GDR economy.

Table 1. Sector Structure of Gainful Employment in East and West Germany
(Percent of Total Gainful Employment)

Sector	Year						
	1991	1992	1993	1994	1995	1996	1997
East Germany							
Agriculture	6.2	4.4	3.7	3.6	3.5	3.4	3.5
Manufacturing	40.8	35.7	34.9	34.9	34.9	34.2	33.7
Trade and Transportation	17.0	17.9	18.2	17.9	17.5	17.5	17.5
Services	12.7	15.8	17.9	19.3	20.4	21.4	22.0
Government	23.3	26.1	25.3	24.3	23.6	23.5	23.3
West Germany							
Agriculture	3.3	3.2	3.0	2.9	2.8	2.7	2.6
Manufacturing	39.2	38.4	37.1	36.1	35.6	34.7	34.0
Trade and Transportation	19.0	19.2	19.3	19.3	19.1	19.1	19.1
Services	19.2	19.9	20.8	21.6	22.4	23.2	23.9
Government	19.3	19.4	19.7	20.0	20.1	20.3	20.5

Source: German Statistical Yearbook, various issues.

Significant adjustments of the employment structure started to take place already in 1992. The employment share of agriculture and the producing sector declined rapidly (the latter below the West German level), whereas the service sector started to catch up to western standards. However, East German convergence on western sector patterns is far from complete after ten years of transition. In particular, the eastern government sector still appears as overstaffed, compared to western standards, as tasks are only hesitatingly transferred to the private sector. The share of the public sector in gainful employment went up significantly with the employment crisis of 1991. This observation suggests that the government sector, not exposed to competition, was able to maintain a high number of low-productive workers, thereby implicitly subsidizing unemployment.

Table 2. Occupational Position of Gainfully Employed in East and West Germany
(Percent of Total Gainfully Employed)

Employment Position	Year							
	1991	1992	1993	1994	1995	1996	1997	1998
East Germany								
Self-Employed	4.6	5.9	6.7	7.2	7.4	7.5	8.0	8.7
Civil Servant	1.2	1.6	2.0	2.3	2.8	3.3	3.7	3.9
White Collar Worker	48.9	49.8	49.1	49.0	47.5	46.2	46.5	47.4
Blue Collar Worker	45.4	42.7	42.2	41.5	42.3	43.1	41.8	40.0
Part-Time Worker[a]	1.9	1.7	2.0	2.4	2.9	3.7	4.3	4.8
West Germany								
Self-Employed	10.8	10.7	10.8	11.2	11.2	11.2	11.5	11.7
Civil Servant	8.2	7.9	7.9	7.9	7.7	7.7	7.6	7.3
White Collar Worker	43.8	44.7	45.4	46.2	46.4	46.6	47.6	48.0
Blue Collar Worker	37.2	36.7	35.9	34.7	34.6	34.5	33.3	33.0
Part-Time Worker[a]	8.9	9.4	9.7	10.1	10.7	11.4	12.2	12.7

Note: (a) Weekly working time 20 hours or less.

Source: German Federal Statistical Office.

What seems more worrying with regard to the future employment outlook is the fact that the trade and transportation sector, where the employment share stagnated, and the service sector have not caught up fully to the West. Since 1995 the share of these sectors in overall gainful employment has been ranging about 3.5 percentage points below the western level. Thus, there appears to be little evidence that the East would leave the West behind as a modern service economy after completion of the transformation process. Of course, this interpretation refers only to the employment structure, not to the actual modernization of the enterprises behind this.

Table 2 surveys changes of the occupational position of the gainfully employed in East and West Germany. Again, the data show comparatively little evidence that employment patterns would converge between the two regions soon. The share of blue-collar workers among the gainfully employed, decreasing since unification, has stayed substantially higher in the East than in the West. In 1998 the fraction of blue-collar workers in East Germany was still 40 percent when the western rate had fallen to less than one third. At the same time, the portion of white-collar workers in the East had fallen below the West German level. The fraction of employees in the government sector, where the machinery of civil servants is building up only gradually, remained substantially smaller than in West Germany.

Two trends revealed in Table 2 might become relevant for the future employment prospects in the East. First, self-employment, starting from a very low level when the GDR economy collapsed, has made great progress after unification. In 1998, 8.7 percent of the gainfully employed in the East ran their own business. However, the level of entrepreneurial activity still lagged behind that in the West substantially. It might well be that the transformation process did not open up sufficient opportunities for private enterprise, in particular in small businesses that would promote dependent employment (Gruhler (1997)).

Secondly, the share of part-time employment, which has been increasing in the whole Germany over the last decade, remains significantly lower on the eastern labor market. Roughly speaking, for each three part-time workers employed in the West (working less than 20 hours a week), there was only one in the East in 1998. This finding hints at unexploited opportunities for labor reorganization in East Germany. Improving the flexibility of employment conditions may open up the chance to additional employment. Obviously, this reading of the current eastern job pattern does not say that there actually would be a demand for additional part-time employment. This has to be discussed further in Section 4. Before doing so, we survey the empirical evidence on the possibilities to improve eastern employment levels through measures of active labor market policy.

3. The Effects of Active Labor Market Policy

As discussed above, one reaction to the labor market problems in East Germany was massive expansion of active labor market policy. The main tools of active labor market policy in the East, educational training programs and ABM, aimed at preserving and improving the qualification of the participants during periods of unemployment, in order to promote rapid reintegration into the first labor market. The effectiveness of active labor market measures in East Germany in reaching this goal has been studied extensively.

A simple analysis of participants' employment status shortly after completion of an ABM or qualification program seems to suggest that active labor market policies were rather successful. According to a specific survey of labor market data that has been conducted regularly in East Germany since the unification (*Arbeitsmarktmonitor Ost*), roughly one third of the participants in qualification programs and one quarter of the participants in job creation programs reentered the regular labor market shortly after termination of the program (DIW et. al. (1999), p. 56).

However, the relative success of active labor market policies is difficult to evaluate on the base of these data, since the labor market performance of the unemployed who did not take part in labor market programs is neglected. Econometric studies, which construct a control-group of non-participants to avoid this bias, have not come to an unanimous conclusion about the effectiveness of active of labor market policies in improving regular employment in the East.

In general, qualification programs seem to have promoted re-employment more successfully than job creation programs. Helberger/Pannenberg (1997), using data from the German Socio-Economic Panel (GSOEP), and Kraus et al. (1999), based on the *Arbeitsmarktmonitor Ost*, have been able to demonstrate positive employment effects (at least in the medium term) of the extensive re-training schemes that were offered by the Federal Labor Office in the first period after unification. Fitzenberger/Prey (1997) come to the same conclusion. However, they show that the positive employment effects were limited to vocational training schemes outside firms. With regard to publicly financed retraining on the job, the employment effect is revealed as insignificant, which suggests that the employment success of program participants was offset by displacement of other workers. Finally, Hübler (1996) has demonstrated that the employment effects of public retraining activities were possibly gender-specific. It appears that the positive employment impact was limited to men, while East German females did not significantly benefit from participation in educational programs.

Challenging the results of previous studies, Staat (1997) and Lechner (1998) who reevaluate evidence from the GSOEP do not observe any significant improvement of chances to employment due to qualification measures. The latter furthermore observes that training and the chance to reenter the first labor market are inversely related in the short-term. One may conclude from this result that financial security during participation in educational programs reduced individual efforts to instantly regain regular employment.

According to the available evidence, public work creation through ABM was less successful in bringing workers back into stable employment on the first labor market than were retraining programs. Empirical evaluations of public works projects in East Germany by Steiner/Kraus (1995), Hübler (1997) and Kraus et al. (1998) uniformly indicate insignificant or even negative effects on the reemployment prospects of ABM participants in comparison to unemployed who did not join the program. There is only one notable exception: Using a regional labor market data set for the eastern state of Saxony-Anhalt, Eichler/Lechner (1998) have observed a positive reemployment effect of public job creation.

One possible explanation for the unfavorable empirical assessment of the ABM measures is again that the participants search less intensively for regular employment. Furthermore, the institutional arrangements of public job creation programs, supporting labor-intensive work and old technologies (or inefficient utilization of new technologies), frequently do not meet with the current demand of the labor market, which promotes individual de-qualification (Schultz (1997)). Thus participation in ABM appears to create a negative signal to potential employers, which reduces the chances for reemployment. The reason for the negative employment outcome, however is *not* a selective targeting of the ABM programs on disadvantaged groups on the labor market. As mentioned above, the terms of eligibility to ABM were less rigid in East Germany. In fact, Kraus et al. (1998) do not find evidence for adverse sample selection.

The weak impact of public job creation programs on individual employment performance casts serious doubt on their role as the central tool of active labor market policy in East Germany. Given that qualification measures are more likely to promote integration into the first labor market, policymakers may consider reallocating resources between the current measures of active labor market policy. This does not say that ABM would not be justified for social reasons. In fact, there is some evidence that provision of active labor market programs is used in East Germany as a social policy instrument cushioning the burdens of unemployment, in particular of long-term unemployment.

According to estimates based on the GSOEP, the net income of eastern households who benefit from active labor market measures amounts to some three quarters of the representative employment income. The income of such households is about as high (and even higher for participants in retraining programs) as that of households receiving passive unemployment support (*Arbeitslosengeld*) (DIW et al. (1999), p. 58). In West Germany, the relative income position of beneficiaries receiving active support is considerably less favorable: Participants in ABM or qualification programs receive only 60 percent and 64 percent, respectively, of the average employment income. Therefore, the household income of eastern participants in active labor market programs is almost equal (97 percent on a weighted average) to that of comparable western households.

Considered that the income support payments by the Federal Labor Office are normally linked to net wage income, which is still substantially lower in the East, this may be a surprising result. It is explained by strong regional disparities in labor market presence (discussed at length in Section 4). As a consequence, households with more than one transfer recipient are much more frequent in the East than in the West. For this reason, the fact that the income status of the eastern unemployed is more favorable relative to comparable westerners than the income status of persons who are in employment is also true for recipients of other transfers from the Federal Labor Office.

The distributional effects of active labor market tools are even more evident considering the development of unemployment income over time. In West Germany, the long-term unemployed typically gradually descend on the transfer income ladder, from unemployment support to unemployment assistance (*Arbeitslosenhilfe*) to social welfare. It appears that this process is slowed down in East Germany through the tools of active labor market policy. During the period from 1990 to 1997, the status of joblessness ended with participation in ABM or educational training programs for more than 40 percent of the eastern unemployed. Furthermore, more than two thirds of the participants in active labor market policy were not reemployed after completion of the measure, or took part in a second program. By the end of 1997, one quarter of the long-term unemployed had participated in active labor market programs for more than 53 months.

This pattern suggests that active labor market policy has been exploited to perforate the period of unemployment (Schultz (1998)). The interruption of unemployment through program participation re-establishes claims on unemployment support payments. Thus, the perforation strategy manages to postpone gradual decline in unemployment transfer levels for the long-term unemployed.

4. Sources of Unemployment

Explaining what causes the high level of joblessness on the East German labor market, observers of the transformation process have referred to demand and supply side arguments. With regard to labor demand, a majority of analysts including Sinn/Sinn (1992), Siebert (1992), Link (1993), Sachverständigenrat (1997) and Lange/Pugh (1998) among others have stressed that the high (and rapidly growing) wages in the East are a major source of high unemployment rates and insufficient investment. Focusing on the supply side, some economists, notably Zimmermann (1993) and Vogler-Ludwig (1997), have argued that differences of labor market participation and hours of work are a major source for the higher level of eastern unemployment relative to the West. In the sequel, some stylized facts are gathered to check the validity of these arguments.

With the economic union, the West German system of trade unions and collective wage bargaining was immediately expanded to the East. Trade unions, lead by the widespread fear of massive east-west migration and the expectation of fast economic recovery, pressed for the rapid convergence of wages.[6] Special collective agreements (*Stufentarifverträge*) were negotiated that adjusted union wages stepwise to the western level over a short period of years. Full convergence

---

[6] The actual size of the migration pressure was certainly overestimated. Migration studies suggest that wage differentials are not so much relevant for migration decisions as unemployment differentials (Wagner (1992), Keil/Newell (1993), Bauer/Zimmermann (1998)). See Pischke et al. (1994) for an opposite position.

of union wages was reached as early as 1995 in certain industries. In some major branches, including banking, construction, the metal and electronic industry, and the iron and steel producing industry full convergence was agreed upon the year 1997, although this still excluded certain extra payments and weekly working hours. In most other sectors, convergence of union wages, usually approaching between 80 and 90 percent of the western level, is also far advanced.

Considering the generally low level of labor productivity after the breakdown of the socialist economy, wage setting in East Germany certainly did not follow the logic of neoclassical equilibrium theory in the first period after unification (Schmidt/Sander (1993)). Nevertheless, the relevance of wage policy for the recovery of employment (or rather the lack of it) seems to have been largely overestimated.[7] Figure 3 allows comparing the development of monthly tariff wages, gross effective wages and labor productivity (measured in terms of gross output per worker) relative to the respective western level.[8]

As the wage drift has been substantial, the focus on union wages seriously exaggerates the actual differential between wage costs and labor productivity. Effective wages have been converging to western standards more slowly than union wages for several reasons. First, payment above tariff, frequent in the West, is very rare practice in the eastern states (DIW et al. (1994)). Secondly, eastern workers often do not receive extra payments (e.g., *Urlaubsgeld, Weihnachtsgeld*) that are quite standard in West Germany. Finally, tariff wages did not prevail on the labor market frequently. A growing number of East German companies seem to exploit opportunities to pay wages below tariff. In 1998, 79 percent of the companies in the producing sector did not participate in collective wage bargaining, many of them paying wages below tariff (DIW et al. (1999), p. 62). In addition, in a significant number of firms that take part in the collective bargaining process formally, internal agreements have been reached with Works Councils and workers to pay less than tariff wages in order to preserve employment

---

[7] Thimann (1996) and Fitzroy/Funke (1998) study the conflict between wage setting and employment in East Germany quantitatively.

[8] Given the complex and confusing system of collective wage agreements, it is very difficult to aggregate union wages on a sector level. Productivity and effective wage measures are not readily available on the industry level. The presentation of Figure 3 claims that productivity growth in the producing sector as a whole would resemble that in the metal and electrical sector. Of course, comparisons on the aggregate level between the East and West are problematic, due to the different industry and employment structures of the two regions.

Figure 3 Union Wages, Effective Wages and Labor Productivity in East Germany
(Index West Germany = 100)

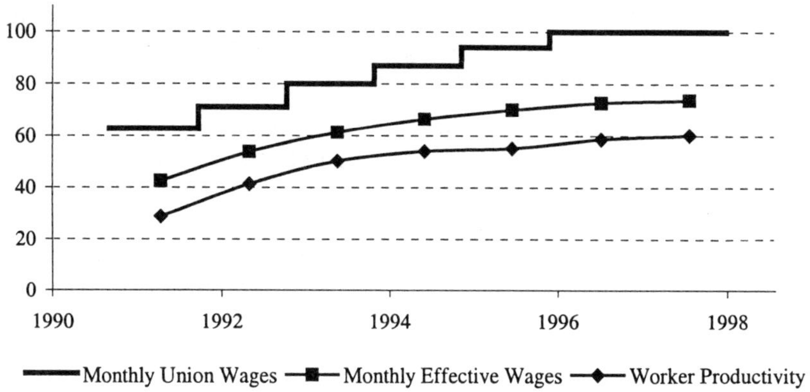

Monthly Union Wages ━■━ Monthly Effective Wages ━◆━ Worker Productivity

Notes: Productivity measured by gross product per worker in the production sector. Monthly effective wages in the production sector. Monthly union wages in the metal and electrical industry.

Sources: *Sachverständigenrat*, Yearly Report, various issues; German Statistical Yearbook, various issues, Boje/Schneider (1995).

The rapid adaptation of the wage setting process to the transformation crisis has been preventing wage convergence as aimed at by the (western dominated) trade unions. As displayed in Figure 3, effective wages in the East had reached only about three quarters of the western level in 1997 when eastern output per worker was close to 60 percent of that in the West. Moreover, since the wedge between effective wages and labor productivity of some 15 percentage points stayed largely unchanged in the course of the transformation process, the productivity gap has been declining substantially in relative terms since unification.

The argument that inadequate wage policy is fundamental to the high level of eastern unemployment might be challenged also for theoretical reasons. Certainly, wages should follow productivity in an equilibrium state. However, it is less certain that the equilibrium concept would provide a valuable answer to the problems of the East German economy during transformation. As the capital stock of the GDR was obsolete, most East German goods would not have sold at any level of socially acceptable real wages. Higher wages, however, should be no problem for a capital stock that is newly built up. Modern technology can pay high wages. In this perspective, the initial rapid wage increase in the East set incentives for creative destruction. A low wage policy in East Germany would have resulted in a low productivity capital stock, associated with very slow convergence to the West. Given that this strategy was no realistic policy option, the question then is why investors hesitated to reconstruct and modernize the eastern capital stock to pay high productivity wages. (Section 5 will provide some possible answers.)

As shortage of employment is a relative phenomenon, the high rates of joblessness reported for East Germany might be due to supply factors. One of the marked differences on the labor market between the former GDR and the FRG was exhibited by the labor force participation rates, which were substantially higher in the East where politics had set strong incentives to encourage employment. Overall labor force participation in East Germany was 78.1 percent in the age group from 15 to 65 in 1988 when the same number was 68.8 percent in the former FRG. Figure 4, which depicts the development of eastern labor force participation rates relative to the western standard, shows that the strong regional differences in labor supply behavior have persisted during the transformation process. The presence of East Germans at employable age on the labor market, although declining after the unification, still was some 8 percent higher than that of representative westerners in 1998. Furthermore, there appears to be little evidence at present that East Germans would adapt to the labor supply behavior of their western countrymen soon.

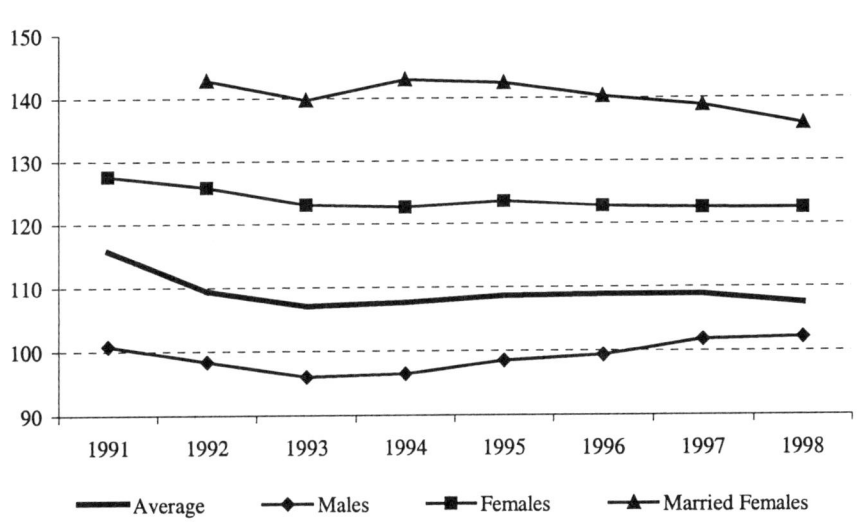

Figure 4   Labor Force Participation Rates in East Germany
(Index West Germany = 100)

Sources: *Sachverständigenrat*, Yearly Report, various issues; German Statistical Yearbook, various issues.

Figure 4 also highlights some considerable gender disparities. While labor force participation of eastern males consistently has been similar to that of western males, the propensity of females to seek employment is still substantially higher in the East than in the West. The communist eastern leaders had tried to overcome traditional gender roles promoting women to work. As a consequence, female labor force participation in the former GDR ranked among the highest in the world. In 1988, 75.7 percent of women at employable age participated in the eastern labor force (most of them employed as there was practically full employment), compared to 55.0 percent in West Germany where the age-pattern of female participation follows the family life-cycle.

In contrast to what many observers of the transformation process had expected, the propensity of East German women to take up a job did not converge on western standards after unification, despite rising obstacles to get employed.[9] Considering the comparatively low eastern wage levels, one explanation for this behavior appears to be the necessity to maintain family income. This may explain why labor force participation of East German married females, which is still ranging more than 35 percent above that of comparable western females, has remained particularly high.

While labor supply was staying at uncommonly high levels, employment opportunities for female workers narrowed substantially. In the consequence, the eastern female unemployment rate was almost double that of males in certain years. Women also had serious trouble to get reemployed. According to estimates by Gladisch/Trabert (1995), as many as 89.6 percent of new regular employment opportunities were taken up by men during the period from 1992 to 1994. The low marginal employment share of females does not necessarily imply discrimination. Other factors, including differences in regional mobility and qualification structure (including retraining possibilities) might have played a role (Lange/Pugh (1998), p. 104).

With strong regional disparities in labor supply persisting, a reduction of eastern unemployment to the western standard certainly cannot be expected. Furthermore, the focus on unemployment rates appears to misrepresent the severity of the employment crisis in East Germany. To assess the actual size of the employment problem, it is only of interest to what extent potential labor is needed. As mentioned above, 6.06 million persons were gainfully employed in the East in 1998. Given the population size at employable age of 10,7 million, the effective eastern employment rate was 56.4 percent, some 5 percentage points lower than the corresponding employment rate for West Germany (61.7 percent). Although the effective employment levels in the East, which had exceeded those in the West

---

[9] In the former GDR, female employment was supported, for example, by generous provision of day care for children. This institution was rapidly dismantled after the unification.

until 1991, have stabilized below the western standard, shortage of employment opportunities in the East is beyond doubt less substantial than the focus on regional differences in unemployment suggests.

This is even more evident considering the effective volume of eastern employment, rather than the share of effectively employed workers. Collectively agreed-upon working hours in East Germany have not converged to the western level. On average, union working time is still exceeding that in the West by about two hours per week. When measured in terms of the yearly hours worked per gainfully employed, the eastern advantage in effective employment volume is even more substantial. As is indicated in Figure 5, labor volume per individual worker in the East consistently surpassed that in the West.[10] Furthermore the individual employment volume is only slowly converging on western standards. In 1998, eastern workers were still occupied longer than western workers by about 6 percent. The regional differences of individual employment volume are only partially due to the less generous tariff agreements. They also reflect the considerable shortage of part-time occupations on the East German labor market.

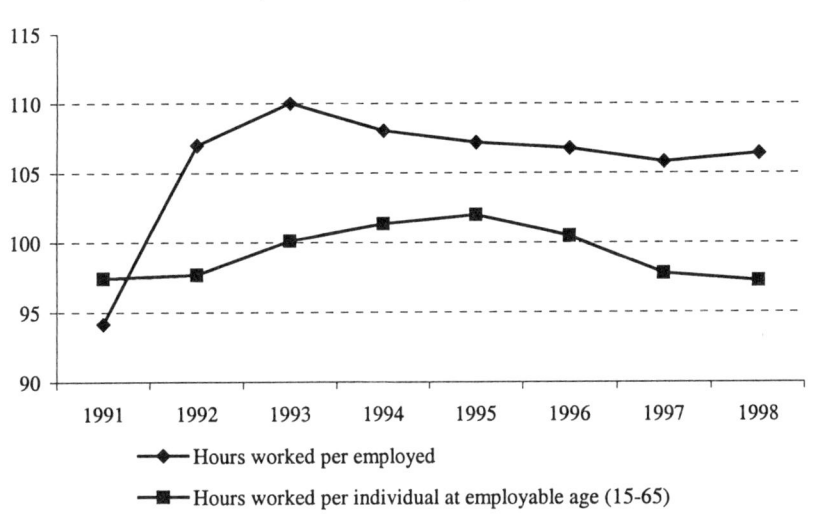

Figure 5   Yearly Employment Volume in East Germany
(Index West Germany = 100)

Sources: Ministery of Labor and Social Affairs, *Statistisches Taschenbuch Arbeits- und Sozialstatistik 1999;* own calculations.

---

[10] The only exception is observed in 1991 when many workers were put on short-term employment. Annual employment volume per worker recovered, as soon as obsolete workers were driven out of their jobs after 1992.

The remarkable advantage of East Germany in terms of individual employment volume suggests that there would be some opportunities for reallocating employment. In fact, had working hours in the East been distributed according to the western standard, the size of gainful employment in 1998 could have been some 390,000 persons higher. The corresponding effective employment quota of 60 percent would have come very close to the observed western employment rate of 61.7 percent. A similar result is displayed in Figure 5. Constructing the volume of hours worked relative to the size of the population at employable age, there appears to be no substantial shortage of employment in the East, relative to the western standards. From this perspective, effective eastern employment volume, which even exceeded the western level during parts of the transformation process, was less than three percentage points below the western rate in 1998.

To avoid misunderstandings, it should be stressed that this type of calculation does not imply that the large size of unemployment in East Germany is not a real social problem. Nevertheless, it has to be emphasized that a remarkable adjustment of the overall employment volume has already taken place. Given that wages and labor productivity are converging on western standards, it is unlikely that the overall employment volume in the East would stabilize above the western level and absorb the more ample eastern labor supply.

5. Missed Opportunities?

The Federal Government policies in the process of unification had the objectives of a fast establishment of the market system, modernization of the eastern capital stock and a smooth adjustment of the labor market. These goals were to be achieved through the monetary, economic and social union which less than eight months after the fall of the Berlin wall expanded the pre-existing West German institutions, standards and practices to the East. Looking back ten years after the unification, there is hardly any doubt that there was no gradualist alternative to the *big bang* approach of fast economic integration taken. Nevertheless, considering the stagnant economic recovery of the eastern states and persisting regional disparities, especially from a labor market perspective, one may ask what opportunities were missed in the course of the economic transformation.

In historical perspective, a major political mistake during the early stages of the unification process was to underestimate and even deny the economic and social costs associated with the eastern transition to a modern market economy. For example, considering the over-employment promoted by the communist system, it was an illusion to believe that gainful employment in the East could have been maintained at the pre-unification level. (It seems that this point is still not well understood by some political decision makers.) As a consequence, individuals' willingness to share in the burdens of unification was substantially weakened in East and West Germany alike.

Due to the political myth of smooth and fast economic integration, the challenge of transforming the eastern socialist command economy was not widely perceived as an opportunity for re-thinking the political and economic system in Germany as a whole. The total collapse of the socialist system rather reinforced confidence that the East German society would adapt to the western institutions without frictions. Thus, a frequent attitude in the West was that the reunited Germany should simply become an enlarged Federal Republic. However, many of the institutions that were expanded to the eastern states without change were impeding economic progress in the West already before unification. It is therefore hardly surprising that the systemic problems aggravated when the eastern transition crisis called for greater flexibility. From the vantage point ten years after unification, it appears that lack of institutional innovation during the transformation process imposed (and is still imposing) the most serious obstacles to recovery of the East German economy which continues to be equipped with too little capital to create sufficient new employment opportunities.

The general reluctance of institutional renewal obstructed, for example, the establishment of efficient government structures. After the dismantling of the communist administrative body, public administration in the eastern states was first largely rebuilt after western examples. Hence the opportunity was missed to immediately install modern techniques of governmental management that could have provided the flexibility required coping with the complex administrative problems occurring in the transformation process. Even at present, (local) administration in the East follows less up-to-date standards on average than in the West (Maaß (1999)).

Ineffective government institutions certainly discouraged private investment. In particular, reconstruction of the mostly outdated eastern infrastructure, prerequisite to foster private capital formation, was slowed down considerably. Public investment, in comparison to transfers for consumption purposes, was dangerously low at the beginning of the transformation process. The gap in public infrastructure, thus, has only partially been closed. At present, the value of public assets in the East is lagging behind the western level by about one quarter (DIW (2000)).

Furthermore slow decision processes, for example concerning the issue of restitution (which had been given preference over compensation of expropriated former owners) caused insecurities that held back investment. The difficult conditions of local administration may provide an explanation why the generous investment incentives introduced by the Federal Government to promote capital formation were only a partial success.

Pressure for convergence of institutions has also prevented East Germany to go ahead with the overdue revitalization of the German education system. Instead, the eastern states swiftly adapted to the unreformed West German educational standards of vocational and university training. (To give credit where it is due, there were certain advancements regarding secondary schooling.) Doing so, East Germany missed the opportunity to obtain a competitive advantage over the West, as shortage of well-trained and well-educated young workers is rapidly getting a bottleneck for economic growth in Germany as a whole. In addition, it seems likely that the network advantages coupled with the foundation of highly competitive research institutions would have enhanced eastern growth prospects, at least in the medium term, by promoting still insufficient private research activities.

A final example of perhaps inadequate convergence is given by the initially unqualified adaptation to pre-existing labor market institutions in East Germany. The practice of universal collective bargaining taken over from the West exerted decisive influence on the rapid increase of eastern labor costs and hence the loss of competitiveness during the first period after unification. In addition, acceptance of the highly regulated working conditions in the West was incompatible with the need for more flexible labor organization acute on the eastern labor market in transition. The mass unemployment in East Germany detected the inflexibilities of the traditional German labor market institutions all too cruelly.

Fortunately, there are some signs that the deep transformation crisis in the eastern states, which discredited many western routines, also fosters institutional renewal. The progressive loss of membership in unions and employers' associations and the establishment of bargaining practices at plant level ignoring industry guidelines demonstrate that the eastern society is capable to independent initiative.

Encouraging such initiative further appears important to solve the problems of transformation, which cannot be achieved through duplication but only through modernization of western structures. If eastern developments catalyzed institutional innovation in West Germany, the challenge of unification could open the opportunity for creative systemic competition, improving the prospects for recovered economic dynamism in Germany as a whole.

References

Akerlof, G. et al. (1991), East Germany in from the Cold: The Economic Aftermath of Currency Union, *Brookings Papers on Economic Activity* 1, 1-87.

Bauer, T./Zimmermann, K. F. (1998), Causes of International Migration: An Overview, in: Gorter, C./Nijkamp, P./Poot, J (eds.), *Crossing the Borders, Regional and Urban Perspectives on International Migration*, Aldershot, 95-127.

Boje, J./Schneider, H. (1995), Der Umbruch am ostdeutschen Arbeitsmarkt, in: R. Pohl (ed.), *Herausforderung Ostdeutschland, Fünf Jahre Währungs-, Wirtschafts- und Sozialunion*, Berlin, 121-138.

Brenke, K./Schmidt, K.-D. (1999), Sektorale Produktions- und Beschäftigungsstrukturen in den neuen Bundesländern, in: E. Wiedemann (ed.), *Die arbeitsmarkt- und beschäftigungspolitische Herausforderung in Ostdeutschland*, Nuremberg, 95-113.

Brinkmann. C./Gottsleben, V. (1994), Labor Market and Labor Market Policy in the Eastern Part of Germany: New Approaches and New Links to Structural Policy, *Labor* 8, 505-520.

DIW (2000), *Infrastrukturausstattung und Nachholbedarf in Ostdeutschland*, Berlin.

DIW et al. (1994), Gesamtwirtschaftliche und unternehmerische Anpassungsfortschritte in Ostdeutschland, Zehnter Bericht, *Kiel Discussion Paper* 231, Kiel Institute of World Economics, Kiel.

DIW et al. (1999), Gesamtwirtschaftliche und unternehmerische Anpassungsfortschritte in Ostdeutschland, Neunzehnter Bericht, *Kiel Discussion Paper* 346/347, Kiel Institute of World Economics, Kiel.

Fitzenberger, B./Prey, H. (1997), Assessing the Impact of Training on Employment: The Case of East Germany, *ifo-Studien* 43, 71-116.

Gladisch, D./Trabert, L. (1995), Geschlechtsspezifische Differenzierung der Erwerbsbeteiligung, *Wirtschaft im Wandel* 1, 8-11.

Gruhler, W. (1997), Beschäftigung in mittelständischen Betrieben Ost- und Westdeutschlands, *iw-trends* 24, 55-66.

Grünert, H./Lutz, B. (1995), East German Labor Market in Transition: Segmentation and Increasing Disparity, *Industrial Relations Journal* 26, 221-240.

Helberger, C./ Pannenberg, M. (1997), Kurzfristige Auswirkungen staatlicher Qualifizierungsmaßnahmen in Ostdeutschland: das Beispiel Fortbildung und Umschulung, in: Timmermann, D. (ed.), *Bildung und Arbeit in Ostdeutschland*, Berlin, 77-97.

Hübler, O. (1997), Evaluation beschäftigungspolitischer Maßnahmen in Ostdeutschland, *Jahrbücher für Nationalökonomie und Statistik* 216, 21-44.

Keil, M./Newell, A. (1993), Internal Migration and Unemployment in Germany: An Anglo-Irish Perspective, *Weltwirtschaftliches Archiv* 129, 514-536.

Kraus, F. et al. (1998), Do Public Works Programs Work? Some Unpleasant Results from the East German Experience, Discussion Paper 98-07, Center for European Policy Research, Mannheim.

Kraus, F. et al. (1999), Employment Effects of Publicly Financed Training Programs – The East German Experience, *Jahrbücher für Nationalökonomie und Statistik* 219, 216-248.

Lange, T./Pugh, G. (1998), *The Economics of German Unification*, Cheltenham.

Lechner, M. (1998), Training the East German Labor Force, Heidelberg.

Link, F. (1993), Lohnpolitik in Ostdeutschland aus ökonomischer und sozialer Perspektive, Cologne.

Maaß, C. (1999), Der lange Weg der Reform – Eine Zwischenbilanz zu den Modellkommunen in Brandenburg, *Landes- und Kommunalverwaltung* Supplement I/99, 23-27.

Pischke, J.-S. et al. (1994), Arbeitslosigkeit, Löhne oder Weiterbildung: Warum pendeln Ostdeutsche in den Westen?, in: König, H./Steiner, V. (eds.), *Arbeitsmarktdynamik und Unternehmensentwicklung in Ostdeutschland*, Baden-Baden, 311-343.

Sachverständigenrat zur Begutachtung der gesamtwirtschaftlichen Entwicklung (1997), Jahresgutachten 1997/98: Wachstum, Beschäftigung und Währungsunion – Orientierungen für die Zukunft, Stuttgart.

Schmidt, K.-D./Sander, B. (1993), Wages, Productivity and Employment in Eastern Germany, in: Ghaussy, A./Schäfer, W. (eds.), *The Economics of German Unification*, London, 60-72.

Schultz, B. (1997), Förderanreize im Widerspruch zu qualifikatorischen Zielen von Beschäftigungsmaßnahmen?, *Wirtschaft im Wandel* 3, 8-12.

Schultz, B. (1998), Hohe Verfestigung der Arbeitslosigkeit in Ostdeutschland, *Wirtschaft im Wandel* 4, 3-8.

Siebert, H. (1992), *Das Wagnis der Einheit*, Stuttgart.

Sinn, G./Sinn, H.-W. (1992), *Jumpstart – The Economic Unification of Germany*, Cambridge.

Staat, M. (1997), *Empirische Evaluation von Fortbildung und Umschulung*, Baden-Baden.

Steiner, V./Kraus, F. (1995), Haben Teilnehmer an Arbeitsbeschaffungsmaßnahmen in Ostdeutschland bessere Wiederbeschäftigungschancen als Arbeitslose?, in: Steiner, V./Bellmann, L. (eds.), *Mikroökonomik des Arbeitsmarktes*, Nuremberg, 387-423.

Thimann, C. (1996), *Aufbau von Kapitalstock und Vermögen in Ostdeutschland: Der lange Weg zur Einheitlichkeit der Lebensverhältnisse*, Tübingen.

Vogler-Ludwig, K. (1997), Arbeitsmarkt Ost: Ist die Beschäftigungspolitik am Ende?, in: Oppenländer, K. (ed.), *Wiedervereinigung nach sechs Jahren: Erfolge, Defizite und Zukunftsperspektiven im Transformationsprozeß*, Berlin, 233-248.

Wagner, G. (1992), Arbeitslosigkeit, Abwanderung und Pendeln von Arbeitskräften der neuen Bundesländer, *Sozialer Fortschritt* 41, 84-89.

Zimmermann, K. F. (1993), Labor Responses to Taxes and Benefits in Germany, in: Atkinson, A. B./Morgenson, G. V. (eds.), *Welfare and Work Incentives: A North European Perspective*, Oxford, 192-240.

I. Analysis of the German Labor Market Problem

1. Wages and Structural Adjustment in the New German States

Michael Burda, Humboldt University, Berlin; IZA, Bonn, and CEPR, London

Michael Funke, University of Hamburg

1. Introduction

Rarely have modern labor markets witnessed wage increases so rapid as in Eastern Germany following the events of November 1989. In the first five years after the unification, nominal wages rose by more than 200 percent and doubled in purchasing power. Measured in terms of the output that labor is used to produce, wages rose by almost 350 percent. Substantial disagreement continues to characterize the discussion of the effects of high wages in the five new German states. On the one hand, the Bundesbank, the *Sachverständigenrat* (Council of Economic Advisors), and major economic research institutes have argued that moderate wage settlements would have been essential for accelerating the process of structural change. According to this position, steep wage increases retarded the retooling of the eastern German economy. Trade unions, in contrast, have replied that high wages were necessary precisely to guarantee that the forces of structural change were brought to bear on industry and to promote investment in skills.

This paper evaluates the wage explosion in eastern Germany in the first period after unification and assesses its potential theoretical effects on structural change, as well as the economic arguments that can be brought for either side. Section 2 takes the first step of evaluating the process of wage convergence in the east and west. Second, we evaluate reasons for the wage explosion: union policy and government intervention (subsidies, postponed structural change, unemployment benefits) as well as the "organic" explanation (Sinn/Sinn (1992)) that would have obtained even in the absence of collective bargaining and other distortions. To the extent that wages are raised exogenously, Section 3 examines two medium to long-run dynamic effects of such an exogenous "high wage" path on structural change. Both stress the impact of wages on the incentives to accumulate different types of capital.

The first model reviews the well-known negative effect of wage policies on physical investment. A robust conclusion is that the initial reduction of employment in the aftermath of a permanent increase in wages is followed by a longer phase of declining employment: Higher wages imply a lower shadow value of capital and will be associated with a protracted period of low investment and greater capital intensity in the East. A second conclusion is that high wage policies reduce the marginal value of capital to the firm, which can explain the massive subsidies and deep selling discounts that were necessary for the *Treuhandanstalt* to dispose of its firm portfolio.

An opposing view held by labor unions and some economists has been that high wages encourage investment in human capital. We present an alternative line of economic reasoning in favor of a high wage policy which is related to incentives for retraining. According to this argument, eastern Germany could achieve rapid development only with human capital endowment similar to that in the West. In a decentralized market economy, this is possible only if sufficient incentives exist for private agents to undertake this investment in human capital on their own. A high wage policy is associated initially with high unemployment, but this unemployment is accompanied by households engaging in retraining in the hopes of improving their earnings prospects. This analysis is conducted in the context of a dynamic model of human capital investment.

It is imperative to distinguish exogenous from endogenous sources of wage increases. Thus while a "wage explosion" occurred for exogenous reasons in eastern Germany, economic forces have been at work to undermine these increases. In Section 4, the arguments of Section 3 are placed in the context of wage endogeneity, and are linked to the developments in the East. In the end, we argue that key factors determining "which view" wins must be related to adjustment costs related to the installation of new plant and equipment, the efficiency of human capital investment, discount and depreciation rates, and the elasticity of labor demand. In addition we examine the sensitivity of wages to local labor market conditions – which determines the extent to which concession bargaining occurs in times of crisis. On the last factor, we examine the evidence on wage convergence. One important fact we stress is that the rapid rates of wage growth in the first few years have not been sustained; full wage convergence has only occurred in isolated cases. The much heralded "Japanese labor costs in eastern Germany" have not been realized, and some evidence suggests that business fixed investment responded to this potential labor cost advantage in the East. Some conclusions are drawn in Section 5.

2. The Wage Explosion in Eastern Germany: Causes

It is ironic that citizens of the ex-GDR – the *Arbeiter- und Bauernstaat* ("proletarian state") – were willing to give up their trade unions so rapidly in the aftermath of the opening of the wall. Only a few months after November 1989, the *Freie Deutsche Gewerkschaftsbund* (FDGB) came under intense criticism for its collaboration with the communist party and for the generous privileges enjoyed by its functionaries. This loss of credibility was exemplified in the indictment of Harry Tisch, the former FDGB head, for embezzlement of union funds and fraud.

At the same time, even before unification was imminent, Western trade unions began to see the danger of a low wage, "right-to-work" region in their backyard. Monetary union without any change in eastern German nominal wages – even at 1:1 exchange of *Ostmarks* for DM – would have implied a dramatic integration shock: an investment boom in the East as western German enterprises took advantage of lower labor costs in the East, and migration, which threatened to send the best workers West looking for jobs. Both developments implied a disruption of western German labor markets, and constituted a threat to the monopoly position enjoyed by the German trade union movement. In response to this historic challenge, the *Deutsche Gewerkschaftsbund* (DGB) staged an impressive organizational campaign so successful that by 1991 the coverage rate in the East was more than 50 percent, compared with about 33 percent in the West (Kleinhenz (1992)).

The DGB's organizational success had several key economic consequences for both eastern and western Germany. The aggressive bargaining position taken by West German unions in wage negotiations certainly bears primary responsibility for the wage explosion. Just before monetary union (June 1990) nominal wages after 1:1 conversion were roughly a third of West German levels; within one year, average wages had reached roughly 50 percent. A number of contracts committed to parity of contractual wages by mid-decade.[1] While workers enjoyed a doubling of real wages measured in consumer goods, labor costs to firms in terms of output prices rose to 450 percent of 1990 levels. (See Table 1 for details.) Almost all of this precipitous real wage growth took place in the first years after unification: relative wages have stagnated at 70-75 percent since 1994.

---

[1] Many of these contracts were renegotiated later on. Moreover, it should be noted that the contractual wage is only one aspect of the compensation package. Eastern German workers work roughly three to five hours per week longer, receive fewer bonus payments and take shorter vacations than their West German counterparts.

Table 1. Wages and Prices Following German Monetary Union

	Monthly earnings[a] (DM/ month)		Weekly earnings[a] (DM/ weeks)		Prices[b]		Real Wages[c]	
	W_E	W_E/W_W	W_E	W_E/W_W	P_0	P_C	W_E/P_0	W_E/P_C
1/90	1184	0.31			-	-	-	-
4/90	1168	0.30			-	-	100.0	100.0
7/90	1393	0.35			64.2	94.5	182.8	124.1
10/90	1588	0.39			62.9	100.6	212.6	132.8
1/91	1667	0.42			63.3	108.9	221.9	128.8
4/91	1926	0.47			63.2	112.6	256.7	144.0
7/91	1996	0.47			63.1	115.1	266.3	146.0
10/91	2086	0.49			63.3	126.9	277.9	138.4
1/92	2211	0.52			63.4	128.5	294.1	144.9
4/92	2477	0.58			63.9	129.8	326.9	160.7
7/92	2618	0.59			63.9	130.6	345.5	168.8
10/92	2710	0.61			64.0	130.7	357.1	174.6
1/93	2704	0.61	578	0.66	64.0	140.0	356.3	162.6
4/93	2918	0.65	631	0.70	64.4	141.5	386.6	175.6
7/93	3027	0.66	652	0.71	64.4	142.2	399.4	180.6
10/93	3122	0.68	673	0.73	64.3	142.4	412.4	186.1
1/94			635	0.70	64.7	145.3	387.4	172.1
4/94			661	0.70	64.7	146.2	403.2	178.1
7/94			691	0.72	64.7	146.7	421.5	185.5
10/94			712	0.74	64.7	146.8	434.3	191.0
1/95			667	0.71	64.9	147.9	405.7	184.4
4/95			713	0.72	65.3	149.1	430.9	196.6
7/95			743	0.74	65.3	149.1	449.0	204.6
10/95			746	0.74	66.0	150.8	446.2	194.8

Notes: (a) W_E = average gross monthly wages of blue and white collar workers in the East (total industry). W_E/W_W = wage ratio East to West in percent; Source: Statistisches Bundesamt, FS 16, Reihe 2.1, various issues.

(b) P_0 (P_C) = price index of industrial producer prices (of the cost of living) in the five Eastern states, 1989 = 100; Source: Statistisches Bundesamt, FS 17, Reihe 3 and Wirtschaft und Statistik, various issues.

(c) W_E/P_0 (W_E/P_C) = real product wages (real consumption wages), 4/90 = 100. Real wages indices for 4/90 were calculated using the price indices for 5/90. W_E (1/93 – 10/95) = average gross weekly wages of blue collar workers in the East (total industry); Source: Statistisches Bundesamt, FS 16, Reihe 2.1, various issues; real wages computed after the two nominal wage series were chained at 1/93.

The economic consequences of such aggressive wage setting were foreseeable. In addition to outmoded production facilities, bloated bureaucracies and nonexistent distribution networks, East German enterprises were faced with sharp increases in unit labor costs. It is surprising that so many enterprises have managed to survive despite this staggering shock.[2] Production fell to a third of 1989 levels, and unemployment rose to roughly 15 percent of the labor force, or 30 percent when make-work, retraining, and early retirement are taken into account.

West German trade unions were apparently well-aware of the impending implications of their actions.[3] Burda/Funke (1993) review reasons why this might be optimal from the perspective of a monopoly union, behaving either as such or as a partner in a noncooperative Nash bargain. If the union simply considers the East as a segmented labor market, it will price labor as a markup on the competitive fallback wage. As usual, the markup depends negatively on the elasticity of demand for labor. Given the situation in the East, however, high labor demand elasticities would predict a much larger wage gap across the two Germanies. Burda/Funke (1993) also adduce econometric evidence that labor demand in the East was indeed more elastic at the time, which is consistent with evidence for declining industries (see Tooze (1976)).

A second reason for a union to raise wage demands is related to East-West migration. If the union takes the competitive wage as a fallback, this wage is likely to be considerably higher after unification, and thus for given markups higher wages in the East were implied. Third, the short-term subsidy policy of the Treuhandanstalt may have played an important role in short-term wage developments. Only this can explain the remarkably high labor shares in East German industry in the early years of unification – for many sectors well in excess of 150 percent (Scheremet (1992)). Finally, simply recruiting members to maintain a viable organizational base must not be overlooked.

Last but not least, there is the "organic" explanation of structural change (Sinn/Sinn (1992)). Besides union policy and government intervention (subsidies, postponed structural change, unemployment benefits), some degree of mobility for

---

[2] Akerlof et al. (1991), for example, forecasted that less than 20 percent of the firms would survive a 1:1 conversion rate.

[3] Former IG-Metall Chairman Steinkühler put it bluntly in 1992: "We knew that there would be firms which could not pay the negotiated wage increases due to their low productivity. We demanded higher wages anyway because consumer prices are rising and you can't pay capitalist prices with communist wages. Therefore wages had to adapt to these higher prices. And we knew someone had to pay.... Everyone wanted reunification – the government, society, all political parties. Therefore everyone has to pay. This means that when firms with low productivity cannot afford these wage increases, then the Treuhand has to pay, that is, the government." *Die Zeit* (No. 42, 1992, p. 30) (authors' translation).

the marginal eastern German worker would lead to an increase in the supply price of labor to the East. At the same time, capital mobility would raise the demand for labor there as investment takes advantage of low labor costs. In the West the converse would occur. Less investment and more labor in-migration would reduce the demand for labor and reduce wages there.

3. The Wage Explosion in Eastern Germany: Consequences

In the following sections we elaborate on some of the effects that a high wage policy might have, taken exogenously, on structural change. We thereby ignore feedback from the consequences of such policies on the wage itself. These factors will be considered in Section 4.

3.1. Wages and Physical Capital Formation

One important implication of a high wage policy is its adverse effect on the value of existing plant and equipment and, more importantly, the valuation of new investment in physical capital. For example, Akerlof et al. (1991) noted that the short term value of firms privatized by the *Treuhandanstalt* would be negatively affected by wages. This point also holds for capital at the margin, or the value of investment. The following model shows in a dynamic context how a high-wage policy can adversely affect investment, on which the economic development of the region crucially hinges.

Consider a representative profit-maximizing firm producing a single output Y with variable factor labor L and quasi-fixed factor capital K, using a neoclassical constant returns to scale production function $F(K,L)$.[4] The firm acts as a price taker in both input and output markets. While labor can be varied costlessly, changing the capital stock is possible only by investing at gross rate I and incurring internal adjustment costs $C(\cdot)$. The strictly convex function $C(\cdot)$ takes the value zero only when gross investment is zero. Capital depreciates exponentially at rate δ ($\delta > 0$). The planning horizon is infinite. Under these assumptions the firm chooses inputs of labor and investment expenditure to maximize the present value of cash flow, solving

$$\max_{L,I} \int_0^\infty [pF(K,L) - wL - I - C(I)]e^{-rt} dt \qquad (1)$$

---

[4] The production function is assumed to satisfy the Inada conditions $\lim_{K\to\infty} F_K = \lim_{L\to\infty} F_L = 0$ and $\lim_{K\to 0} F_K = \lim_{L\to 0} F_L = \infty$.

where p, w are the price of output and the wage rate, respectively.[5] The price of investment goods is assumed to be unity. r is the firm discount rate, here assumed constant for simplicity. Maximization is carried out subject to the capital accumulation constraint

$$\dot{K} = I - \delta K. \tag{2}$$

The problem (1) is solved using Pontryagin's maximum principle. The Hamiltonian is

$$H = e^{-rt}\left([pF(K,L) - wL - I - C(I)] + q[I - \delta K]\right) \tag{3}$$

where q is the (current valued) costate variable associated with (2). The sufficient conditions for the solution to this optimal control problem are:[6]

$$\dot{q} + pF_K(\cdot) = q(r + \delta) \tag{4}$$

$$pF_L(\cdot) = w \tag{5}$$

$$q = 1 + C'(I) \tag{6}$$

and the transversality condition

$$\lim_{t \to \infty} (qK)e^{-rt} = 0 \tag{7}$$

Equation (4) equates the return from holding an extra unit of capital to its opportunity cost. Since the price of capital goods is assumed to be unity, q represents the shadow value of an extra unit of installed capital, or "marginal q." Since $C''(\cdot) > 0$, (6) says that investment is an increasing function of marginal q as in Abel (1979) and Hayashi (1982). We can therefore write

$$I = I(q) \qquad I'(\cdot) > 0 \tag{8}$$

By constant returns $F_L(K,L) = F_L(1,L/K)$ and $F_K(K,L) = F_K(1,L/K)$ so that (5) defines a labor demand curve of the form $K\varphi(w/p)$, which can be inserted into (4) to obtain

$$\dot{q} + pF_K(1,\phi(w/p)) = q(r + \delta) \tag{9}$$

The value of q at time 0, the shadow value of an additional unit of capital in place, can be found by integrating (9) forward and applying the transversality condition (7). It is given by

---

[5] Time subscripts have been supressed whenever possible.
[6] See Kamien and Schwartz (1981). Sufficiency requires concavity of the profit function which is ensured as the production function $F(\cdot)$ is concave and the adjustment cost function $C(\cdot)$ is strictly convex.

$$q_0 = \int_0^\infty [pF_K(1, L/K)] e^{-(r+\delta)t} \, dt$$

$$= \int_0^\infty [pF_K(1, F_L^{-1}(w/p))] e^{-(r+\delta)t} \, dt \tag{10}$$

Notice that current and future real wages enter q negatively. The intuition is that by increasing the capital-labor intensity under constant returns, higher wages reduce the present and future marginal products of capital and therefore the value of capital in place.

Equation (9) and the capital accumulation constraint

$$\dot{K} = I(q) - \delta K \tag{11}$$

are a pair of equations of motion for q and K which can be used to construct a conventional phase diagram.[7] In the steady state, the firm undertakes replacement investment sufficient to maintain a steady-state capital stock K*. This is given as the intersection of the two isoclines

$$q(r + \delta) = pF_K(1, \phi(w/p)) \tag{12}$$

$$I(q) = \delta K \tag{13}$$

at point A in Figure 1. It is straightforward to show that the first locus is flat, the second upward-sloping.

The effect of an unanticipated, permanent increase in wages can be seen in Figure 1. Following the increase in the wage rate from w_0 to w_1, the rate of investment I and the shadow price of capital q jump instantaneously to a lower level (point B). Over time, the capital stock declines to its steady-state value K** (point C). The paths of investment, the capital stock, and employment over time are shown in the second panel of Figure 1. An increase in the wage induces an initial rise in the capital-labor ratio. Convex adjustment costs rule out discrete changes in the capital stock, so the firm accomplishes this objective in the first instance by shedding labor. Thereafter, lower q and lower investment leads to a reduction in the capital stock. It is important to note that, to keep K/L constant along the adjustment path as required, employment and output must further decline over time. This process continues until the capital stock reaches its lower equilibrium

---

[7] The dynamics of the system correspond to a saddlepoint because for any point above or below the $\dot{q} = 0$ locus, the system will blow up asymptotically and the only stable path to the long-run equilibrium lies along this $\dot{q} = 0$ locus. The transversality condition (7) ensures that this stable solution is chosen.

level K*.[8] Capital accumulation therefore reinforces adverse effects of higher real wages on employment; effectively it increases the elasticity of demand for labor, since the supply of the other factor (capital) is perfectly elastic in the long run at price r+δ.[9]

Figure 1. Adjustment of the Physical Capital Stock to an Exogenous Wage Increase and Implied Time Paths of Investment, the Capital Stock, and Employment

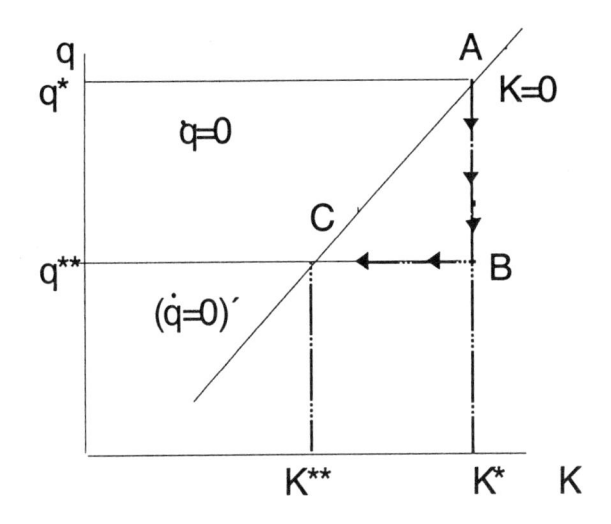

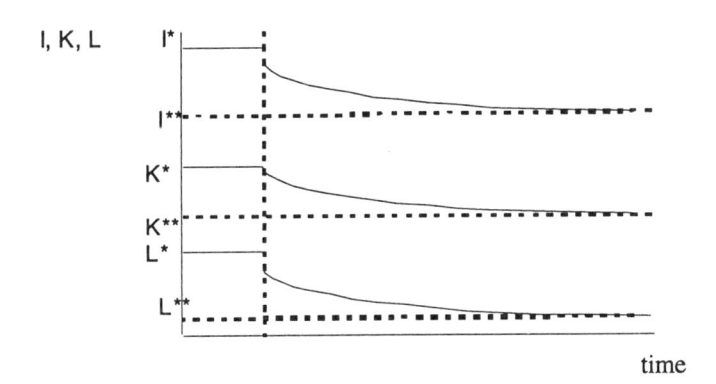

---

[8] With decreasing returns to scale, q and I initially overshoot and afterwards recover and increase towards their new equilibrium levels.

[9] With constant returns in the adjustment cost function as well as the production function, the economy would respond to the wage increase by disinvesting to zero.

3.2. Wages and Human Capital Formation

A claim often made by the leaders of West German trade unions is that high wage levels increase the return to training and thereby induce workers to acquire new skills or a better education. High wages in this sense are ultimately "validated" by an endogenous improvement in productivity. In one sense, the argument is trivially true; moving up along a labor demand curve will result in higher productivity for all those workers who keep their jobs. This also leads to more unemployment, however, so the union argument must be related to favorable shifts in the demand for labor induced by a high-wage policy. In this section we provide a potential rationalization of this argument which focuses on the returns to human capital formation and which has also figured prominently in the literature on endogenous growth.[10]

Consider as an alternative to the model of Section 3.1. the following model of a representative household which supplies $\overline{L}$ units of labor inelastically and is constrained to work whatever hours demanded by the representative firm. This demand is given by the labor demand function $L^D = H\varphi(w)$, where w is the real wage and H is the level of human capital with which workers are endowed, with $\varphi < 0$.[11] Human capital is quasi-fixed; it can be increased only by persistent investment expenditures θ (education, training) which have cost τ. Such training can occur on the job or in unemployment.

The representative household maximizes the present discounted value of income net of investment in human capital, solving[12]

$$\max_{\theta} \int_0^{\infty} \left(wL^D - \tau\theta\right)e^{-rt}\,dt \qquad (14)$$

subject to

$$\dot{H} = \psi(\theta) - \delta H \qquad (15)$$

As before δ is the rate of depreciation of accumulated (human) capital. Note that income in unemployment is set to zero for simplicity and r is fixed real rate of

---

[10] See Lucas (1988), or Barro and Sala-i-Martin (1995).

[11] This function can be derived from the behavior of competitive firms maximizing profits subject to the production function F(H, L) in which L (physical labor) and H (human capital) are imperfect substitutes. As we point out in the next section, this formulation ignores the effect of physical capital on the desirability of human capital investment.

[12] We assume an infinitely-lived household for simplicity; none of the key results is changed if the household has a finite life. Similarly, we assume that utility is equivalent to income; the analysis is made more complicated, but not overturned, when couched in utility terms.

interest used to discount future earnings. Maximization occurs with respect to human capital investment θ, a function of time.

The optimal human capital decision can be solved as in the previous section. The Hamiltonian for problem (14) is

$$H = e^{-rt}\{wH\varphi(w) - \tau\theta + \mu[\Psi(\theta) - \delta H]\} \tag{16}$$

where μ is the costate variable on the human capital accumulation constraint (the marginal value of an additional unit of human capital). Conditions for optimality are:

$$\Psi' = \frac{\tau}{\mu} \tag{17}$$

$$w\varphi(w) + \dot{\mu} = (r + \delta)\mu \tag{18}$$

with transversality condition

$$\lim_{t \to \infty} \mu e^{-rt} = 0 \tag{19}$$

Assuming an interior solution, the optimal human capital investment policy can be written (at least locally) as

$$\theta^*(\mu) \equiv \phi'^{-1}(\tau/\mu) \tag{20}$$

and from the properties of φ, it can be shown that $\partial\theta^*/\partial\mu > 0$ and $\partial\theta^*/\partial\tau < 0$.

The evolution of the costate μ and state variable H are governed by the respective differential equations:

$$\dot{H} = \psi(\theta^*(\mu)) - \delta H, \tag{21}$$

and

$$\dot{\mu} = (r + \delta)\mu - w\phi(w) \tag{22}$$

By integration and applying the transversality condition we can obtain the value of μ in $t = 0$ as

$$\mu_0 = \int_0^\infty e^{-(r+\delta)t} w\phi(w) dt \tag{23}$$

As in the previous section, the dynamics of the system can be investigated using the phase diagram. While the $\dot{H} = 0$ locus is upward sloping, the $\dot{\mu} = 0$ curve is horizontal.

We now study the effect of an exogenous, permanent, unanticipated, once-and-for-all wage increase on H and L. The $\dot{H} = 0$ locus remains unchanged, while the $\dot{\mu} = 0$ locus shifts. To determine the direction of that shift, differentiate the latter isocline to obtain

$$d\mu/dw = (\phi + \phi'w)/(r + \delta), \tag{24}$$

so the steady state value of μ can either increase or decrease in response to the real wage increase. For the union argument to hold at all – for a higher wage to shift the $\dot\mu = 0$ locus upward permanently – requires the elasticity of labor demand to be strictly smaller than unity. The intuition for this result is straightforward. A higher wage has two effects on the value of an additional unit of human capital to an employed worker. It increases the earning power of existing human capital, but it also reduces the level of employment. Assuming that the elasticity condition holds, the outcome is an increase in the shadow value of human capital from μ* to μ**, shown as the jump from A to B in Figure 2. Investment rises, and over time human capital increases to its steady state value H** (point C).

Figure 2. Adjustment of the Human Capital Stock to an Exogenous Wage Increase and Implied Time Paths for Investment, Human Capital Stock and Employment

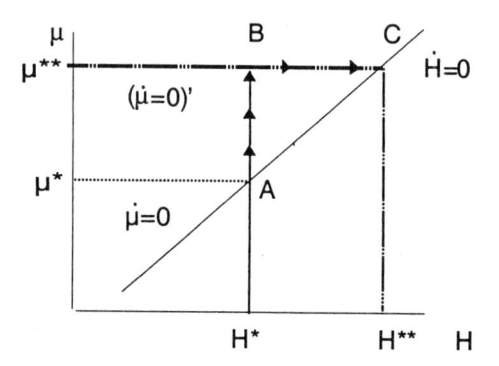

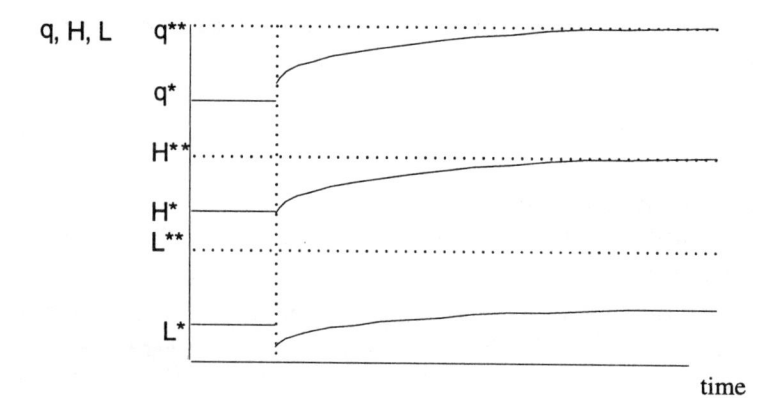

The time paths of employment, human capital investment, and the stock of human capital under the optimistic scenario are displayed in the second panel of Figure 2. The immediate consequence of the wage increase is a decline in employment and an increase in the unemployment rate as firms move back along their given labor demand schedules. At the same time, the shadow value of human capital jumps, inducing retraining investment and an increase in H. As H accumulates, the demand for labor increases and unemployment declines. The steady state value of employment is ambiguous, however, the elasticity condition is insufficient to guarantee that *employment* increases in the steady state. For this, it must be the case that the net effect in the steady state on labor demand is positive, or

$dL^D/dw = \phi(dH/dw) + H\phi' > 0$ which can be rearranged as

$(dH/dw)(w/H) > -w\phi'/\phi \equiv \eta$ (25)

or that the elasticity of human capital formation to wages is greater than η, the elasticity of labor demand at *given* human capital levels. But, using the fact that

$\partial H/\partial \mu = \psi' \theta^{*'}/\delta,$
$dH/dw = (\partial H/\partial \mu)(d\mu/dw)$

$= (\psi' \theta^{*'}/\delta)[(\phi + \phi'w)/(r+\delta)].$

By substitution in (25) we obtain the local condition

$\psi' \theta^{*'} \phi(1-\eta)w > H(r+\delta)\eta\delta$ or

$$\frac{\psi' \theta^{*'}(\eta^{-1}-1)w}{(r+\delta)\delta} > H/\phi$$
(26)

so a small wage increase will lead to higher employment if, among other things, human capital is low to begin with, if the efficiency of resources devoted to training (ψ') is high, if the responsiveness of investment to its shadow value θ^{*} is high, if wages are initially high, and if rates of discounting and depreciation and, most importantly, the elasticity of demand with respect to the wage, η, are sufficiently small. If η exceeds unity, then the union argument can never hold.

3.3. Synthesis: Which Model is Correct ?

The models of the last two sections are limited to the extent that each set of agents ignores the formation of capital undertaken by the other. Firms took their investment decisions given labor productivity, while workers invest in human capital, taking the position of the labor demand curve as given. To model both decisions simultaneously would require considering technologies of the form F(K, H, L) and studying the evolution of the two types of capital in a single framework. Without deriving this model explicitly, which would involve a system of two state and two costate variables, we can draw the following qualitative conclusions.

First, the result will depend on physical capital/human capital complementarities. For the constant returns production case, the steady state shadow value q* can be written as F_K (K/H,1,L/H) / (δ+r), so

$$dq^*/dH = \frac{-(KF_{KK} + LF_{KL})}{(\delta + r)H^2} \tag{27}$$

where the partial derivatives are evaluated at (K/H,1,L/H). Similarly it can be shown that

$$d\mu^*/dK = \frac{w(KF_{LH} + LF_{LL})}{KF_{LL}(\delta + r)} \tag{28}$$

Neither of these two expressions has an unambiguous sign; both depend on relative substitutability with the third factor, physical labor. An increase in the physical (human) capital stock will increase μ* (q*) if human and physical capital are complements, but may decrease it if they are substitutes.

Putting aside issues of capital/labor/skill complementarities, a further conclusion is that even if firms and workers do not interact strategically, expectations of the behavior of other decision makers, and thus of their expectations, will matter. Workers perceiving pessimism among those taking physical investment decisions will, in the complement case, experience a decline in the shadow value of human capital and undertake less investment themselves.

Finally, we have assumed all along that unions set wages with no feedback from the labor market. This is unrealistic, even in countries with highly institutionalized collective bargaining systems. In the next section we examine this last point in more detail with an eye to the development in eastern Germany. Informal evidence suggests that wages do respond to unemployment –that is, are not totally truly exogenous but are determined within the model, even after an exogenous "wage explosion" or shift in the wage setting policies of unions.

4. How "Exogenous" are Real Wages in Eastern Germany?

It is not unfair to say that the ambitious plan to impose wage equality across eastern and western Germany has fallen far short of its goal. Despite widely heralded wage agreements guaranteeing wage parity within a limited time horizon, actual remuneration to workers in the East has stagnated substantially below that in the West (DIW et al. (1999)). While real consumption and especially product wages have risen dramatically, they are far from "Japanese levels" predicted by Sinn/Sinn (1992). One explanation for this discrepancy lies in the considerable differences in hours worked as well as supplemental compensation between the two regions (Vogler-Ludwig, K. (1997)). A second more important reason for the failure of rapid East-West wage convergence seems to be a massive decline in union membership in the East. Just as rapidly as it had risen, the onset of unemployment and the inability of unions to guarantee employment has resulted in a backlash in membership rolls and a dramatic loss of union influence in the new eastern states. Table 2 documents this development in the first years after unification.

Table 2. DGB-Membership in the Eastern German States, 1991-1995

	Membership (000s)			Union density (percent)		
	1991	1993	1995	1991	1993	1995
Berlin & Brandenburg	1085	910	765	38.0	43.8	36.6
Saxony	1342	836	677	59.0	52.1	42.0
Saxony-Anhalt	727	471	376	52.8	52.2	41.4
Thuringia	613	404	327	50.2	50.8	38.5
Mecklenburg-West Pommerania	439	283	224	48.3	49.5	36.7
Total	*4158*	*2906*	*2370*	*50.6[a]*	*48.8*	*39.0*
Memo item: West Germany	7643	7383	6994	32.3	32.5	31.4

Notes: (a) excl. West Berlin 1991: All data as of 30 June 1991; 1993 and 1995: Membership data as of 31 December. For density figures, averages of current and preceding years' membership levels were divided by employment at midyear.

Sources: 1991 numbers from Kleinhenz (1992); 1993 and 1995 -Employment: Statistisches Bundesamt, Fachserie 1, Reihe 4.2.1., June 1996; – Union members: DGB, July 1996.

This decline in influence has resulted in an increased readiness on the part of workers and works councils to engage in US-style "concession bargaining," i.e., accepting wages below contract-determined minimum levels in an effort to save enterprises from bankruptcy. Under West German collective bargaining rules, this development would have been unthinkable, as enterprises which are members of an employers' association are joint signatories to the collective agreement (*Flächentarifvertrag*) and are bound to pay at least minimum wages specified in the contract. Yet in the East, an increasing number of firms, in particular privately run firms, have abandoned their employers' associations, opening up the possibility of enterprise level bargaining (DIW et al. (1999)).[13]

Such unprecedented developments may provide East German industry with a measure of flexibility that is otherwise lacking in the West. Due to the striking variation in fortunes of industrial sectors in the East (Burda/Funke (1995), Pohl (1996)) it is likely that this will show up in a broader differentiation of wages across these sectors. The left hand column of Figure 3 illustrates increased dispersion in a simple way over the years 1991-1993. The points in the diagram represent individual two-digit manufacturing industries, and their location reflects the relative wage levels in that industry. The fact that the points are clustered in the north-western part of the diagram reflects the wage gap. While this situation clearly was improved over time, it did not improve for all sectors, nor at the same rate. In some sectors productivity is increasing dramatically while not at all in others, while productivity increases were achieved by layoffs in some industries and expansion in others (Burda/Funke (1995)). This assessment is confirmed by the evolution of unit labor costs, which is crucial for the viability of enterprises. The right hand side of Figure 3 displays the evolution of unit labor costs for the same set of manufacturing industries. Evidently, the low productivity of eastern German enterprises in many sectors left little room for manoeuvre, but the situation was improving.

These developments – especially the reshuffling of human and capital resources implied by structural change of this magnitude – have important implications for investment, as the models of the previous section discussed. Wage concessions in the light of high unemployment raise the marginal valuation of installed and lead capital to higher investment rates.[14] This can already be seen in the heterogeneity of sectoral investment rates in the eastern states. Figure 4 documents a strong negative correlation between per capita investment rates on the one hand and unit labor costs in East German manufacturing on the other. This would increase productivity in the "right industries." On the other hand, human capital investment – to the extent it occurs as described in Section 3.3. – may be slowed as the incentive to acquire higher skills is dampened.

---

[13] This situation can be changed only if the Minister of Labor declares a contract binding for all firms and workers in a particular sector, should he deem this in the "public interest." The possibility of such an action seems particularly remote at the present time.

[14] See for example the model in Burda (1988), which endogenizes wage setting and capital investment in the same context. Grout (1984) and van der Ploeg (1987) rationalize how wage setting by unions reacts when capital is endogenous.

Figure 3. Hourly Wages (DM/hour) and Unit Labor Costs (percent) in Eastern and Western Manufacturing Industries, 1991 – 1993

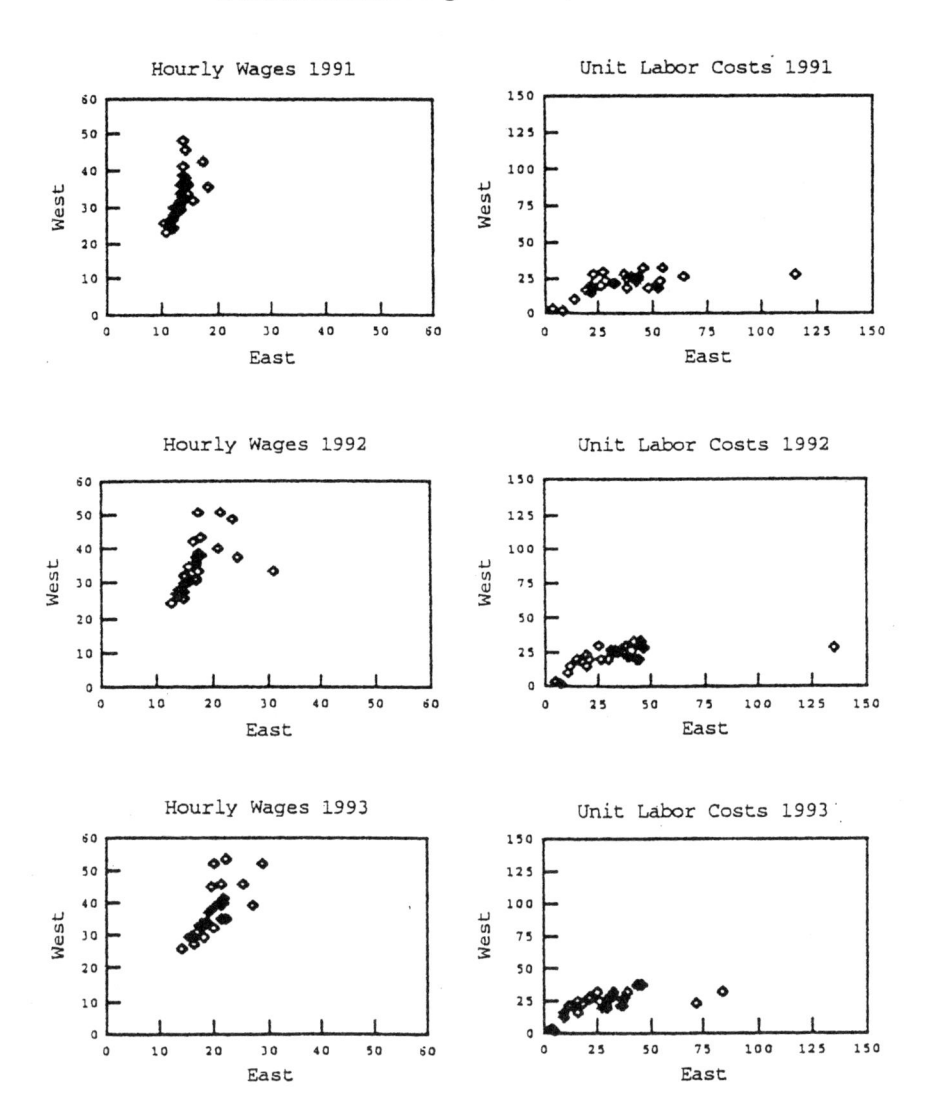

Source: Görzig and Noack (1994)

Figure 4. Unit Labor Costs and Gross Per Capita Investment (1,000 DM, constant 1991 Prices) in East German Manufacturing Industries, 1991-1993

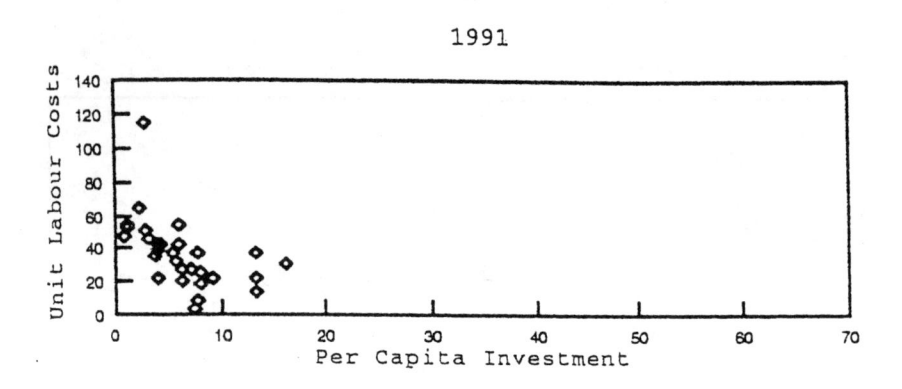

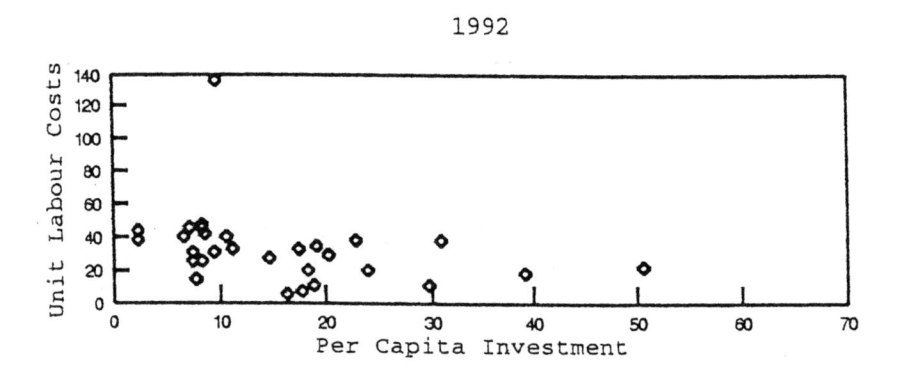

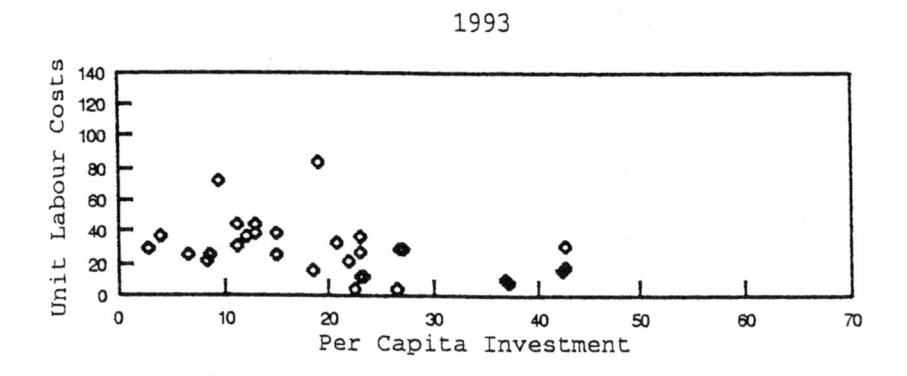

Source: Görzig and Noack (1994)

5. Conclusions

Collective bargaining and wage formation can be related to structural change a number of different contexts. More conventional models (e.g., Djajic/Purvis (1987)) stress the union-driven collective bargaining in a simple two-sector framework. In such models, collective bargaining tends to prolong the course of structural change by preventing the release of workers into the alternative (here: the new private) sector. The results tend to support claims by the *Sachverständigenrat* that wage subsidies "only preserve old structures and the very inefficencies that the reforms are expected to correct." (*Sachverständigenrat* (1991, p.9); authors' translation). On the other hand, a number of less conventional models which stress learning-by-doing reach different conclusions.[15]

In contrast, we have focused on the wage as an exogenous force in the economic integration of Germany and on medium-term incentives to invest in different forms of capital. Arguments presented in this paper suggest that the evolution of wages in the East affected the direction of structural change, as well as the chances for rapid convergence. The more traditional line of argument – high wage policies retard investment and thereby structural change – is well-established. On the contrary, the conditions necessary to justify a "high-wage, high-tech strategy" (Sinn/Sinn (1992)) are sufficiently controversial to warrant further empirical investigation. The central issue is whether an exogenous increase in wages induces enough endogenous investment in human capital to "pay for itself." Besides the interest rate, the rate of human capital depreciation, and the effective resource costs of creating human capital, the central parameter determining the direction of the effect is the elasticity of demand for labor, especially unskilled labor. Provided the elasticity of labor demand sufficiently high, the post-unification wage explosion in Eastern Germany did not only cause high unemployment, but could also leave a poorly skilled labor force in its wake.[16]

Under the pessimistic elasticity scenario, the patterns of wage moderation reported in Section 4 have salutary effects on both types of investment. Rather than East-West wage parity, it now appears that wage flexibility is emerging in the new states in a form which has rarely been seen in post-war Germany. These developments are likely to have far-reaching effects on the traditional German

---

[15] For example, in the "learning-by-doing" model it could be argued that the industrial sector of East Germany is characterized by a higher exogenous growth rate (see for example, Chadha (1991)). It may be well be the case that the "competitive sector" has the fastest growth potential, either due to Schumpeterian dynamics or more rapid adoption of new technologies by competitive firms.

[16] Fitzroy/Funke (1998) report both short and long-run point estimates for unskilled blue-collar workers which are in excess of, but not always statistically significantly different from unity.

industry-wide system of pattern bargaining. Economic historians may judge German unification as the Trojan horse that introduced "right to work" to the collective bargaining landscape, just as southern U.S. states rejected closed shop in the 1970s, or as Swedish metalworkers brought down nationwide bargaining in the mid-1980s. Rather than asking how long East German wages will take to converge to Western levels, the appropriate question may be: How long will the bargaining system in the West require to converge to the East?

Acknowledgements

This research was undertaken with support from the European Commission's Phare ACE Program. This paper is an updated and revised version of CEPR Discussion Paper No. 652 "Trade Unions, Wages and Structural Adjustment in the New German States". We are grateful to Munich conference participants as well as Jürgen Jerger and Jochen Michaelis for comments and suggestions. Matthias Almus and Ulrike Handtke provided useful research assistance.

References

Abel, A.B. (1979), *Investment and the Value of Capital*, New York.

Akerlof, G. et al. (1991), East Germany in from the Cold: The Economic Aftermath of Currency Union, *Brookings Papers on Economic Activity* 1, 1-105.

Barro, R./Sala-i-Martin, X. (1995), *Economic Growth*, New York.

Burda, M. (1988), Is there a Capital Shortage in Europe?, *Weltwirtschaftliches Archiv* 124, 38-57.

Burda, M./Funke, M. (1993), German Trade Unions after Unification: Third-Degree Wage Discriminating Monopolists?, *Weltwirtschaftliches Archiv* 129, 537-560.

Burda, M./Funke, M. (1995), East Germany: Can't We Be More Optimistic?, *Ifo-Studien* 41 (3), 327-354.

Chadha, B. (1991), Wages, Profitability and Growth in a Small Open Economy, *IMF Staff Papers* 38, 59-82.

DIW et al. (1999), Gesamtwirtschaftliche und unternehmerische Anpassungsfortschritte in Ostdeutschland, Neunzehnter Bericht, *Kiel Discussion Paper 346/347*, Kiel Institute of World Economics, Kiel.

Djajic, S./Purvis, D. (1987), Intersectoral Adjustment and the Dynamics of Wages, *Weltwirtschaftliches Archiv* 123, 216-231.

Fitzroy, F./Funke, M. (1998), Skills, Wages and Employment in East and West Germany, *Regional Studies* 32(5), 459-467.

Görzig, B./Noack, G. (1994), Kennziffern für das verarbeitende Gewerbe Ostdeutschlands, DIW, Berlin.

Hayashi, F. (1982), Tobin's Marginal q and Average q: A Neoclassical Interpretation, *Econometrica* 50, 213-224.

Kamien, M. I./Schwartz, N. L. (1981), *Dynamic Optimization: The Calculus of Variations and Optimal Control in Economics and Management*, New York/Oxford.

Kleinhenz, G. (1992), Tarifpartnerschaft im Vereinten Deutschland, *Aus Politik und Zeitgeschichte. Beilage zur Wochenzeitung das Parlament* No. B12/92, 14-31.

Klodt, H. (1990), Wirtschaftshilfen für die neuen Bundesländer, *Wirtschaftsdienst* 70, 617-622.

Lawrence, C./Lawrence, R. Z. (1985), Manufacturing Wage Dispersion: an End Game Interpretation, *Brooking Papers on Economic Activity* 1, 47-106.

Lucas, R.E. (1988), On the Mechanics of Economic Development, *Journal of Monetary Economics* 22, 3-32.

Pohl, R. (1996), Situation und Perspektiven der Wirtschaft in den neuen Bundesländern, *Wirtschaft im Wandel* 8, 2-15.

Sachverständigenrat zur Begutachtung der gesamtwirtschaftlichen Entwicklung (1991), *Marktwirtschaftlichen Kurs halten. Zur Wirtschaftspolitik für die neuen Bundesländer*, Sondergutachten, April, Wiesbaden.

Scheremet, W. (1992), Der Arbeitsmarkt in Deutschland, *DIW-Wochenbericht* 59, 49-57.

Sinn, G./Sinn, H.-W. (1992), Jumpstart – The Economic Unification of Germany, Cambridge.

Tooze, M.J. (1976), Regional Elasticities of Substitution in the United Kingdom in 1968, *Urban Studies* 13, 35-44.

Van der Ploeg, R. (1987), Trade Unions, Investment and Employment, *European Economic Review* 31, 1465-1492.

Vogler-Ludwig, K. (1997), Arbeitsmarkt Ost: Ist die Beschäftigungspolitik am Ende?, in: Oppenländer, K. (ed.), *Wiedervereinigung nach sechs Jahren: Erfolge, Defizite und Zukunftsperspektiven im Transformationsprozeß*, Berlin 233-248.

2. East/West-Wage Rigidity in United Germany

Karl-Heinz Paqué, University of Magdeburg

The aim of this paper is to analyze the causes of the rapid wage equalization between eastern and western Germany following in the first years after economic unification in 1990. The paper is divided into four parts. In Part 1, we summarize the basic facts of the eastern German labor market after economic unification as far as they are relevant for the purpose at hand. In Part 2, we recapitulate the causes of the sharp rise of unemployment in eastern Germany after unification. In Part 3, we turn to the reasons for East/West-wage equalization. We evaluate a few different theories, which have been advanced to explain the observed rapid rise of the eastern real wage level in the face of drastically increasing unemployment. In particular, we discuss whether the observed facts should be seen as the logical consequence of historically unique economic circumstances (e.g., due to the high East/West-mobility of the labor force or to the end-game characteristics of eastern German wage bargaining), or whether they are better viewed as the 'natural' outcome of German-style corporatism. In Part 4, we evaluate some normative economic arguments that have been advanced in favor of a rapid East/West-wage equalization. Particular emphasis is put on matters of interregional mobility, human capital accumulation, and the path of structural change.

1. Stylized Facts of the Eastern German Labor Market

Immediately after German economic unification in mid-1990, underemployment in eastern Germany reached and probably even surpassed the dimension of the Great Depression in the early 1930s. Table 1 gives a rough quantitative picture of the various categories of open and hidden unemployment as they developed in the three consecutive years 1990, 1991, and 1992. Before 1990, unemployment in the command economy of the German Democratic Republic can safely be assumed to have been negligible – though, of course, the employed labor force was heavily underutilized on the job. From this starting-point of close to zero percent, the 'open' unemployment rate, i.e. the number of registered unemployed persons divided by the labor force (unemployment rate U I) rose to a yearly average of 2.6 percent in 1990, 10.9 percent in 1991 and close to 15 percent in 1992. Including short-time work in the definition of unemployment (weighted by the average non-working time of short-time workers), one obtains an adjusted unemployment rate U II, which moved up much sharper than U I to 6.4 percent in 1990 and 21.7 percent in 1991. It declined again thereafter to 17.3 percent in 1992. However, this adjusted measure is still quite misleading. While the sharp rise of short-time working practice in 1990 and 1991 rightly signals a substitution of employment by a specific form of underemployment, the even more drastic decline of this practice between 1991 and 1992 was accompanied not by a massive rise of genuine employment, but a quite substantial increase of the number of people in work creation programs, requalification measures and early retirement schemes. Extending the definition of unemployment to include these supplementary forms of 'hidden' unemployment – in the table: U III covering people in work creation and requalification programs, U IV in addition covering people in early retirement schemes – the picture is one of a sharp increase of unemployment between 1990 and 1991 (from around 6-9 percent to 23-30 percent), and roughly a stagnation between 1991 and 1992.[1]

Although these extended measures U III and U IV do give a first impression of the true magnitude of actual underemployment, they are to be interpreted very cautiously because they still neglect important categories of joblessness in the eastern Germany of 1990-92. At least two categories stand out in importance. First, a significant part of the labor force in *Treuhand* firms was still threatened by lay-offs as these plants were highly subsidized and many would close down eventually. At the time, there were still about half a million employees in *Treuhand* firms – 50 percent of them in industrial plants that were very hard to privatize or restructure[2] and it would not be surprising if that amounted to a further potential of 300,000 unemployed persons. Second, many unemployed persons – notably females – had withdrawn from the labor force into household work. In the labor market, they represented a 'reserve of discouraged workers', which went well beyond the extent of de-activation that typically happens in cyclical downturns in the West. The fact that the rate of labor force participation – measured as the share of the labor force in the population – had decreased from almost 60 percent in 1989 to roughly 48-50 percent in 1992 suggests that this discouraged worker effect may have been quite substantial. It is remarkable that female labor force participation in the East had already more or less reached the lower western level by 1992/93 – despite the probably better than average educational standards and labor market experience of women in the East.

At the same time, a rather broad measure of unemployment such as U IV may also be regarded as overstating the true dimension of joblessness because it includes persons, who retired early and who were likely to be removed from the

---

[1] Note that extending the definition of unemployment to include people in requalification programs and early retirement schemes also requires a redefinition of the labor force to cover not only the persons in employment (including those in work creation programs and in short-term work), unemployed persons and the net balance of East/West-commuters, but also persons in the requalification programs and early retirement schemes, which are usually not counted as part of the labor force.

[2] See DIW et al. (1999)

labor force for good. On the other hand, the massive use of early retirement led to a decline of the average age of the remaining employed labor force, thereby reducing the scope for the natural shrinkage of the labor force through age-induced exits in the next decade or so. Thus, in the short run, early retirement may not have increased unemployment. In the medium and long run, however, it deprived the labor market of a natural relief from the labor supply side. Hence if one focuses on the medium and long run of market absorption of surplus labor, then it makes good sense to include persons in early retirement schemes in the definition of unemployment and the labor force. Taking all these speculative considerations into account, it does not appear unrealistic to assume that about one third of the eastern German labor force were unemployed in one form or another by 1992/93.

Table 1. Underemployment in Eastern Germany 1990-1992[a]

		1989	1990	1991	1992
(1)	labor force	9858	9188	8382	7896
(2)	unemployed persons	0	240	913	1170
(3)	East/West commuters[b]	0	80	290	350
(4)	short-time workers	0	758	1616	370
(5)	average short-time work[c]	0	45.6	55.9	52.1
	Number of persons in ...				
(6)	work creation programs	0	3	183	388
(7)	requalification measures	0	11	223	432
(8)	early retirement schemes	0	239	543	812
(9)	unemployment rate U I[d]	0	2.6	10.9	14.8
(10)	unemployment rate U II[e]	0	6.4	21.7	17.3
(11)	unemployment rate U III[f]	0	6.5	25.3	25.0
(12)	unemployment rate U IV[g]	0	8.9	29.6	31.4
(13)	population	16,600	16,215	15,908	15,702
(14)	rate of labor participation LPI[h]	59.4	55.2	52.7	50.3
(15)	rate of labor participation LPII[i]	59.4	54.7	50.9	48.1

Notes: (a) Annual average of quarterly data (1)-(4), (6)-(8) and (13) in '000; (5) and (9)-(12), (14), (15) in percent. (b) Net balance. (c) In percent of normal working time; for 1992 estimated by Sachverständigenrat (1992/1993, p.101). (d) Defined as (2)/(1). (e) Defined as [(2)+(4)(5)]/(1). (f) Defined as [(2)+(4)(5)+(6)+(7)] /[(1)+(6)+(7)]. (g) Defined as [(2)+(4)(5)+(6)+(7)+(8)]/[(1)+(6)+(7)+(8)]. (h) Defined as (1)/(13). (i) Defined as [(1)-(3)]/(13).

Source: Institut für Weltwirtschaft; Sachverständigenrat (1992/1993, p.101).

A sectoral breakdown of the early contraction of employment is given in Table 2. It shows that, between the last quarter of 1989 and the fourth quarter of 1992, there was a clear-cut sectoral pattern in the magnitude of the shrinkage. Employment declined most sharply in agriculture and forestry (-67.6 percent), followed by industry (-48.9 percent), trade and transport (-27.7 percent), and services in the narrow sense, including government (-20.8 percent). Due to its previously very high share in total employment (44.6 percent), the absolute decline was most dramatic in industry, which released more than two million workers, followed by agriculture (662,000). In turn, the decline in the service sectors (in the broad sense) was relatively moderate. The intersectoral pattern becomes even more accentuated, if one distinguishes three main branches of industry, namely construction, energy (including mining) and manufacturing. While employment in construction and energy remained roughly constant, employment in manufacturing declined almost as sharply as in agriculture.

Table 2. Quarterly Employment in Eastern Germany 1989/IV – 1992/IV

	level		share		change	
	(in '000)		(in %)		89/IV-- 92/IV	
	89/IV	92/IV	89/IV	92/IV	(in'000)	(in %)
Total	9754	6297	100.0	100.0	-3457	-35.4
of which:						
agriculture, forestry	980	318	10.0	5.1	-662	-67.6
industry	4350	2225	44.6	35.3	-2125	-48.9
trade, transport	1651	1193	16.9	18.9	-458	-27.7
services, government	2773	2195	28.4	34.9	-578	-20.8
work creation programs	0	366	0.0	5.8	366	•

Source: Own calculations from Deutsches Institut für Wirtschaftsforschung/Institut für Weltwirtschaft, (1993, Table 1, p.4).

Parallel to the dramatic contraction of employment, real wages rose substantially. The first wave of collective agreements in major branches of industry and services in the summer of 1990 generally fixed the contractual minimum wage at around 50 percent of the western level in the respective branches, in construction even up to 72 percent.[3] As early as spring 1991, most collective agreements stipulated a stepwise increase of the contractual minimum

---

[3] For details, see Sachverständigenrat (1990/91), Table 20, pp.70-75.

wage up to 100 percent of the western level as of spring 1994.[4] In terms of actual earnings, the rise of nominal and real wages in the years 1990 and 1991 is portrayed in Table 3. Roughly speaking, the monthly wage of an average industrial employee (white and blue collar taken together)[5] rose from around 30 percent to about 50 percent of the respective western level within less than two years. Over this period, the respective ratio of hourly earnings was probably somewhat lower because average working time in the East (excluding short-time work) has been persistently higher than in the West, roughly by a margin of 5-10 percent. However, there is no doubt that the sharp upward trend of nominal wages relative to the West applies equally to all standard measures of worker remuneration.

The rise of the eastern nominal wage translates into quite divergent developments of the real wage, depending on whether nominal earnings are deflated by the eastern producer price index, which declined sharply in mid-1990 and remained roughly constant thereafter, or the consumer price index, which rose continuously over the sample period covered in the table. Thus the producer real wage shot up by more than 80 percent between May and July 1990 and by another 50 percent in the following months up to October 1990. In turn, the respective upward adjustments of the consumer real wage were more moderate, about 24 percent and 11.5 percent respectively. Of course, given the statistical difficulties of calculating price indices in an early post-socialist environment, characterized by heavily distorted prices and thus widespread shortages in submarkets as was still the case in East Germany in the spring of 1990, these calculations must be taken with more than a grain of salt. Nevertheless, there can hardly be any doubt that German economic unification in mid-1990 was accompanied by something like a free fall of producer prices that by itself led to a dramatic rise of producer real wages. Equally, it is indisputable that, from mid-1990, both producer real wages and consumer real wages rose quite continuously, and that the former did so considerably faster than the latter.

---

[4] For details, see Sachverständigenrat (1991/92), Table 32, pp.112-115, and (1992/93), Table 30, pp.107-110. Note that these agreements were later reversed so as to allow for a somewhat slower pace of East/West-wage equalization.

[5] For 1990 and 1991, the data on eastern wages as compiled by the Federal Statistical Office do not disaggregate according to white or bluecollar-status in the comparative statistics for East and West, because the dividing line between the two categories would have been quite arbitrary in the early post-socialist eastern economy.

Table 3. Changes in Wages and Prices Following Currency Union

	W_E^a	W_E/W_W^a	P_0^b	P_C^b	W_E/P_0^c	W_E/P_C^c
1/90	1184	0.31	•	•	•	•
4/90	1168	0.30	98.4	98.3	100.0	100.0
7/90	1393	0.35	64.2	94.5	182.8	124.1
10/90	1588	0.39	62.9	100.6	212.6	132.8
1/91	1667	0.42	63.3	108.9	221.9	128.8
4/91	1926	0.47	63.2	112.6	256.7	144.0
7/91	1996	0.47	63.1	115.1	266.3	146.0
10/91	2086	0.49	63.3	126.9	277.9	138.4

Notes: (a) W_E = average gross monthly wages of blue and white collar workers in the East (total industry). W_E/W_W = wage ratio East to West in percent; Source: Statistisches Bundesamt, FS 16, Reihe 2.1, various issues.

(b) P_0 (P_C) = price index of industrial producer prices (of the cost of living) in the five Eastern states, 1989 = 100; Source: Statistisches Bundesamt, FS 17, Reihe 3 and Wirtschaft und Statistik, various issues.

(c) W_E/P_0 (W_E/P_C)= real product wages (real consumption wages), 4/90 = 100. Real wages indices for 4/90 were calculated using the price indices for 5/90. W_E (1/93 – 10/95) = average gross weekly wages of blue collar workers in the East (total industry); Source: Statistisches Bundesamt, FS 16, Reihe 2.1, various issues; real wages computed after the two nominal wage series were chained at 1/93. Due to missing data the real wages indices for 4/1990 were calculated using the price indices for 5/1990.

Source: Burda/Funke (1993).

The contents of most collective agreements as of 1991 pointed to an equalization of contractual minimum levels between West and East in most industries by the year 1994. Later on, major contracts were renegotiated and then envisaged the respective wage equalization by 1996. However, this does not imply that actual earnings were equalized by then either. This is so for three reasons. First, the contractual agreements cover the core elements of remuneration only. Many contractual fringe benefits have not been negotiated to reach the western level or have simply not been subject to collective bargaining at all. Second, there is a persistent, cyclically rather stable 'layer' of supercontractual payments in the West, mostly built up in the time of overemployment in the 1960s and never melted away since then. Obviously, there have not been any market forces which could have helped to build up such a layer in the East as well. Hence, even with contractual minima equalized, a significant wage difference between West and East is in existence even now (DIW et al. (1999)). A highly tentative guess based on the role of fringe benefits and supercontractual payments in the West is that this residual difference is still in the range of 20-30 percent. Third, part of the labor force in the East – and probably a larger part than in the West – is not covered by contractual agreements at all. In all likelihood, this part will be more subject to market forces than the rest, which may prevent the actual East/West-wage equalization to come about.

2. The Causes of the Crisis

Briefly summarized, the breakdown of the eastern German labor market may be described and interpreted as follows.[6] With German unification in mid-1990, the East German economy was subjected to a huge liberalization shock, both internally and externally. Internally, the system of centrally administered price setting, production controls, and trade management was abolished in basically one stroke so that a completely new price system and incentive structure in virtually all newly emerging markets put heavy adjustment pressures on the factors of production. Externally, the economy was stripped off its almost watertight system of protection, which had kept it isolated from western capitalism. The opening up accentuated the adjustment pressures further, especially in manufacturing industries, which were suddenly facing fierce international competition in their home markets. It is clear that this once-and-for-all jump into a liberal market order was bound to lead to a wholesale devaluation of all physical and human capital, or more precisely, an immediate disclosure of the real value of all assets at world market prices. Naturally, large parts of the capital stock – above all in industries producing tradeable goods – were to become obsolete almost overnight at the prevailing wages, which were converted 1:1 from the 'soft' Ost-Mark into the 'hard' D-Mark. As a consequence, a vast, almost universal capital shortage emerged with the concomitant open or hidden unemployment. On top of this, wages rose rapidly from their original 1:1-D-Mark-level at the day of economic unification, and thus further worsened the extent of capital obsolescence and unemployment.

Except for the subsequent wage push, the 'core' of the crisis – not, of course, its sheer size and its abruptness – resembles the classical 'terms-of-trade'-crises that sunset industries in western Germany faced in the mid-1970s and early 1980s. Given the structure of world demand and the extent of competition from abroad, domestic products could not be sold at a price that covered at least short-run average cost. At a given physical productivity of labor, the declining product prices reduced the respective value productivity of labor at given employment.

---

[6] The following line of reasoning is rather uncontroversial in the literature. See, e.g., Akerlof et al. (1991), Sinn/Sinn (1992), Giersch/Paqué/Schmieding (1992), Chapter 6, Siebert (1992), Sachverständigenrat (1997), Lange/Pagh (1998).

Note that the terms-of-trade loss revealed through liberalization in eastern Germany was probably much more dramatic than the roughly 30 percent-decline visible in the statistics (Table 3) because that decline – and the subsequent stability – took place at rapidly shrinking levels of production and employment, i.e. at a steeply decreasing market supply of domestic goods. To soften the landing of the liberalization in terms of employment, a very dramatic nominal wage cut would have been necessary, much more dramatic than the often quoted physical productivity differential between West and East. E.g., if one assumes that the ratio of physical labor productivity between East and West was somewhere between 1:2 and 1:3, a number often floated in the public discussion at the time, and that this would have been the guideline for the East/West-differential, then not all that much would have been gained in terms of a softer landing. In fact, the actual earnings differential up to late 1991 (see Table 3) was approximately in this range, and nevertheless, the crisis took shape in its actual dimension.

In view of this diagnosis, one can conclude that German economic unification pushed the eastern German economy into a deep structural supply-side crisis with a capital shortage of a previously unknown dimension. Some authors[7] claimed that, on top of this dramatic supply-side crisis, there was also a lack of demand which severely aggravated the emerging downturn. This lack of demand was mainly identified with the immediate demand shift of eastern consumers away from 'shabby' eastern consumption goods to the more 'fancy' products manufactured in western Germany, which took place as soon as the Easterners received 'hard' D-Marks for their previously non-convertible East-Mark balances. Although, of course, such a demand shift or preference revelation did take place, it is misleading to attribute anything more to a genuine demand factor than a very short-run crisis in the consumer goods industries. The rationale for our judgment is simple. Only to the extent that the East/West-preference shift was a strictly temporary phenomenon which corrected itself as soon as the first glamour of western products was fading away, one might speak of a temporary lack of demand for domestic, i.e. eastern consumer goods.[8] To the extent that the shift remained permanent, however, it was nothing else than another indicator for the overall terms-of-trade loss of eastern industry. Given the price ratio of any pair of (imperfectly) substitutable East/West-goods at the day of economic unification, there was an oversupply of the eastern and an undersupply of the western goods so that equilibrium could have been restored only by a readjustment of this price ratio to the disadvantage of the East, considered the totality of characteristics (quality, design etc.) of the two products. Thus the apparent lack of demand, properly

---

[7] See, e.g., Akerlof et al. (1991).

[8] Even then, one might argue that it is far from clear why this lack of demand in the market for consumption goods should have translated into a lack of aggregate demand, i.e. a decline in aggregate absorption.

reinterpreted, boils down to another variant of supply-side deficiencies of the eastern products.

Apart from this conceptual argument against the lack-of-demand interpretation of parts of the crisis, it is questionable on empirical grounds how much the eastern German consumer goods industry really suffered from such-like shifts. After all, the inter-industrial pattern of production decline shows consumption goods industries (except textiles) and the food industries in particular to have experienced a much less pronounced downturn in production than the investment goods industries where demand shift effects due to preference revelation are unlikely to have played a significant role. In fact, the pattern of production activity after unification nicely confirms that the main determinants of the strength of the downturn are to be found in the tradability of the respective products and their degree of genuine qualitative and functional inferiority relative to the West. Thus investment goods industries in general experienced the sharpest contraction, much sharper than most basic materials industries (notable exception: chemicals), which are often naturally protected by the high transportation costs of their products and which are likely to have profited disproportionally from the relatively early upturn in construction activity, and much sharper than many consumption goods industries, notably the food industry, where products are relatively homogenous so that the East/West-difference in quality proved not very dramatic and often easily curable through a simple repackaging and restyling according to the new consumer preferences.[9]

3. The Causes of the Eastern Wage Push

The really puzzling fact about the eastern German labor market after unification is not the extent of the emerging unemployment, but rather the immediate sharp rise of nominal and real wages after economic unification and the envisaged contractual wage equalization between East and West. Quite a few different attempts were made in the literature to explain this fact, most of them identifying some 'special' historical circumstances that distinguished the eastern German situation from that of a 'normal' labor market. In the academic and public debate, there were four prominent explanations of this kind, which focus on (a) the conditions of German monetary union, (b) the pressure of East/West-migration, (c) the asymmetry of collective bargaining, i.e. the strength of the unions and the weakness of employers, and (d) the end-game characteristics of wage bargaining.

---

[9] For statistical details on the development of industrial production from the second half of 1990 to December 1992, see Deutsches Institut für Wirtschaftsforschung/Institut für Weltwirtschaft (1993), Table A1, p.64.

We shall review and evaluate these four non-exclusive explanations in the following paragraphs.

3.1. The Role of German Monetary Union

It was argued notably before and right after German economic unification that the 'generous' conversion rate of the formerly non-convertible Ost-Mark into D-Mark of 1:1 (instead of, say, 1:2 or 1:3) raised eastern labor costs to disastrously high levels and thus aggravated the labor market imbalance quite dramatically.[10] This argument is not plausible because it is based on assumptions about wage bargaining that appear to be very unrealistic precisely for the specific case of post-socialist eastern Germany. On theoretical grounds, a different starting-level of the wage can only make a difference for the outcome of subsequent wage bargaining if, roughly speaking, the subject of collective agreements is the *rate of change* of the wage, not its *level*. If it is the level alone, the mere establishing of a different starting-point does not give a reason for a different outcome beyond the very short run, i.e. the time span up to the first bargaining round. To be sure, eastern German wage bargaining after economic unification is an almost classical example of bargaining about wage *levels*, not relative wage increases, with the negotiated wage agreements usually formulated as a share of the western level in the same industry or, especially in the early bargaining rounds, as a fixed minimum DM-level. This was not surprising since from the very beginning, the public looked at eastern German wages almost exclusively in terms of the eastern share of the western level and not in terms of marginal improvements that were to be achieved. In fact, the implicit percentage increases were hardly discussed and went largely unnoticed in the public. Thus, a lower starting point would most likely have induced no more than a sharper once-and-for-all upward shift in the first bargaining round.[11]

---

[10] For an academic statement along these lines, see Akerlof et al. (1991), p.64.

[11] Note that, in such circumstances of almost complete calculation in terms of an exogenous wage standard ('the West'), even the preservation of a separate currency like, say, a convertible Ost-Mark would by itself have changed very little. Any exchange rate adjustment would have been fully compensated by a corresponding opposite change of the wage level in Ost-Mark so that the wage ratio East to West would have remained roughly constant at the ratio agreed upon in collective bargaining. Of course, assuming the survival of the Ost-Mark alone is a purely hypothetical exercise because, if it had happened, it is very likely that some forms of trade and mobility restrictions would also have been preserved and that the institutional merging of East and West would have been much slower than was in fact the case. Given the political constraints of the time, it is doubtful whether this ever was a realistic political option.

Even if the conversion rate were accepted as an important determinant of the early outcomes of wage bargaining after unification (say, those of summer and fall of 1990), it does not help to explain why – from this then collectively agreed base level – wages continued to rise all throughout 1991, despite a clearly visible dramatic worsening of the labor market conditions. To repeat, the actual starting-level of the eastern wage was around 1/3 of the western level in the early summer of 1990 (see Table 3) – much too high to avoid a severe employment contraction, but still way off parity so that a very substantial inner-German wage difference could have been preserved even at this stage. In fact, hardly anybody advocating a different conversion rate made a case for a substantially larger wage differential than 1:3, which roughly conformed to the East/West-physical productivity differential floated at the time. Hence, clearly, the major wage push took place well after German monetary union was established, at a time when the extent of the employment contraction had become quite evident.

3.2. The Pressure of East/West-Migration

By far the most widespread and popular view on the eastern wage push is that it was a reaction to the pressure exerted by large parts of the eastern German labor force which stood ready to move or did move in fact to western Germany to find work there.[12] In the light of the early heavy waves of East/West-migration right after the opening of the inner-German border, this view has some prima facie plausibility. On closer inspection, however, it is not convincing. As a market phenomenon, migration can only exert an upward pressure on the wage if the labor force that moves or threatens to move is in fact a scarce resource, not an abundant one. Roughly speaking, this happens whenever the economy finds itself in a state of full employment. This has manifestly not been the case in eastern Germany after 1989 where employers can hardly be assumed to have paid workers mobility premia to stay in the East simply because competition for jobs on the labor supply side was so intense. If there were partial scarcities in some segments of the labor market, i.e. for highly skilled workers with excellent prospects of finding jobs in the West, then premia might have been paid in these particular segments, but not for the workforce at large. Given the high unemployment in virtually all labor market segments of the eastern German economy – even among highly skilled workers – it is hard to see much market rationale for any such selective premia.[13]

---

[12] This view was expressed by many journalists and politicians on numerous occasions. For an early academic statement and a formal analysis of it, see Burda/Funke (1993), and Burda/Wyplosz (1992), who also provide some statistics on East/West-migration in the crucial year 1990 (p.334). For more current analysis see Burda et al. (1998).

[13] For a similar line of reasoning, see Akerlof et al. (1991), pp. 62-63.

It is important to realize that, if migration were the driving force behind the trend towards inner-German wage equalization, then collective bargaining would only have a passive role to play – just more or less reproducing what market forces would have achieved anyway. Given the very puzzle of fast real wage growth at dramatically rising unemployment, such an interpretation of the facts looks close to absurd. On the other hand, one might make a case for an indirect, non-market impact of migration on union wage policy. With western-dominated unions recognizing the threat of massive East/West-migration and its consequent depressive effects on western wage levels, they put priority on a rapid wage equalization to remove the economic rationale for the migration streams.[14] Plausible as it is on first glance, this argument makes a very unrealistic implicit assumption, namely that unions completely misjudged the economic rationale of the East/West-movements. As all standard migration models recognize, it is the expected income differential that matters for the migration decision of the individual agent, not the actual wage differential.[15] If a monopoly union representing western labor interests and facing a downward-sloping labor demand curve in the East takes this into account, then wage equalization is obviously not an optimal strategy to achieve the aim of minimizing the number of East/West-migrants. Instead, in setting the eastern wage, the union has to weigh the expected decline of the number of migrants from the pool of employed persons against the expected increase of the number of migrants from the pool of unemployed persons, which expands due to the aggressive wage policy. Given an elasticity of the labor demand function with respect to the real producer wage in the empirically relevant range (say, around -1), it is then quite unlikely that the union would choose wage equalization as an optimal strategy. Anticipating that a large part of the eastern workers would be pushed into unemployment, i.e. a state where they receive in the German framework less than 70 percent of their previous net wage (which at the time was still no more than 50 percent of the western level), a union that aims at minimizing migration flows from the labor supply side would hardly opt for the actually observed pattern of sharp wage growth in the East. Only if one assumed an implausibly thick veil of ignorance on the union's side about the labor market consequences of wage demands one could be hopeful to reconcile the observed wage growth with a rational anti-migration union policy. Then, however, the question arises why the unions did not reverse their course as soon as the sheer extent of the labor market crisis became visible.

---

[14] For a formal analysis along these lines, see Burda/Funke (1993).
[15] See very clearly on this point, Meckl (1992).

3.3. Asymmetry of Bargaining Power

It has been argued by Akerlof et al. (1991) that one major reason for the sharp rise in wages was a kind of organizational asymmetry between the labor side and the employers' side at the bargaining table of all major industrial branches. While labor was represented by the newly founded eastern German wings of powerful and experienced western unions like, e.g., the metal workers' union (*IG Metall*), most of the eastern managers at the bargaining table were still survivors of the old regime whose future professional destiny was largely independent of the actual outcome of the wage negotiations. In these circumstances, the resistance of the employers against wage demands was naturally very weak.[16]

This argument is certainly correct in the sense that the wage negotiations which took place were not genuine bargaining rounds with parties that have at least partially conflicting aims. Nevertheless, the argument begs the question because it does not give a rationale why unions should opt for wage equalization on their own. In standard monopoly union models, the wage is unilaterally determined in an optimization by the union under the constraint of a labor demand curve which then fixes the level of employment.[17] Hence what the argument says is that, basically, the situation of bargaining after unification is best described by a monopoly union model, with employers taking the union-set wage as given. However, this kind of model does only predict sharp wage increases, if, in the relevant range, the labor demand curve is quite inelastic so that there is in fact much scope for the monopolistic union to appropriate rents. Thus one has to search for reasons why labor demand was perceived as inelastic by the unions with respect to the real producer wage.

One obvious candidate to explain such a perceived lack of elasticity is the extent of subsidization, i.e. the 'soft budget constraints' of eastern firms.[18] All along the time of the decisive wage bargaining rounds from about summer 1990 to autumn 1991, virtually all firms of the state-owned holding company, the *Treuhandanstalt*, were heavily subsidized to keep up production and employment. Most of the subsidies were paid out in the form of liquidity grants so that, roughly speaking, the degree of subsidization was directly linked to the extent of the losses made. As a consequence, a very large part of the non-privatized firms in eastern Germany was simply not pursuing a profit-maximizing calculus in any meaningful sense so that, for the time being, there was certainly not anything like a downward sloping labor demand curve resulting from any such calculus. Although this was in fact the state of affairs at the time of collective bargaining, it is much less clear how long this state of heavy subsidization was expected to continue. An

---

[16] For details, see Akerlof et al. (1991), pp. 63-64.
[17] See, e.g., Farber (1986).
[18] See Burda/Funke (1993), and Sinn/Sinn (1992).

assessment of the debate at the time would almost certainly suggest that the state of affairs was widely perceived as a temporary emergency, not as anything like a long-term equilibrium. In fact, the already drastic rise of unemployment and short-time work in the 15 months of decisive wage bargaining following economic unification makes it quite implausible to assume that unions did not actually recognize the growing unemployment risks for their clientele entailed in an all too aggressive wage policy.

Other candidates than subsidization to explain a low real wage elasticity of labor demand lead to the fourth hypothesis, namely that wage bargaining had the characteristics of an end game.

3.4. End Game Bargaining

So-called end game situations arise in wage bargaining whenever a firm or an industry is clearly dying in the sense that there are no realistic prospects of recovery under any feasible adjustment scheme. Prospective investment in such a firm or industry will be zero whatever the level of wages simply because there is already more capital engaged in production than is actually needed. As a consequence, the long-run real wage elasticity of labor demand will also be low so that it pays off for unions to appropriate the quasi-rents of the firm by raising the wage.[19] In a way, the situation is the opposite of a soft budget constraint. Precisely because everybody knows that the firm will stop producing, labor has an incentive to 'plunder' the remaining capital stock.[20]

Though intriguing in its own right, this model does not properly describe the eastern German situation either. While for many state-owned eastern German firms the market prospects were very bad indeed, there were probably very few cases where it was clear from the beginning that an eventual return to profitability was altogether impossible. By far most of the firms found themselves somewhere between the prospect of extinction and a more or less successful restructuring. In addition, the wage at which bargaining started (say, 30 percent of the western level) was probably high enough to appropriate a large chunk of all quasi-rents of existing firms[21] so that any further increase would really just mean 'appropriating subsidies' for which case we are back at the question of the likely duration of government support.

---

[19] For an exposition of a model along these lines, see Lawrence/Lawrence (1985).
[20] The end game-model has been proposed i.e. by Burda/Funke (1993, 2000) to explain the peculiarities of the East German labor market.
[21] See Akerlof et al., (1991), pp. 61-62.

A more fundamental objection to the end game interpretation is that collective agreements set wages not only for the existing firms, but – as usual in Germany – also for all future firms of the respective industrial branch, provided they are members of an employers' association. Thus, analytically, the bargaining could never be of an isolated end game character. Rather it also fixed the conditions for future investments of other firms in the same branch. If the employment effects of these prospective future investments are taken into account in the union monopoly calculus – and there is no reason why unions should have disregarded them – then the end game model loses much of its appeal. To be sure, the model appears to be much better designed to describe a plant-level bargaining in the face of a prospective plant closure than industry- or nation-wide bargaining, which sets the conditions for continued employment and/or reemployment of all relevant union members.

In a different context, however, a specific variant of the end game interpretation may shed light on the puzzle of sharply rising wages. In view of the fact that large-scale lay-offs were expected to happen in eastern Germany in any case, wage increases were a means to secure higher benefit levels for the laid-off workforce in the prospective spell of unemployment. As German unemployment benefits are calculated as a share of the terminal net wage – roughly speaking 68 percent for the first year and 58 percent thereafter – the wage increases in fact improved the 'entrance conditions' into the benefit system quite dramatically. As unemployment benefits are regularly adjusted upwards according to the rate of increase of the old-age insurance benefits, which, in turn, are more or less indexed to the level of net wages, the stepwise increase of the wage level was really a major move towards opening the door to the welfare state for the eastern German labor force.

Plausible as this welfare state variant of the end game interpretation appears to be, it is very hard to speculate about its actual relevance. Empirically, there is no direct clue in the facts and the data that could help to determine how important these considerations were in the back of union leaders' minds compared to the standard trade-off between job security and income of the union membership. Two indirect facts, though, may speak against an all too dominant role of them. First, if they had been really dominant, then it would even be hard to explain why unions agreed to stretch the adjustment process over a few years. After all, the bulk of the prospective lay-offs was likely to happen in the two years following economic unification when the East/West-wage ratio was still generally below 60 percent. Second, there was no attempt made by unions to lobby for a temporary de-linking of the level of unemployment benefits (together with old-age pensions) from the general rise of wages. If the unions had simultaneously aimed at improving the lot of those members, who unavoidably lost their jobs, and of those, whose jobs were endangered by high wage rises, then a generous provision of unemployment benefits at a more moderate pace of wage growth would have been an attractive option. Under the special circumstances of eastern Germany, another temporary deviation from standard practices might have been accepted rather easily by the public at large, not least if it had been coupled with a rise of old-age pensions because pensioners were generally perceived as the real losers of unification.[22]

So much for the four major hypotheses that seek to find the explanation for the eastern wage push in the particular historical circumstances of German unification. All of them shed light on some peculiar economic characteristics of the unification process, with the social end-game interpretation having the lead in terms of plausibility. Taking an intuitive view of the matter, however, it is hard to consider even a combination of all four hypotheses as a satisfactory explanatory account of the events. The main reason for this judgment lies in the almost deterministic appearance of the path towards wage equalization. From the very beginning right after the currency union was established, wage negotiations in the East appeared to be strangely unaffected by the dramatic change of external conditions. All major wage rounds in the fall of 1990 and the spring of 1991 proceeded swiftly, without much public controversy on their content and without much press coverage. Remarkably enough, the partly parallel wage negotiations in the West received much more public attention – thus indicating that the West was widely regarded as the wage pacemaker for a united Germany and the East as following suit in due course through East/West-wage equalization.[23] Apparently, it looked much less unusual to the general public than to economists to see wages move up sharply in the face of rising unemployment in the East. This raises the question whether the fact to be explained was not so unusual after all. It may just as well have been a logical consequence of an ever present deep-rooted union philosophy on which wage policy was based for a long time and which was simply applied again under somewhat extreme circumstances. In a sense, this is our interpretation of the matter, and we shall elaborate in the following section what a rough explanatory account along these lines may look like.

3.5. Union Philosophy: The Principle of Equal Pay for Equal Work

Economically speaking, the basic rationale of unionism is to correct the outcome of (free) labor markets in a way that is perceived as desirable by union members.

---

[22] Far-reaching special rules were applied to eastern Germany anyway because laid-off persons in the East had never contributed to the western insurance system during their time of employment.

[23] Of course, this point can hardly be proven in an empirically rigorous manner since it concerns general moods and attitudes in the population, the political elite and the press rather than hard economic facts. However, a glance through the press archives of the Kiel Institute of World Economics on the relevant subject ('wages and collective bargaining') and the relevant time span (1990-1992) confirms the view expressed in the text.

As to wage setting, the union task falls into two different strands, an aggregate one – concerning the wage level and its growth over time – and a structural one – concerning the wage structure and its change over time. Taking a long-run perspective against the reference system of a completely free labor market, the structural task is likely to be the more fundamental one. After all, competitive forces will tend to drive up the wage level roughly with the growth of labor productivity, and to the probably large extent that unions' optimal wage policy follows just the trend growth of labor productivity, the presence of unions will not make much of a difference. Of course, unionism may persistently keep the wage level above its equilibrium by exploiting some monopoly market power,[24] but there is no obvious point in assuming that there is a systematic change of this 'monopoly mark-up' over time. Things look different with respect to the wage structure, where market forces do not necessarily pull in the same direction as union preferences: if some structure is considered as 'fair' or in another sense advantageous by the union membership, and if this structure is not established by the market or is disturbed in a market-driven process of revaluation of manpower and human capital, then there may be a persistent or a recurring clash of the union task with market forces, which is not "accommodated' by any common trend growth.

What matters for our purpose here is the regional element of the wage structure, because the puzzle of East/West-wage equalization is defined in terms of a regional dimension. Looking over the pre-unification experience, it is clear that the broad pattern of the regional wage structure was remarkably stable and undifferentiated in West Germany. This can be seen from Table 4, which depicts the average hourly earnings of an industrial worker in the different German states in ten-year intervals as a share of the West German average (in percent). Overall the differentiation was rather small – in the range of a coefficient of variation between 2.7 and 7.1 percent depending on the year chosen and on whether or not city states are included in the sample. More importantly, the pattern of the inter-state wage structure remained rather constant over time and it barely reacted to regional crises.[25] Taking into account that most of the inter-state variation is likely to be due to differences in the composition of industries – e.g. relatively high-capital intensity industries in Northrhine-Westfalia compared to Bavaria or Schleswig-Holstein – then one has to conclude that the West German economy experienced very little regional wage differentiation and flexibility all along its history.[26] Hence the regional equilibrium structure of wages that survived for so

---

[24] How large this monopoly mark-up happens to be empirically has been the subject of extensive econometric research on American unionism. For a survey of this literature, see Lewis (1986).

[25] See Paqué (1991).

[26] This picture is roughly confirmed when a different wage variable is used, namely the yearly gross income per employee (Table 4).

long should be interpreted as deliberately chosen by wage bargaining and thus fully backed by what may be called an egalitarian preference of the relevant industrial unions and the union umbrella organization.

In this sense, it is legitimate to speak of a long-standing German union philosophy based on a principle of equal pay for equal work ('PEPEW') which means that, whatever different market conditions prevailed in different regions of West Germany, the same type of work should be remunerated with the same wage. Given the regional structure of union organization on the industry level, this principle has never been explicitly formulated or made part of a programmatic statement because this would have meant officially denying the independence of the regional bargaining units. Apart from the factual constancy and rigidity of the regional wage structure, the principle can only be inferred from the many programmatic union statements against any kind of outsider 'wage dumping' under conditions of locally concentrated economic crises. As any such outsider compe-tition does invariably have a strong regional dimension, the case against it implicitly establishes a case against regional differentiation.

Why did German unions quite strictly adhere to the PEPEW in the past? In our view, it would be rather farfetched to search for a rationality of the PEPEW in the standard model world of wage bargaining, where unions basically decide upon the short- or medium-run trade-off between the likelihood of employment and the wage of some representative member. It seems much more reasonable to search for the rationality of the PEPEW in very long-term considerations of political economy, of group ethics (or 'social insurance'). Considerations of political economy creep in as soon as the government can be anticipated by unions to stand ready to take over the responsibility for the equality of living conditions all over the country and to carry out a 'regional policy' that at least partly compensates for the locational disadvantages of a specific region. If the government commitment to such a stance is strong and credible enough, then it is a reasonable strategy for unions to minimize the use of wage moderation as an instrument to improve locational conditions for production and investment in regions hit by crises and to leave the task to the government. Prima facie, this seems to be a quite realistic description of the basic regional policy assignment in West Germany. The West German government always had a rather strong commitment to the use of instruments of regional policy to improve the locational conditions in backward areas or in regions hit by industrial crises. To some extent, this commitment is even part of the German constitution.[27]

---

[27] See the sections on fiscal federalism (articles 106-107), which prescribe a redistribution of tax money to equalize living conditions across the country, and the so-called common tasks of the Federal State Government concerning the improvement of the regional economic structure (article 91a).

Table 4. Regional Wage Level as a Share of West German Average (in percent)

	1950	1960	1970	1980	1990
(a) Hourly Earnings of Industrial Workers					
Non-city states					
Schleswig-Holstein	96	96	96	99	96
Lower Saxony	98	98	101	101	101
Northrhine-Westfalia	103	107	106	102	101
Hesse	104	97	101	101	102
Rhineland-Palatinate	93	91	95	98	99
Saar	•	105	100	101	103
Baden-Württemberg	101[a]	93	98	100	102
Bavaria	93	87	90	93	94
City states					
Hamburg	117	105	111	113	110
Bremen	107	103	102	103	109
Berlin	•	90	101	99	99
Coefficient of variation[b]					
non-city states	4.3	6.5	4.6	2.7	3.0
all states	7.1	6.7	5.3	4.6	4.5
(b) Yearly Gross Income per Employee					
Non-city states					
Schleswig-Holstein	•	96	93	92	91
Lower Saxony	•	94	94	94	93
Northrhine-Westfalia	•	106	106	103	101
Hesse	•	100	104	103	104
Rhineland-Palatinate	•	97	95	98	97
Saar	•	112	100	103	100
Baden-Württemberg	•	99	99	101	103
Bavaria	•	94	93	94	96
City states					
Hamburg	•	110	114	116	117
Bremen	•	109	104	100	100
Berlin	•	95	100	105	103
Coefficient of variation[b]					
non-city states	•	5.9	4.8	4.4	4.5
all states	•	6.5	6.2	6.3	6.6

Notes: (a) 1951

(b) Standard deviation from non-weighted average divided by non-weighted average (in percent).

Source: Own calculations with data from Statistisches Bundesamt, *Bevölkerungsstruktur und Wirtschaftskraft* (various issues); Gemeinschaftsveröffentlichung der Statistischen Landesämter, *Volkswirtschaftliche Gesamtrechnungen der Länder*, Heft 9 (1960-76); and data provided by the Statistisches Landesamt Schleswig-Holstein.

As to group ethics (or 'social insurance'), it is realistic to assume that the vast majority of union members and even of the population at large would subscribe to the moral postulate that an equal type of work should also be paid equally in different locations, even if unemployment rates differ. In fact, the PEPEW is so widely accepted as an abstract principle that there has never really been a controversial discussion of it in the public.[28] Hence it is reasonable to interpret German unions as 'insurance agencies' that, among other things, guarantee a 'fair' treatment of labor across the country by making the same conditions of remuneration prevail everywhere. Of course, this does not mean that, under circumstances of high regional unemployment, an individual unemployed person may not be ready to work for conditions that she considers to be unfair on moral grounds, simply because her personal destiny is even more important to her than keeping up an accepted abstract principle. However, it means, that ex ante, i.e. behind a kind of Rawlsian veil of ignorance[29] where she did not know her future position in the labor market, she would prefer the PEPEW to prevail.

It is against this background of strong government commitment to regional policy and an ethical consensus on the matter of equal pay for equal work in different regions that the events following German unification may sensibly be interpreted. In this light, unification did not mean more than a redefinition of the geographical boundaries of the country in which the PEPEW applies between regions. Any deviation from the PEPEW was regarded as an unusual and unsustainable state of affairs that had to be corrected in due course. In a way, the burden of proof is thus turned upside down. The sharp eastern wage increases are no longer the extraordinary consequence to be explained by peculiar historical circumstances, but rather the logical implication of a long-standing practice of ensuring equal pay for equal work, and of assigning the responsibility to the government to carry out a compensatory regional policy. As long as this practice is not questioned in principle, there is no point in expecting anything else than a fast East/West-wage equalization. Given the vast subsidization of the East right from the start after unification, the unions had every reason to assume that the government stood ready to carry out a large – in fact, a gigantic – 'regional' program to support investment in the new eastern states. Hence there was really no powerful countervailing force which could have driven unions to rethink their philosophy.

It is important to recognize that the actual union wage policy defies any categorization as rational or non-rational in the sense of some simple constrained

---

[28] Remarkably enough, the issue of interregional wage equality does hardly receive any attention in a recent union-edited history of unionism in West Germany (Hemmer/Schmitz (1990)). In our view, this simply shows that PEPEW has become a fact of life, which is taken for granted rather than discussed controversially or preserved as an important item on the union agenda for the future.

[29] See Rawls (1971).

optimization. Given the great uncertainty about the future economic development, unions opted for preserving their role as a guarantor of the PEPEW into the future. By doing so quickly and decisively, they could create early facts and thus avoid being drawn into a quagmire of regional labor market responsibilities that might have endangered their traditionally unambiguous egalitarian position. On the other hand, they risked to worsen the regional labor market plight beyond the point that the public would see it as a sole responsibility of the government, and thus undermine their own position in the long run. A similar combination of pros and cons of this strategy applies to the support of the union members. On the positive side, unions could expect to be seen as unyielding supporters of a widely accepted ethical principle that, viewed from the perspective of western members, helped to suppress "unfair wage dumping'. On the negative side, the personal interests of union members in the East were brushed aside. While they shared the basic moral belief in the PEPEW,[30] they were ready to trade off this job security against the realization of an abstract principle.[31] By sacrificing a large number of union jobs in the East, the uncompromising wage policy could be seen as undermining union dominance in at least part of the united country. At any rate, a difficult conflict for unions between holding up important principles and risking to overdo the case by overstretching government responsibilities and undermining the membership base is clearly visible.

To sum up, the rapid wage push in eastern Germany after economic unification should be viewed first of all as the natural consequence of the interregional egalitarianism that collective agreements used to impose on the wage structure in West Germany. In being confronted with a regional crisis of so far unknown dimensions – both with respect to the size of the area and the restructuring requirements – unions chose a strategy of 'business as usual' so as to underline their traditional role as guarantors of fairness principles and the government's role as a source of regional support for investment. Sticking to this strategy was made very attractive in the short run by the historically unique circumstances of unification, notably the social end-game situation resulting from imposing standard western welfare state rules onto the new eastern states that started at much lower wage levels. However, the driving force of the process is to be located in the traditional structural rigidity of German-style corporatism.

---

[30] See the results of opinion polls carried out by Akerlof et al. (1991), which point to a majority of eastern employees regarding the payment of a lower wage in the East for the same work by the same company as a form of exploitation.

[31] See again the opinion polls by Akerlof et al. (1991).

4. A Normative Economic Case for East/West-Wage Equalization?

Prima facie, the vastly different unemployment rates in western and eastern Germany speak for a substantial wage differentiation between the two parts of the united country. In essence, it is the case of an industrial crisis which has not been accommodated by sufficient sectoral wage moderation in the short and medium run and which has thus turned into a long-term regional labor market disequilibrium, i.e. into a rise of the natural rate of unemployment in the region previously hit by the crisis. Given an insufficient mobility of the unemployed labor force, regional wage differentiation can help to make investment in the respective region profitable enough to close the 'regional capital gap' in the long run.[32]

There are basically two strands of economic arguments that have been put forward against a long-term wage differentiation between East and West. Both point to the detrimental effects of such a differentiation on the long-term growth dynamics of the eastern German economy. In doing so, however, they focus on different issues, namely (a) the need to mitigate East/West-migration to avoid a drain on the resources of the eastern economy, and (b) the need to steer structural change in the direction of industries with a high labor productivity, which is due either to a high physical capital- or a high human capital-intensity of production. We shall evaluate these two arguments in the following paragraphs.

4.1. Meeting the Migration Threat

It is a popular view that a significant East/West-wage differentiation and a massive East/West-migration would have deprived the East German economy of its most important long-term asset, namely a highly skilled workforce, and thus would have impeded its future growth prospects. To prevent this from happening, a rapid wage equalization was warranted.

In our opinion, this view is mistaken for essentially two reasons. First, by identifying the wage differential and not the difference in expected incomes as the main empirically relevant motive for migration decisions, it neglects the rise of migration that results from the rise of unemployment in the East as a consequence of wage equalization.[33] Second, by pleading for across-the-bord wage equalization, it misses the superior option of a market-driven wage equalization in those labor market segments where scarcities actually emerge. E.g., highly skilled workers may be paid supercontractual premia so as to prevent them from moving

---

[32] For a more detailed account of the case for regional flexibility, see Paqué (1991).
[33] See Section 3.2 above.

to the West. Hence, if anything, there is a case for a wage stratification between scarce (mostly skilled) and abundant (mostly unskilled) labor in the East, with the scarce part reaching western wage levels or even beyond (given the better living conditions in the West!), and the abundant part lagging well behind. Such a policy of wage stratification would preserve the eastern locational advantage of low-cost manpower and at the same time prevent outmigration of the complementary human capital. Compared to this, a strategy of minimizing all kinds of East/West-migration irrespective of the labor market segment appears to be suboptimal on welfare economic grounds. Only if one introduces further restrictions of fairness on the interpersonal wage differentiation within the East – e.g., between skilled and unskilled workers – might an East/West-wage equalization be justified as a second-best solution to mitigate migration. Then, however, the real rationale for wage equalization is to be found in considerations outside normative economics.[34]

4.2. Steering Structural Change

Among economists, the most common case against East/West-wage differentiation is based on the view that it would drive the eastern German economy into a pattern of specialization with a higher labor intensity of production and thus, at any given level of technological knowledge in the united country, a lower labor productivity than the western German economy. This prospect is judged to be undesirable because the historical pattern of structural change has shown and the future pattern is likely to show further that, in highly developed Central Europe, there is no place for labor intensive production lines, mainly because the growth potential lies in branches that produce with a relatively high intensity of physical and/or of human capital, but not of manpower. This is why the course was to be set early on in the direction of the inevitable, to avoid an untimely obsolescence of the newly installed capital stock and a poor growth performance of young eastern industries.[35]

---

[34] Burda/Wyplosz (1992) show within a model of the endogenous growth theory that an East/West-migration of the skilled workforce could be desirable if only the extent of human capital externalities is larger in the West than in the East due to, say, agglomeration effects. While their basic point is valid, their analysis starts from a policy-irrelevant framework of maximizing the present and future output of East and West taken together. Thus, within their model, massive migration flows of skilled labor from the East to the West are not excluded a priori: A complete depopulation is within the range of feasible and potentially desirable policy outcomes, partly even calling for the subsidization of migration from the East to the West. For a more detailed critique, see Paqué (1992).

[35] An authorative statement of this kind can be found in Sachverständigenrat (1991/1992), §§538-542, notably §539) with respect to the consequences of wage subsidies.

To evaluate this line of reasoning, we shall assume a simple model economy with two geographically distinct regions ('West' and 'East'), two homogenous factors of production (capital and labor) and a possibly large number of sectors of economic activity ('branches') that are characterized in the West by a large array of different capital intensities and wage levels. Let us then assume that the old capital stock of the East is completely obsolete for whatever reason so that the long-term equilibrium structure of the eastern economy will solely depend on future investments. Let us further assume that the prospective wage level in the East is only a fraction – say, two thirds – of the western level, but with the same inter-sectoral wage structure between 'high'- and 'low'-capital intensity sectors. Hence, basically, labor in the East is devalued across the board.

Within this setting, there are three channels through which the East will end up with a high labor intensity of production. First, branches with a high labor intensity of production will profit disproportionately from the low labor costs in the East, and they will have the strongest incentive to choose the East as a future location for investment and production ('branch selection effect'). There may even emerge altogether new branches in the East (e.g., in low-productivity services) that could not profitably produce in the West at the prevailing wage level. Second, in any single branch with a production technology that allows for a substitution of labor for capital, firms will have an incentive to move to higher labor intensities in the East than in the West, even without switching technologies ('factor substitution effect'). Third, independent of the production technology (whether substitutional or fixed coefficient), firms will tend to use technologies in the East that make a more intensive use of the factor labor ('technology switch effect').

On the normative grounds of a static efficiency of the allocation between eastern and western Germany, it is very hard to argue against any of these effects. After all, the East has a stock of underemployed labor that the West does not have, and it would be completely arbitrary to take the western standard of labor intensity as anything like a relevant normative yardstick for the prospective eastern one. Economically, eastern Germany is simply to be treated like another country whose equilibrium wage level at the given migration propensity of the population happens to be below the western German one. To be sure, there have not been any serious calls in the past for a sharp rise of the labor costs in, say, Austria, Belgium, Britain or Holland up to the western German level so as to remove the 'distortions' in these economies. Although firms in these countries produce for roughly the same international goods markets as West German firms, there is apparently a different equilibrium structure of production, factor use and technology application that cannot sensibly be criticized as inefficient only because it takes account of the specific national, regional or local conditions of the labor market. Without introducing non-economic considerations and restrictions, the same is to apply to the eastern German industrial structure once it will have developed on the basis of a wage level that is persistently lower than the West German one.

Note that the same conclusions apply even if one thinks of labor not being a homogenous production factor that is abundant, but of different types of labor ('skilled' versus 'unskilled') with different degrees of scarcity due to different labor market options in case of migration to the West. If the eastern German industry would tend to produce with a relatively low intensity of physical capital and skilled labor for the three reasons given above, this would have to be considered as an efficient reaction to genuine scarcities, not as a distortion away from the 'appropriate' factor proportions given in the West.

On the grounds of dynamic efficiency, it is widely believed that a higher labor intensity of production would have deteriorated growth prospects for the eastern economy in the long run so that the prospect of convergence of per capita incomes between East and West would have been further postponed into the future. To evaluate this argument, it is convenient to distinguish between two variants of it, the physical capital- and the human capital-version. The former interprets high labor intensity as meaning a relatively low average ratio of physical capital to labor. The latter takes it to mean above all a low human capital intensity of production, i.e. roughly speaking, a low ratio of skilled to unskilled labor.

The physical capital-version of the argument is quite obviously unconvincing. To see this, let us again distinguish the three different effects that lead to a lower aggregate capital intensity: branch selection, factor substitution, and technology switching. As to branch selection, the empirical picture of the past does not confirm the view that branches with higher capital intensities of production are the ones which tend to grow faster. If anything, the reverse holds: most of the sunset industries of the 1970s and 1980s in West Germany – notably iron and steel, mining, shipbuilding etc. – are branches which produce with a high capital intensity and a high physical labor productivity, and which traditionally pay relatively high wages. As a consequence, the geographical growth centers have typically not been regions where these high-wage industries are concentrated – say, Northrhine-Westfalia, the Saar, the northern coastal shore – but rather those areas like southern Bavaria, Baden-Württemberg or Hesse where other industrial or service activities are located. Of course, it is very hard to make a forecast whether this trend will continue in the future because this would require a more or less accurate prediction of the sectoral incidence of the supply side shocks to come. However, it appears to be plausible to assume that producers in newly industrialized countries and increasingly also in developing countries will be able to compete in those high-capital intensity production lines that use standard technologies.[36]

As far as the factor substitution effect is concerned, the argument has hardly any basis at all. The mere profitable employment of some more lower-paid

---

[36] This has been a long-standing prediction of the 'structural reports' of the German economic research institutes. See, e.g., Donges et al. (1988).

workers at the same capital stock and level of technology at any point in time does not give any reason for a change of the long-term productivity growth prospects. An analogous case can be made with respect to technology switching. If the use of a more labor intensive technology becomes profitable precisely because labor is relatively abundant, this has no identifiable implications for the future growth of the respective branch.[37]

The human capital-version of the argument is the much more interesting one and deserves some closer examination. Empirically, there is substantial evidence that those sectors which produce with a high intensity of human capital had a better growth performance than the average in the last two decades in West Germany, and as in the case of high physical capital intensity, there is hardly any reason why the path of structural change in the East should be different in this respect. The normative consequences of this for an East/West-wage differentiation in Germany crucially depend on the types of labor in question. If wage differentiation is uniform for both skilled labor (as a proxy for human capital) and unskilled labor (as a proxy for pure manpower), the relative price of human capital to manpower will be the same in both parts of the country so that no distortion of factor use in favor of manpower should be expected in the East. However, to the extent that the East/West-differentiation is more pronounced for unskilled than for skilled labor, which may have better prospects of employment in the West, then some such distortion will come about. It is an open empirical question to which human capital intensity the economy will converge, because migration flows and threats are very hard to predict. A rough guess is that human capital will be somewhat scarcer in the East than manpower, but that – for a long time to come – there will remain a large-scale unemployment of both skilled and unskilled labor.

---

[37] All this seems so obvious that the question arises why, in the public and in the political discussion, the link between (physical) capital intensity and the growth prospects seems to be taken for granted. Probably, there are two major reasons for this. First, observers tend to confuse the ever-present trend towards capital intensification in the growth process with the choice of an appropriate capital intensity as a startingpoint of this process. Clearly, economies may have very different average capital intensities, but they may all more or less go through the same process of capital intensification over time in all relevant branches of economic activity. The question at hand is clearly one to fit the eastern German economy into the right slot of capital intensity, with no apparent implication for the future performance in the growth race. To put it bluntly, the question is whether eastern Germany should follow the 'example' of western Germany or of another European country with somewhat lower value added per working hour in its economy (say, Austria, Belgium, Britain). Second, observers tend to somehow 'define' the labor abundance in eastern Germany as a strictly temporary phenomenon so that any pattern of specialization which reduces this abundance is almost by definition wrong-headed. Such a view simply assumes that there are other feasible and possibly superior ways to reach full empoloyment than via a lower wage in the East.

Hence the resulting downward bias of human capital intensity and the concomitant loss of growth potential may not be all that dramatic.

Even if one were ready to accept the rationale for a corrective measure to raise the human-capital intensity of production in the East, a 'policy' of general rapid East/West-wage equalization would hardly be a first-best solution. In fact, if the policy aim were, roughly speaking, to reach full employment of both skilled and unskilled labor and a maximum speed of income convergence through essentially market-driven growth processes between West and East, a policy of preserving a market-determined East/West-wage differential for unskilled labor and paying wage subsidies for skilled labor that just neutralized the market-determined wage differential between the two types of labor, would be preferable to an East/West-wage equalization across the board.

Up to this point, we interpreted the human capital version of the argument as concerning the long-term pattern of specialization at a given supply of manpower and human capital. There is another strand of thought based on ideas of endogenous growth theory,[38] which focuses on the role of a high-wage level as a device to raise the profitability of investment in human capital.[39] The rationale of this argument is very simple. Within a standard model of optimization of human capital investment by a representative individual household, it can be shown that, ceteris paribus, a higher wage involves a higher shadow value of human capital, which, in turn, makes for a greater incentive to invest time in costly training, both on the job and in unemployment. Hence, while a wage rise increases unemployment in the short and medium run through the standard labor demand effects,[40] the greater incentive for human capital investment accelerates human capital formation and thus labor productivity growth. Under a set of additional assumptions, the model implies that a large part of an original wage increase thus 'validates itself' in the subsequent endogenous improvement of labor productivity.

Without going into any details of this model type, there are some major objections to its use as a standard of judgment and policy guide in the case of eastern Germany or any other economy in a similar situation. First, the theory does not make an explicit distinction between training on the job and training in unemployment, at least not in the form presented by Burda/Funke (2000). In fact, it is assumed that both kinds of training incur the same training costs and lead to the same productivity enhancing effects, which is probably quite unrealistic. Instead, it is likely, that, for many industrial jobs, training on-the-job is the more effective method to acquire skills than some publicly financed requalification programs that cannot be targeted precisely enough at the future labor market

---

[38] Notably Lucas (1988) and Barro/Sala-i-Martin (1995).

[39] See Burda/Funke (2000).

[40] In the model of Burda/Funke (2000), it is assumed that employment is labor demand constrained in the relevant range.

needs. While appropriate model variations to take account of this difference may be technically feasible, they would somehow run counter to the whole philosophy of the approach. After all, the more the process of training presupposes the state of employment in the first place, the less the idea of a positive long-run effect of the wage increase on growth as put against the negative short-run effect on employment can be upheld.

Second, it is doubtful whether the state of human capital has been really anything close to a relevant constraint on employment and growth in eastern Germany. Sure enough, there is a widespread consensus among economists that the eastern German labor force has in general a rather high level of skill. In terms of formal education, it is not much worse than the labor force in the West, and the initial gap in expertise with modern technical equipment has been perceived to be relatively small. What matters for employment and growth are apparently much more the general locational conditions than a lack of human capital, which makes the situation of eastern Germany quite different from that of a developing or a newly industrialized country.[41]

Third, if human capital were a constraint in eastern Germany in a free market wage regime with a relatively low wage level, then a market-determined wage differentiation between skilled and unskilled labor would do the job of providing the required retraining incentives. Beyond that, there is no justification for a general rise in wages. In fact, wage differentiation is preferable to the (probably large) extent that training-on-the-job is the more effective and cheaper method of human capital accumulation than requalification in unemployment (see above).

Finally, while theoretically sound in terms of abstract optimization, the argument lacks an empirical reference which could give at least a clue, where the appropriate wage level could be located to initiate an intertemporally optimal growth process. To put the problem in the form of a policy question: How far is one to deviate from the traditional reference of full employment to speed up human capital formation? On intuitive grounds, an argument of this kind might possibly justify a surpassing of the full employment benchmark by, say, up to 5 percent of the labor force for a few years. The dimensions of eastern German unemployment (20-30 percent), however, appear to be well beyond the plausible scope for any such policy advice.[42]

All in all, the argument for speeding up human capital accumulation through an aggressive wage policy looks rather farfetched when applied to the actual case of

---

[41] Burda/Funke (2000) quote the case of Singapore in the 1980s as an example for a human capital oriented policy via high wages. For different accounts of the Singapore experience, see Fischer/Spinanger (1986), Suhr (1989), and Chadha (1991).

[42] This is why the frequent reference to wage policy in Singapore in the 1980s as an example for this kind of policy is misleading. After all, Singapore had never to cope with unemployment levels in the range of the eastern German labor market.

eastern Germany. It appears to be a mere ad-hoc rationalization of an observed development, which would never have been recommended as sensible policy in the first place. Remarkably enough, no such policy has been proposed for the economy of the Czech Republic, which, in many respects, started off from very similar conditions in terms of factor endowment and industrial structure as eastern Germany.[43]

In a more general sense, the aura of ad-hoc rationalization of an observed fact surrounds all normative economic cases for a rapid inner-German East/West-wage equalization, simply because the very fact to be justified is so obviously dependent on the legalistic, not the economic preconditions created by the nation state. If history had taken a different turn after the iron curtain had come down and the two Germanies had remained separate nation states with market economies – say, with free goods and factor mobility between them within the European Community – it is very hard to imagine that any economist would have recommended to equalize the wage levels between the two Germanies as soon as possible, be it on the grounds of 'excessive' migration or of the future path of structural change. After all, there has never really been a serious discussion on abruptly raising the wage levels in, say, Austria, Belgium, the Netherlands or the United Kingdom or, more recently, the post-socialist eastern European countries to the high (western) German level. If this is so, however, then one may well ask, whether in the last resort all normative economic considerations were no more than instruments to give some moral or legal considerations an intellectually attractive underpinning.

References

Akerlof, G. et al. (1991), East Germany in from the cold: the economic aftermath of currency union, *Brookings Papers on Economic Activity* 1, 1-87.

Barro, R./Sala-i-Martin, X. (1995), *Economic Growth*, New York.

Burda, M. (1991), Labor and Product Markets in Czechoslovakia and the Ex-GDR: a Twin Study, in: Directorate General for Economic and Financial Affairs (ed.), *The Path of the Reform in Central and Eastern Europe*, Commission of the European Communities Luxembourg, 111-128.

Burda, M./Wyplosz, C. (1992), Labor Mobility and German Integration: Some Vignettes, in: Siebert, H. (ed.), *The Transformation of Socialist Economies*, Tübingen, 333-359.

Burda, M./Funke, M. (1993), German Trade Unions after Unification: Third Degree Wage Discriminating Monopolists?, *Weltwirtschaftliches-Archis 129(3)*, 537-560.

---

[43] For a comparison of the two cases, see Burda (1991).

Burda, M. (1998), Semiparametric Analysis of German East-West Migration Intentions: Facts and Theory, *Journal of Applied Econometrics*, 13, 525-541.

Burda, M./ Funke, M. (2000), Wages and Structural Adjustment in the New German States, in: R. T. Riphahn/D. Snower/ K. F. Zimmermann (ed.), *Employment Policy in Transition: The Lessons of German Integration for the German Labor Market*, Heidelberg, 31-51

Chadha, B. (1991), Wages, Profitability, and Growth in a Small Open Economy, *IMF Staff Paper* 38, 59-82.

Deutsches Institut für Wirtschaftsforschung, Berlin/Institut für Weltwirtschaft, Kiel (1993), Gesamtwirtschaftliche und unternehmerische Anpassungsprozesse in Ostdeutschland, Achter Bericht, *Kiel Discussion Papers* 205/206.

DIW et al. (1999), Gesamtwirtschaftliche und unternehmerische Anpassungsfortschritte in Ostdeutschland, Neunzehnter Bericht, *Kiel Discussion Paper 346/347*, Kiel Institute of World Economics, Kiel.

Donges, J. et al. (1988), *Mehr Strukturwandel für Wachstum und Beschäftigung. Die deutsche Wirtschaft im Anpassungsstau*, Tübingen.

Farber, H. (1986), The Analysis of Union Behaviour, in: Ashenfelter, O./Layard, R. (eds.), *Handbook of Labor Economics*, Vol. 2, Amsterdam, 1039-1089.

Fink, U. (1992), Aufschwung durch Arbeitnehmer-Kapital, in: *Die Zeit*, May 8, 1992.

Fischer, B./Spinanger, D. (1986), Factor Market Distortions and Export Performance: an Eclectic Review of the Evidence, *Kiel Working Papers* 259.

Giersch, H. et al. (1992), *The Fading Miracle, Four Decades of Market Economy*, Cambridge.

Hemmer, H./Schmitz, K. (eds.) (1990), *Geschichte der Gewerkschaften in der Bundesrepublik Deutschland: Von den Anfängen bis heute*, Köln.

Lange, T./Pagh, G. (1998), *The Economics of German Unification*, Cheltenham.

Lawrence, C./Lawrence, R. (1985), Manufacturing Wage Dispersion: an End Game Interpretation, *Brookings Papers on Economic Activity* 1, 47-106.

Lewis, G. (1986), Union Relative Wage Effects, in: Ashenfelter, O./Layard, R. (eds.), *Handbook of Labor Economics*, Vol. 2, Amsterdam, 1139-1181.

Lucas, R. (1988), On the mechanics of economic development, *Journal of Monetary Economics*, Vol. 14, 3-42.

Meckl, J. (1992), Lohnpolitik und innerdeutsche Arbeitskräftewanderung. The Influence of Politically Determined Wage Rates on Migration Between Germany's New and Old States, *Jahrbücher für Natio alökonomie und Statistik* 209, 407-418.

Paqué, K.-H. (1991), Structural Wage Rigidity in West Germany 1950-89. Some New Econometric Evidence, *Kiel Working Papers* 489.

Paqué, K.-H. (1992), Comment on Michael C. Burda and Charles Wyplosz, Labor Mobility and German Integration: Some Vignettes, in: Siebert, H. (ed.), *The Transformation of Socialist Economies*, Tübingen, 365-367.

Rawls, J. (1971), *A Theory of Justice*, Cambridge, Mass.

Sachverständigenrat zur Begutachtung der gesamtwirtschaftlichen Entwicklung, *Annual Reports* (various issues), Stuttgart.

Sachverständigenrat zur Begutachtung der gesamtwirtschaftlichen Entwicklung (1997), Jahresgutachten 1997/98: Wachstum, Beschäftigung und Währungsunion – Orientierungen für die Zukunft, Stuttgart.

Siebert, H. (1992), *Das Wagnis der Einheit: Eine wirtschaftspolitische Therapie*, Stuttgart.

Sinn, G./Sinn H. (1992), *Jumpstart – The Economic Unification of Germany*, Cambridge.

Suhr, W. (1989), Singapurs Rezession 1985: Resultat eines lohnpolitischen Experiments?, *Kiel Working Papers* 391.

3. Early Retirement in East and West Germany

Axel Börsch-Supan, University of Mannheim, and NBER, Cambridge

Peter Schmidt, University of Bremen

1. Introduction

This paper provides an analysis of the retirement patterns in East and West Germany in the first period after German unification. The study is driven first by a general interest in retirement behavior in East Germany, and in the characteristics which distinguish it from its counterpart in West Germany. Secondly, we investigate whether the incentives in the German public retirement system to retire at certain ages were strong enough to change the customary East German retirement patterns even in a brief period of time.

Average retirement age is very low in Germany. In 1981, it reached its minimum with 58.4 years for men and 59.7 for women. In spite of several changes in the German public retirement system, it has increased only very little since then and is still around age 60 although the official retirement age begins at 63. As a result of the political and economic changes in East Germany, average retirement age there has been even lower. In the first years after unification it was down to age 55. Very early retirement was possible after the unification due to a generous interpretation of the rule that workers may retire not only because of health reasons but also because of the inability to work in precisely the job one is qualified for.

This paper claims that peaks in retirement transitions at specific ages that were observed in East and West Germany after unification are an outcome of actuarially unfair design of the age adjustments in the replacement rate. The paper proceeds to quantify this effect and to investigate the impact of changes to these age adjustments. We estimate the probability of early retirement conditional on socio-demographic variables and on the option value of postponing retirement by combining the option value approach with a Gompertz-type hazard model of early retirement.

The model is applied to the West German Socio-Economic Panel (GSOEP), 1984-1990, and to the East German GSOEP, 1990-92. We restrict the sample to those workers who were at risk of retiring during the panel period. These samples permit reliable imputations of the pre-retirement incomes relevant for benefit computations and feature a sufficient number of retirement transitions.

The article has the conventional setup. In the following section, we describe the German public pension system for those not familiar with it, with particular emphasis on the transition rules in East Germany between 1990 and 92. In section 2 we talk about differences and similarities in retirement patterns between the eastern and the western part of unified Germany. Section 4 introduces the option-value-hazard-rate model. The variables used for our analysis as well as the estimation results are presented in section 5. These estimates reveal a strong response of retirees to economic incentives. Although the observed retirement patterns in the East were dominated by retirement due to unemployment, the estimates strongly reveal that the German public pension system at that time had strong and very specific impacts on retirement behavior. Section 6 translates the elasticities estimated by the option value model into changes in retirement age due to the 1992 Pension Reform. In section 7, we draw some policy conclusions.

2. A Brief Description of the German Pension System

Germany has a pay-as-you-go public pension system which features a very broad mandatory coverage of workers. Only the self-employed are not subject to mandatory coverage. As opposed to many other countries (such as the United Kingdom and the United States), public pensions in Germany are designed to maintain the household standard of living after work life and not to provide a subsistence income. Public pensions are therefore roughly proportional to labor income averaged over the life course and feature only few redistributive characteristics, much less than e.g. in the United States. This is the reason why the German pension system is termed "retirement insurance" rather than "social security" as in the United States.

Public pensions provide the major source of income after retirement. Although firm pensions exist in Germany, their role is small. In West Germany, in the period 1984 to 1988, only 16 percent of the elderly received private pension income at all (mainly annuities from a life insurance bought by the household or by the firm on the household's behalf) while 84 percent received public pensions as the only income source. 8.5 percent had both social security and firm pension income and 7.6 percent had only private pension income.[1] Moreover, private pension income is small. The average contribution to total retirement income is slightly more than 3 percent for the German elderly.

---

[1] Estimates from the German Socio-Economic Panel.

We can therefore essentially abstract from private pensions and attribute all incentive effects for retirement behavior to the public pension system. This is quite different from the United Kingdom or the United States and considerably facilitates the analysis of retirement behavior in Germany.

The incentives for early retirement provided by the public pension system are strong indeed. First, the system provides a rather generous retirement income. The average net replacement ratio – after-tax retirement income as a percentage of the preceding after-tax labor income – has been larger than 70 percent, resulting in a social security income which is about 33 percent higher than the comparable social security income in the United States.[2] The high German replacement ratio gives an incentive for Germans to retire early, *ceteris paribus*. Second, the German public pension system is not actuarially fair because it has very small adjustments of retirement income by retirement age. This also creates strong incentives to retire early. We describe this in detail in the following paragraphs.

While retirement at age 65 was prescribed by rather strict rules until 1972, the social security reform of 1972 introduced the opportunity to retire at different ages during the so-called *window of retirement*. The first year of this window, i.e. the earliest retirement age, depends on the group a worker belongs to. Retirement at age 60 is possible for women and for those male workers who are unemployed and/or cannot be appropriately employed for health or other reasons ("*erwerbsunfähig*" or "*berufsunfähig*"). The latter rule has been interpreted very broadly and was used as a device to keep unemployment rates down. For instance, it applied when no vacancies for the worker's specific job description were available. Retirement at age 63 is possible after 35 years of contribution. Finally, everybody can retire at age 65. In theory, there is no upper limit to the window except for about a quarter of the German labor force which is still subject to a mandatory retirement age. This mainly includes the public sector. In effect, however, labor force participation is very low beyond age 70.

The 1972 Social Security Reform introduced only implicit adjustments to the level of retirement benefits with respect to retirement age as benefits were dependent on the number of years of contribution into the system. Explicit adjustments of social security benefits with respect to the retirement age chosen were only introduced with the 1992 Social Security Reform. Table 1 displays these adjustments. They relate the retirement income for retirement at age 65 (normalized to 100 percent) to the retirement income at earlier or later ages. The table compares the statutory German adjustments after 1972, the changed ones

---

[2] Recent measures to reduce pension replacement rates coming into effect from the year 2000 are not in the focus of our analysis.

after the 1992 Social Security reform, and the adjustments in the United States. Moreover, as a reference, column 1 displays actuarially fair adjustments.[3]

Table 1. Adjustment of Public Pensions by Retirement Age

		Pension as a percentage of the pension that one would obtain if one had retired at age 65		
Age	Fair	Germany 1972	Germany 1992	United States
60	59.8	(87.5)	(69.5)	(0.0)
61	65.8	(90.0)	(75.6)	(0.0)
62	72.6	(92.5)	81.7	77.8
63	80.4	95.0	87.8	85.2
64	89.5	97.5	93.9	92.6
65	100.0	100.0	100.0	100.0
66	112.5	109.9	108.5	105.6
67	127.5	120.1	117.0	111.1
68	145.9	123.0	125.5	120.0
69	168.9	125.8	134.0	128.9
70	198.5	128.7	142.5	137.8

Notes: Adjustments in parentheses indicate restricted or no eligibility.
Source: Börsch-Supan (1992).

While neither the German nor the American system are actuarially fair, the public retirement system in Germany is particularly distortive. There is less economic incentive for Americans to retire at one age or another in the window of

---

[3] Actuarially fair in the sense that the adjustments would not provide an incentive to retire at any specific age during the window period given that the worker has worked until the beginning of the window period. Hence, these adjustment factors $ADJ^{Fair}(R)$ are defined by the condition that they keep the present discounted value of retirement benefits minus pension contributions the same for all retirement ages. They are computed by solving the following equations for the adjustment factors $ADJ^{Fair}(R)$ of retirement ages R = 60,...,70:

$$PDV(R) = \sum_{t=R}^{\infty} ADJ^{Fair}(R) \cdot Y_t^{Ret}(65) \cdot a_t \cdot \delta^t - \sum_{t=0}^{R-1} c \cdot Y^L \cdot a_t \cdot \delta^t = PDV(65)$$

where PDV(R) present discounted value of net retirement benefits, R retirement age, Y^{Ret} retirement income for R=65, $c \cdot Y^L$ contribution to pension system at labor income Y^L, a_t probability to survive at least until age t, and δ discount factor.

early retirement and only a small disincentive to retire later than at age 65, while the German social security system tilts the retirement decision heavily towards the earliest retirement age applicable.[4] The 1992 Reform has diminished but not abolished this incentive effect.

Since January 1992, Germany has a unified public pension system with the same replacement ratios and the same adjustment factors for new retirees in eastern and in western states. This does not imply the same level of pension benefits, however, because the replacement ratio refers to the relative wage level in either part of the country. Before January 1992, the situation was complicated by the transition of the old GDR system to the West German one. Between 1990 and 1992, existing pensions in East Germany were revaluated several times. In the rest of this section we will describe this process and briefly comment on some of the problems during the transition.[5]

The entire social security system of the GDR was organized in one comprehensive institution ("*Sozialversicherung*"),[6] financed in equal parts by the state budget and by contributions from workers. This system had to be integrated into the western one which consists of several independent institutions notably the social health, unemployment and retirement insurance, each of which is separately financed by earnings-related contributions and partly subsidized by the federal budget.

As opposed to the West German system described above, the comprehensive GDR social security system aimed at reintegrating people into the labor force, and at keeping them working as long as possible. As a consequence, the relative financial position of pensioners in the GDR was poor by international standards although most comparisons do not account for the high subsidization of every-day goods in the GDR.

The retirement system of the GDR included a mandatory and a voluntary part, which made the transition to the completely mandatory West system even more problematic. The mandatory part covered the first 600 Marks of income, about 45 percent of the average GDR income. In 1971, a voluntary public insurance ("*Freiwillige Zusatzrentenversicherung*") was introduced. In addition, there existed more than 60 supplementary insurances for certain sectors (e.g., medical doctors, teachers, and – controversial after unification – police, army and the intelligence service). Taking mandatory and voluntary insurance together, the

---

[4] Curiously, the German system before 1992 provided a large increase in retirement benefits for work at ages 66 and 67. However, it was ineffective because the inducements to early retirement offset this incentive by far.

[5] For details see Schmähl (1991, 1992).

[6] More exactly there were two institutions, the *Sozialversicherung der Arbeiter und Angestellten* and the *Sozialversicherung bei der staatlichen Versicherung der DDR*.

typical replacement rate varied between 49.9 percent for workers retiring in 1970 and 62.7 percent for workers retiring in 1990.[7] Retirement age was fixed at age 60 for women and 65 for men.

As a result of the different supplementary insurances, existing pensions in the GDR were partly higher, partly lower compared to their value had they been calculated under West German rules. The transition process involved two simultaneous changes. First, pensions had to be recalculated on the basis of West German law. Then the thus obtained pension level had to be revaluated based on the currency exchange rate and the relative income standard in East Germany. These revaluations were governed by political, not economical decisions. Pensions below their West German equivalents were immediately increased to the West German level or at least to the level of social assistance payments. Pensions higher than their West German equivalents were reduced in a stepwise fashion to the West German level. This reduction was achieved by at least partly excluding the involved workers from the general income increases in the process of wage and pension revaluation.

Taking both adjustments together, East German pensions on average increased by about 60 percent between mid-1990 und mid-1991, the first year after the introduction of the DM. Only two thirds of this increase were covered by payroll contributions, so that a considerable subsidy had to be paid out of the West German federal budget (Schmähl (1992)).

At the same time, the fixed retirement age in the former GDR was abolished in favor of the West German 1972 window rules, as described above. Moreover, special pre-retirement regulations ("*Vorruhestandsregelungen*") were introduced to keep the statistical unemployment rate down. They permitted retirement at age 55 in East Germany with a net replacement rate of about 65 percent. This is not actuarially fair as can be seen from column 2 in Table 1. The distortive effect is smaller than under the 1972 social security rules, but considerably larger than under the 1992 rules, as seen from colums 3 and 4 in Table 1.

3. Retirement Patterns in East and West Germany

Figures 1 and 2 depict retirement patterns in East and West Germany. They are computed from the German Socio-Economic Panel (GSOEP). We used seven waves of the West German GSOEP, 1984-1990, and three East German waves, 1990-1992. This yields six possible dates of a labor force transition in the West,

---

[7] Comparing standard workers with equal income and years of service (Schmähl (1992, Table 1)).

two in the East. We observe 401 transitions in the East for 965 workers, and 608 transitions in the West for 2,369 workers.

In Figure 1, we find the well known West German retirement pattern with pronounced peaks at ages 60 and 63, and with a much smaller peak at age 65, the 'normal' retirement age.[8] Note that the maximum occurs at age 60, for both male and female workers.

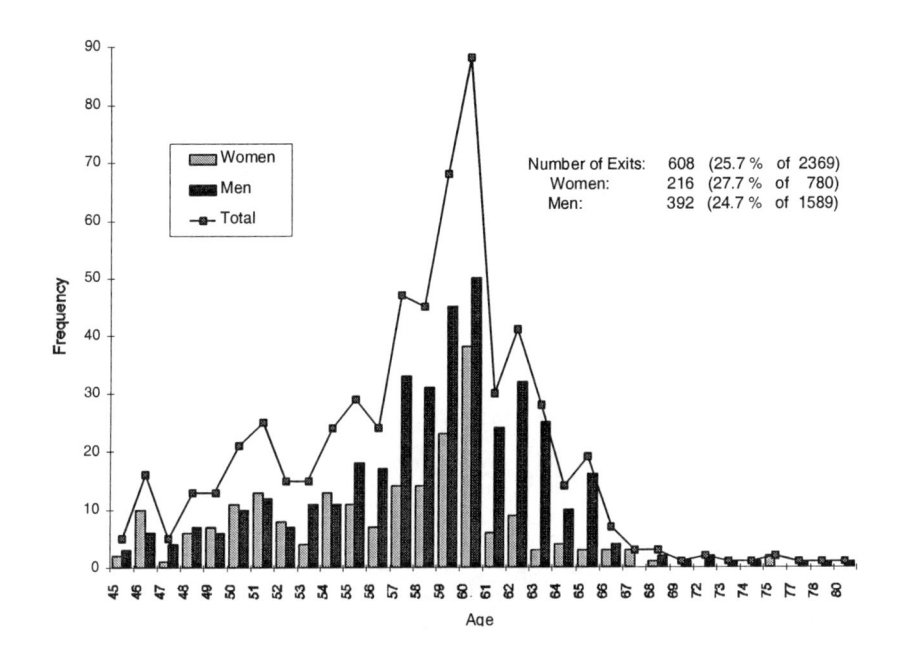

Figure 1. Age at Labor Force Exit in West Germany

Source: GSOEP, West; 7 Waves 1984-1990 (6 transitions).

The picture for East Germany, Figure 2, looks totally different. It reflects the rather dramatic decline in labor force participation immediately after unification, particularly among women. Two observations stand out. Average retirement age

---

[8] A very similar picture can be seen in Börsch-Supan (1992), who uses the official data of the *Verband Deutscher Rentenversicherungsträger*. Deviations result from the impossibility to determine the exact age for the individuals in the GSOEP as mentioned below.

was much lower than in the West. Furthermore the peaks were less pronounced and occur at ages 57 and 60 for men and at age 54 for women, respectively.

The main reason for these differences is of course the break-down of the East German economy following the unification, resulting in a dramatic decline in labor force participation, as is displayed in Table 2. Within only three years, the number of persons not in the labor force nearly doubled. Table 3 shows that the transition rates out of the labor force were around five times as high in East Germany compared to the western part of the country. The dramatic decline is also reflected in the different mean retirement age, which was more than 3 years lower in the East than in the West.

Figure 2. Age at Labor Force Exit in East Germany

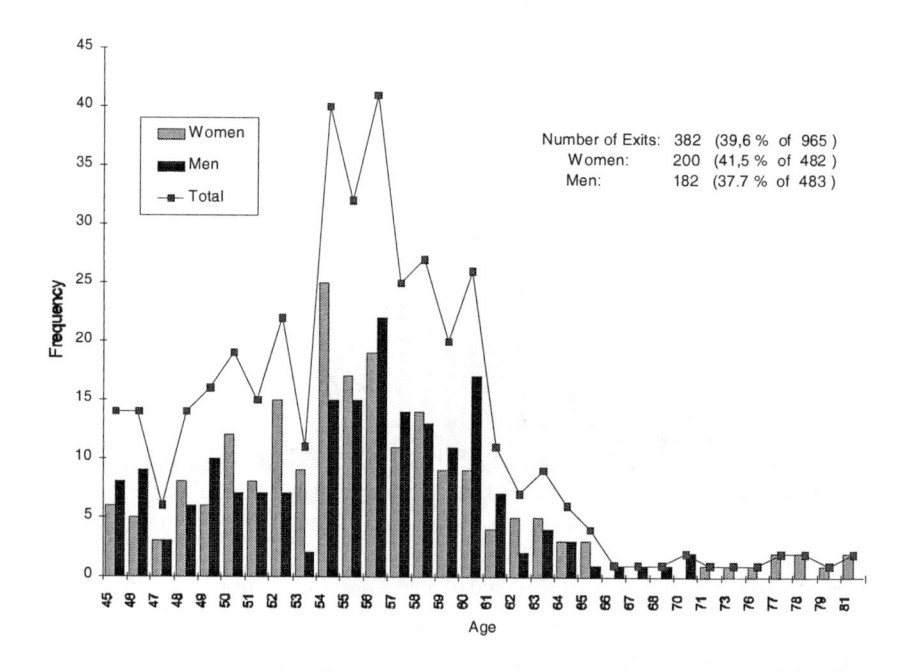

Source: GSOEP, East; 3 Waves 1990-1992 (2 transitions).

These observations set the stage for the analytic part of this paper. Can we explain the retirement behavior observed after unification by the incentives set by the public pension system as outlined in the previous section? Are the differences between East and West Germany at least partially justified by the differences that existed in the pension systems between 1990 and 1992? To answer these questions, we embed an option value computation of retirement incentives into a hazard rate model of early retirement, being aware that any estimates based on East German data have to be interpreted with care. The data reflect a period of transition in which the political system was completely changed. Since the entire institutional system had broken down, decisions had to be taken under large uncertainty.

Table 2: The Rapid Decline in Labor Force Participation in East Germany

	1990	1991	1992
Full Time employed (in percent)	56.9	44.5	37.4
Not in Labor Force (in percent)	33.6	48.3	59.1
Observations:	3,764	3,456	3,328

Source: GSOEP-East, based on all panel-members aged 44 and above in 1990.

Table 3: Transitions out of the Labor Force in East and West Germany

	West Germany 1984-1990			East Germany 1990-1992		
	Male	Female	Total	Male	Female	Total
Initially in labor force	1589	780	2369	483	482	965
Transitions per year	65.3	46.9	101.3	95.0	105.0	200.5
Transition rate (in percent)	4.1	6.0	4.3	19.0	21.0	20.0

Source: GSOEP, based on all panel-members aged 44 and above in the first wave.

4. An Option Value – Gompertz Hazard Rate Model of Retirement

We capture the economic incentives provided by the pension system by the option value to postpone retirement (Lazear/Moore (1988), Stock/Wise (1990)). This value captures, for each retirement age, the trade-off between retiring now (resulting in a stream of retirement benefits that depends on this retirement age) and keeping all options open for some later retirement date (with associated streams of first labor, then retirement incomes for all possible later retirement ages).

Consequently, the option value for a specific age is defined as the difference between the maximum attainable consumption utility if the worker postpones retirement to some later year, minus the utility of consumption that the worker can afford if she would retire now. If $R^*(t)$ denotes the optimal retirement age if the worker postpones retirement past age t, the option value is therefore

$$G(t) = V_t(R^*(t)) - V_t(t) \qquad (1)$$

where $V_t(R)$ denotes the expected discounted future utility at age t if the worker retires at age R. Since a worker is likely to retire as soon as the utility of the option to postpone retirement becomes smaller than the utility of retiring now, retirement probabilities should depend negatively on the option value.

The expected utility arises from income financing consumption and leisure before and after retirement:

$$V_t(R) = E_t \left[\sum_{s=t}^{R-1} u(Y_s^L) \cdot a_s \cdot \delta^{s-t} + \alpha \cdot \sum_{s=R}^{\infty} u(Y_s^{Ret}(R, Y^L)) \cdot a_s \cdot \delta^{s-t} \right] \qquad (2)$$

where Y_s^L Labor income at age s = t,..,R-1
$Y_s^{Ret} = (R, Y^L)$ Retirement income at age s = R,...,D
R   Retirement age
α Marginal utility of leisure
a_t Probability to survive at least until age t
δ Discount factor
E_t Expectation at age t.

To capture the utility from leisure after retirement, utility during retirement is weighted by $\alpha > 1$, where $1/\alpha$ may be interpreted as the marginal disutility of work. We ignore saving in old age by specifying utility from consumption directly as an iso-elastic function of current income, $u(Y) = Y^\sigma$ Retirement income Y^{Ret} depends on the retirement date R (according to the adjustment factors displayed in Table 1) and on previous labor income Y^L (according to the applicable replacement ratio). It is also necessary to impute labor income in the computation of utility for the hypothetical case that the worker had worked longer than s he actually did. This imputed labor income is characterized by a cubic age-profile estimated by a semi-logarithmic regression of labor income on human capital and age, again using the GSOEP 1988-1990.[9] We emphasize that these are cohort-

---

[9]   Estimates can be obtained from the authors upon request.

corrected age-income profiles which do not substantially fall in old age as opposed to the potentially misguiding age-income profiles estimated from cross sectional data.

Because the consumption attainable depends on the ratio of labor income to retirement income as well as on the adjustment of pensions to retirement age and on an age-specific labor income, the option value captures the economic incentives created by the pension system and the labor market. The option value is computed for each person, using the applicable pension regulations and the personalized labor income profiles. Additional private pension income is ignored because it represents only a very small proportion of retirement income as described above.

We describe the probability to retire using a parametric hazard rate model. Hazard rate models of retirement have been estimated by Sueyoshi (1989) and Meghir/Whitehouse (1997), however, not in combination with an option value describing the incentives to retire.

Since the German panel data reveals very little return transitions – almost all workers who are retired at one time stay in retirement and only very few have another job at some later stage – we can confine ourselves to a one-spell analysis. Moreover, because Germany has very few part-time employees (Börsch-Supan (1991)) we model only two states, in and out of the labor force, unlike the competing risk analysis of Sueyoshi (1989). In order to accommodate increasing or decreasing hazard rates, we employ a Gompertz hazard with the following survival probability:

$$\text{Prob (Not yet retired at age } t) = \exp[(\exp(X'\beta)/\gamma) \cdot (1 - \exp(\gamma t))] \qquad (3)$$

The explanatory variables X are weighted by the parameter vector β and include the option value as well as other socio-demographic variables influencing the retirement decision.

The model (1)-(3) is much less computationally involved and more practical than the estimation procedure employed by Stock/Wise (1990) which in turn much closer approximates the underlying dynamic programming structure, see Lumbsdaine/Stock/Wise (1992). We go this route because our interest is mainly in obtaining precise results for the distribution of retirement ages, not so much in a reproduction of the kink points in the observed retirement distribution. Rather than estimating the parameters in the option value (α, δ, σ) simultaneously with β and γ, we recycle the parameters obtained from previous research (Börsch-Supan (1992)) and estimate the base hazard rate γ and the parameters in β using the PARAT package (Schneider (1991)).

5. Variable Definitions and Estimation Results

The dependent variable is the age at transitions from the employment status 'employed' (full- or part-time) or 'unemployed' to 'retired' for employees who were 45 years and older when first observed. However, the definition of 'retired' is problematic, although less so in Germany than in other countries. Retirement definitions commonly employed in the literature include the retirement status self-reported by the respondent, the fact that there are few work hours, or the receipt of retirement benefits, among other definitions. We use the first concept, as opposed to Börsch-Supan (1992) who defines retirement as working less than 15 hours per week. Since Germany has very little part time work and the transition from work to retirement is rather quick, there are much fewer contradictions between different retirement concepts than in the United States. We employ the annual employment status rather than the monthly employment calendar of the GSOEP data because it turns out that respondents change rather frequently between retirement and employment, which is institutionally impossible in Germany.

A further complication arises from the fact that only the year but not the month of birth is reported in the data. Because most interviews are taken in April, the age of about one third of the individuals is one year too young, smoothing the retirement age profiles in Figures 1 and 2, and adding noise to the econometric estimates.

The independent variables consist of the option value as described in the previous section and the socio-economic variables listed in Table 4. Demographic variables include gender, marital status, and year of birth, the latter to describe cohort changes during the panel period. Human capital is described by two dummy variables reflecting education and vocational training. Health is poorly reported in the GSOEP. We use the degree of legal disability as a rough measure for health. In the West German SOEP, this is measured on a scale from 0 to 100 percent, in the East German SOEP, in several categories.

The next group of variables in Table 4 describes the employment status in the period preceding retirement or in the last period before censoring. The reference category is 'only temporarily in the labor force'. We also include a set of dummies for the industry of the most recent job. A further group of variables describes the social status of the job and is closely related to the human capital variables above. The reference category here is very low job quality (*"ungelernt"*). Finally, we describe the economic position of the sample person by a set of indicator variables for housing and financial wealth. Again, like health, these variables describe wealth only poorly, a weakness of the GSOEP.

Estimation results for East and West Germany are presented in Table 5. Positive coefficients indicate higher transition rates to retirement, negative signs a longer duration of the current state, mostly employment, sometimes unemployment.

Table 4. Definition of Independent Variables

Variable name	Description	Variable Mean (at year of decision) West	East
Female	1 = female, 0 = else	0.33	0.50
Cohort	year of birth (- 1900)	31.97	36.11
Married	1 = married, 0 = else	0.57	0.84
School	1 = more than "Hauptschule" (West)	0.20	
	1 = > 8 years in school (East)		0.41
Training	1 = more than vocational training	0.24	
Disabled	Degree of disability (0-100%)	9.04	
	– " – computed on basis of categories		5.80
FullTime	1 = full time employed	0.12	0.11
PartTime	1 = part time employed	0.79	0.86
Unempl	1 = unemployed	0.04	0.01
Reference:	irregularly employed		
Agricult	1 = agricultural sector	0.02	0.04
Mining	1 = mining sector	0.01	0.01
Manufact	1 = manufacturing sector	0.37	0.09
Trade	1 = trade sector	0.08	0.02
PubServ	1 = public service ("Angestellter")	0.11	0.05
CivServ	1 = civil servant ("Beamter")	0.07	0.00
Services	1 = services, unless otherwise spec.	0.07	0.00
BankIns	1 = banking and insurances	0.02	0.00
Educ	1 = educational sector	0.05	0.03
Health	1 = health sector	0.04	0.01
Social	1 = social sector	0.03	0.00
Reference:	Construction sector	0.08	0.01
LowQual	1 = job quality low ("angelernt")	0.34	0.43
MedQual	1 = job quality medium ("gehoben")	0.11	0.22
SelfEmpl	1 = self employed ("selbstaendig")	0.11	0.06
Reference:	= no qualification ("ungelernt")	0.45	0.00
Owner	1 = owns home	0.43	0.40
LifeIns	1 = has life insurance	0.54	0.41
Assets	1 = owns bonds or stocks	0.18	0.07
OptVal	Option Value to postpone retirement	139.65	106.40

Note: Variables are evaluated at the period before an exit or the last period before truncation.

Table 5. Gompertz Hazard Rate Model of Retirement

Variable	West Parameter	West t-Statistic	East Parameter	East t-Statistic
γ (base hazard)	0.5050	30.2225	1.6718	22.9866
Constant	-42.5590	-30.4514	-151.2875	-23.0810
Female	0.1374	1.3110	0.0403	0.3791
Cohort	0.3876	23.2559	1.6618	22.7377
Married	0.0679	0.6763	-0.1525	-1.0822
School	-0.2725	-2.1200	0.2133	1.8753
Training	0.1735	1.7362	–	-
Disabled (%)	0.0072	4.3757	–	-
Disabled (cat)	–	–	0.5336	3.1891
PartTime	0.1988	1.1180	0.6602	2.0695
FullTime	0.6395	3.8546	0.4911	1.6629
Unempl	1.8783	10.9142	0.7352	1.6590
Agricult	-0.6010	-1.9973	2.9415	13.4169
Mining	-0.0594	-0.1511	3.7599	10.0517
Manufact	-0.1528	-1.3677	2.8144	16.5043
Trade	-0.3763	-2.1184	3.0762	11.4588
PubServ	-0.2790	-1.6617	2.8337	14.6758
CivServ	0.4785	2.3443	-	-
Services	-0.5614	-2.8329	-	-
BankIns	-0.0351	-0.1252	-	-
Educ	-0.6217	-2.6568	2.7155	10.4379
Health	-0.6468	-2.3903	-	-
Social	-0.3118	-1.1874	-	-
LowQual	-0.2878	-2.7403	-0.1802	-1.5681
MedQual	-0.0134	-0.0797	-15.1938	-0.0846
SelfEmpl	-1.1158	-6.0131	-14.6006	-0.0468
Owner	-0.0191	-0.1947	-0.2569	-2.2540
LifeIns	0.0931	1.0314	0.1808	1.5955
Assets	-0.0060	-0.0498	-1.2915	-4.3603
OptVal	-0.0054	-4.7263	-0.0065	-4.2906
α (1/marginal disutility of work)	1.196	1.43	1.196	1.43
δ (discount factor)	0.862	1.63	0.862	1.63
σ (elasticity of income in utility)	1.011	1.82	1.011	1.82
Individuals:	2369		965	
Exits	608		382	
Log Likelihood	-2076		-665	
Log Likelihood at 0	-3871		-2260	
Pseudo R-squared	0.46		0.71	
Chi-squared	3590		3190	

Both models fit the data well. The pseudo-R^2, one minus the ratio of the likelihood at the estimated parameters over the likelihood at zero, is 0.46 for the West German sample and even 0.71 for the East German sample. As visible in Figures 1 and 2, East Germany features a more homogenous retirement behavior than West Germany, resulting in a better fit.

The baseline retirement hazard rate, as indicated by γ, is strongly positive. Since the retirement hazard rate is well known to increase quickly with age, this is of course expected. It is much larger for East Germany, a reflection of the rapid decline in labor force participation in East Germany as described in section 3.

Our most important result relates to the coefficients of the option values. In both samples, they are statistically highly significant. The sign is negative, as expected, indicating a longer duration of employment when the option value to postpone retirement is large. Hence, retirement behavior is well described by the option value, the main economic incentive for retirement, in both East and West Germany. This result is particularly remarkable for the East German panel surveyed in a period of political instability and high uncertainty. Also remarkable is the similarity of the two coefficients. Although the coefficient in East Germany is a bit larger than the West German one, the difference is not significant.

Comparing Figures 1 and 2 with the estimation results, two seemingly contradictory observations emerge. On the one hand, the unconditional retirement profile in East Germany was very different from the West German one, with an even larger percentage of very early retirees. This is reflected in the larger baseline hazard rate γ in the East German estimation results. On the other hand, however, we realize the very similar influence of the economic retirement incentives as measured by the coefficient of the option value. Hence, *conditional on the different incentives* in East and West Germany, the response to these incentives was similar and very strong in both parts of the country.

The other economic incentives for retirement, the wealth variables, are not significant in the West. This is disappointing because life cycle considerations indicate an unambiguously earlier retirement age for wealthy workers. Of course, the weak results may well be due to the poor measurement of wealth by the set of dummy variables.

At least the least insignificant variable, i.e., ownership of life insurance, has a positive sign, prompting earlier retirement, as predicted by theory. In the East, life cycle considerations initially were hardly relevant. Rather, the negative coefficients reflect that the few who had accumulated wealth under the communist regime were also less likely to lose their jobs for early retirement after unification. Female heads of household retired earlier, while marital status had no influence.

Poor health has the expected implication for earlier retirement. This variable is highly significant in spite of the poor measurement. The significant coefficient may also indicate an endogeneity problem. The desire for early retirement may prompt workers to seek disability status.

The significance of the cohort variable is a statistical artefact. This variable only controls for a selection bias. Because we only observe employees who were not retired at the beginning of the panel period, members of the early cohorts must be very old to enter the sample.

The highest significance in the West German sample is found for the dummy variable for being unemployed in the year preceding retirement. This reflects that unemployment is an important pathway to eligibility for early retirement, as described above. In East Germany, the early retirement rules generated transitions directly from work to retirement which would have resulted in an unemployment spell under West German rules. Hence, the coefficient of unemployment in the East German regression is insignificant.

The signs of the human capital variables differ between East and West Germany. In the West, higher education is related to later retirement, as is higher job quality. In the East, workers with more than eight years of schooling retire earlier. Vocational training is not known in our East German data set. It has a surprising negative effect on retirement age in West Germany, although it is only barely significant. The sectoral indicators vary in sign, with civil servants retiring relatively early, and workers in the agricultural, education and medical sector relatively late.

The parameters in the option value itself are taken from Börsch-Supan (1992). The estimated value of α means that a person is indifferent between receiving a dollar in cash transfer and earning \$1.20 by working. While the disutility of work appears rather small, the discount rate implied by the estimated δ is 13.8 percent which in turn appears rather large. As a matter of fact, however, identification between α and δ is weak. Increasing α by simultaneously reducing δ produces very similar retirement probabilities. Finally, the estimated σ translates into a utility function that is about linear in income.

6. Policy Implications

What do these coefficients tell us about the retirement system? As is well-known, the population aging process will strain the pay-as-you-go social security systems up to the point of infeasibility at the peak of population aging. An important question is whether changes of the system can induce later retirement thus releasing the strain on contribution rates to the system.

The retirement model of the preceding section can be used as a micro simulation model to predict retirement ages under alternative retirement age-dependent adjustment formulae. For each sample person, we change the option value from its actual value to the value that results from inserting alternative adjustment factors in the retirement income Y^{Ret} of equation (2). The results are based on the population-weighted sum of the East and West German estimates.

Table 6 summarizes the simulated effects by computing the average retirement age and the percentage taking very early retirement (before age 60) implied by the micro simulation exercise. The first row gives the baseline retirement age under the old German public pension system as observed in 1984. The low average retirement age is due to (physical and economic) disability retirement.

Table 6. Retirement Age and Early Retirement

	Mean Retirement Age	Early Retirement (Retirement Age<60)
System Before 1992 Reform	58.5	32.2 %
After 1992 Reform	59.0	28.2 %
Non-distortionary System	60.6	17.8 %

Source: Own computations using population-weighted coefficients from Table 5.

The second row predicts the effects of the 1992 German Social Security Reform. This reform will remove some but by no means all of the distortions towards early retirement, when it finally will be fully implemented in 2002. It will increase the average retirement age by about half a year. The micro simulation also reveals that retirement before age 60 is reduced from 32.2 percent to 28.2 percent.

The third row shows the effect of switching to a non-distortionary system defined in section 2 with adjustment factors computed for the discount rate estimated in the retirement probability model. The simulation reveals a strong reaction to this change in the social security system. A non-distortionary system would shift the retirement age by more than two years. The effects of a non-distortionary system are most powerful in the reduction of early retirement, i.e., retirement before the official window period. Retirement at ages 59 and below would drop from 32.2 percent to 17.8 percent.

Since the responses are rather large, one may be suspicious of the estimation results. However, a brief look at the historical data reveals similarly large responses to the 1972 Social Security Reform in Germany. Although no micro data is available, the time series of retirement ages provided by the annual employment survey of white collar workers show that retirement age declined in a plunge from age 63 to age 58.5 after the 1972 reform.[10]

Moreover, introduction of the window replaced the almost universal 65 year retirement age before 1972 by an almost even split between age 63 and age 65 six years after the reform. In the eighties, the disability rule was increasingly evoked among blue collar workers, leading to the pattern discussed in section 3 with more workers retiring at age 60 than at ages 63 and 65.

7. Conclusions

In the wake of unification, descriptive retirement profiles in East and West Germany were very different. East Germany featured an even larger percentage of early retirees than West Germany. As a result of the political and economic changes in the East, average retirement age in East Germany dropped to 55.8 years. On the other hand, however, the economic retirement incentives seem to have had strikingly similar impacts as measured by the coefficient of the option value. Hence, *conditional on the different incentives* in East and West Germany, the response to these incentives was rather similar and very strong in both parts of the country.

The responsiveness of the choice of retirement age to the incentives offered by the pension system has strong policy impacts. The public pension system in the just unified Germany did not only dispense with using the retirement-age-dependent adjustments as policy instruments for balancing the budget of the pension system, it even yielded incentives that worked against this because the adjustments were not actuarially fair. Rather than awarding later retirement to moderate the labor supply disincentives created by quickly rising social security taxes, social security regulations encouraged early retirement, thus aggravating the imbalance between the number of workers and pensioners.

The 1992 social security reform, fully effective from 2002, will remove some but by no means all of these distortions. According to the estimates presented in this paper, it is predicted to increase the average retirement age only by about half a year. A truly age-neutral system, in contrast, could shift the retirement age by up to four times as much. It is remarkable that this estimate is supported by both East and West German evidence.

Of course, this is an issue for the long run. In the past decade, the short-run consideration of reducing statistical unemployment by early retirement provisions

---

[10] See Riphahn/Schmidt (1997) or Schmidt (1995, chapter 4) for a detailed description of the development of age-specific retirement rates in West Germany over a 20 year period starting in 1970.

seems to have dominated policy in Germany. However, one should keep in mind that reducing incentives for early retirement becomes ever more complicated due to changes in the politics of the social security system. The political power is gradually shifting from the working population to the retired population, i.e. to an electorate which is unlikely to vote for a reduction of benefits in order to keep labor supply disincentives at a reasonable limit.

Acknowledgements

We thank Jens Köke for his excellent research assistantship. The first author is grateful for financial support by the National Institute on Aging (grant no. 3 PO1 AG05842-01) and the hospitality of the Department of Economics at the University of California at Berkley where most of the research was performed.

References

Börsch-Supan, A. (1991), Implications of an Aging Population: Problems and Policy Options in the US and Germany, *Economic Policy* 12, 103-139.

Börsch-Supan, A. (1992), Population Aging, Social Security Design, and Early Retirement, *Journal of Institutional and Theoretical Economics (Zeitschrift für die gesamte Staatswissenschaft)* 148, 533-557.

Lazear, E. P./Moore, R. (1988), Pensions and Turnover, in: Bodie, Z. et al. (eds.), *Pensions in the U.S. Economy*, Chicago, 163-188.

Lumbsdaine, R. L./Stock, J. H./Wise, D. A. (1992), Three models of Retirement: Computational Complexity versus Predictive Validity, in: Wise, D. (ed.), *Topics in the Economics of Aging*, Chicago, 19-60.

Meghir, C./Whitehouse, E. (1997), Labor Market Transitions and Retirment of Men in the UK, *Journal of Econometrics 79(2)*, 327-354.

Riphahn, R. T./Schmidt, P. (1997), Determinanten des Rentenzugangs – Eine Analyse altersspezifischer Verrentungsraten, *Review of Economics (Jahrbuch für Wirtschaftswissenschaften), 48*, 133-147.

Schmähl, W. (1989), Labor Force Participation and Social Pension Systems, in: P. Johnson, C./Thomson, D. (eds.), *Workers versus Pensioners: Intergenerational Justice in an Ageing World*, Manchester, 137-161.

Schmähl, W. (1991), Alterssicherung in der DDR und ihre Umgestaltung im Zuge des deutschen Einigungsprozesses – Einige verteilungspolitische Aspekte, in: Kleinhenz, G. (ed.), *Sozialpolitik im vereinten Deutschland*, Berlin, 49-95.

Schmähl, W. (1992), Public Pension Schemes in Transition: Germany's Way to Cope with the Challenge of an Ageing Population and the German Unification, Discussion Paper, Centre for Social Policy Research, University of Bremen.

Schmidt, P. (1995), *Die Wahl des Rentenalters – Theoretische und empirische Analyse des Rentenzugangsverhaltens in West- und Ostdeutschland*, Frankfurt.

Schneider, H. (1991), *Verweildaueranalyse mit GAUSS*, Frankfurt.

Stock, J. H./Wise, D. A. (1990), The Pension Inducement to Retire: An Option Value Analysis, in: Wise, D. (ed.), *Issues in the Economics of Aging*, Chicago, 205-224.

Sueyoshi, G. T. (1989), Social Security and The Determinants of Full and Partial Retirement: A Competing Risk Analysis, NBER Working Paper 3113, Cambridge.

4. Employment Effects of Newly Founded Businesses in East Germany

Thomas Hinz, University of Munich
Rolf Ziegler, University of Munich

1. New Firms as Promotors of New Employment

The creation of new firms represents an important aspect of the economic restructuring in East Germany. High hopes were attached to the new businesses: They were expected to stimulate a competitive market economy, implement product and process innovation, create opportunities for capital accumulation and, last but not least, to relieve the strain on the labor market imposed by German unification. Especially this last function explains why new business creation has been a main target of German economic policy after unification. The financial support allocated to create a tapestry of small businesses in East Germany by far outweighed expenditures in West Germany. The programs promoting new firm establishment in East Germany were seen as part of the overall employment policy (Bundesministerium für Wirtschaft (1996), DIW (1999)).

This paper analyzes the employment dynamics of new firms in East Germany on the basis of a panel study. Were the high hopes concerning job creation justified? More specifically, we focus on three points: (1) We describe the process of job creation in the first three years after a business is established. (2) We identify some important factors influencing the job creation process. (3) Finally, we analyze the effects of governmental funding programs on employment dynamics.

The creation of new firms in East Germany was embedded in the transformation from a planned to a market economy. Whereas the condition of "economic normality" might be characterized by the entry of new firms into a pool of established enterprises showing a mixed distribution of size, the situation in East Germany was distinctly different. We are confronted with a high mortality of large firms established during the socialist past. The surviving industrial "giants" – formerly integrated into the *Kombinate* system – drastically cut down on employment after privatization. Additionally, there were only a few small-sized firms remaining that were founded in the GDR (Bannasch (1990)). Their chances of survival in the new market environment were doubtful. When we consider the establishment of small businesses our attention must also be drawn to those firms which registered as new businesses, but were not actually new. In the course of privatization a hybrid form of new firms was constituted: *Ausgründungen*, split-off firms. For example, small parts of former GDR economic organizations, such as worker cooperatives, state owned firms and the trading organization (*HO*), were privatized.

Further extraordinary conditions for the constitution process can be characterized by an uncovered demand for consumer goods, and by imponderabilities and problems resulting from the dramatic change of the economic system. The latter included a shortage of private capital, the destruction of networks (Albach (1993), Hinz/Ziegler (1996)), uncertainty associated with property titles and a lack of important infrastructure.

2. Theoretical Sketches

The research of David Birch (1987) is one of the best known studies on employment effects of newly founded firms. His findings demonstrate that new and small businesses create a proportionally high number of new jobs. Although there is a broad discussion about data problems in his studies (Eckart et al. (1987)), his main conclusions have been confirmed (Berney/Phillips (1994)). In West Germany, similar findings have been reported (Cramer (1987), Boeri/Cramer (1991)). Brüderl/Bühler/Ziegler (1993) report a net growth of jobs over a four year period in the region of Munich and upper Bavaria, primarily due to a small group of highly expansive firms.

Theories about organizational growth mainly focus on the size of the firm.[1] Empirical studies show that larger organizations grow more slowly. A second influence on the growth of organizations is their age. Older organizations show a reduced growth rate. We will discuss four additional dimensions concerning employment dynamics:

1. Market conditions (demand and competition). The theoretical background for the relationship between market conditions and employment growth stems from industrial and regional economics (Storey (1994)), as well as organizational ecology (Hannan/Freeman (1989)). Favorable conditions for growth emerge depending on the market situation. In industries characterized by a great demand, the development of employment should be influenced positively. A competitive setting should influence the growth of firms by two different mechanisms. While a higher density has a negative impact on survival chances,

---

[1] See Wagner (1994) for a review.

firms surviving in competition tend to grow if the firm strategies fit the environment.

2. Types of firms. As mentioned above, the creation of the small business sector in East Germany consisted of two parts – "top-down" privatization and a "bottom-up" process of creating new businesses. To the former group belong those hybrid firms that were split-offs from former GDR economic organizations. We discussed the pressures on these firms adjusting their businesses to the market. Dismissals were one part of the necessary adjustments. Newly founded firms, however, begin relatively small in size, having a greater chance of employment growth.

3. Human capital. Although human capital theory concentrates on the returns of educational investment in employment relations (Becker (1975)), we can transform the core idea into the context of self-employment. Firms founded by persons with higher qualifications are supposed to have a higher productivity and show a better performance (Brüderl/Preisendörfer/Ziegler (1996)). Thus employment growth as a crucial variable of economic success should be influenced by human capital that the founder brings in. It can be argued that human capital of the GDR labor force was devaluated in the course of German unification.[2] Firm-specific knowledge clearly could not be transferred to a new business, for the business routines of a planned (shortage) economy differ from the activities which are more important in a market economy. The main focus shifted from organizing goods and labor supply (often through informal networks) to selling products and services on the market.

4. Institutional setting. The introduction of a market economy in the former GDR was orchestrated by introducing the West German institutional system (Lehmbruch (1993)). Parts of this system of laws, associations, and organizations may have supported or impeded the constitution of new firms. We will discuss the governmental financial allocations to promote the creation of new firms.[3] Did governmental credit programs affect employment growth in newly founded firms?

In the following analysis we ask how employment growth in new East German firms was affected by these factors. Which firms were most promising with regard to job creation? Which organizational and individual characteristics influenced the employment potential? Before starting the formal analysis, however, data and variables used in our empirical study need to be discussed.

---

[2] For a discussion of the transferability of human capital see Bird et al. (1992), and Scheuer et al. (1992))

[3] For an overview of programs see Brandt et al. (1991), or Gruhler (1997).

3. Data and Variables

Employment dynamics need to be studied longitudinally, and new firms should be observed over a longer period of time after starting their activities. The number of jobs created when a business starts up can be diminished by two processes – firms may shrink and new businesses may fail. Additionally, we have to take into account that new firms compete with firms that are already in the market. Newly created jobs may replace the jobs in firms which could not withstand competition. Although our data cannot address the argument of job replacement, the problem should be kept in mind.

Our analysis is based on panel data containing 624 cases, the *Leipziger Gründerstudie* (founder study)[4]. Each case represents a firm registered in the second half of 1991. Data was collected during two interviews, one in 1992 (about nine months after registration) and one in 1995. The panel was based on official records of business registrations (including the entries to the *Handwerksrolle*).[5] We conducted a screening survey of all the 4,162 businesses registered at that time and received responses from 48 percent (N=2,011) of those firms. From about 1,500 firms willing to participate in our study, we selected a stratified random sample of 840 (stratification criterion: Industry). 742 interviews were conducted in the first fieldwork period (summer 1992), and 624 could be successfully re-interviewed in the second survey. For 600 firms we have complete data on the number of existing jobs (including the entrepreneur herself). The reported number of employees corresponds to the *average number of employees* in each of the years 1991-1994. This figure represents a weighted "full-time equivalence" calculated on the reported full-time and part-time workers including the founding person(s).[6]

In our analysis we focus on a specific aspect of the employment dynamics. We analyze the *employment potential* represented by the firms at the *time of starting their business activities*. When analyzing the overall effect, this approach requires us to include the businesses which were shut down during the observation time. A shut-down firm is regarded as having zero employees. The combined analysis of surviving and non-surviving firms enables us to evaluate the employment potential of the firms at the time of their "births" in a more realistic way.

---

[4] The *Leipziger Gründerstudie* was supported by the *Deutsche Forschungsgemeinschaft* (DFG). In addition to the authors, Christoph Bühler, Frigga Dickwach, Peter Preisendörfer and Steffen H. Wilsdorf were part of the research team at the Universities of Munich and Leipzig.

[5] According to German laws, firms in certain industries (traditionally, in which craftsmen are working) have to be registered in the *Handwerksrolle* based on occupational qualifications of the founder(s).

[6] A part-time worker equals .5 and a full-time worker 1.0.

Employment growth is studied in two dimensions. First, in an OLS-model we analyze the growth rate which is defined by the difference of the (log) number of employees in 1994 minus the (log) number of employees in 1991. A second dimension of growth we distinguish is the probability of growing fast: We analyze the probability of increasing the number of jobs by a factor of 5 between 1991 and 1994.[7] The starting size in 1991 is measured by two control variables: The (log) number of employees and the (log) start-up capital.

As independent variables we use a set of dummies indicating industries (construction, metal, trade; category of reference: services), the regional site (city of Leipzig; category of reference: rural areas). Several other dummies are included to measure some organizational characteristics: Legal form (*Kapitalgesellschaften*; reference category: firms not in the register of commerce); degree of independence (complete independence; reference category: subsidiary firms); business partner (reference: no business partner engaged); full-time business (reference: part-time business to get a second income); and the type of the founded firm (newly created; reference category: split-off), which is a variable of specific interest.

Another set of variables characterizes the founder of the firm. In addition to demographic variables (sex and age), we include some measures of human capital: (1) Years of labor force experience, (2) years of schooling, (3) experience in the branch of industry (reference: no experience) and (4) previously self-employed (reference: no previous self-employment). Two other dummies are included: Being from West Germany (reference: Living in the GDR in 1989) and the labor market position before founding (unemployed, not participating in the labor force; reference category: employed). The latter refers to the hypothesis that firms founded by unemployed persons perform more poorly than firms founded by employed people (Hinz (1996)).

4. Empirical Results

The empirical section of our paper consists of three parts. First, we describe job creation at the time the new businesses started. How many jobs did new firms have just after starting their activities? Additionally, we try to compare this figure with the overall loss of jobs in the region Leipzig at the same time (4.1.). Second, the dynamics are investigated following the outline discussed in section 2: What factors – such as environmental conditions, types of founded firms and human capital – had an impact on employment growth? (4.2.) Third, attention is given to the employment effects of supporting programs (4.3.).

---

[7] The factor of 5 indicates an extraordinary growth rate.

4.1. Job Creation at the Time of "Birth"

The size of the firms at the time of starting the business is a crucial indicator for the evaluation of the employment effects. Large firms obviously create a larger number of jobs but they show a lower growth rate. About one half of the firms (49.6 percent) belongs to the category "self-employed", i.e. only one person (the founder) is working in the firm when the business gets started. 23.6 percent of the firms have 1.5-3 employees, 7.5 percent belong to the category 3.5-5 employees. A similar proportion (7.2 percent) has 5.5 to 10 jobs. More than 10 workers are employed by 12.1 percent of the new firms in the panel.

Table 1 gives an overview of the means and medians for the different branches of industry. There exist clear differences. Firms in construction and metal industry were relatively large at the time of founding. Trading and services, which cover large parts of the small business sector, started with a significantly smaller number of employees.

Another clear difference exists between newly created firms and the split-offs, some of them doing the same business as in the GDR. The mean and the median differ significantly.

Table 1. Average Number of Jobs When Starting Business (Mean and Median)

	Mean	Median	N
Construction	15.3	3.3	162
Industry/Metal industry	40.3	3.0	36
Trading	3.2	1.0	172
Services	4.1	1.0	227
Newly Founded	3.9	1.0	492
Split-off	33.0	5.0	105
All firms	9.1	1.5	597

Source: Leipzig founder study, second panel survey.

Before we focus on the dynamics of employment, we compare the number of new jobs created by all the businesses that were established in the second half of 1991, with the loss of jobs in the region of Leipzig within the same time period. For this purpose we extrapolate the number of jobs created by the firms participating in our study to all the 4,162 business registrations. This extrapolation relies on the problematic assumption that the probability of taking part in the survey is independent of firm size. Analyses of the selection process, however, indicate that very small businesses (often started to provide an extra income) have a low response rate (see Hinz/Preisendörfer/Ziegler (1995)). Hence the extrapolated total number of jobs is an optimistic overestimation. We compare this figure with the estimated 40,000 job losses during the second half of 1991 according to official unemployment statistics (Arbeitsamt Leipzig (1992)).

The extrapolated figure of 28,500 jobs is mainly due to the split-off firms, while only 8,400 jobs were newly created. The new jobs could only compensate for one fifth of the registered entries into unemployment. Therefore, in the second half of 1991, the estimated net change in total employment was significantly negative in the Leipzig region.

Table 2. Net Job Change (Second Half of 1991)

	Newly created (*Neugründungen*)	Maintained by split-off (*Ausgründungen*)
Number of jobs (time of business registration)	8,400	20,100
Entries into unemployment	40,000*	
Net change	-32,400	

Source: Estimations based on Leipzig founder study; interviews of the first survey 1992; weighted data; *Arbeitsamt Leipzig (1992): All entries into unemployment from July to December 1991 were summed up. Note that the regional boundary of *Kammerbezirk* that formed the basis for the registration does not exactly match the *Arbeitsamtsbezirk*.

4.2. Employment Effects in the First Three Years

Let us first look at the employment dynamics in Table 3. During the first three years we observe a continuously increasing number of jobs in our new businesses. This holds for both the median and the mean. The total number of jobs increased from about 5,400 to 6,500. There is marked growth during the first year, which diminishes in the following years. One fifth of the firms continuously increased employment while one fifth saw a reduction of jobs between 1992 and 1994.

The first column of Table 3 shows the proportion of firms with no employees for each year. From 1991 to 1992, the proportion of firms reporting zero employment first decreases from 13.3 percent to 1.7 percent – this means that the firms started gradually. Then, the proportion increases to 10.5 percent in 1994 – reflecting the growing number of firms shut down.

In Table 2 we distinguished between newly created jobs and jobs maintained by split-off firms. Analyzing the employment dynamics of these two types of firms shows opposing trends. Newly created firms increased their employment from 1,900 to 3,800 jobs, whereas split-off firms significantly reduced the number of jobs from 3,500 to 2,700 (see Figure 1). There was a remarkable job gap in 1991 between these two types of firms, but only two years later, the number of jobs in newly created firms exceeded those in the split-off firms. This result is even more striking considering the fact that firms which failed within the first three years are included in the analysis. Figure 1 also indicates the high pressure exercised on the split-off firms. One way to raise productivity was by dismissing employees.

Table 3. Job Creation 1991-1994

	Firms with job number=0 (in %)	Median	Mean	Total number of jobs	Number of firms
Number of jobs 1991	13.3	1.5	9.0	5411	600
Number of jobs 1992	1.7	2.0	10.0	6026	600
Number of jobs 1993	4.5	2.5	10.7	6440	600
Number of jobs 1994	10.5	3.0	10.8	6490	600

Source: Leipzig founder study, second panel survey.

Notes: Note that firms with job number zero in 1991 showed a low business activity in the year of registration. However, none of these firms had been shut down by the end of 1991.

Figure 1. Job Creation in Newly Founded Firms and Split-off Firms

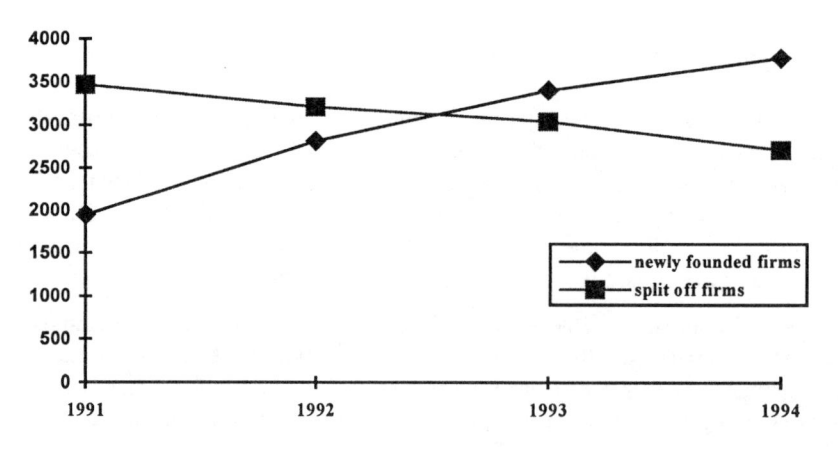

Source: Leipzig founder study, second panel survey; total number of jobs, failed businesses included (N=600)

The following figures show changes in the distribution of firm size during the observation period. Notice, however, that shut-down firms are excluded from the analysis. The proportion of very small firms sharply decreases during the first three years. This decline was perhaps caused by a growth of "one-person firms",[8] and by a higher failure rate of very small businesses (liability of smallness).

Figure 2 gives an impression of the overall dynamics. In 1991, about 50 percent of the firms started as one-person-firms. By 1994, the category "one-person firm" is reduced by 25 percentage points, indicating remarkable employment growth of very small firms. The category 1.5-3 employees remains constant. Firms with 3.5-5 employees increase in number (7,5 percent to 12.7 percent), similar to the firms with 5.5-10 employees (7.2 percent to 13.3 percent).

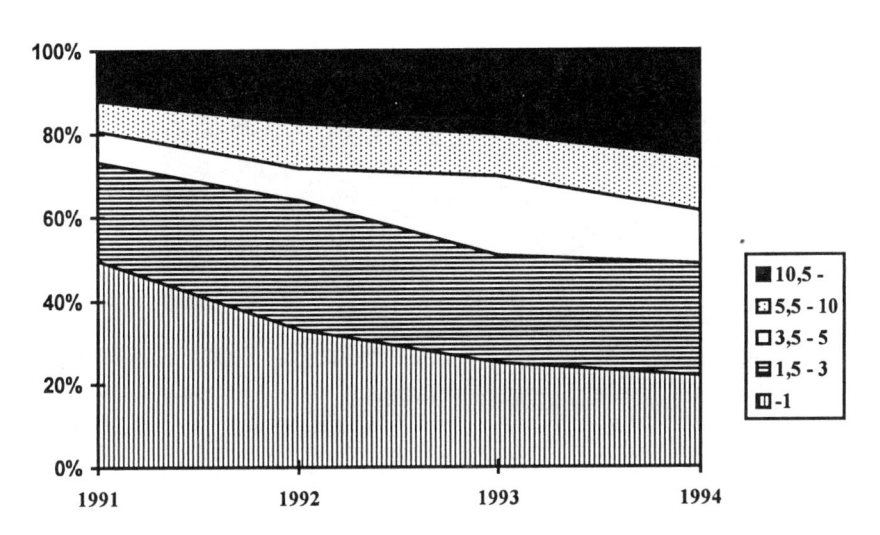

Figure 2. Firm Size 1991 – 1994 (all firms)

Source: Leipzig founder study, second panel survey; survivors only; N(1991)=597; N(1992)=573; N(1993)=540; N(1994)=503

Figures 3, 4, 5, and 6 show the distribution of firm size in different industries. Only some trends shall be highlighted. In the construction industry, the initial proportion in the largest category (more than 10 employees) was 25 percent,

---

[8] Firms in which the founder is the only employee are called "one-person firms".

increasing to 50 percent.[9] In construction, an entrepreneur without employees is an exception. Trading and services, however, were characterized by an enormous proportion of "one-person firms" in 1991. Both industries show similar growth patterns. When one compares the situation at the beginning with that in 1994, the proportion of "one-person firms" is reduced by 50 percent in each of the two categories. A look at the figures for trading and services shows the differences between the industries. Services have a higher proportion of very small firms, and a higher proportion of firms in the largest group (the mean increases in trading from 3.2 to 6.0, in the service sector it rises from 4.1. to 6.7). Firms in the metal industry show a continuous increase in the group of firms with more than 10 employees. The mean number of jobs in the metal industry decreases from 40.3 to 28.1, while the median shows a contrary pattern. It increases from 3.0 to 8.5.

Figure 3. Firm Size 1991 – 1994 / Construction

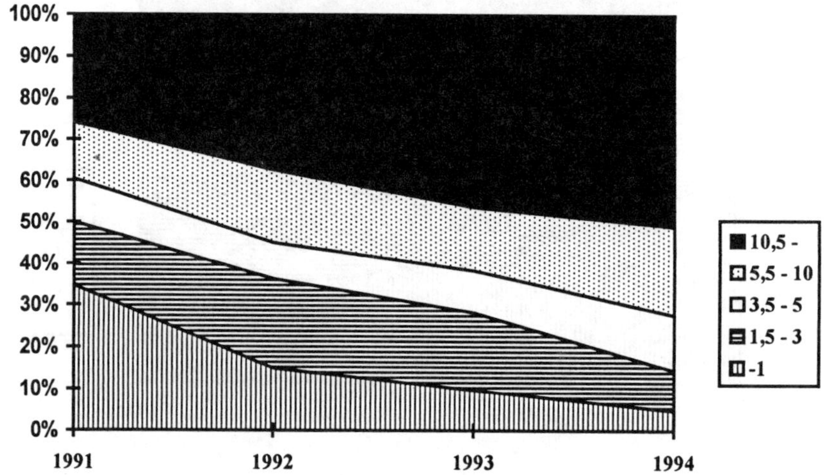

Source: Leipzig founder study, second panel survey; survivors only; N(1991)=162; N(1992)=160; N(1993)=152; N(1994)=145

---

[9] At the same time the mean shifted from 25.9 in 1991 to 23.6 because large "outliers" significantly reduced the number of employees.

Figure 4. Firm Size 1991 – 1994 / Metal Industry

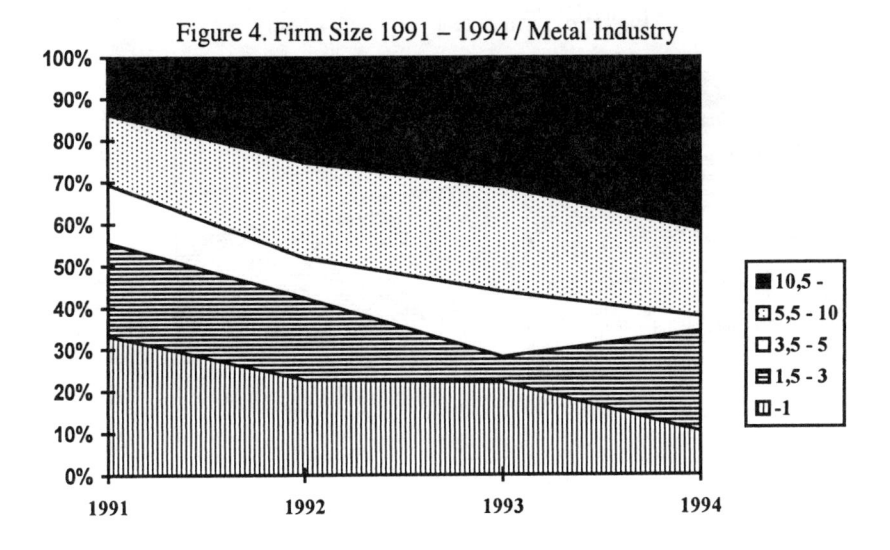

Legend: ■ 10,5 - ; ▣ 5,5 - 10 ; ▢ 3,5 - 5 ; ☰ 1,5 - 3 ; ▥ -1

Source: Leipzig founder study, second panel survey; survivors only; N(1991)=36; N(1992)=32; N(1993)=26; N(1994)=25

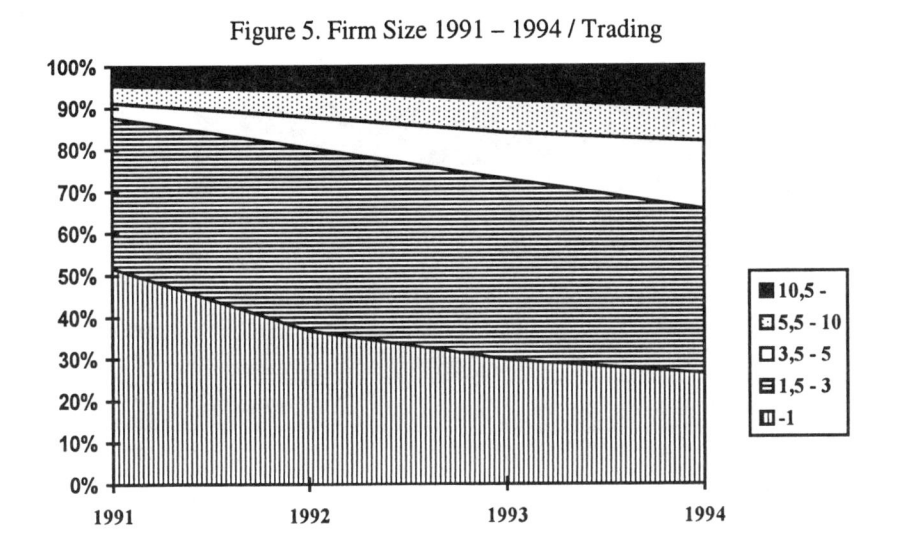

Figure 5. Firm Size 1991 – 1994 / Trading

Legend: ■ 10,5 - ; ▣ 5,5 - 10 ; ▢ 3,5 - 5 ; ☰ 1,5 - 3 ; ▥ -1

Source: Leipzig founder study, second panel survey; survivors only; N(1991)=172; N(1992)=163; N(1993)=155; N(1994)=137

Figure 6. Firm Size 1991 – 1994 / Services

Source: Leipzig founder study, second panel survey; survivors only; N(1991)=227; N(1992)=215; N(1993)=201; N(1994)=192

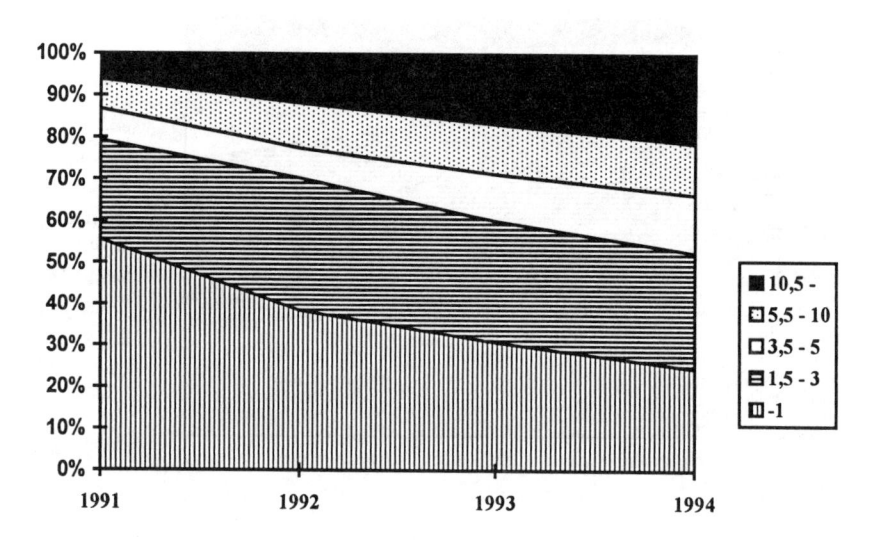

Figure 7. Firm Size 1991 – 1994 / Newly Founded Firms

Source: Leipzig founder study, second panel survey; survivors only; N(1991)=162; N(1992)=160; N(1993)=152; N(1994)=145

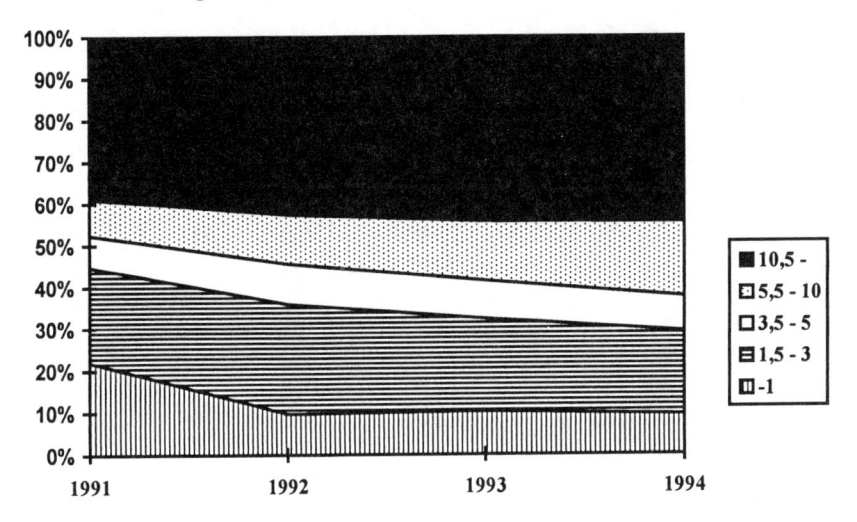

Figure 8. Firm Size 1991 – 1994 / Split-off Firms

[Chart showing firm size distribution 1991-1994 with categories: 10,5-; 5,5-10; 3,5-5; 1,5-3; -1]

Source: Leipzig founder study, second panel survey; survivors only; N(1991)=162; N(1992)=160; N(1993)=152; N(1994)=145

When we compare how firm size developed in newly founded firms and in split-off firms we notice a different size distribution. Initially only 5 percent of the new firms were in the category with more than 10 employees, whereas about 40 percent of the-split off firms are found in this size group (see Figures 7 and 8). The new firms increased their average size from 3.9 (in 1991) to 9.0 (in 1994). The mean number of jobs in split-off firms fell slightly, from 33.0 to 28.1.

We now turn to a multivariate analysis – beginning with two OLS-models which estimate the change of employment over the whole period of observation, i.e. from 1991 to 1994 (Table 4). The interpretation concentrates on the signs and statistical significance of the estimated coefficients. A positive value indicates employment growth. Model (1) takes the branches of industry and the organizational characteristics into account. In model (2) we additionally analyze the effects of individual characteristics. The employment level of 1991 is included in the models to control for initial size. The coefficient is – as expected – negative and highly significant. This means that larger firms had negative growth rates.

Industries differed in growth rates. The construction and metal industry experienced significantly positive employment growth. The effect for the construction sector is stronger. This outcome is related to very high demand that was stimulated by tax incentives and public investment into infrastructure. If one wants to speak of an East German "job machine", it could have existed only because of the construction boom.

Table 4. Job Change Rate 1991-1994 (OLS-Regressions)

	(1) coeff.	t-value	(2) coeff.	t-value
initial number of jobs 1991 (log)	-.70**	24.812	-.70**	24.953
construction	.79**	7.908	.71**	6.806
metal	.52**	3.054	.44*	2.581
trading	-.08	.826	.04	.378
city of Leipzig	.13	1.761	.11	1.413
legal form	.68**	5.028	.69**	5.064
business partner engaged	.11	1.077	.07	.625
newly founded	-.06	.598	-.05	.466
completely independent	.20	1.664	.14	1.186
founder working full-time	.48**	3.532	.54**	3.979
start up capital (log.)	.09**	5.554	.07**	4.749
sex (1 = female)			-.14	1.442
age (years)			-.003	.470
founder from West Ger-many			-.12	.783
labor force experience (years)			-.01	1.332
education and vocational training (years)			.01	.748
experience in branch of industry			.28**	3.262
previously self-employed			.18	1.567
labor market position before founding: unemployed			-.35**	3.871
no labor force participation			-.08	.410
constant	-.59*	2.537	-.51	1.288
N	492		480	
R-Square	.61		.64	

Source: Leipzig founder study, first and second panel surveys; survivors only; dependent variable: log (number of employees in 1994) – log (number of employees 1991); categories of reference are explained in section 3,* p < .05, ** p < .01.

The coefficients representing the influence of organizational characteristics on employment growth show a similar pattern. Controlling for the initial number of employees (in 1991), we find a positive relation between the other variables which measure size and employment growth. The larger the capital stock, the higher the job growth. The dimension that characterizes the specific situation of East German transformation, however, does not seem to be meaningful. Newly founded firms did not perform better than split-off firms, if initial firm size is taken into account.

However, entrepreneurial human capital is relevant. Experience in the industry is related to a positive growth rate. Occupational qualification and experience, even if made in the context of the old command system, seem to have been important factors for running a successful business in the new market environment. Notice that the effect of experience in the industry indicates continuity in a rapidly changing social and economic system. If (analyzing new businesses) we focus on the individuals who were involved in the process of restructuring, we have to conclude that the transformation of the eastern economy was far away from being characterized by a complete reshuffling of market chances.

Being unemployed before founding a firm is not conducive to employment growth. Our results allow two interpretations: (1) The motivation of unemployed persons to engage in business was a sort of "defensive" strategy. The founders created a small firm to earn her own living. The explicit strategy says: The firms should stay very small, without taking greater risks. (2) The persons who were unemployed before founding the firm were negatively selected. They could have been less productive than founders who started the business out of employment. However, one has to consider unemployment in East Germany as a mass phenomenon. Thus becoming unemployed did not necessarily mean being less productive. Other factors were prevalent. In the period after unification, certain industries were closed almost completely, and certain individual characteristics (e.g., sex) not automatically connected with a lower productivity did influence the risk of being dismissed.

Let us now focus on fast-growing firms, the "winners" of the system change. We define as fast-growing businesses those firms that increased the number of employees by a factor of 5 from 1991 to 1994. About 20 percent of our surveyed firms showed such marked growth. We use a logistic regression model analyzing the effects on the probability of belonging to this subgroup of new firms. The results are presented in Table 5. We will only discuss the statistically significant variables.

The environmental conditions had strong impact on employment dynamics. Construction firms were more likely to be fast-growing than firms of the reference category (services). Businesses in the metal industry also show a fast growth, due to the fact that many of these firms were working in the wider field of construction. The "newness" again is not a crucial variable to determine chances of growth. Split-off firms did not perform worse than newly founded firms. The only disadvantage split-off firms had with regard to employment dynamics is their large number of employees at the beginning. Furthermore, we find two other effects of individual variables confirming our previous results. Experience in the industry makes fast growth more likely. Again, the labor force position before the business got started affects the likelihood of growth. Firms of unemployed founders had a significantly lower chance of fast growth.

Table 5. Fast Growing Businesses (logistic regression)

	coeff.	t-value
initial number of jobs 1991 (log.)	-2.14**	8.568
construction	2.19**	3.729
metal	1.54*	1.961
trading	-.13	.230
city of Leipzig	.78	1.876
legal form	.89	1.132
business partner engaged	.34	.560
newly founded	-.05	.074
completely independent	.73	1.008
founder working full-time	.88	1.227
start up capital (log.)	.13	1.411
sex (1 = female)	-.35	.651
age (years)	-.01	.267
founder from West Germany	-1.26	1.516
labor force experience (years)	-.03	.493
education and vocational training (years)	-.09	.969
experience in the branch of industry	.92*	2.060
previously being self-employed	.80	1.283
labor market position before founding: unemployed	-1.17*	2.321
no labor force participation	.66	.807
constant	-4.72**	2.27
N	480	
Pseudo R-Square	.59	

Source: Leipzig founder study, first and second panel surveys; survivor firms only; dependent variable: increasing employment by factor 5; categories of reference are explained in section 3,* p < .05, ** p < .01.

Summarizing the results concerning human capital, we have to stress that the occupational experience of the founder positively influences employment dynamics. Continuing to work in the same industry distinctly raises the chance of higher growth. People who moved into self-employment out of unemployment seem to have behaved minimalistic. They did not want to expand. Such firms would not have been created without the dramatic labor market collapse characterizing the East German transformation.

4.3. Effects of Credit Programs (EKH and ERP)

When analyzing the effects of state-supported credit programs on employment dynamics we concentrate on the two most important programs: *"Eigenkapitalhilfe"* (EKH) and *"European Recovery Program"* (ERP) providing credits under favorable terms. Firms receiving normal bank credits only or with no outside capital at all serve as control groups. This design makes it possible to distinguish between a real *supporting effect* that derives from program participation and a *selection effect*, i.e. that potentially more successful firms are selected to take part in the programs (Brüderl/Preisendörfer/Ziegler (1993)). There is an underlying and plausible assumption. The criteria to get credit approval look the same applying for a bank credit or a credit financed by the government. In the period under investigation, an enormous proportion of firms was supported by the credit programs (about 35 percent),[10] a third of the firms took bank credits only, while the other third started up without any outside capital.

Patterns of employment dynamics differ among the three groups. Figure 9 shows the mean number of jobs in the years 1991 to 1994. Firms without any outside capital started relatively small (about 5 jobs) and remained on this level until 1994. New businesses having received normal bank credits are characterized by a stable development on a higher level (about 14 jobs). Firms supported by credit programs raised their number of employees from 8 to 14 persons. At first glance, this result seems to indicate a clear and strong effect of program participation on employment growth. We have to test this relationship with a multivariate model. Growth is measured as a continuous increase of employment during the observation period, i.e. firms having a growing number of jobs for each year.

---

[10] Most of these firms received additional "normal" bank credits.

Figure 9. Mean Number of Jobs by Sources of Outside Capital (1991-1994)

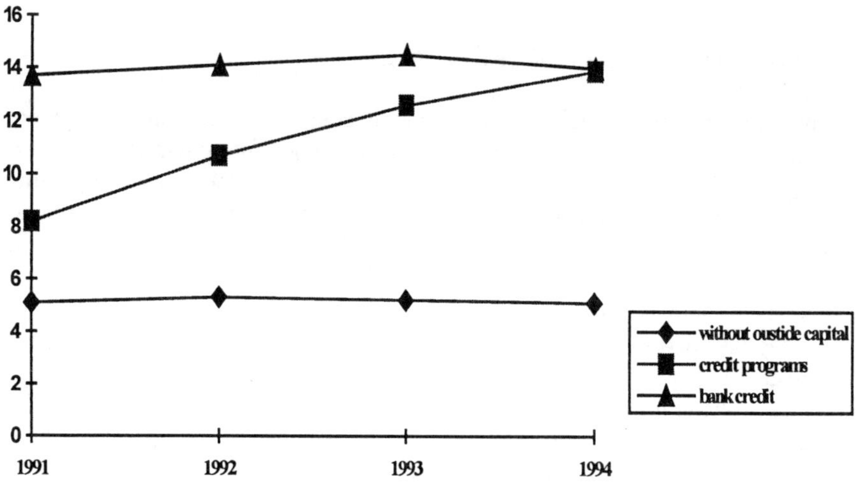

Source: Leipzig founder study; calculations of mean values include firms shut-down; without outside capital: N=199, credit programs: N=214, bank credit: N=200

Table 6 shows that firms without outside capital performed worse than firms partly financed by credits. A specific, though weak, program supporting effect exists (t-value 1.864).

These results may be explained by the favorable credit conditions of the supporting programs. Interest rates were rather low, credit contracts exempted the founders of an immediate repayment, and credit lines were shifted upwards when a firm was supported by the "EKH". Nevertheless, a selection effect exists, as indicated by a comparison of the coefficients. The variable indicating firms without outside capital shows a stronger effect.

The creation of new firms was influenced by government policies that tried to stimulate economic development. Ironically, the reintroduction of the market and "the revolutionary installation of a class of entrepreneurs" (Offe (1994, p. 60)) were accompanied by a strong intervention of the state. It appears that not only the mere transfer of the market system to the East that was responsible for the process of creating new firms, but also the specific institutions of a market economy like the banking system and the supporting programs that determine the success of new firms.

Table 6. Effects of Credit Programs on Continuous Employment Growth
(binomial logistic regressions)

	employment growth	
	coeff.	t-value
credit programs	.58	1.864
without outside capital	-.76	1.951
construction	1.06**	3.286
metal	.62	1.206
trading	-.50	1.217
city of Leipzig	.40	1.448
legal form	.69	1.693
founder working full-time	1.23*	2.119
newly founded	.77	1.158
complete independence	.68	1.803
business partners	.11	.330
start-up capital (log.)	.01	.137
initial number of jobs in 1991 (log.)	-.03	.363
sex (1=female)	-.71	1.795
founder from West Germany	.69	1.563
years of educational and vocational schooling	-.08	1.568
experience in the branch of industry	.17	.559
previously self-employed	-.07	.187
labor market position before founding: unemployed	-.73*	2.108
no labor force participation	-.13	.207
constant	-2.53	1.749
N		478
Pseudo R Square		0.22

Source: Leipzig founder study, first and second panel survey; categories of reference: see section 3; the model of employment growth was estimated for survivor firms only;* p < .05, ** p < .01.

5. Summary

To sum up, we find a growing number of jobs in newly created firms. However, these new jobs did not compensate the dramatic job loss that occurred due to the economic restructuring after unification. All four dimensions we studied influenced the employment dynamics. We demonstrated that environmental conditions determined the development of the firms. Employment effects of new firms in East Germany were, to a high degree, the outcome of a booming construction industry. The two types of the founded firms differ. Split-off firms perhaps played an important role in maintaining regional economic potential. However, they had to reduce their employment drastically over time. Notwithstanding this sharp reduction of employment, it does not seem that split-off firms were less successful in the first period after unification. In addition, our results underline the positive impact of higher capital investment on firm growth.

Occupational experience and qualifications had an impact on economic performance of the firms, too. This result has to be stressed, since the human capital gathered in the socialist system was frequently devaluated in the course of the economic transformation. Our empirical findings show that the occupational history of the founder played an important role in determining firms' success in terms of an increasing number of jobs. What is responsible for this effect of human capital? Discussing the participation in governmental supporting programs we would argue that education and occupational experience served as credentials. Furthermore, experience in the branch of industry consisted of specific technical knowledge and skills, and facilitated network support. It could be derived that human capital helps to raise productivity. Empirical studies on labor market transitions show that occupational education and experience are key factors stabilizing the labor force participation. We can apply this result to the transition into self-employment: Occupational experience seems to be a prerequisite for a successful step into entrepreneurship.

Previous labor market position as "unemployed" negatively influenced the growth rate of new firms. Unemployed persons were motivated in a specific way: They became self-employed in order to secure their labor force participation. Their motivation largely was to create one single job – for themselves. Unemployed founders did not act like entrepreneurs, they just wanted to make their living and explicitly refrained from growing too big. The stability of new firms, however, was not influenced by the labor market position (Hinz (1996)). This result is related to the poor labor market situation in general which did not provide alternative employment opportunities. On the whole, our study shows a great number of growing firms in the start-up period after unification. Unfortunately, many of the first booming industries got into trouble all too soon. Frequently firms, like in the construction sector, had to pay for relying too much on an extraordinary economic situation with a high demand supported by financial transfers, tax reductions, and investments into infrastructure, at the same time neglecting innovations.

References

Albach, H. (1993), *Zerrissene Netze: eine Netzwerkanalyse des ostdeutschen Transformationsprozesses*, Berlin.

Arbeitsamt Leipzig (1992), Der Arbeitsmarkt – das Jahr 1991, Leipzig, mimeo.

Bannasch, H.-G. (1990), The Role of Small Firms in East Germany, *Small Business Economics* 2, 307-311.

Becker, G. S. (1975), *Human Capital*, 2nd ed., Chicago.

Berney, R.E./Phillips, B.D. (1994), Small Bunisess and Job Creation – An Update, Washington D.C., mimeo.

Birch, D. (1987), *Job Creation in America*, New York.

Bird, E./Schwarze, J./Wagner, G.G. (1992), The Changing Value of Human Capital in Eastern Europe: Lessons from the GDR, Discussion Paper No. 55, Deutsches Institut für Wirtschaftsforschung, Berlin.

Boeri, T./Cramer, U. (1991), Betriebliche Wachstumsprozesse: Eine statistische Analyse der Beschäftigtenstatistik 1977-1987, *Mitteilungen aus der Arbeitsmarkt- und Berufsforschung* 24, 70-80.

Brandt, M./Herrmann, B./Sabathil, M. (1991), *Förderhilfen für die neuen Bundesländer*, Bonn.

Brüderl, J./Bühler, C./Ziegler, R. (1993), Beschäftigungswirkungen neugegründeter Betriebe, *Mitteilungen aus der Arbeitsmarkt- und Berufsforschung* 26, 521-528.

Brüderl, J./Preisendörfer, P./Ziegler, R. (1993), Staatliche Gründungsfinanzierung und der Erfolg neugegründeter Betriebe, *Jahrbücher für Nationalökonomie und Statistik* 212, 12-32.

Brüderl, J./Preisendörfer, P./Ziegler, R. (1996), Der Erfolg neugegründeter Betriebe. Eine empirische Studie zu den Chancen und Risiken von Betriebsgründungen, Berlin.

Bundesministerium für Wirtschaft (1996), Mittelstandspolitik für mehr Selbständigkeit und Beschäftigung, Bericht an den Ausschuß für Wirtschaft des Deutschen Bundestages, *BMWi Dokumention* No.394 (März), Bonn.

Cramer, U. (1987), Klein- und Mittelbetriebe: Hoffnungsträger der Beschäftigungspolitik?, *Mitteilungen aus der Arbeitsmarkt- und Berufsforschung* 20, 15-29.

DIW et al. (1999), Gesamtwirtschaftliche und unternehmerische Anpassungsfortschritte in Ostdeutschland, Neunzehnter Bericht, *Kiel Discussion Paper* 346/347, Kiel Institute of World Economics, Kiel.

Eckart, W./v. Einem, E./Stahl, K. (1987), Dynamik der Arbeitsplatzentwicklung: Eine kritische Betrachtung der empirischen Forschung in den Vereinigten Staaten, in: Fritsch, M./Hull, Ch. (eds.), *Arbeitsplatzdynamik und Regionalentwicklung*, Berlin, 21-47.

Gruhler, W. (1997), Beschäftigung in mitteldeutschen Betrieben Ost- und Westdeutschlands, *iw-hends, 24*, 55-66.

Hannan, M.T./Freeman, J. (1989), *Organizational Ecology*, Cambridge.

Hinz, T. (1996), Existenzgründungen in Ostdeutschland: Ein erfolgreicher Weg aus der Arbeitslosigkeit, in: Diewald, M./Mayer, K. (eds.), *Zwischenbilanz der Wiedervereinigung*, Opladen, 111-133.

Hinz, T./Preisendörfer, P./Ziegler, R. (1995), Die Rolle von Kleinbetriebe bei der Schaffung von Arbeitsplätzen in den neuen Bundesländern, in: Andreß, H.-J. (ed.), *Fünf Jahre danach. Zur Entwicklung von Arbeitsmarkt und Sozialstruktur im vereinten Deutschland*, Berlin, 277-301.

Hinz, T./Ziegler, R. (1996), Businesses Founded in East Germany: Economic Activity and Capital Investment, in: Brezinski, H./Fritsch, M. (eds.), *The Economic Impact of New Firms in Post-social Countries: Bottom-up transformation in Eastern Europe*, Cheltenham, 233-252.

Lehmbruch, G. (1993), Die Transformationsdynamik der Schnittstellen von Staat und Wirtschaft in der ehemaligen DDR, *BISS-Public* 3, 21-41.

Offe, C. (1994), *Der Tunnel am Ende des Lichts*, Frankfurt.

Scheuer, M. et. al. (1992), Ein Beitrag zur Bewertung der in der DDR erworbenen beruflichen Qualifikation in den Bereichen Metall und Elektro, *Mitteilungen aus der Arbeitsmarkt- und Berufsforschung* 25, 553-574.

Storey, D.J. (1994), *Understanding the Small Business Sector*, London.

Wagner, J. (1994), The Post-Entry Performance of New Small Firms in German Manufacturing Industries, *Journal of Industrial Economics* 42, 141-154.

5. Earning Dynamics in the East German Transition Process

Johannes Schwarze, University of Bamberg and IZA, Bonn

Gert G. Wagner, University of Frankfurt/Oder; DIW, Berlin, and IZA, Bonn

1. Introduction

In Eastern Europe a rapid transition which increases productivity, the level and the distribution of wages would satisfy the aims of full employment as well as the income preferences of the labor force. But such a development has been far away in East Germany. In this paper we look at the wage structure as an indicator for the progress made in the first years of the transition process from a planned to a market economy. We evaluate empirically to which degree the wage structure in East Germany became responsive to the qualification of employees. We find such adjustments in the wage structure mainly with newly established firms. While this positive development for new firms, who mostly employ younger workers, is generally viewed as beneficial, it also may have problematic social implications for older workers.

The paper is set up as follows. In section 2 we outline a theoretical framework by applying human capital theory (HC) to the dynamics of earnings within the transition process from a "socialist" to a market economy. An extension of standard HC models which takes into account the problem of a misallocation of human capital is discussed. Section 3 starts with a brief description of our data, which is the German Socio-Economic Panel (GSOEP). Then the empirical results of the dynamics of wages following unification are discussed. The paper ends with a short discussion of the social implications of these dynamics and with some suggestions for economic policy in transition processes (Flassbeck/Horn (1996), Hauser/Wagner (1997)).

2. Theoretical Framework

In contrast to other transformation economies in Eastern Europe, that of Germany was marked by a special development. In the first period after unification, many enterprises, especially the *Treuhand* firms (afterwards called trust firms),[1] but also most of the privatized firms that were formerly state-owned were heavily subsidized and mainly working with old-fashioned physical and human capital, including management which had not been trained for a market economy (Dyck (1993), DIW et al. (1999)). Often they produced products which were not tradable or only tradable at a loss (Bös (1991)). On the other hand there were new firms, often founded by western companies, which mainly worked with modern technology and efficient management that provided retraining and continued to train their employees. These firms produced tradable goods at a high level of productivity. Other new firms supplied services, whereas most trust firms and privatized firms belonged to the industrial sector.

Table 1 provides indicators which show the very different development of those different types of firms within the industrial sector.[2] While the overall level of employment was declining, the managers of newly founded firms could expect an increase. The investments made in 1992 support these expectations. But because newly founded firms were small, their impact on employment was small in 1992: Whereas the new firms made up a quarter of all firms in the industry, the share of employees working in new firms was only four percent. It is also noteworthy that in the East German economy as a whole, the share of employees working in newly established firms was higher than in the industrial sector. The reason is that most newly founded firms belonged to the service sector. With respect to the indicators "expected employment" and "investment" in 1992, the privatized firms did better than the trust firms. This result is plausible because the firms already privatized represented a positive selection of more viable firms, compared to firms that were not privatized at this early stage.

In 1995, most of the former trust firms had been privatized. Thus the share of employees employed by new firms vastly exceeded that of 1992. This result is not surprising. The high level of per capita investment might be surprising. It is due to a selection process. The worst-performing trust firms were no longer in business.

---

[1] The *Treuhandanstalt* was founded in 1989 by the government of the GDR (Flassbeck/Horn (1996, p. 101)). This trust owned most of industrial enterprises in East Germany. The aim of the trust was the restructuring and privatization of those firms.

[2] Table 1 is based on a survey conducted in the summers of 1992 and 1995 for industry and manufacturing firms (*verarbeitendes Gewerbe*). Due to a high attrition rate of the firms and a lack of other statistical information it is unknown to what extent this survey represents the universe of firms (DIW et al. (1999)).

Table 1. Indicators of Industrial Firms in the New German States by Type of Firm. Results from a Firm-Survey in 1992 and 1995

Indicator		Trust Firms	Privatized Firms	New Firms	All Firms
Expected increase of employees per firm in	1993	-14	0	20	-6
Investment per capita (DM)	1992	11,070	23,340	47,360	18,000
	1995	24,900	26,800	29,100	26,800
Percent of employees	1992	55	36	4	100
	1995	5	73	20	100
Distribution of firms	1992	28	47	25	100
(in percent)	1995	1	54	45	100

Source: DIW et al. (1999).

Our first research question is whether differences in the fundamental economic indicators of the firms did lead to different wage levels and wage structures. In the former GDR the wage structure was very flat for ideological reasons. It can be assumed that for the case of trust firms a change in the wage structure did not occur, as these firms were in a kind of "waiting position", when in privatized and new firms the GDR wage structure were replaced by a more dispersed one, in order to create work incentives. On the other hand, the privatized and newly founded firms, which were doing better, could afford to pay their less qualified employees more than trust firms did, despite the wage structure being more unequal in those firms.

Changes in the wage structure can be analyzed by different concepts. In this paper we estimate models which are based on human capital theory. We will not discuss here whether this approach is appropriate for a deeper analysis of the former GDR (Schwarze (1993), Newell/Reilly (1996)). When analyzing the wage structure in planned economic systems human capital theory may fail, because free market conditions are not satisfied. But our main purpose is to study the development of the East German wage structure under the conditions of an emerging market system. Therefore estimates for the former GDR are obtained only for reasons of comparability.

When estimating earnings regressions for an economy under transition, it is necessary to quantify whether and to what extent misallocation of human capital affects the measured returns to human capital. Misallocation of human capital occurred because the level of formal qualification in the GDR was very high. The communist regime made a point of providing a better education to its population than "capitalist societies". But due to the low efficiency of the East German economy, the demand for higher qualification was often lower than skills supplied. Therefore employees in the former GDR were frequently employed on jobs where they could not use their qualifications in a proper way – we call them "overqualified". The actual value of the "old" GDR human capital is evaluated in the new market system through the level of pay, and through the decision of whether to hire a worker at all.

The standard model of human capital theory does not address the phenomenon of overqualification, because supply side restrictions are ignored. We make an attempt in our wage regressions to control for overqualification as misallocation of human capital (Schwarze (1993), Bird et al. (1994)). The estimated wage regression can be expressed as follows:

$$\ln(Y) = b_0 + b_1 E + b_2 \text{OVER} + b_3 \text{WE} + b_4 \text{WE}^2 + b_5 \text{WF} + b_6 \text{OTHERS} + e$$

where Y is monthly gross wage income and e is an error term. E is years of education, where education means schooling and vocational training. WE is work experience. The quadratic form for WE is included because of the declining accumulation of such capital with age. WF is firm experience, i.e. the time spent with the current employer. OTHERS stand for additional demographic characteristics such as working time, size of firm. b_0 through b_6 are the related coefficients to be estimated. b_1, for example, is the estimated rate of return to human capital.

Overqualification will be controlled by OVER, which stands for a vector of dummy variables and indicates whether an employee is overqualified or not. In the simplest case OVER might have the dimension one. Then the overqualification of a specialist worker would matter the same as the overqualification of an employee with a university degree. In this paper OVER has a dimension equal to four, which means that overqualification is controlled for by four different types of occupational certificates – specialist worker, master worker, engineer, and university degree. The related vector of coefficients b_2 can be interpreted as a correction of the overall rate of return to human capital, and the coefficients should have negative signs. On the other hand the overall rate of return should be higher after the correction.

We estimate a simple wage regression[3] for all male employees[4] in the GDR in 1989 and compare the results with regression estimates for wages surveyed in the

---

[3] All wage regressions are estimated by simple OLS. The reason for this procedure is theoretical. In our analysis the structure of wages is an indicator for economic performance of the whole economy and for the performance of different firm types. Thus we are interested in employed persons only. The wage structure of any enterprise can be analyzed only for the employees who are actually working there and not for those who will work there in the future, or those who worked there in the past. In this sense, the parameters derived from the simple OLS estimator are consistent estimates for the population being considered.

spring of 1992. These estimates are then compared with identically specified regressions for a so called "real" market economy, namely West Germany in 1989, which is our "benchmark". We will not discuss here whether the West German wage structure is an "optimal" one in terms of employment and earnings. Quantifying such an optimal wage structure seems to be impossible. But it also seems to be clear that the West German wage structure will eventually determine the wage structure of the East German economy, which is only a small share of the united German economy. This does not mean that a distinctive East German wage structure could not arise. But with respect to the structure of earnings, a long-term segmentation into an eastern and a western structure seems not very likely, because the regional labor markets are highly integrated. The institutional settings are the same for East and West Germany, and wage bargaining is highly centralized (although regional practice of collective bargaining differs). Moreover, five percent of the East German labor force is commuting to West Germany, which contributes to reducing labor market differences.

3. Empirical Evidence

3.1. Data

We use survey data of employees, who are asked not only about their personal characteristics, but also about some key variables for their employers. The data we use are drawn from the eastern and western subsamples of the German Socio-Economic Panel (GSOEP). The GSOEP was started in West Germany in 1984 and expanded to the GDR in June 1990, immediately before the Monetary, Economic and Social Union (Wagner et al. (1993)). All respondents were asked about their income and earnings one year before, i.e. before the fall of the wall. Thus, the first cross-section for East Germany refers to May 1989 and is a measure for the old "socialist" economy. The second and third cross-sections come from spring 1992 and 1995. The sample of 1992 gives us a picture of the economy 18 months after the economic unification of Germany, which occurred three months before the political unification. The sample of 1995 describes the situation 4.5 years after economic unification when East Germany had entered into the recovery phase of the economic transition.

---

[4] An analysis for female employees would be very difficult, because more detailed information for the female career trajectories is required which is not available for the sample of 1992.

All information we need is available from the GSOEP. Most of the variables are well known and need no further comment.[5] In 1992 and 1995 all employees were asked whether they are working in a trust firm, a privatized firm or a firm which was founded after 1989. Overqualification is estimated by the following procedure: First, we compute for each employee in the sample the highest degree of formal qualification she holds (the levels are specialist worker (*Facharbeiter*), master worker (*Meister*), and engineering or university degree). In a second step we use the answer to the question "What type of training is usually necessary for the job that you do?" to compute dummy variables for each level of formal qualification which are equal to one for overqualified workers and zero otherwise.

In our sample the number of cases is comparatively small, especially for employees in newly founded firms in the year 1992 (cf. Table 4). But it will turn out that our main findings are significant. Because our estimates are conditional, the question of whether this small sample allows estimates of population values does not matter.[6]

3.2. Results

Table 2 shows the dramatic increase of the level of earnings in East Germany in the first 18 months after economic unification. In nominal terms, it has nearly doubled (row 2). In real terms, this means an increase of more than 50 percent (column 3). Rows 3 to 5 show that the differences in the increase in earnings between the different types of firms were substantial. Workers in newly founded firms were earning 12 percent more than workers in privatized firms, in real terms.

---

[5] It is noteworthy that years of education include vocational training. We do not use the actual years a person needed to get a certain qualification but we assign the minimum number of years, which are necessary to get this qualification to the observed case. Because we do not yet know the number of years a person was gainfully employed we estimate work experience as "Age – Years of Education – 6". The years of firm experience (tenure) are calculated on the basis of the date of hiring, which is surveyed directly.

[6] Nevertheless, it is of interest whether the sample is representative. In general the GSOEP is a random sample of high quality. The question about the representation of particular firms is difficult to answer nonetheless, because in the beginning the quality of the official economic statistics for East Germany was poor. The comparison of the distribution of employees in the survey of firms that is the basis for Table 1 above and the corresponding distribution in the GSOEP (Table 4) shows considerable differences. But due to the small number of cases in both samples the differences are not statistically significant. Moreover the differences are in the expected direction. Because the GSOEP includes new firms in the service sector whereas the survey of firms does not, the share of employees in new firms should be larger in the GSOEP, as it in fact is.

In 1995, the picture is different. The employees in privatized firms earned more than the employees of the new firms. This reflects two different processes. First, the wage bill of privatized firms was still subsidized by the government. Second, the number of newly founded firms was bigger than in 1992 (see Table 1), i.e. the new firms do not represent any longer a positive selection of firms.

Table 3 presents the basic information about the determinants of the earnings distribution in East Germany.[7] The coefficients of the variables controlling for overqualification have the expected sign and are significant. Comparing columns 1 to 3 of Table 3 shows the surprising result that in the five years after the economic unification, the overall rate of return to education did not rise. The return to work experience was still flat, but its influence significant. Other structures changed in the course of the transformation process. First, in 1992 firm experience (tenure) was unimportant for the average (the coefficient is extremely small and is insignificantly different from zero), but in 1995 tenure mattered again. Second, the negative coefficients which control for overqualification were larger than they had been in the GDR, and they were of the same size as in West Germany. Both these changes are very plausible, because the 'old' human capital may have become inappropriate in a market economy.

Table 2. Dynamics of Monthly Gross Earnings of Male Employees (1989 = 100)

	Nominal Earnings		Real Earnings[b]
	M[a] / DM	Index	Index
GDR 1989	1241	100	100
East Germany 1992 by type of firm	2300	185	155
- Trust	2319	187	157
- Privatized	2283	184	155
- New	2466	199	167
East Germany 1995 by type of firm	3287	265	194
- Trust	3157	254	186
- Privatized	3288	265	194
- New	3171	255	186

Notes: (a) M: Mark of the GDR in 1989.

(b) Consumer price index for the average four-person household.

Source: GSOEP (1990, 1992, 1995); Statistisches Bundesamt (1993).

---

[7] Column 1 which displays the results for the GDR should be interpreted with caution. In the GSOEP, as in other disaggregated data sets, we could observe only paid earnings and not in-kind-transfers or access to western goods. It is likely, therefore, that the results for the GDR underestimate the real inequality of compensation for work. But even then the conclusion that unification did not change rapidly the overall flat earnings profiles holds true.

Table 3. Wage Regressions Accounting for the Misallocation of Occupational Qualifications (Male employees)

Variable	GDR 1989	FRG 1992 new states	FRG 1995 new states	FRG 1989 old states
Constant	4.3293*	5.1402*	6.7136*	4.8595*
	(0.041)	(0.2731)	(0.1880)	(0.1622)
Education	0.0452*	0.0438*	0.0312*	0.0692*
	(0.0036)	(0.0055)	(0.0048)	(0.0029)
Work Experience	0.0123*	0.0126*	0.0084**	0.0339*
	(0.0022)	(0.0042)	(0.0048)	(0.0024)
(Work Experience)**2/10	-0.0020*	-0.0018*	-0.0013	-0.0058*
	(0.0004)	(0.0008)	(0.0010)	(0.0004)
Firm Experience	0.0020*	0.0003	0.0028*	0.0040*
	(0.0007)	(0.0009)	(0.0011)	(0.0008)
Overqualification Status, by Level of Qualification:				
Specialist Worker	-0.0322*	-0.0533*	-0.1052*	-0.0497*
	(0.0165)	(0.0234)	(0.0237)	(0.0148)
Master Worker	-0.1410*	-0.1189*	-0.1042	-0.1601*
	(0.050)	(0.0613)	(0.0741)	(0.0453)
Engineer	-0.0173*	-0.1894*	-0.1613*	—
	(0.0542)	(0.0554)	(0.0421)	
University Degree	-0.0705	-0.2237*	-0.2961*	-0.1862*
	(0.0412)	(0.0589)	(0.0688)	(0.0602)
R^2	0.391	0.288	0.316	0.539
Sample size	1134	719	747	1800

Notes: Dependent variable is ln(Y), standard errors in parentheses; work experience = age − education − 6; other variables in the regression include: Work hours, civil service employment, firm size, white collar employment, tenured civil servant status, and whether married. *(**) Statistically significant at the 5 (10) percent level.

Source: GSOEP (1989, 1990, 1992, 1995).

We argue that not only the dynamics of wage levels, but also the development of the wage structure differed by firm types. In order to test this hypothesis, we run earnings equations for different firm types. Table 4 shows the sample means, Tables 5a and 5b display the regression results, which are remarkable. Table 5a presents the results for the year 1992. In the old firms (trust firms and privatized firms) the rate of return to education was as low as it was in the GDR in 1989,[8] while in the newly founded firms it was about the same as in West Germany. In fact the latter coefficient is higher than for West Germany, but the difference is not significant.[9] On the other hand, trust firms and privatized firms did not differ in a statistically significant manner. This result is unexpected. It might be due to heavy government subsidies for privatized firms which were thus protected from market forces.

In 1992, general work experience was significant for privatized firms only. For trust firms, the coefficients are as expected and of the same size as for the whole sample (cf. Table 3). Insignificance might be caused by the relatively small number of observations. The insignificant cofficients for new firms do not surprise, because in those firms experience with obsolete methods should not matter too much.

Tenure (firm experience) did not matter in the old firms, but it seems to have mattered strongly in new firms. This is plausible because the new firms would train their employees in new technologies as well as in new organizational methods. It seems that in the beginning the marginal returns to training were high. It is obvious that the coefficient for tenure, which is estimated for observed tenures between 0.1 and 1.9 years, cannot be compared easily with the same coefficient for trust and privatized firms. Perhaps the impact of tenure in old firms must be split into two effects, one for the short tenure (say between 0 and 2 years) and a second one for longer tenure. We tested this hypothesis for old firms, but the coefficient for short tenure was still close to zero and not significant. Our main result that tenure matters only in newly founded firms is strongly supported. Short as well as long tenure in old firms does not matter.

---

[8] These results hold true for firm averages only. Within the trust and the privatized firms there might have been firms that did well, but we were not able to identify them.

[9] This result is supported by an analysis of East German workers who were employed in West Germany as permanent or temporary migrants (commuters). The coefficient of education for this group is 0.057.

Table 4. Averages of Selected Worker Characteristics by Employer Type in 1992 and 1995

Characteristic	Trust Firm		Privatized Firm		New Firm	
	1992	1995	1992	1995	1992	1995
Age in Years	39	38	40	42	36	37
Age brackets (in percent)						
16 to 29	23	21	17	15	28	25
30 to 39	34	41	30	29	42	35
40 to 49	25	22	31	29	17	23
50 to 55	16	11	17	17	12	13
56 and older	(2)	(6)	5	10	(1)	(4)
Years of Education	11.6	11.3	11.5	12.0	11.5	11.9
Work Experience (Years)	20.8	20.7	22.6	23.7	18.4	19.8
Firm Experience (Years)	10.3	9.3	12.8	13.0	0.8	2.3
Percent Overqualified	26	27	24	32	39	43
Sample size	198	140	242	192	76	237

Note: Parentheses indicate a cell size of less than 10 observations.
Source: GSOEP (1992, 1995).

Table 5a. Wage Regressions for Male Employees in Different Enterprises 1992

Variable	Trust Firm	Privatized Firm	New Firm
Constant	4.5530*	5.3811*	5.3248*
	(0.6342)	(0.5299)	(0.8710)
Education	0.0435*	0.0338*	0.0847*
	(0.0131)	(0.0105)	(0.0267)
Work Experience	0.0113	0.0164*	-0.0192
	(0.0099)	(0.0075)	(0.0158)
(Work Experience)**2 / 10	-0.0017	-0.0027	0.0056
	(0.0021)	(0.0015)	(0.0059)
Firm Experience	0.0008	0.0016	0.1714*
	(0.0021)	(0.0016)	(0.0605)
Overqualification Status, by Level of Qualification:			
Specialist Worker	-0.0268	-0.1135*	-0.0233
	(0.0498)	(0.0421)	(0.0789)
Master Worker	-0.1567	-0.1199	-0.0361
	(0.1038)	(0.1243)	(0.3111)
Engineer	-0.0839	-0.2709*	0.1785
	(0.1480)	(0.0894)	(0.3056)
University Degree	-0.2617*	-0.1788	-0.3054
	(0.1122)	(0.1465)	(0.2422)
R^2	0.254	0.284	0.241
Sample size	198	242	76

Notes: Dependent variable is ln(Y), standard errors in parentheses; work experience = age − education − 6; other variables in the regression include: Work hours, civil service employment, firm size, white collar employment, tenured civil servant status, and whether married. * Statistically significant at the 5 percent level.

Source: GSOEP (1992).

Table 5b. Wage Regressions for Male Employees in Different Enterprises 1995

Variable	Trust Firm	Privatized Firm	New Firm
Constant	7.6279*	7.9233*	6.0682*
	(0.3891)	(0.4631)	(0.3012)
Education	0.0121	0.0252*	0.0418*
	(0.0138)	(0.0108)	(0.0104)
Work Experience	0.0107	0.0094	0.0008
	(0.0121)	(0.0098)	(0.0086)
(Work Experience)**2/10	-0.0020	-0.0013	0.0006
	(0.0024)	(0.0019)	(0.0018)
Firm Experience	0.0024	0.0039*	0.0097
	(0.0025)	(0.0018)	(0.0121)
Overqualification Status, by Level of Qualification:			
Specialist Worker	-0.1391*	-0.0633	-0.0423
	(0.0576)	(0.0480)	(0.0404)
Master Worker	-0.1544	0.3374**	-0.1521**
	(0.1883)	(0.1801)	(0.0902)
Engineer	-0.2330*	-0.2352*	-0.1547**
	(0.1072)	(0.0700)	(0.0862)
University Degree	0.4571	-0.4231*	-0.5775*
	(0.2954)	(0.1577)	(0.1310)
R^2	0.276	0.301	0.314
Sample size	140	192	237

Notes: Dependent variable is ln(Y), standard errors in parentheses; work experience = age – education – 6; other variables in the regression include: Work hours, civil service employment, firm size, white collar employment, tenured civil servant status, and whether married. *(**) Statistically significant at the 5 (10) percent level.

Source: GSOEP (1995).

For the year 1992 the coefficients that control for overqualification do not differ significantly across the different types of firms.[10] But their size and signs are still as expected. A look at the share of overqualification in the different firm types

---

[10] Due to the small numbers of cases most of them do not differ from zero significantly.

gives us an important insight into the early dynamics of wages in East Germany (see Table 4). In newly founded firms the occupational certificates of about 40 percent of the employees were downgraded, whereas the share of downgraded workers in the old firms was only slightly higher than it had been in the GDR (21 percent in the GDR, compared to 25 percent in the old firms).[11] It is not surprising that newly founded firms hired on average younger workers (see Table 4). Workers who were 56 years and older had only negligible chances to find a job in such a firm.

For the year 1995, the results are different from the results for 1992 (cf. Table 5b). The return to education is still higher in newly founded firms (as expected), general experience does not matter in all types of firms (as expected), and the coefficients for the control of overqualification are about the same as in 1992. But tenure matters for privatized firms and, surprisingly, it does not matter for the new firms in a statistically significant manner. The latter result might be the outcome of the increasing heterogeneity of newly founded firms who had become the most important employer (outside the public sector) then. Within the sector of new firms, the share of service firms was important (i.e. those firms not considered in Table 1).

The personal characteristics of the employees in the different types of firms did not change between 1992 and 1995 (see Table 4). This means older workers had only a small chance to be employed by a newly founded firm.

4. Conclusions and Policy Outlook

In the first two years after the economic unification of Germany, wage levels changed significantly in East Germany, but the overall structure of wages did not. A closer look shows noteworthy developments. Earnings moved much more dynamically in newly founded firms than in either privatized firms or trust firms. New generations of capital were the driving force for restructuring the East German economy. This result, which is well known from the restructuring of the labor market in West Germany after World War II, is not surprising. What is surprising is not only the importance of the growth of earnings differentials for given qualifications, but also of the reallocation of workers. It appears that the new evaluation of occupational qualifications by employers was used as a central tool reallocating workers in the now market-oriented economy.

The re-evaluation of certificates in new firms was much easier than within the old structures of trust firms and privatized firms. Making sure that re-evaluation of

---

[11] Although the number of observations in the new firms is small the differences in the shares between new and old firms are significant on the 10 percent level.

occupational certificates is possible without great social troubles might be one of the important lessons that can be drawn from the transition process in East Germany.

Because the wage structure changed rapidly in new firms only, it seems the subsidization of trust firms seems was an inefficient policy. On the basis of additional empirical evidence (Schwarze et al. (1995), Grabka/Schwarze/Wagner (1999)), which shows that previously unemployed workers who obtained substantial occupational retraining (longer than 6 months) during their lay-off did become better-off than previous short-time workers (*Kurzarbeiter*), it seems clear that short-time work, very popular at the beginning of the transition process, was inefficient as well. Subsidization of trust firms and short-time work did neither improve the capital stock of the firms, nor the human capital of the work force.

Rapid modernization of the capital stock and retraining caused a social problem. After unification, older workers faced not only the problem of finding a new job, they earned much less than their colleagues in West Germany due to the devaluation of their "socialist" work experience and their old firm-specific human capital. Thus older workers might be considered as the losers of the transformation process, not only in the short run: In the long run, also contribution-based old-age pensions would be affected by low wages.

Acknowledgements

The authors wish to acknowledge helpful comments by Richard V. Burkhauser, Jan I. Ondrich, and by participants of seminars at Syracuse University and the University of Wisconsin at Madison. We are grateful for support by the Deutsche Forschungsgemeinschaft (DFG) and the Metropolitan Studies Program (Syracuse University).

References

Bird, E. J./Schwarze, J./Wagner G. G. (1994), Wage Effects of the Move Towards Free Markets in East Germany, *Industrial and Labor Relations Review* 47, 390-400.

Bös, D. (1991), Privatization in East Germany – A Survey of Current Issues, *Paper of the IMF Fiscal Affairs Department*, Washington, D.C.

Büchel, F./Schwarze, J. (1994), Die Migration von Ost- nach Westdeutschland – Absicht und Realisierung. Ein sequentielles Probitmodell mit Kontrolle unbeobachteter Heterogenität, *Mitteilungen aus der Arbeitsmarkt und Berufsforschung* 27, 43-52.

Dyck, A. (1993), Imperfect Information, *Ownership and Incentives Theory and Practice in Eastern Germany*, Dissertation, Stanford.

DIW et al. (1999), Gesamtwirtschaftliche und unternehmerische Anpassungsfortschritte in Ostdeutschland, Neunzehnter Bericht, *Kiel Discussion Paper* 346/347, Kiel Institute of World Economics, Kiel.

Flassbeck, H./Horn G. A. (eds.) (1996), *German Unification – an Example for Korea?*, Dartmouth.

Grabka, M. M./Schwarze, J./Wagner, G. G. (1999), How Unification and Immigration Affected the German Income Distribution, *European Economic Review, 43,* 867-878.

Hauser, R./Wagner, G. G. (1997), Die Einkommensverteilung in Ostdeutschland: Darstellung und Determinanten im Vergleich, in: Glatzer, W./Kleinhenz, G., *Wohlstand für alle?* Opladen, 11-61.

Newell, Andrew/Reilly, B. (1996), The Gender Wage Gap in Russia: Some Empirical Evidence, *Labor Economics* 3, 337-356.

Schwarze, J. (1993), Qualifikation, Überqualifikation und Phasen des Transformationsprozesses, *Jahrbücher für Nationalökonomie und Statistik* 211, 90-107.

Schwarze, J./Rendtel, U./Büchel, F. (1995), Income Effects of Unemployment and Short-Time Work in the East German Transformation Process, *Vierteljahreshefte zur Wirtschaftsforschung*, 64, 477-486.

Statistisches Bundesamt (1993), *Zur wirtschaftlichen und sozialen Lage in den neuen Bundesländern*. Special Edition April 1993, Stuttgart.

Wagner, G./Burkhauser, R./Behringer, F. (1993), The English Language Public Use File of the German Socio-Economic Panel, *Journal of Human Resources* 28, 429-433.

II. Policy options

1. Eastern Germany Since Unification: Wage Subsidies Remain a Better Way

David Begg, Birkbeck College, London, and CEPR, London
Richard Portes, London Business School, and CEPR, London

1. Introduction

German unification, according to Bismarck, was achieved by blood and iron. Over a century later, the reunification of Germany in 1990 was secured without war, but blood has again been shed: the economic cost of unification has exceeded all expectations. In this chapter we argue, that the policy response to unification has been inappropriate, and hence unnecessarily expensive; the adoption of a universal, temporary wage subsidy in Eastern Germany would have been the preferred solution (Begg and Portes (1991)).

Although we focus solely on events in Germany, our analysis is motivated by the desire to clarify the theoretical issues to which the unification problem gave rise, and this analysis also has a wider relevance. In principle, it applies in any situation where the prospect of mass migration is suddenly raised by a change in political regime. This prospect may be greatest, but need not only occur, where the regime change is reunification. The eventual reunification of North and South Korea is only one possible example.

The paper is organized as follows. Section 2 describes the reasons for the performance of the Eastern German economy since unification. Section 3 assesses the basis for policy intervention: where exactly were the market failures specifically attributable to unification? We try to pin these down, and then argue that the host of policy interventions were poorly targeted. Section 4 sets out our alternative proposal, explains why it is more efficiently targeted on the market failures and hence would have introduced smaller distortions elsewhere, and deals with common objections to proposals for a wage subsidy. Section 5 concludes.

2. Eastern Germany Since Unification

German unification was more difficult and costly than most Germans anticipated. First, the inherited levels of East German output and productivity were much lower than expected: West Germans were genuinely surprised that official statistics about the GDR proved so misleading. In turn, this helps to explain why the ex-GDR had difficulties in finding western markets for its products. Second, problems in acquiring western export markets were significant precisely because export markets to the east were rapidly curtailed: the ex-GDR was hit both by the implosion of the former Soviet Union and by austere stabilization programs in its nearer neighbours Poland, the Czech Republic, and Hungary. Third, and also in common with these neighbours, the ex-GDR faced a substantially adverse terms of trade shock: its exports no longer attracted Soviet subsidies.

We reject the view that the lack of competitiveness of Eastern Germany was caused by that region's exchange rate appreciation implicit in the chosen rate of conversion between the DM and the Ostmark (see also Sinn (1996)). We do not deny that Eastern Germany did experience a nominal exchange rate appreciation at that time. However, we contend that real wages in Eastern Germany would have risen to uncompetitive levels whatever the chosen level of monetary conversion at the time of unification.

Two key pieces of evidence support this interpretation. The first is the evolution of wages and unemployment in the labor markets. If the root cause of the problem was an "excessive" nominal exchange rate appreciation for Eastern Germany in 1990, one would then have expected to see the emergence of rising unemployment but then falling wages: it is the latter that forms the standard mechanism of adjustment in a fixed exchange rate regime. Instead, rising unemployment was accompanied by rising wages. Wages rose in nominal terms, in real terms, and relative to Western Germany. Neumann (1992) calculated that, to permit zero profits at unchanged productivity, nominal wages in Eastern Germany would have had to fall by 60 percent after unification. Instead they rose by 18 percent in the second half of 1990. Franz (1995) estimated that the product wage increased by 31 percent in the year between the third quarter of 1990 and of 1991.

The second piece of evidence concerns the avowed objective of both government and trade unions, namely to achieve near parity of wages between Eastern and Western Germany. It is this, not monetary conversion, that was the real force driving wages in Eastern Germany, and it would have been the dominant force whatever the initial rate of monetary conversion.

This simple observation may be elaborated in several dimensions. First, unification was a political affirmation of a previous entity, intrinsic to which was a perception that moves to equalize living standards between east and west, or at least remove blatant disparity, were "fair". Initially at least, West Germans accepted this duty to pay for their Eastern siblings.

Second, there was a perceived need to limit migration from East to West Germany by reducing existing wage differentials. Migration would have left Eastern Germany deserted and Western Germany congested, an outcome desired by neither. Only the fear of migration can explain the extreme speed with which the timetable of unification was conducted.

Third, in addition to any social benefit, one critical group of private agents had a vested interest in the rapid mitigation of wage differentials: the trade unions of Western Germany, whose members were potentially vulnerable to competition from cheap labor from the east. When these unions "assisted" their Eastern siblings to negotiate higher wages, they were not only reducing the danger of substantial migration but also acting in the self-interest of their own members. Under such pressure, it was official policy to achieve complete parity of contract wages between east and west by 1994, and huge steps in this direction were taken. Although bonuses still allow a disparity of earnings even since contract wages are almost equalized, this in no way alters the substance of this argument.

Fourth, we must recognise a feature of the "end game" during adjustment that is present throughout Central and Eastern Europe but that was likely to be quantitatively more significant as a direct result of German Economic and Monetary Unification. When a (state-owned) enterprise seemed likely to be doomed, workers expected to lose their jobs at some point. If entitlement to unemployment benefits is tied to the wage prior to dismissal, workers had an incentive to press for high wages even if this marginally brought forward the date at which the enterprise was closed. If, moreover, the agency charged with restructuring enterprises (the *Treuhandanstalt*) believed it can obtain government subsidies to maintain enterprises and employment in the short run, it might have had little incentive to resist such wage claims. In this end game, wages were likely to be high whether or not that was the objective of a wider policy.

3. Where is the Market Failure?

In reforming command economies there are many instances in which market failure is acute. The market for corporate control hardly exists, and privatization per se may be insufficient to establish a well-functioning market (see e.g. Carlin/ Mayer (1992); Bolton/Roland (1992)). There may be important externalities in the creation of human and physical capital, the central theme of the "new growth economics" (for a survey, see Crafts (1992)). There are certainly significant failures in the capital market impeding attempts to borrow by households, firms, and even governments themselves: Central and Eastern European countries are still a long way off from the textbook solution of intertemporal consumption smoothing. Product and labor markets are segmented, allowing significant pockets of domestic monopoly power. The absence of a housing market further impedes labor mobility and competition. Concern for equality has compressed income differentials to such an extent that incentives for effort or for investment in human capital have been largely removed. Environmental disasters reflect the complete failure to price or to regulate environmental externalities.

We set out this familiar list to emphasize that there have been many legitimate grounds for intervention in such an economy of which some are still in existence. Many policies can be defended on one or other of these grounds. However, what was special about Eastern Germany was the scale of the initial unemployment and its probable link with German unification. Thus, in what follows, we focus on additional difficulties to which unification gave rise. Whatever they were, they must have been substantial, for in other respects Eastern Germany benefited enormously from the deeply-lined transfer pockets of its Western sibling, from a supply of managerial and advisory talent from the same source, and from instant access not merely to Western German markets but to the entire European Union (EU). Indeed, by 1991 Eastern Germany was classified as a lagging region of the EU. Over 1.5 billion ecu of the EU's regional funds were earmarked for Eastern Germany during 1991-93, a substantial share of the EU's regional budget which was just over 5 billion ecu in 1990.

We have little doubt that unification has mitigated, though by no means removed, three of the generic market failures described above. West German money has enabled East Germans to borrow; West German money and expertise has allowed the *Treuhandanstalt* to undertake corporate restructuring and to establish the beginning of a market in corporate control; and wide market access has swept away local monopoly power.[1]

Where unification specifically exacerbated market failure is in the labor market. Whereas countries such as the Czech Republic were able to pursue a low-wage strategy, keeping labor costs tightly in check until productivity improvements were secured, unification committed Eastern Germany immediately and dramatically to a high-wage strategy in which, for years, wages exceeded productivity. The lack of competitiveness of Eastern German enterprises in turn was responsible for both the extent of recession and the need for a host of ad hoc policies as damage limitation.

In Section 2 we distinguished four reasons for excessive wages in Eastern Germany. We now discuss whether they should be characterized as market failures attributable directly to unification.

---

[1] Though in many cases GDR monopolists have been taken over by the leading firm in the same industry in Western Germany.

Consider first the motive based on fairness. Both Western and Eastern Germans believed that Eastern Germans have suffered during four decades of central planning and should, after unification, share in the prosperity of Western Germany. Applying the standard welfare economics of the second best, this should be interpreted as a justification for a consumption subsidy. High eastern wages did subsidize consumption of Easterners but also incurred the deadweight burden of taxing the employment of Easterners until their productivity would have catched up to Western levels; further, taking an intertemporal view, high wages and thus low profitability also distorted investment decisions and might had perpetuate a low capital stock for an inefficiently long time. Thus, if the motive is redistribution of consumption, high wages were an inefficient solution, a consumption subsidy is better.

Second, consider the important channel through which Eastern wages were raised essentially to Western levels by actual or threatened migration. Several arguments need to be distinguished carefully. First, after the wall came down, protection was removed. There was the potential for gains from trade, most of which might have been expected to accrue to Eastern Germany, or to those owning assets there, since Western Germany was already trading extensively with other countries. In the absence of migration externalities, it might not have been very important in the long run whether trade creation between east and west took the form of trade in people (migration, tending to equalize wages) or trade in products (indirectly promoting factor price equalization). At this level, trade is beneficial, and unification should have been welcomed.[2] High wages are merely a symptom of improved opportunities. To identify a market failure, we need to probe more deeply. First, one can evaluate externalities connected directly with migration itself. An influx of Eastern immigrants to Western Germany imposed congestion in markets such as housing, where the stock supply can be changed only slowly. And the new economic geography, with its stress on external benefits of agglomeration, might be used in reverse to demonstrate considerable social costs of depopulation, especially if that process had a selection bias, providing the greatest emigration incentives to the best and the brightest, the young and the fit.

These externalities both to immigration and emigration gave both Easterners and Western Germany a rationale for wishing to limit migration westwards. Raising eastern wages sufficiently was one way to achieve this. In principle, it would have been more efficient to change the cost of migration than to raise the price of working in Eastern Germany: High wages also deter employment and unnecessarily distort the incentives of those for whom, for whatever reason, migration was not a consideration.

---

[2] With the collapse of the CMEA, trade diversion is scarcely an issue, such trade is good anyway.

The most obvious way to target policy intervention on the externality itself would have been to rebuild the wall. Its optimal height would have fallen over time, and eventually it would have disappeared. Combining a barrier to labor migration, whilst ensuring free movement of products would have permitted gains from trade without the adverse migration externalities. As output, productivity and investment rose in the east, equilibrium wage differentials would have fallen and the optimal height of the wall would have come down, until, at last, regional disparities would have been reduced to the levels normal within an European Union member state.

This efficient solution was evidently incompatible with the political and ethical judgements bound up in German unification. The policy problem was therefore to produce the most efficient solution that observed these additional constraints. We shall argue that, although German policy set itself this objective, a better way did in fact exist.

The third reason we gave earlier for Eastern Germany's high wages was activity by Western German labor unions. The GDR unions were tainted as collaborators with the old order. Following the collapse of communism, West German unions quickly inserted themselves into the vacuum, achieving higher union density than even in Western Germany (see Table 1). These unions had forced this pace in pressing for rapid movement towards parity of contract wages between Eastern and Western Germany.

One obvious motive for Western German workers was defence of their insider status against a possible assault by low-wage outsiders from the East. If so, then the exercise of union power had implications both for efficiency and distribution. It prevented full exploitation of the gains from trade and it imposed costs directly on Eastern Germany (low competitiveness, employment, and investment). If the source of the market failure – restrictions on labor market competition because of the power from organized unions from Western Germany – could not be directly addressed, it might have been wise to cushion Eastern Germany from its full effects.

Our fourth explanation of high eastern wages can also be traced in part to unification. State-owned enterprises faced the threat of closure throughout Central and Eastern Europe, and this gave rise to an end game in which workers had every incentive to grab what they can while they could get. In countries where the government is struggling to establish macroeconomic stability and to bring the budget under control, there is an upper limit to the ability of workers to raise wages in excess of productivity. In Eastern Germany such enterprises were ultimately backed by the fiscal might of Western Germany, a deep if not limitless pocket. In such circumstances, it might have been proved difficult for those running state-owned enterprises (ultimately the *Treuhandanstalt*) credibly to resist wage demands. The relative ease with which the *Treuhandanstalt* was able to overspend its allocated budget reinforced this concern. In this instance, the inefficiency arose from the effect of unification in reducing the state's ability to precommit to a policy of enforcing sensible wages once the time horizon had closed in. A robust policy would have been to address head on the issue of credibility.

Table 1. Union Density in Eastern Germany, June 1991

Federal States (*Bundesländer*)	Union Density (percent of employment)
Berlin & Brandenburg	38
Saxony	59
Saxony-Anhalt	53
Thuringia	50
Mecklenburg – West Pomerania	48
Total Eastern Germany (excluding West Berlin)	51
Western Germany	32

Source: Burda/Funke (2000)

4. A Simple Proposal

German policy after unification faced two binding constraints: Barriers to movement of people as citizens and workers had to vanish, yet in equilibrium Easterners had to be induced to stay put. Together, these requirements implied that Easterners had to attain consumption levels tolerably close to what they could have obtained by migrating to the west. Equally clearly, in the first years after unification such living standards exceeded labor productivity in the east.

There were three possible responses to this inevitable pressure. First, there was the possibility to do nothing. Wages would have risen to provide adequate consumption but large numbers of workers would have become unemployed. Second, they could allow wages to rise and then introduce a battery of policies to cushion the adverse effects. This is essentially what German policy did so far. Third, recognize from the discussion of market failures in Section 3 that what was required is a divorce of consumption levels and labor costs. High consumption was required, high labor costs were not; the latter were inefficient because they were unnecessary, distort employment and investment, and foster other policy interventions which themselves brought additional and quite avoidable distortions.

Germany was drawn into a wide range of interventionist policies in Eastern Germany. Nevertheless, the design of policy seemed inadequately targeted on the market failures that would have justified intervention. In consequence, it was possible to do the same job more efficiently.

Since the major disortion arose in the labor market, it could have been tackled most efficiently in the labor market. Our proposal would have been a simple, uniform, universal wage subsidy declining over time according to a prespecified schedule. The subsidy would have been 75 percent of the wage bill in the first year, 50 percent in the second year, 25 percent in the third year, and would have been disappeared thereafter.

The stark simplicity of the policy has several advantages. First, it would have not required any complicated evaluation or monitoring. It would have been therefore much more credible than a complicated formula that ex post offered scope for blurring criteria and shading definitions. This in turn would have made its removal according to the specified timetable much more likely. Second, conditional formulae would have set up moral hazard problems: our subsidy, being unconditional, provides no such incentives. Thus, although in an ideal world it might have been preferable to make the extent of subsidy depend on the difficulty of the transformation process or the speed of productivity catch up, in practice that more sophisticated formula would have been likely to bias reported productivity and discourage genuine adjustment.

Similarly, an ideal policy might have hoped to differentiate between regions, for example according to estimates of the extent of the restructuring problem faced, the amount of social infrastructure available, and so on. However, such a scheme would have invited widespread rent seeking, and this disadvantage in our view would have outweighted any possible advantages.

Our temporary wage subsidy in Eastern Germany would have been accompanied by the scrapping of the plethora of ad hoc subsidies which were largely introduced to cushion inappropriate labor costs, and which could now become unnecessary. We would have scrapped investment subsidies, export guarantees, and credit guarantees.

In fact, there would have been only one other measure necessary to adopt: bad debts inherted from the past should not be allowed to infect the present and the future. In Begg and Portes (1993) we discuss more generally the credit market failures that are acute in Central and Eastern Europe. There, as here, we advocate the use of taxpayers' money to clean up balance sheets of banks and enterprises. In fact, the taxpayers' money was lost when state-owned enterprises ran operating losses. Making the books honest to recognize that reality did not incur any additional economic cost, though it would have increased the declared fiscal deficit and public debt if the basis for previous calculations was a mistakenly optimistic assessment of the value of state assets.

4.1. Advantages of Our Proposal

By construction, our proposal focuses policy intervention on eliminating the first-order distortion, the discrepancy between the market wage and social cost of labor, during the period in which that distortion is greatest. Investment, rising output, and rising productivity would have steadily eroded that disortion over the years to come.

Our proposal would have stimulated employment in Eastern Germany in the first years after unification by bringing the private cost of labor much closer to its at that time low social cost. But we do not believe that it would have impeded the transformation of Eastern Germany. Given access to capital markets on anything like terms available to Western Germany – and many joint ventures or takeovers achieved precisely that – a three-year wage subsidy should have done little to affect longer term investment calculations not only for physical capital but also for human capital. Labor mobility towards expanding sectors within Eastern Germany should not therefore have impeded; there would have been little security in a dead-end job temporily kept alive by subsidies.

The momentum of transformation could have been maintained in this way, and the dead-end jobs should not have been forgotten. First, since in the first years after unification, people were a little more modest about the certainty of picking winners, they could not have been sure that some apparently unsaveable enterprises might not have survived and prospered. Second, and likely to be quantitatively more significant, the real choice was between some current output (from enterprises with positive value added) and zero output from such enterprises and consequently much higher unemployment. In common with policy and the *Treuhandanstalt* in the first years after unification, we took the (self-evident) view that some output would have been better than none. However, our method of realizing this outcome would have been better targeted and consequently both simpler and more efficient.

Consider how much more straightforward it would have been to operate the *Treuhandanstalt* itself under such a regime. With the largest distortion removed, there would have been a closer correspondence between market equilibrium and the socially efficient outcome. It would have been easier to organize private-sector bidding for *Treuhandanstalt* firms, more credible for the *Treuhandanstalt* to threaten to close those which continued to sustain losses, and, with fewer special cases, opportunities for rent seeking would have been fewer. These were important advantages.

Similarly, the temporary, uniform wage subsidy would have provided a more efficient solution to incentives for new private businesses than did the battery of ad hoc subsidies at that time. It would have combined substantial initial help – when unemployment was high and a less than perfect capital market made early cash flow significant – with a clear signal that longer-run decisions should have been based on eventual market prices; and it would have avoided unnecessary and inefficient promotion of capital intensity (the investment incentives route) and the proliferation of rent seeking (the special cases route).

4.2. Theoretical Objections

Burda and Wyplosz (1992) and Burda and Funke (2000) consider whether there are any circumstances in which subsidies to wages or employment would be inappropriate. They do manage to construct cases, embedded in the new literature on endogenous growth, in which there are externalities to investment in either human or physical capital. High wages, if the wage structure is appropriate, may provide incentives to investment in human capital. Subsidies for physical investment may be appropriate when there are externalities to physical capital accumulation. If either or both of these effects are sufficiently powerful, then theoretically these could dominate the case for a wage subsidy we made out above.

Although this logic is infallible, there are two reasons we do not find its practical relevance compelling. First, in spite of all the theoretical interest in the new growth economics, to date we have only very weak empirical evidence of its significance. Second, if these externalities are prevalent and large, they would already be reflected in the policy of most countries.

From such a baseline, we ask: How should previous West Germany policies have been amended once they were inherited by the united Germany? The effect that is additional in this experiment is the labor market externality we discussed in Section 3. The consequence for policy should therefore have been the adoption of the temporary wage subsidy.

4.3. How to Adhere to the Timetable for Subsidy Removal

The simpler the policy, the more easily it is monitored and the larger the political cost of reneging on any prior pledge. That is why we would have proposed a uniform, unconditional wage subsidy declining over a period of three years so that decline would have been highly visible.

This deliberate simplicity may be contrasted with the more complicated proposal of Akerlof et al. (1991) in which the subsidies would be set automatically by a formula that took account of the remaining divergence between East and West Germany. Formally, we would have advocated an open-loop path for subsidies, they propose a closed-loop feedback. Whilst their scheme has the attractive feature that the degree of subsidy would gradually die out as convergence occured, for reasons that we shortly discuss we think that proposals for subsidies should do everything possible to make credible their subsequent removal. The difficulty with any complex formula is that it relies on measurement and may build in incentives to mismeasure or misreport in order to increase the eligibility for subsidy. Such fears were especially acute in the first years after unification given the discovery of the extent to which previous data on the GDR turned out to be wildly off the mark. For this reason alone, we conclude that a simple, open-loop subsidy would have been much more cheaply monitored, less easily manipulated, and hence its removal according to plan would have been much more likely.

The objective of precommitting to the maximum possible extent can usefully be supplemented by conditionality. This requires an external institution to act as monitor and threat. The natural body to undertake such a role is the European Union. Indeed, European Union acquiescence would in any case have been essential for our proposal. Wage subsidies must not get outlawed as 'state aids.' Perhaps the most promising route would have been for the European Commission to allow a temporary derogation for the purpose of the declining wage subsidy, subject to the condition that any further departure from the agreed timetable of withdrawal would then render Germany liable to forfeit of access to the European Union structural funds. Since Eastern Germany would have been otherwise likely to be recipient of European Union regional and social funds for some years, this deal would have had a real deterrent effect and hence a precommitment value.

4.4. Why Do Wage Subsidies Have Such a Bad Name in Germany?

An obvious reason to object to a universal wage subsidy is its probable budgetary cost. This objection is largely fallacious. Any candidate for a policy package had to prevent substantial migration from east to west. This had tied down the minimum consumption Eastern Germany should have received. Moreover, for a given level of Eastern consumption, greater Eastern output would have reduced the cost of unification for Germany as a whole. Thus, although a partial analysis might attribute large direct costs to the financing of wage subsidies, general equilibrium analysis suggests that the money spent on wage subsidies would have been recouped somehow or other. Some of these channels were evident – lower unemployment payments, higher profits tax, greater revenue from *Treuhandanstalt* sales (where the present value of subsidies to such enterprises should have been recouped in full), higher revenue from income and value-added tax – but it was not essential to have been able to detail all of them in advance. Provided only that wage subsidies (i) increase output and employment, and (ii) do not lead to wages unnecessarily above those required to prevent migration, there should not have been any significant budgetary problem of wage subsidies relative to the cost of alternative policies for meeting the no-migration constraint.

A second fear commonly expressed is that wage subsidies will follow after the bargaining power of organized labor. Unions will simply appropriate all the extra liquidity as higher wages without any change in employment. There are two reasons this fear was largely misplaced. First, high wages were not themselves avoidable. The particular constraint imposed by unification was precisely that it was the threat of migration that makes "unjustifiably high" wages in the East inevitable. Second, given this constraint, one should have asked which conjectured response by employers one would have liked to instill in union bargainers. Our proposal would have confronted unions with a uniform wage subsidy but no other support; driving wages too high would have been then a recipe for job loss for insider-workers. In contrast, the system in the first years after unification, precisely because it was ad hoc, and since the *Treuhandanstalt* was also open-ended in support, it was likely to lead union wage bargainers to assume a less elastic demand for labor, and hence this was a system more likely to lead to higher wages and lower employment.

Whether a regime of wage subsidies would have augmented union power relative to an unsubsidized competitive labor market was not the issue, and was no argument against wage subsidies. The question was and still is how to maintain an adequate level of Eastern wages whilst credibly maintaining the threat that, at the margin, employment remains sensitive to the cost of labor. Only this would have provided high employment subject to the wage (migration) constraint. Our proposal would have achieved this more efficiently than the policy in force.

A third objection (e.g. Dornbusch (1991); Siebert (1991)) is that wage subsidies would have frozen the existing industrial structure, thereby inhibiting restructuring. We also find this objection unconvincing. First, like Flemming (1993), we have little sympathy with the view that big bang would have been the most efficient form of restructuring. When adjustment costs are substantial, and increase at the margin with the attempted rate of progress, one should have traded off benefits of going more slowly against the danger that the commitment to ultimate reform would have become less credible.[3] Second, because our wage subsidies were meant to be time-limited, they are unlikely to inhibit either investment or the reallocation of labor. Such sclerotic effects would have been likely only if the scheduled removal of subsidies was incredible. In Section 4.2 we argued this was not the case.

Fourth, the simplicity of our approach depends not merely on targeting wage subsidies on the market failure itself, but on the accompanying removal of a host of less efficient interventionary measures. It was argued that continuation of the status quo (for example the range of special incentives for investment in Eastern Germany) was as much a political constraint as the constraint that widespread

---

[3] And, when mistakes can be fatal, trying to go more quickly might not have enhanced the credibility of reaching the target in the shortest possible tine.

migration should have been avoided. One could always fall back on such an argument to defend the status quo. The role of economics is to identify situations in which policies are so inefficient that the battle for change should be waged.

5. Conclusion

We put the case for a temporary wage subsidy in East Germany, accompanied by removal or simplification of the host of other subsidies and interventions being applied in that region in the first years after unification. Wage subsidies would have been a better form of intervention because they would have tackled the problem where it occured. The design of a practical scheme should have paid attention to the form of a subsidy that was least likely to become entrenched. A simple, unconditional path for a declining subsidy would have maximized the political cost of defaulting on its subsequent removal, and minimized the economic opportunities for moral hazard or rent seeking.

Right after unification the economy of East Germany was in free fall, today expansion is in sight and in some sectors has begun. It would of course have been preferable to have introduced wage subsidies earlier, but even now the case for them remains compelling. Growing output is not in itself a reason to abandon policy intervention. Significant productivity differentials between east and west are still in existence. The market failure we identified in Section 3 has not disappeared completely till now. While it remains, it is best to counter it in the most efficient manner possible.

References

Akerlof, G. et al. (1991), East Germany in from the Cold: The Economic Aftermath of Currency Union, *Brookings Papers on Economic Activity* 1, 1-105.

Begg, D./Portes, R. (1991), There is a Better Way to Help Germany's New Länder Catch Up, *International Herold Tribune* 19/8/91.

Begg, D./Portes, R. (1993), Enterprises Debt and Economic Transformation: Financial Restructuring of the State Sector in Central and Eastern Europe, in: Mayer, C./Vives, X. (eds.), *Capital Markets and Financial Intermediation*, Cambridge, 230-255.

Bolton, R./Roland G. (1992), Privatization Policies in Central and Eastern Europe, *Economic Policy*, 15.

Burda, M./Funke, M. (2000), Wages and Structural Adjustment in the New German States, in: Riphahn, R.T./Snower, D. J./Zimmermann, K. F. (2000), *Employment Policy in Transition: The Lessons of German Integration for the Labor Market*, Heidelberg, 31-51

Burda, M./Wyplosz, C. (1992), Labor Mobility and German Integration: Some Vignettes, in: Siebert, H. (ed.), *The transformation of socialist economies: Symposium 1991*,Tübingen, 333-359.

Carlin, W./Mayer, C. (1992), Restructuring Enterprises in Eastern Europe, *Economic Policy*, 15.

Crafts, N. (1992), Productivity Growth Reconsidered, *Economic Policy*, 15.

Dornbusch, R. (1991), Discussion of Akerlof et al., *Brookings Papers on Economic Activity*, 1.

Flemming, J. (1993), Price and Trade Reform: The Economic Consequence of Shock Therapy and Possible Mitigating Measures or why Liberalization is not enough, *National Westminster Bank Quarterly Review*, 4-12.

Franz, W. (1995), Central and East European Labor Markets in Transition: Developments, Causes and Cares, *CEPR Discussion Paper, No. 1132*, London.

Neumann, M. J. (1992), German Unification: Economic Problems and Consequences, *Carnegie-Rochester-Conference-Series on Public Policy, 36(0)*, 163-209.

Sinn, H.-W. (1996), Macroeconomic Aspects of German Unification, in: Welfens, P. (ed.), *Economic Aspects of German Unification: Expectations, Transition Dynamics and International Perspectives*, Heidelberg, 135-189.

Siebert, B. (1991), German Unification: The Economics of Transition, *Economic Policy*, 13.

2. Economic Efficiency and Social Acceptance of Wage Subsidies

Henning Klodt, Kiel Institute of World Economics

1. Introduction

Is it a common feature of economists to think and to argue in economic terms – who wonders. Their view of life is governed by the pre-eminence of economic efficiency; their view of men is based upon the utility-maximizing individual who turns a completely blind eye on the merits of justice, fairness, solidarity and other social values. Starting from there, the economist develops his policy recommendations and is completely dazzled by the low acceptance of his proposals in the policy arena. The shelves of libraries and the bookcases of ministries are packed with analyses and recommendations which contain sound economic reasoning, but are completely ignored in the design of actual economic policy.

To give a concrete example: direct subsidies for pit-coal mining in Western Germany account for roughly 100,000 DM per head, which significantly exceeds average annual gross earnings of employees (86,000 DM). Everybody would be better off, therefore, if the coal mines were shut down and the subsidies were directly paid to the miners (Neu (1995)). Although economically efficient, there is no realistic change for public adoption of this proposal, because it is not socially acceptable. There is good reason for economists to take better into account the determinants of social acceptance when presenting their policy advice.

In the following, the potential clash between economic efficiency and social acceptance shall be exemplified for the case of labor market policy. The paper concentrates on the concept of wage subsidization schemes, which increasingly gains ground in the economic literature and which allows the design of various reform proposals for actual labor market policies (section 3). Before entering this subject, however, it seems appropriate to take a closer look at the German labor market in order to evaluate the potential contribution of wage subsidization schemes for solving the particular German unemployment problems (section 2). Based on this analysis, the final section 4 picks up again the potential tension between economic efficiency and social acceptance.

2. The Core of the Labor Market Problem: Structural Unemployment

2.1. The Size of German Unemployment

In 1998 on average 4.3 million people were registered as unemployed in Germany, of which 2.9 million were registered in Western Germany and 1.4 million in Eastern Germany (Bundesanstalt für Arbeit (1999)). There is an additional number of persons, who are not registered as unemployed, but who would probably show up in the labor market if labor demand would improve. Finally, there is a significant amount of "disguised" unemployment, especially in Eastern Germany, because massive active labor market programs have been launched to mitigate the social consequences of the transformation crisis. All in all, the difference between the total German labor force and regular employment can be estimated at about 8 million persons, which amounts to a "true" unemployment rate of more than 20 percent.

Of course, it would be an overambitious goal for economic policy to completely eliminate this difference, because a certain amount of frictional unemployment is a natural accompanying phenomenon of structural change in a growing economy. It would also not be reasonable to strive for the creation of employment opportunities for those persons who have registered as unemployed because they are looking for unemployment benefits or other social support and who are not actively searching employment. If the available estimates on frictional and voluntary unemployment are added up, the "natural" rate of unemployment in Germany appears to be in a range of about 3 percent of the total labor force, which corresponds to the actual unemployment rate as it was achieved on average in Western Germany in the 1970s. Hence, full employment in Germany would require the creation of more than 5 million additional jobs, which can be regarded as the benchmark for labor market policy (Table 1).

2.2. Structural Change and Labor Market Adjustment

The calculation of aggregate figures for job creation requirements seems to be an appropriate procedure to evaluate the dimension of the total unemployment problem. In a sense, however, these figures are misleading because they tend to suggest that unemployment is primarily a macroeconomic phenomenon which would call for macroeconomic policy responses. As a matter of fact, the German unemployment problem appears to be rather independent from macroeconomic imbalances over the business cycle. Unemployment in Western Germany is obviously a long-term phenomenon and cannot be explained by the current stage of the business cycle. The unemployment rate has reached its present level in three major steps after the recessions of 1975, 1982 and 1993 and which were only partly removed in the subsequent cyclical upswings. Since 1990, a substantial amount of unemployment emerged also in Eastern Germany, which can mainly be attributed to the transformation crisis (Figure 1).

Table 1. Labor Market Account for Germany 1996 (million persons)

	Germany	Western Germany	Eastern Germany
Unemployed	5.9	4.3	1.6
Registered	3.9	2.7	1.2
Non-registered	2.0	1.6	0.4
Persons in active labor market programs	1.9	0.6	1.3
Supported employment (ABM, short-time work etc.)	0.6	0.2	0.4
Reduced participation (early retirement, re-training etc.)	1.3	0.4	0.9
Employed (incl. supported employment)	34.7	28.3	6.4
Labor force[a]	41.9	33.0	8.9
"Natural" unemployment	1.3	1.0	0.3
Additional jobs required for full employment[b]	5.9	3.7	2.2

Notes: (a) Unemployed plus reduced participation plus employed.

(b) Labor force minus employed and "natural" unemployment.

Source: Own calculations based on estimates provided by the joint business cycle forecast of the leading German economic research institutes.

There is a lively debate among German labor economists about the reasons of the strong increase and high persistence of unemployment in Germany, but most observers agree that the major part is structural unemployment.[1] This view is supported by the fact that the risk of becoming unemployed is closely related to the level of formal training (Table 2). Obviously, the labor market problem of the German economy is mainly a problem of inadequate qualification of the labor force. There is a substantial gap between the qualification requirements of labor demand and the qualifications actually provided by labor supply. Hence, the main reason of unemployment seems to be a mismatch between the structural attributes of available jobs on the one hand and of the unemployed on the other hand (Paqué (2000)).

---

[1] See, e.g., the contributions to Franz (1992).

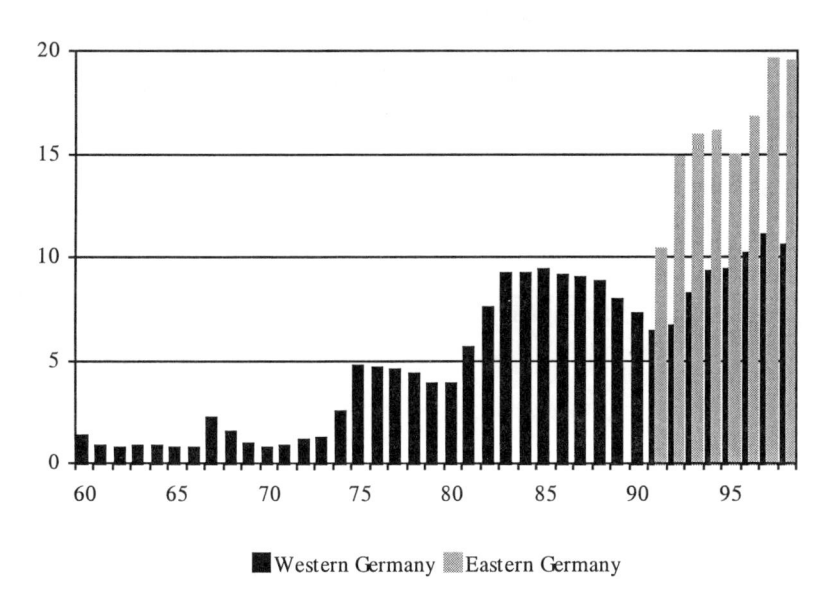

Figure 1. Unemployment Rates in Germany

■ Western Germany ▨ Eastern Germany

Mismatch unemployment may occur for several reasons: Individuals may be unwilling or unable to move from high-unemployment regions to regions where the majority of new jobs is created (*regional mismatch*). New jobs may require higher qualifications than the unemployed can provide (*qualification mismatch*). And workers may be regionally mobile and sufficiently qualified, but the type of their qualification may be ill-adjusted to the qualification patterns of labor demand (*occupational mismatch*). Presumably, all three types of mismatch-unemployment are of some importance in Western Germany. Above-average unemployment rates can be observed in Northern regions such as Lower Saxony and North-Rhine-Westfalia, whereas job creation is most vivid in Hesse, Baden-Württemberg and Bavaria, i.e. in the South, which points to the existence of regional mismatches. Nevertheless, the data on unemployment by qualification level clearly indicate that qualification and occupational mismatch are obviously the most important components of structural unemployment in Germany.

A sound analysis of the specific properties of occupational mismatch is hampered by highly insufficient statistical data. There is some evidence from sectoral shifts in employment, however, which tend to support the occupational mismatch hypothesis (Figure 2): The evolution of structural change over the four major business cycles in Western Germany reveals that the expansion of service sector activities took place in a rather smooth manner, whereas the reduction of industrial employment was concentrated on phases of recession. Since the 1970s, there is a pronounced sectoral asymmetry between job losses during recessions and job creation during subsequent booms. Hence, it can be argued that the above-described stepwise increase of total unemployment was mainly fed by the dismissal of industrial workers whose qualifications were rather unsuitable for expanding service sector activities. A similar development of structural adjustment and changing qualification requirement was experienced by the Eastern German economy in a quick-motion procedure in the first years after German unification.

Table 2. Unemployment Rates[a] by Formal Qualification in 1997 (in percent)

Qualification level	Western Germany	Eastern Germany
Without completed formal training	24.2	55.5
Vocational training	7.4	20.1
Technical school	2.8	6.8
College	3.9	4.3
University	4.1	6.3
Total	9.5	15.8

Notes: (a) Unemployed per employee of the respective qualification category.

Source: Parmentier et al. (1995); Institut für Arbeitsmarkt- und Berufsforschung (1995).

The occupational mismatch hypothesis also provides consistent explanations for some other statistical observations discussed above:

The North-South disparity in regional unemployment may not only result from regional immobility, but also from considerable job losses in ailing industries such as mining, iron and steel, and shipbuilding, which are mainly located in North-Rhine Westfalia and in coastal regions. If labor demand in the South refers to different qualifications than labor supply in the North, an increased regional mobility would not solve the labor market problem.

The stepwise increase of total unemployment during recessions presumably reflects the basic employment strategies of manufacturing firms, which tend to concentrate their restructuring and rationalization processes on periods of weak economic activity. Significant lay-offs are less difficult to achieve if employers can argue that cost-cutting strategies are unavoidable due to reduced production and market potentials. In this case, rules on job protection and financial compensation entitlements of dismissed workers are much less restrictive in the legal framework of the German labor market.

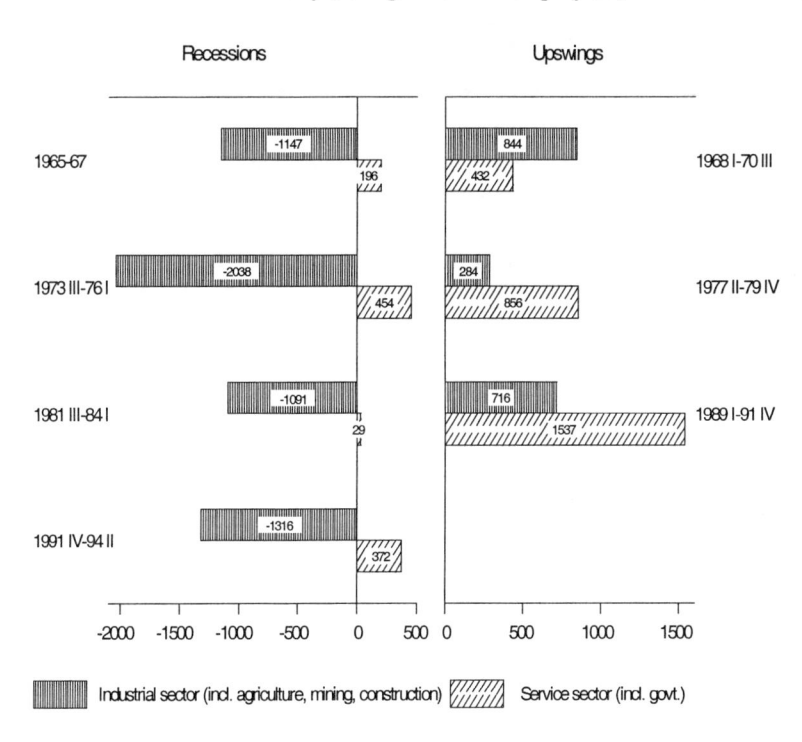

Figure 2. Sectoral Employment Patterns over the Business Cycle in Western Germany (changes in 1000 employees)

	Recessions	Upswings	
1965-67	-1147 / 196	844 / 432	1968 I-70 III
1973 III-76 I	-2038 / 454	284 / 856	1977 II-79 IV
1981 III-84 I	-1091 / 29	716 / 1537	1989 I-91 IV
1991 IV-94 II	-1316 / 372		

Industrial sector (incl. agriculture, mining, construction)   Service sector (incl. govt.)

Source: Statistisches Bundesamt; own calculations.

The implications of this view for the future of the German labor market are rather unpleasant. If the current business cycle will follow previous patterns, new jobs will again be created mainly in service industries, where the employment opportunities for industrial workers are limited. A market-oriented response to the rise in mismatch-unemployment would call for a significant increase in qualification-specific wage differentials. Such an "American" way of solving the labor market problem is hampered, however, by relatively high reservation wages of industrial workers, which are backed by rather generous social security standards. Depending on individual circumstances unemployment benefits account for 53 to 67 percent of net income, which is quite high by international standards. And every person without own income is entitled to receive means-tested welfare benefits, which in some cases may exceed the labor income that could be earned in low-productivity service jobs.

Table 3 presents some evidence on this issue for two typical low-productivity service industries by comparing the labor income of the lowest wage group to the claims upon the welfare system. Apparently, there is no financial incentive to work for married persons with more than one child, because disposable income would be lower than social benefits. Although there is no minimum wage legislation in Germany, the system of social security establishes significant factual minimum wages.

With these considerations in mind, the improvement of the flexibility and qualification of workers appears to be the most important part of a far-sighted strategy for fighting structural unemployment. In the long run, improvements in the stock of human capital are indispensable for coping with the challenges of structural change in highly developed countries. Such a long-term strategy surely has to be complemented by a re-engineering of the system of social security, which was basically established in periods of high industrial growth and low unemployment and which increasingly hampers labor market flexibility by imposing factual minimum wages and restricting the exploitation of job opportunities provided by the service sector.

Both components of this two-handed strategy could significantly be supported by active labor market policy, if it were reoriented at the specific problems of integrating low-qualified industrial workers with rather high reservation wages into the expanding service sector. For these persons, the acquisition of appropriate qualifications could be supported by a process of learning-by-doing, which would require temporary wage-cuts below industrial wage levels and presumably also below acceptable social standards. The solution to this problem could be the substitution of existing active labor market policy measures by a system of wage subsidization, which will be discussed in the following section.

Table 3. Labor Income of Low-Qualified Workers and Social Benefits in German Service Industries 1995[a]

	Hotels and restaurants			Retail trade		
	Single	Married children		Single	Married children	
	none	one	two	none	one	two
Gross monthly earnings	1947	1947	1947	2510	2510	2510
Income tax	99	-	-	267	122	-
Social security contribution	394	394	394	508	508	508
Child support	-	200	400	-	200	400
Housing benefits	12	143	378	-	73	270
Disposable income	1465	1896	2331	1735	2153	2672
Social aid income	1095	1823	2753	1095	1828	2753

Notes: (a) The data on gross earnings and social aid refer to Hesse in 1995. The difference between gross earnings and disposable income is calculated according to the laws of 1996, which are more favorable to low-wage earners than previous laws.

Source: Deutsche Bundesbank (1996, p.65)

3. Policy Concepts for Structural Unemployment

3.1. The Case for Wage Subsidization

Already in the early 1990s, it became obvious that system transformation in the former GDR would be associated with a dramatic breakdown of old industrial structures and a severe increase in unemployment. The Federal Government then decided to foster the reconstruction of the Eastern German economy mainly by massively supporting private investment. This approach was backed by the recommendations of the German Council of Economic Advisors (Sachverständigenrat (1991)), but there also appeared a number of studies which demonstrated that a direct subsidization of labor input would have been more favorable to employment and to the fiscal burden as well (Akerlof et al. (1991); Klodt (1990a), Schmieding (1991)).

The advantage of wage subsidization over investment subsidization can easily be illustrated within the framework of neoclassical production theory. Figure 3 presents the production function (*PF*) of Eastern Germany after unification. For simplicity, linear homogeneity is assumed in order to allow the graphical illustration in the per-capita version. Labor productivity (y) and capital intensity (k) are shown on the axes.[2] The slope of T_1 represents the real interest rate, which is basically determined on world capital markets. Without transfers from Western Germany and with flexible real wages, the production point would be in a, which implies a capital intensity of k_1 and a real wage rate of w_1.

Due to euphoric expectations of the Eastern Germans about the economic promises of unification, which were further fed by corresponding promises of Western German politicians, and due to the specific properties of Eastern German wage negotiations, the real wage rate rapidly increased to a level of w_2. Hence, T_1 shifted towards T_2, which drove the marginal productivity of capital below the world market real interest rate. To stabilize investment activities and to prevent the Eastern German labor market from a complete breakdown, massive financial transfers from Western Germany were required.

As noted above, these transfers were mainly paid as investment subsidies, which closed the gap between the low marginal productivity of capital and the real interest rate on financial markets.[3] Due to this intervention, the Eastern German economy was enabled to reach point b as the production equilibrium, where the rate of return on capital for private investors (including investment subsidization) is given by the slope of T_3, which is equal to the slope of T_1. Without transfers, there would have existed no production equilibrium at all, whereas the investment grants at least preserved the remaining jobs after the transformation shock. The same result could have been achieved, however, by subsidizing real wages, which would have reduced producer real wages to a level of w_1. In this case, the production equilibrium would again have been in a.

---

[2] It should be noted that the production function in this context does not describe the physical production frontier of Eastern Germany, but the available production technology, because the factor endowment of an economy with open borders is not fixed. After unification, Eastern Germany got access to world capital markets and workers got the opportunity to migrate in both directions.

[3] According to calculations of Sinn (1995), investment support even made the cost of capital negative for East German industry.

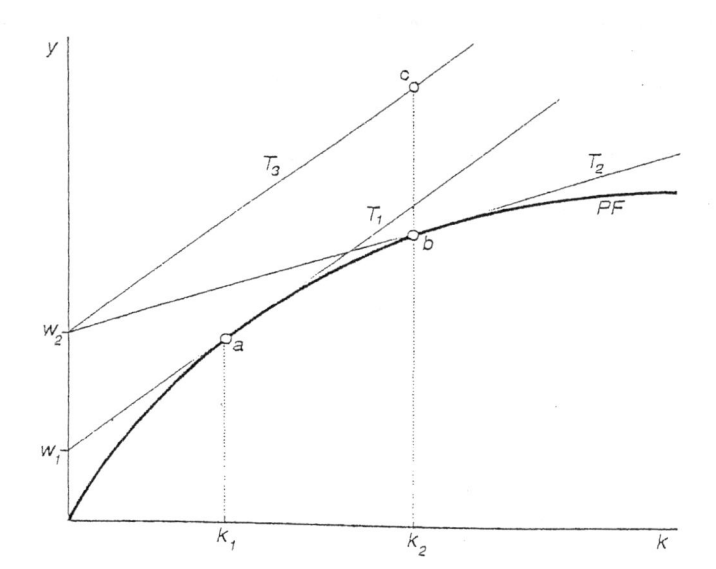

Figure 3. Wage and Investment Subsidization

Both workers and investors in Eastern Germany can be assumed to be indifferent to these two systems of transfer payment, because each system generates an equilibrium consumer real wage of w_2 and a rate of return on capital corresponding to the world real interest rate. Wage and investment subsidization differ, however, with respect to the fiscal requirements for stabilizing labor demand:

- The amount of wage subsidization per head is depicted in Figure 3 as the distance w_1w_2.

- The size of capital subsidization per workplace corresponds to the distance bc, because this amount is required for closing the gap between the slopes of T_2 and T_3 at a capital intensity of k_2.

Irrespective of the specific properties of the production function, bc always exceeds w_1w_2 if only the fundamental neoclassical assumptions hold (i.e. if PF is convex). Hence, the costs of protecting jobs are higher under a system of investment subsidization than under a system of wage subsidization. To put it differently, the total amount of transfers from West to East Germany could have protected more Eastern German jobs if the Federal Government had adopted a wage subsidization approach.

3.2. Qualification Vouchers

Presumably, direct financial support to the labor input of firms would also have been superior to the active labor market policy which was established in Eastern Germany and which mainly rested upon classroom requalification and public employment (ABM). The formal qualification levels of Eastern German workers on average even exceeded the corresponding levels in Western Germany; the central problem was the lacking adaptation to the specific working conditions in market-oriented surroundings. The typical Eastern German construction worker was mainly experienced in handling ferro-concrete sheets, the car mechanic was practiced in the repair of two-stoke engines, and the secretary was accustomed to mechanical type-writers. These workers primarily needed practical training under market conditions rather than classroom teaching. For initiating such a "training-on-the-job," it would have been much more effective to establish a wage subsidization scheme instead of simply transferring the traditional and well-established Western German system of active labor market policy to Eastern Germany.

In order to foster the qualificationary component of wage subsidization, the Kiel Institute of World Economics repeatedly proposed to launch a system of qualification vouchers, which would have been handed out to the unemployed for submitting them to a new employer of their own choice (Klodt (1990b, 1991), Siebert/Klodt (1991)). The details of this proposal shall not be described here; it should be noted, however, that such an approach would have opened up better opportunities for the unemployed to unfold individual activities for being reintegrated into the labor market.

There was a lively discussion about the qualification voucher proposal not only in academics, but also among politicians. In the end, however, the hysteresis of traditional institutions of active labor market policy prevailed against the prospects of an innovative policy approach. For instance, it was argued that the financial requirements of a qualification voucher scheme would have been too high, which is hardly a convincing argument in the light of the extent of actual labor market policy in Eastern Germany and the amount of investment subsidies that were paid. Furthermore, it was argued that it would have been too difficult to prevent massive abuse of vouchers. Finally -- and this was presumably the decisive point -- Eastern German workers could not be trusted to make their own choices of how to spend the vouchers; they had to be led by labor administration to not get lost in the concealed world of a market economy.

Needless to say, the author of this paper is not convinced by any of these objections. Instead of diving into this debate again, however, it may be more useful to explore the prospects for carrying over some elements of the policy proposals originally developed for coping with the transformation crisis, to actual labor market policy in re-united Germany.

3.3. Wage Subsidies to the Long-Term Unemployed

The central task of labor market policy at the end of the century is to reintegrate those workers into the production process who are incapable of coping with the challenges of structural adjustment in both parts of Germany. This group of persons is rather heterogeneous, therefore a certain variety of labor market policies is surely appropriate. For instance, there is a significant number of persons who actually need fundamental vocational qualifications as well as social qualifications which are indispensable for participating in the labor market. In this area, the existing programs of active labor market policy seem to be well-designed and superior to a system of wage subsidies.

On the other hand, there is a presumably much larger group of long-term unemployed who would be capable of re-entering the labor market under a different institutional setting, but are excluded from participating because the social welfare system imposes factual minimum wages. These persons are clearly beyond the reach of traditional active labor market programs. To simplify matters, wage subsidies could significantly contribute to the reintegration of those long-term unemployed in Germany who would have been absorbed in low-production service activities under U.S. labor market conditions (Phelps (1997)).

A concrete proposal in this direction was developed by Paqué (1994). He suggests that the long-term unemployed should be forced to accept low-paid jobs, even if wages would fall short of individual unemployment benefit claims. The difference between labor income and unemployment benefits should be granted to them by the labor administration (including a certain bonus to promote work incentives). Thus, no unemployed would have to face financial losses if accepting a low-paid job. For the employers it would pay to provide jobs which would otherwise not be profitable under the general German labor market conditions. The labor administration may even save money, because it could substitute the payment of unemployment benefits by this specific form of wage subsidization. And first and foremost, the social costs of mass unemployment would be reduced, and the respective workers would be enabled to escape the vicious circle of increasing duration of unemployment and ever-decreasing prospects for re-entering the labor market.

A combination of this proposal and the above-described concept of qualification vouchers was proposed by Snower (1997). According to his "benefit-transfer-program" every long-term unemployed is entitled to take part of his unemployment benefits as an employment voucher to a new employer, who in turn will be paid for the face value of the vouchers from public funds.

- The value of the vouchers increases with the duration of unemployment of the respective person, because it can be expected that both the individual qualification deficiencies and the discounted present value of future unemployment benefits will be positively related to the duration of unemployment.

- The value of the vouchers decreases with the duration of the new employment, because the qualification deficiencies can be expected to be reduced via learning-by-doing and the risk of unemployment will decline correspondingly.

- In order to promote the qualification aspect of learning-by-doing, a specific premium on the vouchers is paid to those firms which engage in specific measures for qualifying and training the subsidized workers.

It can be expected that the fiscal burden for the labor administration will be reduced by this concept, because the voucher payments are more than matched by saved unemployment benefit payments. In part, this may be compensated by those cases where long-term unemployed would have found new jobs also without public assistance. But it can be expected that the net balance would still be positive. There is also no reason for the unemployed to reject the Snower model because it is ultimately in their self-interest to improve their own long-term employment and income opportunities. And last not least, every unemployed still has the choice of not accepting the voucher option under the Snower model.

It is the basic lesson of this section that a variety of alternative policy measures is available, which would leave everybody better off, but which nevertheless are most unlikely to be adopted by actual labor market policy. The reasons behind this disparity between theory and practice, which was already addressed in the introduction, cannot be fully explored on the remaining pages, but it shall at least be discussed how they can be dealt with using the analytical tools of economic theory.

4. Economic and Ethical Efficiency as Determinants of Social Acceptance

In traditional economics, there are basically two sets of hypotheses for explaining why actual economic policy may differ from economically efficient policy designs:

- The first type of explanation refers to the limited intellectual capacity of policy makers, who are incapable of recognizing the advantages and benefits of the policy recommendations of economists. This is the common hypothesis in the framework of traditional neoclassical economics.

- The second type of explanation is concerned with the selfishness of politicians and bureaucrats, who are more interested in maximizing votes, personal competence and public budgets than in improving national welfare. This is the basic hypothesis of public choice theory.

It is not easy to completely deny the relevance of such explanations in the area of labor market policy. However, it would probably go too far to ascribe the whole disparity between potential and actual efficiency in labor market policy to them.

Presumably, the resistance against policy proposals which rests upon the motivation of the unemployed and on market forces mainly results from a general distrust in the outcome of market processes by the public. The market economy is esteemed for its capacity of providing high income and wealth, but at the same time many individuals feel subjected to the mercy of anonymous market forces. The market is viewed as cold-blooded and heartless as compared to the cosiness of families and other social institutions. It is a widespread concern that this cosiness should also prevail in the area of social policy if it wants to strengthen social welfare after all.

Essentially, such social phenomena are behind the horizon of economic theory. There are some empirical studies, however, which tend to support the view that the invisible hand of Adam Smith is often perceived as unfair and unjust. For instance, more than four fifth of surveyed individuals declared it to be unfair that a shop-keeper raised the prices of snow shovels the morning after a blizzard, although the economist would argue that such a kind of rationing is indispensable for allocating scarce snow shovels to those who are really in need of them right then (Frey/Pommerehne (1988)).[4]

The true determinants of individual economic choices are systematically investigated by the new game theory, which more and more departs from its initial neoclassical origins towards new domains at the borderline to psychology. Several laboratory experiments have provided a bulk of evidence for the hypothesis that most people are not rigorous individual utility maximizers, but value ethical standards such as fairness and justice higher than traditional economic theory is aware of (see, e.g., Carter/Irons (1991)). Reinhard Selten, who has been awarded the nobel prize for his contributions to neoclassical game theory, even states that the concept of the neoclassical utility function must be regarded as falsified (Rheinisch-Westfälische Akademie der Wissenschaften (1985, p. 64)).

Even Selten would not conclude, however, that all economic analyses based upon the assumption of individual utility maximization are misspecified and completely useless. Nevertheless, economists should learn to acknowledge the importance of non-economic determinants of individuals' economic choices. The relevance of such an extended approach for designing an appropriate labor market policy is illustrated in Figure 4.

---

[4] The reader may find a number of further empirical examples for the widespread distrust in market-oriented allocation procedures.

The horizontal axis displays the economic efficiency of available policy measures, whereas the vertical axis integrates all non-economic objectives of people into one aggregate index. These objectives may include justice, fairness, solidarity, and other non-economic values, which all are more or less related to ethical value-judgements. The extent to which specific policy measures contribute to those objectives is labelled as "ethical efficiency", which is regarded as an additional determinant of social acceptance.

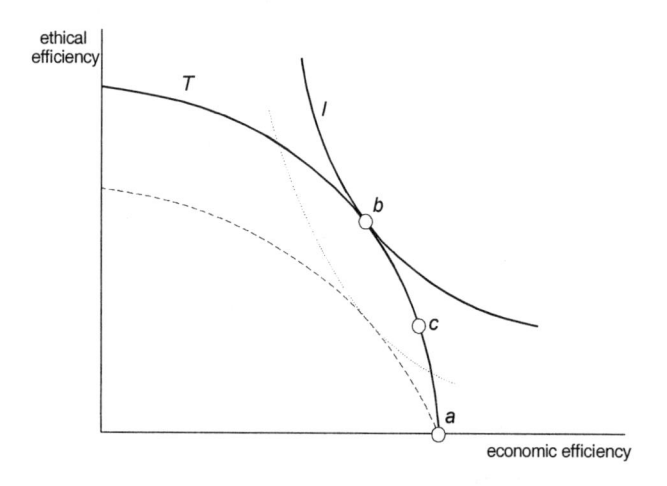

Figure 4. Social Equilibrium

It is the basic idea of Figure 4 that there exists a trade-off between economic and ethical efficiency.[5] Hence, a transformation curve (T) can be constructed which allows to evaluate the contribution of specific policy measures to both economic and non-economic objectives. In accordance with conventional production theory postulates, T is assumed to be concave.

If T correctly describes the available policy options, a textbook homo oeconomicus would always choose point a on the transformation curve, which coincides with the policy recommendations of economists. For true-to-life individuals, however, this solution is unacceptable, because it completely sacrifices ethical values for plain economic efficiency. Their preferences for

---

[5] This trade-off can be interpreted as an extension of the well-known trade-off between equality and efficiency (see e.g., Okun (1975)).

ethical and economic values are represented by the indifference curve *I*. For them, point *b* constitutes the equilibrium, because at that point forgone economic efficiency is just compensated by the gains in ethical efficiency.

With respect to labor market policy, point *a* probably represents a solution where structural unemployment is eliminated by increasing wage flexibility, spreading wage differentials and reducing social standards. Point *c* can be interpreted as a wage subsidization concept, which is less efficient than point *a* from a strict economic viewpoint, but includes some social elements. Finally, point *b* may represent traditional labor market policy, which is less suitable for fighting unemployment, as discussed above, but is more in line with public apprehensions about socially oriented labor market policy.

In the first instance this graphical illustration does not provide any additional information on the above-described reasoning. If the assumptions behind the graphs are true, however, they allow to derive two further conclusions:

- First, policy recommendations as described by point *a*, which represent flawless corner solutions, have almost no chance of ever being socially acceptable. Hence, insisting again and again on the responsibility of unions for reducing excessive real wage claims does not contribute very much to solving the unemployment problem.

- Second, the readiness to take economic efficiency more into account may rise when the transformation curve is shifting downwards. Such a shift (which is indicated in Figure 4 by the dotted line below *T*) is probably under way due to the above-described structural changes in the labor market and the ongoing globalization of the world economy. If international factor mobility rises, redistributive and other socially oriented policies are increasingly difficult to achieve without substantial losses in economic efficiency.

Hence, the social acceptance of wage subsidization schemes and other market-oriented concepts of labor market policy can be expected to rise in the future. In this context, the ongoing debate in Germany about the reform of the welfare state and the "alliance for jobs" may probably be interpreted as first steps towards shifting the social equilibrium from point *b* into a south-eastern direction.

References

Akerlof, G. et al. (1991), East Germany in from the Cold, *Brookings Papers on Economic Activity* 1, 1-87.

Bundesanstalt für Arbeit (1999), Arbeitsmarkt 1998, Amtliche Nachrichten der Bundesanstalt für Arbeit, Nürnberg.

Carter, J.R./Irons, M.D. (1991), Are Economists Different, and If So, Why? *Journal of Economic Perspectives* 5, 171-177.

Deutsche Bundesbank (1996), Die Wirtschaftslage in Deutschland um die Jahreswende 1995/1996: Konjunkturlage, *Monatsberichte* 2, 51-66.

Franz, W. (ed.) (1992), *Structural Unemployment*, Heidelberg.

Frey, B.S./Pommerehne, W.W. (1988), Für wie fair gilt der Markt? – Eine empirische Untersuchung von Einschätzungen in der Bevölkerung, *Hamburger Jahrbuch für Wirtschafts- und Gesellschaftspolitik* 33, 223-237.

Institut für Arbeitsmarkt- und Berufsforschung (1995), *Arbeitsmarktmonitor für die neuen Bundesländer*, Nürnberg.

Klodt, H. (1990a), Wirtschaftshilfen für die neuen Bundesländer, *Wirtschaftsdienst* 70, 617-622.

Klodt, H. (1990b), Arbeitsmarktpolitik in der DDR: Vorschläge für ein Qualifizierungsprogramm, *Die Weltwirtschaft* 1, 78-90.

Klodt, H. (1991), Wirtschaftsförderung für die neuen Bundesländer: Qualifizierungsgutscheine als Alternative, *Die Weltwirtschaft* 1, 91-103.

Neu, A. (1995), Subventionen ohne Ende? Steinkohlenbergbau und Energieverbrauch in Deutschland, *Kieler Diskussionsbeiträge* 248, Institut für Weltwirtschaft, Kiel.

Okun, A.M. (1975), Equality and Efficiency – The Big Tradeoff, *The Brookings Institution*, Washington, D.C.

Paqué, K.-H. (1994), Unemployment and the Crisis of the German Model, A Long-Term Interpretation, *Kieler Arbeitspapiere* 655, Kiel.

Paqué, K.-H. (2000), East/West-Wage Rigidity in United Germany, in: Riphahn, R.T./Snower, D. J./Zimmermann, K. F. (2000), *Employment Policy in Transition: The Lessons of German Integration for the Labor Market*, Heidelberg, 52-82.

Parmentier, K. et al. (1995), Beschäftigungssituation und -perspektiven von Hochschulabsolventen, *IAB-Arbeitspapier*, Nürnberg.

Phelps, E. S. (1997), Wage Subsidy Programmes: Alternative Designs, in: Snower, D. J./De La Dehesa, G. (eds.) *Unemployment Policy: Government Options for the Labor Market*, Cambridge, 206-247.

Rheinisch-Westfälische Akademie der Wissenschaften (1985), *Vorträge*, Natur-, Ingenieur- und Wirtschaftswissenschaften N 336, Opladen.

Sachverständigenrat zur Begutachtung der gesamtwirtschaftlichen Entwicklung (1991), *Marktwirtschaftlichen Kurs halten. Zur Wirtschaftspolitik für die neuen Länder*, Sondergutachten, Stuttgart.

Schmieding, H. (1991), Die ostdeutsche Wirtschaftskrise: Ursachen und Lösungsstrategien, Anmerkungen im Lichte der westdeutschen Erfahrungen von 1948 und des polnischen Beispiels von 1990, *Kieler Arbeitspapiere* 461, Kiel.

Siebert, H./Klodt, H. (1991), Qualifizierungsgutscheine: Eintrittskarten in den Arbeitsmarkt, *Kieler Diskussionsbeiträge* 175, Kiel, Institut für Weltwirtschaft.

Sinn, H.-W. (1995), Factor Price Distortions and Public Subsidies in East Germany, *CEPR Discussion Papers* 1155, London.

Snower, D.J. (1997), The Simple Economics of Benefit Transfers, in: Snower, D. J./De La Dehesa, G. (eds.) *Unemployment Policy: Government Options for the Labor Market*, Cambridge, 163-198.

3. Revenue-Sharing Subsidies as Employment Policy: Reducing the Cost of Stimulating East German Employment

Dennis J. Snower, Birkbeck College, London; IZA, Bonn, and CEPR, London

1. Introduction

This paper provides a brief overview of the East German employment problem and the deficiencies of the employment policies in the first years after unification, and then builds a simple model in which alternative policy proposals can be analyzed. Only two proposals are considered here: (i) wage subsidies, which many economists recommended to replace the array of employment stimuli,[1] and (ii) revenue- or profit-sharing subsidies, which this paper seeks to draw to policy makers' attention. Revenue- or profit-sharing subsidies had received as good as no consideration in the public debate on how to raise East German employment efficiently. This paper suggests that this might have beean a serious omission. Given the labor market conditions in East Germanyin the first years after unification, it appears likely that the social and budgetary costs associated with revenue- or profit-sharing subsidies would have been and still may be significantly lower than those associated with wage subsidies.[2]

There is little if anything in the present analysis that ties the conclusions of this analysis more to East Germany than to other East European economies in the process of transformation to a market system. The case for revenue-sharing subsidies appears equally applicable to, say, Czechoslovakia, Hungary, and Poland.

Section 2 provides a brief summary of East Germany's employment problem in the first years after unification. Section 3 presents a simple model of the East

---

[1] See, for example, Akerlof et al. (1991)

[2] It would be trivial to analyze other employment policies - particularly output, investment, export, and credit subsidies in the context of the mode l - and to derive the associated social and budgetary costs, although for brevity I do not do so here. Suffice it to say that the reasons that make revenue-sharing subsidies attractive relative to wage subsidies also apply, with a few modifications, to output and investment subsidies.

German labor market and uses it to document the need for government intervention by describing the problems that would arise in the absence of such intervention. Sections 4 and 5 analyze the effects of wage subsidies and revenue-sharing subsidies in this context. Section 6 concludes.

2. The East German Employment Problem Since Unification

It is widely recognized that the policies the German government implemented in the first years after unification thus far to stimulate East German employment were inefficient and incurred an unduly high budgetary cost. The problem, in the opinion of many observers, was not that the government's wage targets were set inappropriately high. It was clear from the outset that the political process of German unification would not have been meaningful unless it was accompanied by a rapid fall in the wage differential between East and West Germany. It was equally clear that it would have taken some time for the productivity differential between East and West Germany to disappear. Needless to say, the creation of new firms in the east, the dismantling of inefficient organizational practices, the modernization of existing plant and equipment, and the retraining of workers all took time.

Thus most German policy makers considered it inevitable that East Germany would have went through a substantial transition period in which (a) labor incomes exceeded productivity and (b) employment was sustained at a level where the marginal product of labor fell far short of the marginal value of time. The implication was that East German employment would have been to be subsidized. On all this there was wide agreement. The contentious policy problem was what form these subsidies were to take.

2.1. Sources of Inefficiency in Employment Policies Thus Far

The policies that were in fact implemented were wide-ranging and diverse. There were subsidies for investment, research and development, exports, and credit; these were supplemented by work-creating measures, vocational training schemes, early retirement and transitory retirement regulations, and subsidies for short-time work. In addition, the *Treuhandanstalt* sought to create employment opportunities through transfers to loss-making firms, debt write-offs, and privatization. This vast array of policies has proved to be seriously wasteful in several important respects.

The absence of clear-cut and general rules on which subsidies to offer to which enterprises in which amounts over which period of time meant that the *Treuhandanstalt* had to consider each case independently. As a result, policy implementation has been costly and unnecessarily slow. The process of keeping loss-making enterprises in business through individually negotiated hand-outs has diverted manpower and resources from the privatization process, and has kept resources tied to inefficient production processes and unwanted outputs.

In addition, the case-by-case approach has vastly increased the returns from redistributional battles. Many inefficient East German enterprises found that the payoff from lobbying was higher than that from restructuring. The upshot was doubtlessly a sizeable waste of potential managerial resources and a socially undesirable incentive to use political pressure to maintain the status quo rather than to reorganize production in accordance with consumer demand.

Policy makers made little attempt to subsidize loss-making firms through a cost-minimizing set of policy instruments and managers saw little need to respond to given policies in a cost-minimizing way.

2.2. Unemployment and Productivity

As it turned out, the policies above were unable to prevent a dramatic rise in East German unemployment. From the third quarter of 1990 to the third quarter of 1991, the number of registered unemployed in East Germany rose from 359,000 to 1,053,000, leading to a rise in the official unemployment rate from 4.1% to 12.0%. Since then, the East German unemployment rate remained over two times as high as that in West Germany.

Since unification, East German average productivity, measured in terms of GDP per man hour, has remained far beneath that of West Germany. In part, this productivity gap was due to inefficient use of management and administrative practices as well as the large number of East Germans previously employed in the political arms of enterprises and the armed services and national security. In part, it was due to an obsolete capital stock and insufficient industrial infrastructure.[3] These problems have been augmented by a sectoral misallocation of East German workers (for example, with too many employed in agriculture and forestry, and too few in banking and insurance).[4]

2.3. The Wage Setting Process

Wage settlements turned out to be unexpectedly high, for a variety of complementary reasons. West German unions exerted a strong influence on East German wage negotiations after March 1990. Their objective was the equalization

---

[3] See, for example, Franz (1995) and Koldt (1990).

[4] See, for example, Siebert (1991).

of East and West German wages. In this regard, they had the support of most politicians. Both the West German unions and the politicians appeared to think that the elimination of the wage gap was the most effective way of preventing large migration flows from East to West Germany.

This approach seemed curious to many economists, who pointed out that a closing of the wage differential would lead to a widening of the unemployment differential and that migration tends to be more sensitive to the latter differential than the former. This argument, however, does not take account of the German unemployment benefit system, which makes the size of the unemployment benefits highly dependent on the previously earned wage. Consequently, workers who faced the likely prospect of plant closure had a powerful incentive to press for high wages in order to secure maximal unemployment benefits in the future. This incentive, incidentally, was equally strong for the managers of loss-making firms. Thus none of the parties to these negotiations stood to benefit substantially from wage restraint. For its part, the *Treuhand* did little to lean against the wind; on the whole, it tried not to get involved in wage negotiations.

The resulting high wage settlements and the associated, generous unemployment benefits undoubtedly did much to moderate migration flows. In view of this effect, the narrowing of wage differentials may well have had a stronger effect in keeping East German workers at home than a narrowing of unemployment differentials would have had.

Bargaining over contractual wages throughout Germany has been conducted primarily by sector and geographic region. Moreover, actual wages can exceed the negotiated contractual levels on account of wage drift. The geographical differentiation meant that there was no overriding institutional reason for an abrupt equalization of East and West German earnings. Indeed, the sectoral differentiation combined with wage drift meant that the narrowing of the earnings differential between East and West Germany proceeded unevenly across sectors.

On the basis of these observations, we now proceed to build a simple model of the East German labor market.

3. A Simple Model of the East German Employment Problem

Our model deals with labor market activity in an individual sector of the economy (e.g. construction, food, retail trade). It focuses attention on the value of a job to the firm and the worker. We consider two types of jobs, "old" ones with low productivity and "new" ones with high productivity. Let $a(N)$ be the real marginal revenue product from a new job in a particular sector, where N stands for aggregate East German employment in that sector and $a' < 0$ (diminishing returns to labor), and $\gamma \cdot a\,(N)$ be the real marginal revenue product from an old job, where $0 < \gamma < 1$.

In line with the German wage setting process, we assume that wage bargaining is sector-specific, so that old and new jobs in each sector command the same wage, W. Let b (a positive constant) be the real non-labor cost associated with each job.[5] Then the real profit generated by an old job is

$$\pi_0 = \gamma \cdot a\,(N) - b - W, \tag{1a}$$

whereas a new job yields

$$\pi_n = a\,(N) - b - W. \tag{1b}$$

Let E be the real fixed cost of creating a new job, H be the real cost of hiring and training a newly hired worker, and F be the real cost of firing an incumbent worker. Then, under single period optimization,[6] an old job is kept open as long as

$$\gamma \cdot a\,(N) - b - W + F \geq 0, \tag{2a}$$

which will be called the "incumbency constraint" (IC). A new job is created when

$$a\,(N) - b - W - E - H \geq 0, \tag{2b}$$

which is the "entry constraint" (EC).

We assume that wages and employment are determined in a Nash equilibrium setting. Specifically, employment decisions are made taking wages as given and wage decisions are made taking employment as given. This setup differs from the standard analysis in which wage-employment decisions are made in two stages, with wages set first (taking the employment repercussions into account) and then employment (taking wages as given). The relative merits of these alternative frameworks depend on the relative frequency with which wage and employment decisions are made. Given significant costs of creating new jobs as well as significant costs of hiring, training, and firing – a particularly important assumption even now when considering the East German employment problem – it is often unrealistic to view wages as precommitted when employment decisions are made. Our setup implicitly presupposes that neither wages nor employment

---

[5] We could have assumed that b(N), with b' > 0, i.e. a rising non-labor cost per worker, but for expositional simplicity we include any such effects in a(N).

[6] This is not an assumption of substance. It is easy to show that the qualitative conclusions of our analysis also hold under multi-period optimization.

can be renegotiated instantaneously and that they are generally not set simultaneously.[7]

Wages are assumed to be set by a Nash bargain between the employers and employees in a sector. The employers cover both old and new jobs in that sector, and the employees are represented by a union which seeks to maximize the utility of its representative member. Under bargaining agreement, each employee receives the real wage W (taking employment (N) in that sector as given). Under disagreement, each employee is assumed to look for another job. With probability ρ he finds another job and then receives the real "outside wage" $\hat{W}$. The employment probability ρ depends on labor demand and supply not only in East Germany, but also in West Germany and, to a lesser extent, abroad. Both the employment probability ρ and the outside wage $\hat{W}$ are exogenously given when the wage W is determined. With probability $(1-\rho)$ the worker finds no job and he then receives an exogenously given unemployment benefit B.[8] Thus the worker's fall-back income is $\hat{Y} = \rho \cdot \hat{W} - (1-\rho) \cdot B$ which, under the assumptions above, is exogenous to the bargain. Since the employment probability ρ depends, in part, on the sectoral employment N, the fall-back income may be written as $\hat{Y} = \hat{Y}(N)$, where $\hat{Y} = 0$. In this context, the union's bargaining objective may be specified quite simply as

$$\Omega_W = W - \hat{Y}(N). \tag{3a}$$

Under bargaining agreement, an old job generates profit π_0, given by (1a). Under disagreement the job is kept vacant, yielding no revenue and generating the cost b. A new job under agreement generates profit π_n, given by (1b), and yields neither revenue nor cost under disagreement. Given that there are M old jobs and N jobs in total in the sector under consideration, the employers' bargaining objective may be specified as

$$\Omega_f = \left[\frac{M}{N}\right] \cdot [\gamma \cdot a(N) - W + F] + \left[1 - \frac{M}{N}\right] \cdot [a(N) - W - H - E]. \tag{3b}$$

Given the bargaining objectives (3a) and (3b), the wage may be derived as the outcome of the following Nash bargain:[9]

---

[7] Non-simultaneous wage-employment decisions are assumed in the monopoly union and right-to-manage bargaining literature, but generally not in the efficient contract bargaining models.

[8] In accordance with German practice, this may be viewed as positively related to the worker's previous wage; but as long as this latter wage is exogenously given in the bargaining process, we are justified in assuming that the unemployment benefit is exogenous as well.

[9] The wage W in our analysis is defined as the real wage. Whereas it is unrealistic to assume that employers and employees bargain over the real wage, it would be trivial to

$$\underset{w}{\text{Maximize}} \; \Omega = (\Omega_w)^{\mu} \cdot (\Omega_f)^{1-\mu}, \tag{4}$$

where μ (a constant, $0 \leq \mu \leq 1$) is a measure of the bargaining strength of the employees relative to the employers. Let the proportion of old jobs be

$$\beta \equiv (M/N) \tag{5a}$$

and define the average productivity factor as

$$\Gamma \equiv \beta \cdot \gamma + (1 - \beta). \tag{5b}$$

Then the negotiated wage, that solves the bargaining problem (4) may be expressed as

$$W^n = \mu \cdot [\Gamma \cdot a(N) + \beta \cdot F - (1-\beta) \cdot (H + E)] + (1-\mu) \cdot \hat{Y}(N), \tag{6}$$

which will be called the "negotiated wage function" (WN).

Figure 1 illustrates the labor market equilibrium for relative parameter values that appear to be relevant to the East German unemployment problem. The negotiated wage function (WN) may be upward or downward sloping since $a' < 0$ (diminishing returns to labor) and $\hat{Y}' > 0$ (fall-back income depends positively on the employment level N). The entry constraint (EC), $W \leq a(N) - b - H - E$, has a slope that is less than the WN curve.[10] The incumbency constraint (IC), $W \leq \gamma \cdot a(N) - b + F$, is parallel to the entry constraint. The figure implicitly assumes – as is probably realistic in most cases – that the productivity differential between new and old jobs exceeds the cost of job turnover:

$$(1 - \gamma) \cdot a(N) > E + H + F. \tag{7}$$

---

restate our model in terms of bargaining over the nominal wage, with prices set by the employers under perfectly or imperfectly competitive conditions in the product markets.

[10] The reason is that even if $\hat{Y}$ were equal to zero (so that the wage setting function WS would be unambiguously downward sloping), the EC curve would be steeper than the WS curve since $\mu<1$.

Figure 1. Labor Market Activity in the Absence of Government Intervention and under the Wage Subsidy Scheme

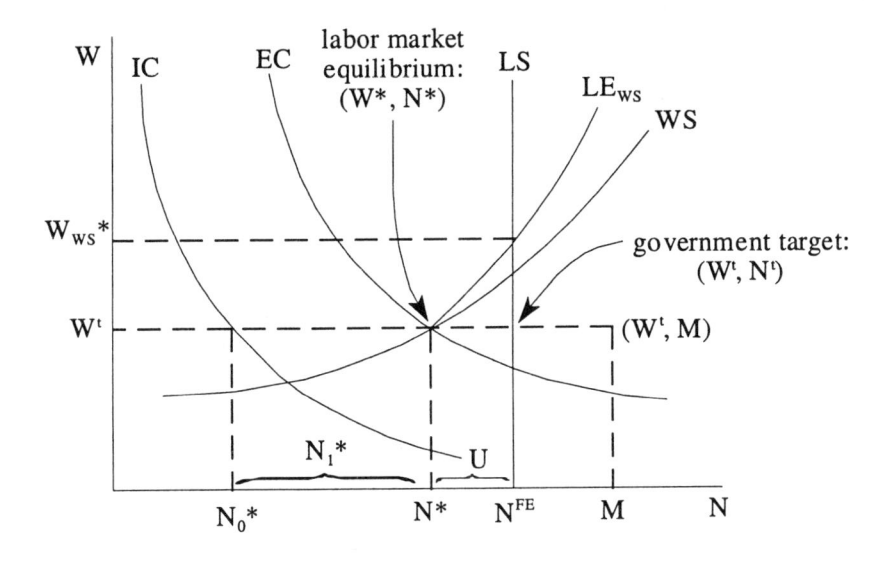

Then the entry constraint lies above the incumbency constraint and the labor market equilibrium is given by the intersection of the negotiated wage function (6) and the entry constraint (2b).[11] Specifically, at the equilibrium wage W*, new jobs will be created until employment is N*(as determined by the entry constraint); and at the equilibrium level of employment N*, the negotiated wage will be W*(as determined by the wage setting function). By the negotiated wage function (6), the entry constraint (2b), and the definitions (5a) and (5b), the equilibrium wage is

$$W^*_{AG} = \left[\frac{1}{1-\mu\cdot\Gamma}\right] \cdot [\Gamma \cdot b + \beta \cdot F + (\beta \cdot \gamma) \cdot (H+E)] + \left[\frac{1-\mu}{1-\mu\cdot\Gamma}\right] \cdot \hat{Y},$$
(8a)

where the superscript "*" in W^*_{AG} stands for "equilibrium" and the subscript "AG" stands for the wage in the "absence" of "government" intervention. If we assume that a(N) takes the Cobb-Douglas form $a(N) = A \cdot N^{-\alpha}$, the equilibrium employment level is

$$N^*_{AG} = A^{\alpha} \cdot \left[\left(\frac{1}{1-\mu\cdot\Gamma}\right) \cdot [\Gamma \cdot b + \beta \cdot F + (\beta \cdot \gamma) \cdot (H+E)] = \left(\frac{1-\mu}{1-\mu\cdot\Gamma}\right) \cdot \hat{Y} + b + H + E\right]$$
(8b)

---

[11] If, on the contrary, $(1-\gamma) \cdot a(N) < E + H + F$, then the incumbency constraint lies above the entry constraint and the labor market equilibrium is given by the intersection of the WS and IC curves. Under these conditions no new jobs are created.

In the absence of the fixed cost (b = 0) and all entry barriers (F = H = E = 0), the equilibrium wage reduces to

$$W^*_{AG} = \left(\frac{1-\mu}{1-\mu \cdot \Gamma}\right) \cdot \hat{Y} \quad (8a')$$

and the equilibrium employment level becomes

$$N^*_{AG} = A^{-\alpha} \cdot \left(\frac{(1-\mu) \cdot \hat{Y}}{1-\mu \cdot \Gamma}\right)^{-\frac{1}{\alpha}} \quad (8b')$$

Figure 1 is drawn to illustrate some basic features of the still existing East German employment problem in the absence of government intervention in the East German labor market. Observe that the labor market equilibrium

$$\left(W^*_{AG}, N^*_{AG}\right)$$

lies at the intersection of the EC and WN curves. The full-employment level of employment, N^{FE}, is given by the intersection of the entry constraint (EC) and the labor supply curve (LS). To fix ideas, we assume that the government's employment target, N^t, is equal to the full employment level N^{FE}, and that its wage target, W^t, is equal to the equilibrium wage W^*_{AG}. The latter assumption is probably not unreasonable given the involvement of West German unions in the East German wage setting process. It is generally recognized that, in the absence of any government intervention, most old jobs would become unprofitable, necessitating the firing of most incumbents. It is also widely agreed that, in the short run at least, not enough new jobs would be created to avoid substantial unemployment. In terms of our figure this means that the point (M, W*) lies to the right of the incumbency constraint, so that at the equilibrium wage W^*_{AG} only N^*_0 old jobs survive and $(M - N_0^*)$ incumbent workers are fired. Moreover, the equilibrium level of employment N^*_{AG} falls short of the full employment level N^{FE}, so that there is unemployment of $U = N^{FE} - N^*_{AG}$.

It is to avert such layoffs and unemployment that the German government has instituted its vast, intricate and costly program of subsidies, tax incentives, and transfers to prop up the East German labor market. In the following sections we investigate two rival policy proposals designed to improve the employment performance of the East German economy at lower social and public cost.

4. Wage Subsidies

Perhaps the most prominent policy proposal to revive the East German labor market was to establish a program of wage subsidies and then to auction off East

German firms to the highest bidder.[12] The main line of reasoning in support of this proposal is quite simple: The government's wage target, formulated on the grounds of social acceptability, lied far above the market-clearing wage. Under such circumstances, economic efficiency can be restored by a subsidy that reduces the cost of labor sufficiently to bring the associated marginal product of labor (net of the subsidy) back into equality with the marginal value of time.

The obvious problem with this argument is that it presupposes perfect competition. If wage determination is imperfectly competitive, as it doubtlessly is in East German labor markets, then the imposition of wage subsidies will raise the negotiated wage at any given level of employment. Then, if $W^t = W^*_{AG}$, subsidy sufficiently large to restore full employment will push wage outcomes above the target wage.

Even if $W^t = W^*_{AG}$, there is still a convincing case to be made that the full-employment level of wage subsidies would drive real wages in excess of the government's target. There is widespread agreement that East German real wages have been generally above government targets, and there is good reason to believe that the replacement of the current employment policies by a wage subsidy program would raise real wages, simply because some of the current transfers to East German firms are not related to the magnitude of employment and consequently do not put upward pressure on the outcomes of wage negotiations. In short, it may be impossible to restore efficiency in production and employment at the target wage through wage subsidies.

This, of course, does not imply that wage subsidies are necessarily inappropriate to deal with the East German employment problem. The first-best optimum may be unattainable through any feasible policy intervention. The crucial issue is whether wage subsidies can achieve a second-best optimum, given that East German wages cannot fall beneath the government's wage target. Specifically, the case for wage subsidies must rest on the argument that this policy can achieve full employment with socially acceptable wages at lower social cost and/or lower government budgetary cost than other feasible proposals. It is this issue that the present paper calls into question.

Consider the impact of a proportional wage subsidy s in the context of the labor market described in the previous section. The entry constraint may now be rewritten as

$$W \leq \left(\frac{1}{1-s}\right) \cdot [a(N) - b - H - E], \tag{9a}$$

---

[12] See, for example, Akerlof et al. (1991) and Begg and Portes (2000).

and the incumbency constraint as

$$W \le \left(\frac{1}{1-s}\right) \cdot [\gamma \cdot a(N) - b + F]. \tag{9b}$$

Turning to wage setting, the employees' bargaining objective remains (3a), whereas the employers' bargaining objective now becomes

$$\Omega_f = \left(\frac{M}{N}\right) \cdot [\gamma \cdot a(N) - (1-s) \cdot W + F] + \left(1 - \frac{M}{N}\right) \cdot [a(N) - (1-s) \cdot W - H - E].$$

Thus the negotiated wage becomes

$$W_{WS}^n = \left(\frac{\mu}{1-s}\right) \cdot [\Gamma \cdot a(N) + \beta \cdot F - (1-\beta) \cdot (H + E)] + (1-\mu) \cdot \hat{Y}, \tag{10}$$

where the subscript "WS" in W_{WS}^* stands for the wage under the "wage subsidy" scheme.

Given that the labor market equilibrium is determined by the intersection of the negotiated wage function (10) and the entry constraint (9a), the equilibrium wage is

$$W_{WS}^* = \left(\frac{1}{1-\mu \cdot \Gamma}\right) \cdot \left[\Gamma \cdot b + \left(\frac{1}{1-s}\right) \cdot [\beta \cdot F + (\beta \cdot \gamma) \cdot (H + E)]\right] + \left(\frac{1-\mu}{1-\mu \cdot \Gamma}\right) \cdot \hat{Y}. \tag{11a}$$

The equilibrium employment level becomes

$$N_{WS}^* \, a^{-1}\left[\left(\frac{1}{1-\mu \cdot \Gamma}\right) \cdot [\Gamma \cdot b \cdot (1-s) + \beta \cdot F + (\beta \cdot \gamma) \cdot (H+E)] + \left(\frac{(1-\mu) \cdot (1-s)}{1-\mu \cdot \Gamma}\right) \cdot \hat{Y} + b + H + E\right], \tag{11b}$$

where $\left(a^{-1}\right)' < 0$ since $a' < 0$. One important implication of equation (11a) is that the greater the labor turnover costs (H and F) and the greater the entry cost (E) and the greater the ratio of old to new jobs (β), the more the wage subsidy raises the negotiated wage. Moreover, in the absence of the fixed cost (b = 0) and all entry barriers (F = H = E = 0), the equilibrium wage is unaffected by the wage subsidy (i.e. W* is given by equation (8a')) and the equilibrium employment level is

$$N_{WS}^* = a^{-1}\left(\frac{(1-\mu) \cdot (1-s)}{(1-\mu \cdot \Gamma)}\right) \cdot \hat{Y}. \tag{11b'}$$

Equations (11a) and (11b) indicate that the greater the wage subsidy s, the greater will be the resulting equilibrium employment level N_{WS}^* and, in the presence of some entry barriers (F, H, E > 0), the greater will be the equilibrium wage W_{WS}^*. In fact, as the wage subsidy is raised from s=0 to s=1, we can trace out a locus of labor market equilibrium points denoted by LE_{WS} in Figure 1. The greater the entry barriers (F, H, E), the steeper this locus will be. By (11a), in the extreme case of no entry barriers (F = H = E = 0), the locus is horizontal.

From the figure it is clear that if $W^t = W^*_{AG}$ and some entry barriers exist, it is impossible to achieve the government's wage-employment target (W^t, N^t) through the wage subsidy scheme. A subsidy that raises employment to its target level N^t will necessarily raise the equilibrium wage W^*_{WS} above its target level W^t. In practice, the unwillingness of West German firms to engage in substantial job creation after German unification, despite the massive government incentives to do so, led one to believe that the costs of firm entry (E) and perhaps also the costs of training in East Germany are large, and thus (by (11a) and (11b)) the LE_{WS} locus may be expected to be steep. Then, provided that the wage target W^t is in the neighborhood of the equilibrium wage W^*_{AG} in the absence of intervention, the full-employment wage under the subsidy scheme will far exceed the target wage.

Now turn to the social benefit and the budgetary cost of a wage subsidy that is sufficiently high to raise employment to the full-employment level N^{FE}. One appropriate measure of the social benefit (SB_{WS}) of the scheme is total production minus the direct budgetary cost (DBC) of the scheme. Total production is

$$\Gamma \cdot N^{FE} \cdot \xi(M) + (1-\beta) \cdot N^{FE} \cdot \xi(N), \quad \text{where} \quad \xi(N) = \int_0^N a(N) dN.$$

The direct budgetary cost is

$$DBC_{WS} = s^* \cdot W^*_{WS} \cdot N^{FE}. \tag{12}$$

Thus the social benefit of the wage subsidy scheme is

$$SB_{WS} = \Gamma \cdot N^{FE} \cdot \xi(M) + (1-\beta) \cdot N^{FE} \cdot \xi(N) - s \cdot W^* \cdot N^{FE} \tag{13}$$

The total budgetary cost of the scheme, on the other hand, consists of three main components: (i) the direct budgetary cost of the subsidy scheme, minus (ii) the additional tax revenue generated by the scheme, minus (iii) the rise in the value of firms as result of the scheme, which is an additional value that accrues to the government when the firms are auctioned off. The direct budgetary cost (DBC) is given by (12). Assuming a proportional income tax rate t, the additional tax revenue is $t \cdot (y_{WS} - y_{AG})$, where y_{AG} is income in the absence of government intervention (as determined in the previous section) and y_{WS} is income under the wage subsidy scheme. y_{WS} is the sum of wage income $W^*_{WS} \cdot N^{FE}$ and profit income

$$\left(\Gamma \cdot N^{FE} \cdot a(N^{FE}) - (1-s) \cdot W^*_{WS} \cdot N^{FE} - (1-\beta) \cdot N^{FE} \cdot (H+E) - b \cdot N^{FE} \right).$$

In short, the additional tax revenue is

$$t \cdot (y_{WS} - y_{AG}) =$$
$$t \cdot \left[\Gamma \cdot N^{FE} \cdot a(N^{FE}) + s \cdot W^*_{WS} \cdot N^{FE} - (1-\beta) \cdot N^{FE} \cdot (H+E) - b \cdot N^{FE} - y_{AG} \right] \tag{14a}$$

The rise in the value of firms as result of the wage subsidy scheme is

$$\zeta \cdot [V_{WS} - V_{AG}] =$$

$$\zeta \cdot \begin{bmatrix} \Gamma \cdot N^{FE} \cdot A(M) + (1-\beta) \cdot N^{FE} \cdot A(N) - b \cdot N^{FE} - (1-s) \cdot W^*_{WS} \cdot N^{FE} - (1-\beta) \cdot N^{FE} \\ \cdot (H+E) - V_{AG} \end{bmatrix}$$

(14b)

where ζ is the proportion of firms that remain to be privatized, V_{WS} is the value of firms under the wage subsidy scheme, and V_{AG} is their value in the absence of government intervention. Consequently, the total budgetary cost TBC_{WS} of the scheme is

$$TBC_{WS} = DBC_{WS} - t \cdot (y_{WS} - y_{AG}) - \zeta \cdot (V_{WS} - V_{AG})$$

$$= W^*_{WS} \cdot N^{FE} \cdot \left[\zeta \cdot \left(1 - s^*\right) - t \cdot s^* \right] - t \cdot \Gamma \cdot a\left(N^{FE}\right) \cdot N^{FE}$$

$$+ b \cdot N^{FE} \cdot (\zeta + t) + (H+E) \cdot (1-\beta) \cdot N^{FE} \cdot (\zeta + t)$$

$$- \zeta \cdot N^{FE} \cdot [\Gamma \cdot \xi(M) - (1-\beta) \cdot \xi(N)] \cdot N^{FE} + \zeta \cdot V_{AG} + t \cdot y_{AG}$$

(15)

Equation (15) implies that the total budgetary cost depends positively on the size of the hiring and training cost (H), the entry cost (E), the fixed cost (b), and the equilibrium wage W^*_{WS} and negatively on the tax rate (t) and the marginal revenue product of labor (a(N)).

5. Revenue-Sharing Subsidies

Now consider the labor market implications of government subsidies for revenue-sharing. To begin with, it is useful to note that revenue- and profit-sharing are formally equivalent, provided that the revenue to be shared is net revenue, viz, revenue net of non-wage costs. To see this in the context of our model, note that net revenue-sharing[13] in old jobs gives an incumbent employee a labor income of $Y_o = \lambda \cdot [\gamma \cdot a(N) - b]$ and the employer a profit of $\pi_o = (1-\lambda) \cdot [\gamma \cdot a(N) - b]$, where λ is the revenue-sharing coefficient. Under profit-sharing, the incumbent employee receives $Y_o = \delta \cdot \pi_o$, where δ is the profit-sharing coefficient, and the

---

[13] For brevity, we restrict our attention to the case of "pure" revenue- and profit-sharing, where workers receive all their labor income as a share of the revenues or profits they generate.

employer receives $\pi_0 = \gamma \cdot a(N) - b - Y_0 = [1/(1+\delta)] \cdot [\gamma \cdot a(N) - b]$. Clearly, these two systems are equivalent provided that the revenue-sharing coefficient is set so that $\lambda = [\delta/(1+\delta)]$. The same argument obviously holds for new jobs as well. Thus, in what follows, we can restrict our attention to revenue-sharing without loss of generality.

Let the government's revenue-sharing subsidy to employers be θ_π and to employees be θ_Y, so that the labor and profit incomes from old jobs become

$$Y_0 = (\lambda + \theta_Y) \cdot [\gamma \cdot a(N) - b] \tag{16a}$$

and

$$\pi_0 = (1 - \lambda + \theta_\pi) \cdot [\gamma \cdot a(N) - b], \tag{16b}$$

respectively, and the incomes from new jobs are

$$Y_n = (\lambda + \theta_Y) \cdot [a(N) - b - H - E] \text{ and} \tag{17a}$$

$$\pi_n = (1 - \lambda + \theta_\pi) \cdot [a(N) - b - H - E]. \tag{17b}$$

The entry constraint is therefore

$$(1 - \lambda + \theta_\pi) \cdot [a(N) - b - H - E] \geq 0, \tag{18a}$$

and the incumbency constraint is[14]

$$(1 - \lambda + \theta_\pi) \cdot [\gamma \cdot a(N) - b] + F \geq 0. \tag{18b}$$

To make these constraints comparable with the analysis in the previous sections, it will be convenient to restate them in terms of labor income. Accordingly, by (17a) and (18a), the entry constraint may be expressed as

$$Y_n \leq (1 + \theta_\pi + \theta_Y) \cdot [a(N) - b - H - E], \tag{19a}$$

and the incumbency constraint may be written as

$$Y_0 \leq (1 + \theta_\pi + \theta_Y) \cdot [\gamma \cdot a(N) - b] + F. \tag{19b}$$

Provided that (7) is satisfied, the entry constraint lies above the incumbency constraint in income-employment space, as shown in Figure 2.

The wage setting process now involves negotiation over the revenue-sharing coefficient λ, rather than over the wage W. The employers' bargaining objective[15] is

---

[14] The firing cost (F) in our model falls entirely on the firm; it is generally not feasible to pass it on to the employees when they leave the firm.

[15] Since workers' productivities are independent of one another in this model, the negotiated wage does not depend on whether employers and employees bargain individualistically or in groups.

$$\Omega_f = \beta \cdot N \cdot [\pi_0 + b + F] + (1-\beta) \cdot N \cdot \pi_n$$
$$= (1 - \lambda + \theta_\pi) \cdot [\Gamma \cdot a(N) - b] + \beta \cdot N \cdot (b + F) - (1 - \lambda + \theta_\pi) \cdot (1-\beta) \cdot N \cdot (H + E).$$

The union's bargaining objective is

$$\Omega_W = \beta \cdot N \cdot Y_0 + (1-\beta) \cdot N \cdot Y_n$$
$$= (\lambda + \theta_Y) \cdot [\Gamma \cdot a(N) - b] - (1-\beta) \cdot N \cdot (\lambda + \theta_Y) \cdot (H + E) - \hat{Y}.$$

The revenue sharing coefficient is the outcome of the Nash bargain:

$$\underset{\lambda}{\text{Maximize}}\ \Omega = (\Omega_W)^\mu \cdot (\Omega_f)^{1-\mu}. \tag{20}$$

Solving,

$$\lambda^n = \mu \cdot (1 + \theta_\pi + \theta_Y) + \mu \cdot \beta \cdot [(b+F)/I] - \theta_Y + (1-\mu) \cdot \hat{Y}/I \tag{21}$$

where λ^n the negotiated revenue-sharing coefficient and

$I = \Gamma \cdot a(N) - b - (1-\beta) \cdot (H+E)$ is average income per head.

Substituting the negotiated revenue-sharing coefficient (21) into the expressions for income in (16a) and (17a), we obtain the negotiated incomes that are generated by the revenue-sharing coefficient:

$$Y_n = [a(N) - b - H - E] \cdot [\mu \cdot (1 + \theta_\pi + \theta_Y) + \mu \cdot \beta \cdot (b+F)/I + (1-\mu) \cdot \hat{Y}(N)/I], \tag{22}$$

which we can call the "negotiated income function" for new entrants, denoted by YN_n in Figure 2, and

$$Y_o = [a(N) - b] \cdot [\mu \cdot (1 + \theta_\pi + \theta_Y) + \mu \cdot \beta \cdot (b+F)/I + (1-\mu) \cdot \hat{Y}(N)/I] \tag{23}$$

which can be called the negotiated income function for incumbents, denoted by YN_o in Figure 2. These two functions play an analogous role to the wage setting function in the previous sections. Observe that whereas workers at new and old jobs receive the same remuneration under the bargaining in the wage system described in the previous sections, they do not do so under revenue-sharing for the simple reason that the old firms tend to make less revenue than the new firms. Thus the YN_o curve may be understood as the equivalent of a wage setting function for incumbents and the YN_n curve can be seen as the equivalent of a wage setting function for new entrants.

Figure 2. Labor Market Activity under the Revenue-Sharing Scheme

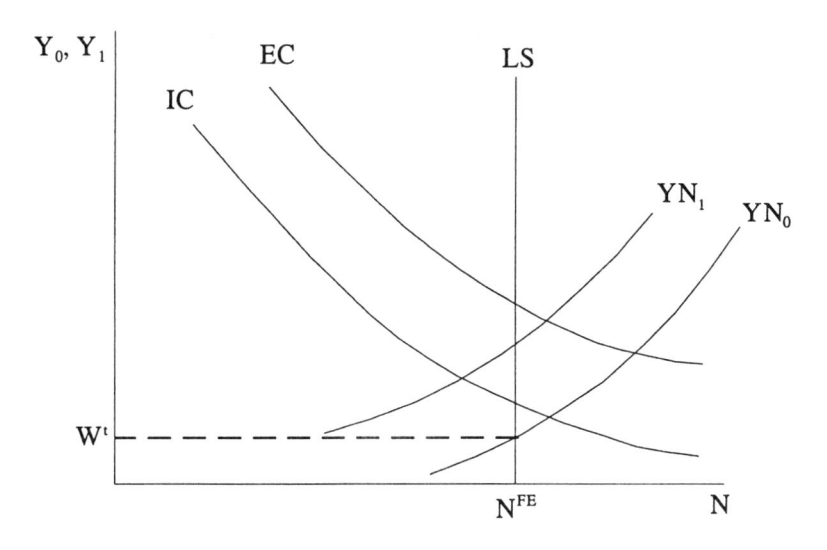

[Figure: Axes labeled Y_0, Y_1 (vertical) and N (horizontal). Curves labeled EC, IC, LS, YN_1, YN_0. Horizontal dashed line at W^t. Vertical line at N^{FE}.]

Figure 2 illustrates the labor market equilibrium under this revenue sharing system. Note that the entry constraint (18a) implies that

$$a(N) - b - H - E \geq 0,$$

i.e. new jobs are created as long as the revenue they generate exceeds the sum of the non-wage costs of production. The incumbency constraint (18b) implies that

$$\gamma \cdot a(N) - b \geq - F/(1 - \lambda + \theta_\pi),$$

i.e. old jobs are retained as long as the revenue they generate exceeds the fixed cost of production. It is reasonable to assume that the entry constraint are compatible with full employment for *any* feasible values of the government subsidies for revenue sharing, even when $\theta_\pi = \theta_Y = 0$. What this means is that all workers seeking jobs at the prevailing revenue-sharing coefficient would be employed if firms would continue hiring workers as long as their marginal revenue products exceeded the associated hiring cost, non-wage factor cost, and job entry cost, *but without taking account of any labor costs*. This assumption is illustrated in Figure 2, where the intersection of the incumbency constraint (IC) with the negotiated income function for incumbents YN_0 as well as the intersection of the entry constraint with the negotiated income function for entrants both occur to the right of the full employment level N.

Consequently, the government's employment objective is achieved automatically under revenue-sharing, and the revenue subsidies can be devoted entirely to attaining the target level of labor income, W^t. Since the YN_n curve lies above the YN_o curve (by condition (7)), the requirement that all workers receive at least W^t reduces to the requirement that

$$Y_o = W^t, \tag{24a}$$

which, by (23), implies that the wage subsidies be set as follows:

$$\theta_\pi^* + \theta_Y^* = \left[W^t/(\mu \cdot \gamma \cdot a(N) - b)\right] - \left[\mu \cdot \beta \cdot (b + F)/I\right] - \left[\hat{Y}(N) \cdot (1-\mu)/(I \cdot \mu)\right]. \tag{24b}$$

Note that it is only the *sum* of the revenue-sharing subsidies to the employers and the employees that are relevant to the achievement of the target labor income. Once this sum is set at the desired level (24b), the YN_o curve intersects the labor supply curve at the target labor income W^t, as shown in Figure 2.

Now consider the social benefit and the budgetary cost of this revenue sharing system. Measuring the social benefit in the same way as in the previous section, we find

$$SB_{RS} = \Gamma \cdot N^{FE} \cdot \xi(M) + (1-\beta) \cdot N^{FE} \cdot \xi(N) - \theta_\pi^* \cdot N^{FE} \cdot I^*, \tag{25}$$

where SB_{RS} is the social benefit under the optimal revenue sharing system and the third right-hand term is the direct budgetary cost. It is easy to show that, for a broad range of plausible parameter values, this social benefit exceeds that from the optimal wage subsidy scheme, as described in the previous section. The main intuitive reason is that the optimal revenue-sharing scheme permits the achievement of both the full-employment target N^{FE} as well as the exact achievement of the labor income target W^t for incumbent workers; however, assuming that $W^t = W_{AG}^*$ the wage subsidy scheme can achieve the full-employment target only when all workers receive more than the labor income target. Consequently the direct budgetary cost (DBC) of the optimal revenue-sharing scheme generally falls short of DBC of the optimal wage subisidy scheme. Comparing the labor remuneration equations under the wage subsidy and revenue-sharing schemes, it is easy to see that the greater the labor turnover costs (H and F) and the greater the entry cost (E) and the greater the ratio of old to new jobs (β) -- all of which are known to be very important in the East German labor market -- the greater will be the direct budgetary cost of the wage-subsidy scheme relative to that of the revenue-sharing scheme.

As in the analysis of the previous section, the total budgetary cost consists of the direct budgetary cost of the scheme minus the additional tax revenue from the scheme minus the additional value of the firms to be auctioned off. It may be expressed as

$$TBC_{RS} = DBC_{RS} - t \cdot (y_{RS} - y_{AG}) - \zeta \cdot (V_{RS} - V_{AG})$$

$$= [\theta_\pi \cdot (1-t) - t] \cdot I^* + (1 - \lambda^* - \theta_\pi^*) \cdot N^{FE} \cdot [b \cdot (\zeta + t) + (H + E) \cdot \zeta \cdot (1-\beta)]$$

$$- (1 - \lambda^* - \theta_\pi^*) \cdot \zeta \cdot [\xi(N^{FE}) - (1-\gamma) \cdot \xi(M)] \cdot N^{FE} + \zeta \cdot V_{AG} + t \cdot y_{AG}.$$
(26)

It is easy to show that this total budgetary cost is less than that under the optimal wage subsidy scheme, provided that the revenue generated (ξ) is small relative to the non-wage costs. There are two counterveiling factors to be taken into account. First, as noted, the direct budgetary cost of the optimal revenue-sharing scheme is generally less than that of the optimal wage subsidy scheme. Second, if the revenue generated minus the non-labor remuneration costs is positive, then the value of the auctioned firms will be larger under the optimal wage subsidy scheme than under the optimal revenue-sharing scheme. The reason, obviously, is that under the revenue-sharing scheme only a fraction of the revenue minus non-labor remuneration costs accrue to the employers, whereas under the wage subsidy scheme all of it does. Consequently, the smaller the value of the firms to be auctioned off (i.e. the lower the revenue generated by these firms or the smaller the proportion of firms yet to be privatized), the lower the total budgetary cost of the revenue-sharing scheme relative to that of the wage subsidy scheme. Since the process of privatization is already far advanced, while the labor turnover costs and entry costs (that raise the direct budgetary cost of the wage subsidy scheme relative to the revenue-sharing scheme) are sizeable, it is to be expected that the total budgetary cost of the revenue-sharing scheme will generally be lower than that of the wage subsidy scheme.

6. Concluding Remarks

The analysis above is meant to provide a simple, tractable framework within which the relative social benefits and budgetary costs of wage subsidies versus revenue- or profit-sharing subsidies can be assessed. It is worth stressing that the implementation of either policy would have probably led to substantial social and budgetary gains in relation to the vast array of policies, implemented on a case-by-case basis, that were in operation in the first years after unification and are partly even now. Nevertheless, which of these policies might have had performed better in a social and budgetary sense is clearly a matter of prime policy importance. The model highlights an important disadvantage of wage subsidies and an important counterveiling advantage of revenue-sharing subsidies: Wage subsidies lead to higher wages as well as to higher employment, and subsidies large enough to achieve full employment may well lead to extravagantly high wages. By contrast, revenue-sharing schemes, even in the absence of subsidies, may be expected to bring the labor market close to full employment, and consequently the subsidies can be set so as to achieve an appropriate level of labor income.

There is good reason to believe, however, that this by no means exhausts the advantages of revenue-sharing subsidies relative to wage subsidies. Wage subsidies distort the labor-capital ratio, whereas revenue- or profit-sharing subsidies do not. Finally, in small enterprises where individual workers' labor inputs can have a noticeable effect on the profits of their enterprise, the revenue- or profit-sharing subsidies may be expected to have incentive effects that the wage subsidies cannot reproduce.

Furthermore, it is important to observe that the above-mentioned deficiency of wage subsidies is generally also shared by output, export, credit, and investment subsidies. All of these subsidies tend to increase the marginal value product of labor[16] and thereby raise the amount of economic rent that may be partially appropriated by workers in the wage bargaining process. Thus these subsidies, like the wage subsidies, lead to wage increases, and subsidies that are sufficiently high to ensure full employment may generate real wages far in excess of government targets. The implications for the budgetary costs of these subsidies are also similar to those of the wage subsidies. As we have seen, when wage subsidies raise wages, they automatically raise the direct budgetary cost of the wage subsidy program, since the total government expenditure on wage subsidies is positively related to the level of wages. By contrast, when output, export, credit, or investment subsidies raise wages, they do not thereby have any direct effect on the magnitude of the subsidy payments. They do, however, have an important indirect effect: The induced rise in wages discourages employment and consequently higher subsidies are now required to achieve full employment than would have been called for in the absence of the wage increase. It is for this reason that the induced wage increase raises the budgetary cost of these subsidy schemes.

Finally, it is significant that many of the most serious criticisms that have been levelled against the establishment of profit- or revenue-sharing schemes in mature market economies appear to lose much of their force with regard to economies that are in the process of transformation to a market mechanism. It has been asserted, for example, that managers of firms may have a substantial incentive to resist switching from a wage system to a profit- or revenue-sharing system, because the latter involves revealing revenue information to the employees. Moreover, the insiders in these firms may also have an incentive to resist, since they may be able to achieve higher remuneration under the wage system.[17] It is

---

[16] Of course, if labor and capital are Edgeworth substitutes then investment subsidies that raise the capital stock will reduce the marginal product of labor, but this contingency appears not to be predominant in practice.

[17] Of course, a two-tier revenue-sharing system could be implemented, whereby insiders are offered a sufficiently large revenue-sharing coefficient to prevent a drop in insider

clear, however, that these problems are likely to be much more pronounced for existing firms that have operated under a wage system in the past and that employ workforces containing a large proportion of insiders. Yet East Germany, like other eastern European economies, has experienced such substantial shifts in final demand that the establishment of a revenue-sharing system would lead to the destruction of most old firms and the creation of many new ones. Thus it is to be expected that most of the jobs operating under the revenue-sharing system would not involve switching from the wage system and reparameterizing insider contracts and thereby would avoid the conflicts with the vested interests of incumbent workers and firms.

In view of these various considerations, the analysis above suggests that revenue-sharing subsidies still deserve more attention in the policy debate concerning employment stimulation in East Germany - as well as in other eastern European economies – than they have thus far received.

References

Akerlof, G. et al. (1991), East Germany in from the Cold: The Economic Aftermath of Currency Union, *Brookings Papers on Economic Activity*, 1, 1-105.

Begg, D./Portes, R. (2000), Eastern Germany since Unification: Wage Subsidies Remain a Better Way, Riphahn, R.T./Snower, D. J./Zimmermann, K. F. (2000), *Employment Policy in Transition: The Lessons of German Integration for the Labor Market*, Heidelberg, 140-153.

Franz, W. (1995), Central and East European Labor Markets in Transition: Developments, Causes and Curves, *CEPR Discussion Paper, No. 1132*, London.

Koldt, H. (1990), Arbeitsmarktpolitick in the DDR: Vorschläge für ein Qualifizierungsprogramm, *Die Weltwirtschaft*, 1, 78-90.

Siebert, H. (1991), German Unification: The Economics of Transition, *Economic Policy 13*, 287-340.

---

income while new entrants receive a lower coefficient. The problem with this approach is that insiders generally resist two-tier systems since they often prove to be time-inconsistent: At a future date, when the current entrants have achieved a comparable productivity to the current insiders - the firm will have an incentive to retain the low-paid entrants and dismiss the high-paid insiders. Besides, a sufficiently large revenue-sharing coefficient for insiders may not be sustainable by the relative bargaining strengths and fall-back positions of the insiders and their firms, in which case firms will have an incentive to reduce the insiders' revenue-sharing coefficient in future bargaining rounds.

4. Investment Wages and Capital Market Imperfections

Gerhard Illing, University of Frankfurt/Main

1. Introduction

The restructuring of firms in Eastern Europe still requires massive amounts of investment. At the same time, the process of restructuring is creating high unemployment. The problems of raising capital and fighting unemployment would have to be faced even if the transformation process were functioning organically and smoothly. They are, however, aggravated by the fact that there hardly existed a financial infrastructure in Eastern Europe. Capital markets needed to be built up at the same time. In the communist regime, private investment and private savings were operating only to a very limited extent. Private firms could not borrow to finance investment, and the main means of savings by households had been either stockpiling of goods or money deposits. The liberalization of financial markets was likely to promote private savings. As long as capital markets were not well established, however, the channeling of savings to the most efficient forms of investment would have been impeded, limiting expected efficiency gains.

Under these conditions, investment wages would have helped to overcome inefficiencies in the provision of capital. In East Germany, the promotion of investment wages were suggested as a simultaneous cure both for the problem of high unemployment and low investment (compare Sievert (1992) or Snower (2000)). Ulf Fink (1992), the head of the *CDU-Sozialausschüsse*, proposed them as a way for raising more capital in order to finance the building up of a modern East German capital stock. In Eastern Germany, financing of new investment turned out to be insufficient, despite the fact that the West German banking system had expanded immediately to the East, and an enormous inflow of transfers occurred. Most of the transfers, however, went into consumption.

In the German policy debate, investment wages were suggested as one way of stimulating new investment. It is argued that they could have attacked both problems at the same time by lowering the burden of high wages for the firms and by providing additional capital needed for investment. It would be naive, however, to expect that such effects would have came about. Investment wages cannot solve the problem of high wages – they simply postpone payment of the wage bill to the future. It is also unlikely that they will increase savings: this would happen only if investment wages force workers to save more than what is individually optimal for them. In an economy with perfect capital markets, however, higher savings via investment wages would be offset by a reduction of savings in other forms, thus nullifying the initial effect. To the extent that aggregate savings are increased, it actually represents a welfare loss under such conditions: if workers are forced to save, rather than to spend their income, they are worse off because they have to deviate from their preferred choice. A far more efficient way to increase aggregate saving would be to make it more attractive (e.g. by raising the real interest rate).

At first sight, this might suggest that investment wages are nothing but a costly intervention into the free market system: If they force workers to accept inferior investment opportunities, they conflict with consumers' sovereignty. The only result would be a forced change of the individual portfolio to an inferior menu of risky assets and, consequently, a reduction in individual welfare. If they provide the firms with capital below market conditions, they cause a misallocation of capital. As will be shown, this view turns out not to be correct if capital market are imperfect. Investment wages may improve upon the allocation for reasons which have to do with the incompleteness of the capital markets. The mechanism is not that aggregate savings will be increased, but rather that capital will be directed to a more efficient use – a task which is not automatically accomplished in an economy with imperfect capital markets. Under certain conditions a switch from paying wages in cash to investment wages may help to achieve this task, thus making all parties better off.

The present paper analyses the role of investment wages as a way to overcome capital market imperfections. It is shown that, by generating liquidity, they can increase efficiency if workers as insiders are better informed about firms than banks, which provide external funding opportunities. Section 2 surveys theoretical arguments about profit sharing and investment wages. Section 3 presents the model of asymmetric information. Section 4 comments on special aspects related to East Germany. A combination of investment wages and subsidies is suggested as an attractive policy option for handling both the problems of liquidity constraints and of excessive wages.

2. Profit Sharing and Investment Wages in the Presence of Frictions

Profit-sharing and investment wage schemes were discussed among German economists for a long time. During the 70es, there were heated debates concerning the allocative and distributional advantages of such schemes. One main argument in favor of such schemes has been that they are a means to introduce more flexibility into the labor market. This argument has been taken up by Weitzman (1984). He shows, that switching from a system of fixed wages to some form of profit-sharing improves the efficiency of capitalist market economies. The intuitive reason why a Pareto-improvement can come about is the following: Bargaining about profit sharing leads to an allocation which is equivalent to a solution of the efficient bargaining model (compare Pohjola (1987)). As is well known, if the union and the employer bargain both about wage and employment, a better outcome can be obtained than via bargaining about wages alone, leaving employment decisions to the firms.

The difficulty with this argument is that it does not explain why the bargaining parties should be willing to switch to a profit sharing scheme, as long as they are not able to agree on an efficient bargaining solution. To show that a change in the rules of the game (a switch from fixing wages to fixing profit- or revenue shares) improves upon the outcome does not help to explain how such a change of rules could be achieved. After all, the bargaining parties agreed on the specific arrangement in the wage negotiations in the first place.

There must be reasons why inefficient bargaining occurs, and an improvement does not come about. It is likely that exactly these reasons (such as asymmetric information about the state of the firm) may prevent a switch to profit-sharing agreements as well. Why should it be easier to introduce a profit-sharing scheme rather than persuading employers and employees to adapt flexible wage contracts? Without modeling explicitly the frictions in the bargaing process, the superiority of profit-sharing schemes is hardly a convincing argument. It is difficult so see why externalities could be internalized via profit-sharing, whereas they impede flexible wage contracts.

The present paper incorporates explicitly informational frictions and shows that in this context, investment wages can improve upon the allocation of capital. It is assumed that private contracts are chosen optimally. Thus, the paper is related to a second argument in favor of profit sharing, put forward by the German council of economic advisers in the 70s. The council argued that profit sharing could improve upon the allocation of risk capital. Sievert/Tomann (1977) formulated this argument as follows: *"The potential scope of optimal risk allocation could be extended if access to risk income would be more easily available to those who only possess human capital."* Again, this statement makes sense only if there is potential for efficient risk sharing between workers and firms which is not taken care of adequately by capital markets. Sievert/Tomann (1977), however, do not model the reasons which may prevent capital markets from providing firms with efficient risk sharing. The model presented below could be interpreted, in a way, as clarifying the conditions under which this claim (or, more generally, the arguments in Sievert (1992)) may be justified.

Sievert/Tomann (1977) have been concerned with profit-sharing schemes. In Eastern Europe, however, profit sharing does not seem to be an attractive option due to short run problems: In the declining industries, there are no profits (rather, there are losses) to be shared. On the other hand, in new sectors with high profit opportunities a huge amount of investment is needed, whereas expected earnings will be realized in the far future. Investment expenses leave no room for current profits. Furthermore, especially in a period of transition as in Eastern Europe, true economic profits can be manipulated to a large extent (e.g., via depreciation allowances). These short run problems can be avoided by investment wages. In contrast to profit sharing schemes, they allow workers to participate in future expected earnings in the long run. By providing internal capital to the firm, investment wages are a superior way to overcome liquidity problems.

The underlying friction modeled in the paper is asymmetric information between the firm and external financiers. This asymmetry causes liquidity problems for the firms. In order to concentrate on the implications of informational frictions, the present paper assumes that all agents are risk neutral. Capital markets are assumed to work smoothly except for the problem of asymmetric information. This is a reasonable assumption when analyzing the problems in Eastern Germany in the first years after unification. There, West German capital markets have been adapted instantaneously. In contrast, asymmetric information is certainly not the only source for the incompleteness of capital markets in Eastern Europe. In this region, lack of experience with the mechanisms of financial markets even now is at least of equal importance.

These structural problems reinforce the arguments in favor of investment wages presented below. Without modeling these frictions explicitly, one should, however, be careful in drawing policy conclusions. Given the incompleteness of capital markets, one might easily argue that government intervention is bound to improve upon risk-sharing. Since firm specific risks (giving rise to risk-averse investment behavior) are cancelled out on the aggregate level, government participation would stimulate investment, acting as a kind of risk-neutral insurance agency. The participation contract suggested in Demougin/Sinn (1994) is based on this argument (which, essentially, is the Arrow-Lind theorem). It is, however, not at all clear why private, profit oriented financial institutions should have more difficulties in establishing risk markets than government agencies.

The firms in Eastern Europe still are in urgent need of new capital to finance investment their indispensable restructuring. In Western economies, the main source of finance are retained earnings. Borrowing external capital is rarely done by issuing public bonds, rather it is done by making use of long-term connections to specific banks (the "house banks"). Many firms are credit constrained. The obvious explanation is asymmetric information about the firm. Insiders (managers, current shareholder, or the "house banks") have better information, and thus more accurate expectations about the state of the firm and its future profitability. For that reason, outsiders demand a higher risk premium when providing capital – being afraid of adverse selection phenomena. Thus, financing via reinvesting profits is much cheaper than issuing new shares to outsiders. For the same reason, banks lacking a long-term relationship to the firm are reluctant to grant credits. The main productive activity of banks is to build up specific 'information capital' about those firms to which they provide credit. As with all capital investment, building up this capital stock takes a long time. In addition to adverse selection problems, disincentive effects coming from a too high debt-equity ratio prevent extension of credit by banks: Dept imposes a burden on the debtor. The larger the share of the return which goes to the creditor, the higher the effective tax on future earnings for the firm, thus reducing incentives to undertake an efficient amount of effort.

Firms in Eastern Europe even now suffer from capital market imperfections much more than Western firms. They are handicapped in any respect: The process of reconstruction needs massive amounts of capital, and there will be a negative cash flow for quite a long time. For those firms, no specific information capital has been built up in the past, as – for obvious reasons – there have been no long term relations to private banks. Most of these firms lack the collateral required to get access to bank credits. Banks have been very reluctant in providing risk capital: In the first years after opening the wall, West German banks played only an extremely limited role in providing capital to East Germany. But eastern firms did not only suffer from severe credit constraints, they did not have the chance to resort to self finance either.

Investment wages may be a way to mitigate liquidity constraints. At first sight, to claim that workers can be a more efficient source of providing finance to their own firm than banks, may appear to be totally absurd. After all, banks are professionalists in this business and – in contrast to workers – they are able to pool risks. The liquidity constraints imposed on firms are the result of allocative optimization by banks. Granting no credits in the presence of insufficient collateral is not necessarily an indication of market failure, rather it may be an efficient answer to incentive and monitoring problems. One of the main advantages of capitalist economies is exactly the discipline imposed on firm's behavior in the presence of hard budget constraints. If workers would provide firms with cheap credit at below market conditions, this would effectively reintroduce a soft budget constraint, now at the expense of workers instead of the socialist state.

But this argument neglects basic insights from the modern theory of finance. As this theory shows, adverse selection problems can lead to inefficiently low investment funding. That is, even firms with attractive profit opportunities may have enormous difficulties in raising capital to finance the investment urgently needed. In the absence of sufficient collateral liquidity constraints threaten to close down firms (or prevent them from taking off) despite the chance of high expected future earnings.

3. Investment Wages under Incomplete Capital Markets

The following model shows that, in the presence of adverse selection problems on financial markets, granting credits by postponing wage payments can be in the interest both of the firm and the workers. If part of the wage payments are transferred in the future, the amount of internal funding can be enhanced. That is, in effect, workers relax the firm's liquidity constraint. Consequently, the risk of bankruptcy will be reduced, implying that the amount of aggregate restructuring investment will be increased.

3.1. The Model

The model extends the adverse selection model of Stiglitz/Weiss (1981) by allowing for inside information of workers about their own firm. In order to work out the implication in the most straightforward way, it is assumed that capital markets work perfectly except for the adverse selection problem due to firms' private information. Thus, it is assumed that banks pool the firms' risks and provide savers with a completely diversified portfolio which ignores firm specific risks. That is, there exists a market portofolio yielding a safe rate of return ρ. All agents (firms and workers) can invest in the safe alternative. Banks have to refinance themselves at this rate. Aggregate savings (A) are assumed to be an increasing function of ρ: $A(\rho)$ with $\delta A/\delta \rho > 0$. All agents are assumed to be risk-neutral. This allows to work out the specific aspects which are due to the problem of asymmetric information. Section 3.2. will comment on how the analysis has to be modified if risk-aversion is taken into account. Section 3.3. takes into account mobility costs arising from the threat of unemployment.

3.1.1. The Firms

There is a continuum of existing firms i. In each firm, one representative worker is employed. Firms can continue operation only if they incur a restructuring investment of K. All firms have initial resources (after paying first period wages y_1) $W < K$ and need additional finance. Restructuring is risky and firms differ in their risk. For firm i, restructuring is successful with probability p_i, yielding a return (net of wage payments) in the second period of x_i. In case of failure, the return net of wage payments is assumed to be fixed for all types of firms to x_0. $p_i \in [0,1]$ is distributed among all firms according to the density function $f(p_i)$ with cumulative $F(p_i)$. As in Stiglitz/Weiss (1981), it is assumed that outside investors are able to screen the firms with respect to their expected return, but not with respect to the specific risk involved in the restructuring process. For simplicity, all restructuring projects are assumed to have the same expected value:

$$p_i x_i + (1 - p_i) x_0 = \text{constant}. \tag{1}$$

The specific type of the firm (the success probability p_i) is private information of the insiders of the firm (the owner or the worker). Both the firm's owner and the worker are risk neutral. Those firms which do not get sufficient finance for carrying out the restructuring investment, have to close down.

3.1.2. The Workers

The first-period income of workers is y_1. Workers are assumed to be risk neutral with respect to second-period consumption. They maximize the utility U (c_1, $E(c_2)$). This could be motivated, within the expected utility framework, by the payoff function E U = u (c_1) + β E (c_2) with u' > 0, u'' < 0. More generally, E U should be seen as a special class of the stochastic intertemporal decision rules analyzed by Kreps/Porteus (1979). Throughout the paper, it will be assumed that savings s (ρ) = y_1 - c_1 are strictly positive, and increasing, but s (ρ) < B for all ρ ≤ ρ* with ρ* being defined below.

If the firm gets the funds needed to finance restructuring, the worker will stay employed within the firm in the second period. If the firm has to close down, the worker has to look for another job. At present, it is assumed that the worker can find a job immediately in period 2, earning a competitive wage income y_2. Section 3.3. discusses how the results have to be modified if the worker has to incur moving cost m before getting employed with another firm.

3.1.3. Contracts under Private Information

Under conditions of perfect information, all firms with positive expected net present value will get funding, independent of their initial wealth. With risk neutrality, the efficiency condition is:

$$p_i x_i + (1 - p_i) x_0 = (1 + \rho^*) K. \tag{2}$$

ρ* is the interest rate ensuring equilibrium between investment and savings in case all socially efficient projects are financed. Because all firms have the same expected return, all restructuring projects are socially efficient. Since there is no liquidity problem for any firm, investment wages – being equivalent to payments in cash – have no allocative role.

In reality, informational frictions restrict the set of feasible contracts relative to a world of perfect information. There are two main kinds of informational problems: First, the type of the firm is not known to outsiders. Second, it is costly to monitor the success of the firm: Without incurring monitoring costs, outsiders cannot observe whether restructuring has been successful or not (the owner can always claim that a failure occurred and walk away with the return). As is well known in finance theory (see Harris/Raviv (1992)), under such conditions standard debt with limited liability is the optimal contract for outside finance: These costs have to be incurred only in case of bankruptcy. By delegating the costs to financial institutions (banks), economies of scale in monitoring costs can be exploited. Under such conditions, all external finance will be provided by banks. Let $Z = \theta$ (K-W) be the amount of external finance if workers provide $S = (1-\theta)$ (K-W) of internal finance. When restructuring turns out to be successful, Z $(1-r_i)$ has to be paid to the bank, and the firm and worker get $x_i - (1+r_i) Z$. If restructuring fails, the firm goes bankrupt, and the bank gets a proportion σ x_0, with σ depending on the nature of the worker's contract.

If the bank were informed about the specific risk of each firm it could charge an interest rate such that the expected return of the debt contract, adjusted to the specific risk, is equal to the opportunity cost ρ. This firm specific interest rate is:

$$(1+r_i)p_i + \frac{\sigma}{\theta}\alpha(1-p_i) = 1+\rho. \tag{3}$$

with

$$\alpha = \frac{x_0}{K-W}. \tag{4}$$

as the gross return to K-W in case of bankruptcy. It is assumed that $\alpha < 1 + r_i$ for $\theta = \sigma = 1$. Banks, as outsiders, however, lack detailed information about the firms and have to charge an average interest rate r on their debt contract. This gives rise to an adverse selection problem: Since the debt contract calculates with an average rate r, it is unattractive exactly for those firms with low return, but high success probability. Due to the high repayment in case of success, low risk firms cannot afford to become indebted. A firm applies for debt only if the expected net return (after deducting interest payments to the bank) exceeds the opportunity cost ρ. That is, the following participation condition must hold:

$$p_i\, x_i \geq p_i\, (1+r)[K-W] + (1+\rho)W. \tag{5}$$

(1) and (4) imply that the constraint becomes more severe for firms with higher p_i. Thus, with a given interest rate r, all firms below a critical boundary $\hat{p}$ apply for credit, whereas the remaining firms will not get finance for restructuring investment (as shown in Stiglitz/Weiss (1981), the firms applying for credit, may also be credit rationed). For the marginal firm $\hat{p}$, the participation constraint (5) becomes binding.

If banks lend the amount $Z = \theta$ (K-W) to firms and receive the proportion σ in case of bankruptcy, the zero-profit constraint for banks is:

$$E\pi_B = (1+r)\int_0^{\bar{p}} p_i\, f(p_i)\,dp_i + \frac{\sigma}{\theta}a\int_0^{\bar{p}}(1-p_i)f(p_i)\,dp_i - (1+\rho) = 0. \tag{6}$$

If there is only bank finance [Z = K-W with θ = σ = 1], aggregate restructuring investment will be insufficient for the following reason: The zero-profit constraint (6) implies that, for the marginal project $\hat{p}$:

$$(1+r)\overline{p} + \frac{x_0}{K-W} > 1+\rho.$$ (7)

For the marginal project, the participation condition (5) becomes binding. Using (7), it follows that:

$$\overline{p}\,\overline{x} > (1+\rho)K - (1-\overline{p})x_0.$$ (8)

All projects having the same expected return, this shows that $\rho < \rho^*$. Aggregate investment is inefficiently low, crowding out low risk projects.

As long as workers do not have better information than banks, investment wages could not sustain an allocation different from the one obtained via bank financing – unless workers provide credit to their own firm at a subsidized rate. It is, however, quite likely that workers – as insiders of the firm – may have some inside information about their own firm. An extreme case would be that they have exactly the same knowledge as the owner of the firm. In that case, the firm's liquidity problem could be mitigated simply by workers putting their savings S into the firm as equity, thus raising equity to W + S. Workers could then participate in the return of the restructuring success. Obviously, an increase in equity base can reduce the underlying inefficiency. With equity increasing to W + S, the participation constraint (5) will be relaxed. For given ρ and r, an increase in equity raises $\hat{p}$. The increase in $\hat{p}$ raises the banks' profits for given ρ and r. Consequently, ρ and thus Z(ρ) rises. Thus, more restructuring investment will be financed – debt becoming more attractive for low risk firms.

Such an equity contract would, however, only be feasible if state contingent payments between the owner and the worker could be arranged. But as long as evidence on the success of the restructuring process can be manipulated by the owner of the firm, there is no reason to expect that workers would have a comparative advantage in monitoring relative to banks. After all, private information of the management about the state of the firm is one of the main reasons why labor contracts are distorted (compare Grossman/Hart (1983)). Therefore, in general, equity finance will not be an option in the presence of informational frictions, unless workers can become owners themselves (by some kind of management buyout), in this way internalizing informational externalities.

The main informational advantage of workers as insiders as opposed to banks is the knowledge about current features of the firm, in particular information about the quality and motivation of the workers themselves. For some firms, such knowledge may be obsolete after restructuring, but in general these aspects are of relevance for judging the firm's success probability. Especially in a situation where a local banking system is not yet developed, workers will have a finer partition of the information set concerning the probability distribution of the success than outside banks. In the following, it is assumed that the workers know their own firm's p_i, but they cannot observe the outcome of the restructuring process. In that case, workers can provide insider finance in the form of debt.

The contract may arrange priority claims for workers on the firm's assets in case of bankruptcy, as opposed to the banks' claim. In that case, $\theta > \sigma$. Since such an arrangement affects the banks' profits (6) adversely, it will result in an increase of the bank rate r. If the worker gets a claim $(1-\sigma)x_0$ in case of bankruptcy, the interest rate r_i which compensates the worker for the firm specific risk is:

$$(1+r_i)p_i + \frac{1-\sigma}{1-\theta}\alpha(1-p_i) = 1+\rho. \tag{9}$$

For high-risk firms, this rate exceeds the bank rate $r_i > r$. For those firms, in principle bank finance would be cheaper than financing via investment wages. But if those firms would not accept investment wages, banks could identify them as high-risk firms, charging them a high rate as well. In order to avoid being identified as high risk firms, they have to accept investment wages at the firm specific interest rate.

If investment wages are designed in the form of debt contracts with the firm specific rate of return (9), they can mitigate the adverse selection problem in a way similar to equity. The participation constraint for the owner of the firm is modified to:

$$p_i x_i \geq p_i (1+r)[K-W-S] + p_i (1+r_i)S + (1+\rho)W. \tag{10}$$

Using (9), this reduces to:

$$p_i x_i + (1-\sigma)x_0(1-p_i) \geq p_i (1+r)[K-W-S] + (1+\rho)(W+S). \tag{11}$$

As long as investment wages have no prior claim to the return in case of bankruptcy (that is, if $\theta = \sigma = 1$), investment wages will increase aggregate investment: With the participation constraint relaxed, $\hat{p}$ rises, increasing the bank's profits for given ρ and r. Again, ρ and $Z(\rho)$ rises. This positive effect of investment wages is weakened if workers have a priority claim in case of bankruptcy, that is if $\theta > \sigma$. Then, the zero-profit constraint (6) is negatively affected by investment wages, raising r. Under such conditions $\hat{p}$ does not necessarily increase.

As shown, a debt contract provided by workers of the own firm, can result in a more efficient allocation. Of course, this mechanism works only in case investment wages are invested in the specific firm where the worker is employed. If, in contrast, investment wages were pooled in a fund across firms, exactly the same problems of adverse selection would arise as with private banks. In that case, the funds would be nothing else but financial intermediaries subject to the same problems of asymmetric information. The specific advantage of investment wages

– the relaxation of constraints caused by asymmetric information – requires a firm-specific relationship.

3.2. Risk Aversion

The last section analyzed the case of risk neutral workers. One of the main arguments against investment wages is, however, that they burden risk-averse workers at the same time with both employment and capital risk. This critique has been formulated most clearly by Meade (1986, p. 28): "...on the principle of spreading risk such schemes should not be carried too far since they involve workers in committing any capital which is accumulated in this way to the same basket as their labor eggs."

Again, this argument has to be interpreted with caution as long as the frictions giving an economic role for investment wages are not modeled explicitly. As this section shows, if capital market imperfections impose liquidity constraints on the firms, and workers have inside information, relaxing constraints will be Pareto-improving even when workers are risk averse.

Of course, if well functioning capital markets exist, it makes no difference whether workers are paid in cash or whether they are paid by issuing risky claims with equal expected present value. Under such conditions, the specific arrangement of payments would be completely irrelevant. Whatever the actual arrangement, workers will be indifferent among all options as long as the claims are priced according to the market value of the risk involved. If workers prefer a different proportion of risky assets in their own portfolio or if they prefer consumption instead of savings, they could sell their claims on the capital market, thus rearranging their portfolio according to the preferred choice. By selling her claims, the worker herself can pool the risks according to individual taste.

Obviously, investment wages need to be discussed in the context of an imperfect capital market giving rise to liquidity constraints. As in section 3.2, liquidity constraints are assumed to arise from informational asymmetries. Again, workers of low risk firms with inside information can provide finance to their own firm at a rate below the market rate r. Of course, a risk averse worker would prefer to invest in a safe asset with equal expected return, since this would not force her to take a risk which cannot be diversified away (investment wage being not tradable assets). Thus, she needs to be compensated for investing in the own firm i by a risk premium γ_i. If the risky investment in the own firm yields the return $r_i + \gamma_i$, the worker's expected second period consumption (with the share $(1-\tau_i)$ of savings invested in the own firm) is:

$$E(c_2) = y_2 + \tau_i S(1+\rho) + (1-\tau_i) S p_i (1 + r_i \gamma_i) + (1-p_i)(1-\sigma)\alpha. \tag{12}$$

The worker chooses her optimal portfolio-mix according to her risk preferences. If risk aversion is not infinite, $\tau_i < 1$, provided $\gamma_i > 0$. Firms are willing to pay a risk premium, as long as the return does not exceed the market rate, that is if $r_i + \gamma_i < r$. Since the liquidity constrained firms are exactly those firms with low risk r_i (high p_i), they are the firms which can afford to pay the highest risk premium, having at the same time the lowest risk. Consequently, since τ_i is decreasing in p_i workers in low risk firms will invest the highest share in the form of investment wages.

In this simple set up, the workers' share of investment wages would be a perfect signal of the riskiness of the firm thus allowing perfect screening by banks in the absence of exogenous noise. In a separating equilibrium, the bank could infer the firm's specific risk and charge the adequate interest rate. Under such conditions, a first-best allocation could be obtained. This result, however, is rather special. In general, the participation rate of workers will serve only as an imperfect signal for the firm's risk – this will be true in particular when investment wages are arranged for other reasons as well rather than only because of inside information (such as discussed in next section). Then, banks have to offer a contract pooling different types of risks. In that case, workers of the low-risk firms can relax their firms' liquidity constraint by putting part of their savings in investment wages.

3.3. Moving Costs

The last sections have shown that investment wages can overcome temporary liquidity problems, provided workers have inside information. This result was derived in an economy with a perfectly competitive labor market, thus showing that investment wages may be attractive even if the threat of unemployment has no impact on the worker's choice. If the closure of a firm imposes high mobility costs for the workers, investment wages will become even more attractive, provided they can transform unemployment risk into capital risk. This aspect is still relevant in Eastern Europe, where workers have hardly a chance to find a new job immediately, when a firm has to close down; in addition, unemployment benefits are extremely low. Since the bankruptcy risk of the firm is directly related to the risk of unemployment for the worker, mitigating the firm's liquidity constraint will, at the same time, reduce the worker's risk of being fired.

Under such conditions, investment wages can transform immediate risk of unemployment into future capital risk. Even though, in the future, the capital risk is strongly correlated with the risk of being fired (when profits turn out to be lower than expected, layoffs are likely to occur), taking such a risk will improve individual welfare, given that the alternative is immediate bankruptcy and unemployment. In view of this alternative, to be forced to save at a rate below the market rate will be a preferred choice, because otherwise, the firm would have to close down anyway.

The model of section 3.1. illustrates this in a straightforward way. As was shown, investment wages based on inside information modify the firm's participation constraint to equation (10), thus reducing the number of closures. Those firms closing down could survive only if they get credit at a rate below the market rate. Obviously, in the absence of mobility costs, it would make no sense for workers in those firms to arrange investment wages. Under the threat of unemployment, however, these workers have an incentive to provide loans if that prevents closure, even if the expected return of the loan is below the market rate. Thus, mobility costs provide an additional motive to agree upon investment wages exactly for workers employed in marginal firms, those facing the immediate threat of the closure. To model mobility costs, it is assumed that workers have to incur costs m in the second period before finding a new job. If firms would have to close down, the workers would get a utility level $U(y_1 - S_u, y_2 - m + (1+\rho)S_u)$. Providing loans at a subsidized rate $r_i^s < r_i$ relaxes the firm's participation constraint, thus preventing closure:

$$p_i x_i \geq p_i (1+r)[K - W - S] + p_i (1 + r_i^s)S + (1+\rho)W. \tag{13}$$

The minimum rate at which workers would be willing to provide credit under the threat of unemployment is defined by the following equation:

$$U\left(y_1 - S, y_2 + \left[(1 + r_i^{min})p_i + \frac{1-\sigma}{1-\theta}a(1-p_i)\right]S\right) = U(y_1 - S_u, y_2 - m + (1+\rho)S_u). \tag{14}$$

Evidently, r_i^{min} is decreasing in mobility costs m. Workers are willing to grant credit to their own firm at a return below the market rate, exactly for the same reason why banks extend credit to those firms in which they have stakes already. After a bad shock, it is optimal to concede further loans, in order to recover part of their investments in the future, even though credit by new banks – not yet involved – would not be granted. For obvious reasons, banks had hardly any stakes in Eastern European firms from the past. Workers, however, would lose in the case of bankruptcy – they would need to incur the costs m of mobility and unemployment and thus lose stakes in the present firm. Transforming immediate employment risk into future capital risk via investment wages can help to reduce the loss of rents. In contrast to a wage cut (strengthening the firms equity base), investment wages allow the worker to participate in future profits, thus offering the chance to recapture part of the rent with some probability.

If the risk of immediate bankruptcy and unemployment is transformed into future capital risk, both the worker and the firm will gain. Since such a scheme has to be arranged on a firm specific level, it makes no sense to have general agreements between the union and the employers to introduce investment schemes for the whole industry. Rather, this calls for escape clauses specifying that the contractual wage may be transformed into investment wages in case an agreement between workers and the firm comes about (that is, for marginal firms). In effect, such an agreement would introduce more flexibility in the labor market.

The worker's bargaining position, however, is rather weak under the threat of unemployment. This fact may explain the ongoing strong aversion of German unions against investment wages. Escape clauses can certainly eliminate ex post inefficiencies, once unemployment risk has materialized. But ex ante, such clauses may give rise to the problem of dynamic consistency. In principle, both firms and unions may gain from the union's reputation not to accept escape clauses – for the same reason why both creditors and debtors will be better off, provided the bank is able to commit not to renegotiate in case the firm runs into liquidity problems.

The rejection of escape clauses by unions may be interpreted as an attempt to make a binding commitment not to renegotiate, trying to get around problems of dynamic inconsistency. Thus, in Western economies, such a policy may be sensible. But in the special case of Eastern Germany, or, more generally, Eastern Europe, things were quite different. There, the need for restructuring investment had nothing to do with firm specific liquidity shocks; rather it was the consequence of an economy wide negative shock, resulting in high mobility costs and a low shadow wage for the whole economy. Under these conditions, a reduction in inefficient bankruptcies and layoffs has a high social value.

4. Investment Wages in East Germany

In East Germany in the first years after unification, investment wage schemes had been introduced in several small firms. In nearly all of those firms, capital was provided as direct investment by workers, mostly in the form of minority participation (out of 880 firms established by management buyouts, about 200 introduced such schemes – compare AGP (1992)). As shown in part 3, such schemes were attractive for those firms which suffered from liquidity constraints, but would have been profitable otherwise. Most firms in Eastern Germany, however, were facing problems of liquidity constraints and too high wages at the same time.

One example is the *Motorradwerk Zschopau* (a motorcycle factory in Saxony). In that firm, workers credited part of their net wages to the firm during the first half of 1992 in order to save their own jobs and avoid liquidation. Workers credited 10 percent, managers 15 percent of the net wage exceeding a minimum of DM 1,100 per month. The amount credited has been put on a separate account (which would be paid back to the workers in case of bankruptcy). A council, composed of management and workers, was founded surveying the state of the firm. The plan was to decide in the beginning of July 1992, depending on the firm's state, whether the whole sum saved (about DM 750,000) or only the interest rate earned should be invested in the firm or whether the money should be paid back to the workers. Layed-off workers would get their investment back anyway (whereas in July 1992 about 1200 workers were employed, a reduction of employment by 600 was planned till the end of 1992). This agreement, initiated by the firm's workers council (*Betriebsrat*), had the approval of the IG Metall (the German labor union), even though, in general, there was strong opposition against such schemes from the union.

In public, the agreement in Zschopau was seen as a first step to lower wages in East Germany. But if too high wages rather than liquidity constraints were the cause of the problem, it was evident that investment wages cannot be a cure to reduce the wage bill. In that case, future expected profits would have been negative even when discounted at the lower rate appropriate for insiders. Then, giving credit meant just a postponement of final liquidation. Indeed, despite the fact that the publicity caused by the scheme increased the interest of potential buyers, the investment scheme was cancelled and the *Motorradwerk Zschopau* was privatized with just 200 employees left.

Even though investment wages by themselves are of no help with too high wages, a combination of government subsidies and investment wages could be an attractive option in such circumstances. If a wage cut is not feasible, combining subsidies with a switch to investment wages are a way both to introduce more flexibility in the labor market and, at the same time, to save the rents in a long-term perspective which Eastern workers tried to capture by demanding high wages.

This policy could easily have been realized in East Germany: the Treuhandanstalt has been auctioning off its firms at a lower price under the condition that job guarantees will be given for the next years. Effectively, this is a policy of wage subsidies. In view of the results derived above, the following policy would have been superior: The firms should have been auctioned off at a lower price, yet not under the condition that jobs will be guaranteed, but rather that an agreement on a reduction in *contractual wages* will be reached for the next few years. The subsidy (the reduction in the auction price of the firm) should have been linked to the present value of wage reductions. In return, workers would get a share in the firm equal to that amount.

Such a scheme has several attractive features: By paying the subsidy at the time of privatization, no commitment problem arises with respect to a fading out of subsidies in the future. The subsidy will be paid to the worker, not to the firm, but in a lump-sum fashion, thus avoiding distortions in relative prices. By reducing the wages (not the expected wage bill), it introduces much needed flexibility in the labor market. By introducing investment wages, it improves upon the long run flexibility of the economy (and, by the way, the long run distribution of wealth). By giving workers claims on future profits, it improves upon the incentive structure within the firm. A related scheme has been suggested by Sinn/Sinn (1991). They proposed – among other elements – to introduce investment funds giving asset claims to the whole East German population. The advantage of the scheme presented here is that it is much easier to adopt on a firm by firm base: Since the expected wage bill is not reduced, workers may be more willing to accept it. Furthermore, by giving participation rights to the workers, the scheme makes full use of the informational advantages within a specific firm.

References

AGP (Arbeitsgemeinschaft zur Förderung der Partnerschaft in der Wirtschaft) (1992), *Mitarbeiterbeteiligung im Freistaat Sachsen – 15 Praxisbeispiele*, Kassel.

Demougin, D./Sinn, H.W. (1994), Privatization, Risk Taking and the Communist Firm, *Journal of Public Economics 55(2)*, 203-231.

Fink, U. (1992), Aufschwung durch Arbeitnehmer-Kapital, *Die Zeit*, No.20, 8.5.1992.

Grossman, S./Hart, O. (1983), Implicit Contracts under Asymmetric Information, *Quarterly Journal of Economics* 98, Supplement, 123-156.

Harris, M./Raviv, A. (1992), Financial Contracting Theory, in: Laffont, J.J. (ed.), *Advances in Economic Theory: 6th World Congress*, Vol. 2, Cambridge.

Kreps, D./Porteus, E. (1979), Dynamic Choice Theory and Dynamic Programming, *Econometrica* 54, 91-100.

Meade, J. (1986), *Different Forms of Share Economy*, London.

Pohjola, M. (1987), Profit Sharing, Collective Bargaining and Employment, *Journal of Institutional and Theoretical Economics* 143, 334-342.

Sievert, O. (1992), *Für Investivlöhne. Plädoyer für ein vernachlässigtes Konzept*, Frankfurt.

Sievert, O./Tomann, H. (1977), Allocational Aspects of Profit Sharing, *Zeitschrift für die gesamte Staatswissenschaft*, Special Issue, 19-42.

Sinn, G./Sinn, H.-W. (1991), *Kaltstart*, Tübingen.

Snower, D. J. (2000), Revenue-Sharing Subsidies as Employment Policy: Reducing the Cost of Stimulating East German Employment, in: Riphahn, R.T./Snower, D. J./Zimmermann, K. F. (2000), *Employment Policy in Transition: The Lessons of German Integration for the Labor Market*, Heidelberg, 172-191.

Stiglitz J./Weiss, A. (1981), Credit Rationing in Markets with Imperfect Information, *American Economic Review* 71, 393-411.

Weitzman, M. (1984), *The Share Economy*, Cambridge, Massachussetts.

5. Public Sector Sponsored Continuous Vocational Training in East Gemany: Institutional Arrangements, Participants, and Results of Empirical Evaluations

Martin Eichler, University of Mannheim

Michael Lechner, University of St. Gallen and IZA, Bonn

1. Introduction

After unification of the East and West German economies in July 1990 the public sector conducted an active labor market policy to ease the transition from the formerly centrally planned East German economy to a West German type of system. The basic intention was to adjust the skills of the labor force of former East Germany to the demands of the future structure of the economy as well as to western technologies. Additionally, substantial resources were devoted to smooth the impact of the rapidly contracting economy on the labor markets, in order to avoid even higher unemployment than actually occurred.

In this paper we concentrate on the training-related aspects of active labor market policy. The paper contributes to the ongoing discussion about the effectiveness of training in two ways: One part gives an (almost) complete and hopefully accessible account of the institutional rules and regulations effective between 1990 and 1994. This is supplemented by descriptive statistics to show major trends and empirical facts in the first years after unification. Since the situation in East Germany was fairly different from that of almost any other country, knowing these facts – which changed rapidly over time – is very important before any credible evaluation of the labor market policies can be performed. Such evaluations are reported in the second part of the paper. They are based on data on individual labor market histories before and after training on a monthly and yearly basis, respectively. The evaluations look at the effects of subsidized training courses for the participants. These effects are measured in terms of labor market outcomes after the completion of training, such as earnings, employment status, and career prospects. Our general conclusion will be that at least for training beginning between mid 1990 and early 1993 no positive effects can be found. However, there is some evidence that trainees expect positive returns over a longer time horizon that is beyond the sampling period used in this paper.

The paper is organized as follows: The next section outlines basic features of the East German labor market in the first years after unification. Furthermore, it describes briefly the organisational structure of the labor offices (*Bundesanstalt für Arbeit*) in East Germany. Section 3 describes empirical facts and institutional rules and regulations for the active labor market policy in East Germany as far as they relate to training. The econometric evaluations are reported in Section 4. Section 5 concludes.

2. The Institutional Framework

2.1. The East German Labor Market and Labor Market Policy

The centrally planned economy of the GDR was not prepared for unification in 1990. The institutional settings of the West German market economy, the relative prices, and the international competition came as a shock. The GDP per capita, already far below that of West Germany, dropped sharply after the Economic, Monetary, and Social Unification in July 1990:[1] In 1991 it was about a quarter of that in West Germany. From 1991 to 1994 GDP rose with an annual rate of 6-8 percent and GDP per capita reached approximately 50 percent of the West German level in 1994. At the same time labor productivity increased from 31 percent to 51 percent of the West German level. However, this was offset by the development of wages rising from 48 percent of the West German level in 1991 to 73 percent in 1994, which led to economic disequilibria, especially on the labor market. We will provide some information on the resulting movements in the labor market as well as on adapted active labor market policies (ALMPs).[2] The East German active labor force dropped from 9.7 million in 1989 to 5.6 million in

---

[1] The GDP figures given in this section are taken from Statistisches Bundesamt (1992, 1995), the data on productivity and wages from Bundesministerium für Wirtschaft (1995).

[2] The most important types are training, short time work (STW), "*Arbeitsbeschaffungsmaßnahmen*" (ABM), i.e. make-work-measures, and early retirement. STW benefits are payed by the labor office (LO) to workers who have to reduce working hours temporarily because of a company-specific shortage of labor demand. The LO replaces the loss of earnings at the same rate as in the case of unemployment. An exception frequently used in East Germany allows a non-temporary reduction to 'zero percent working time' under certain circumstances. In the case of ABM the LO offers a wage subsidy to the employer. There are several regulations in the AFG allowing such a subsidy, for example §§91-99 or §249h. Early retirement are "*Altersübergangsgeld*" and "*Vorruhestand*". All paragraphs (§) mentioned refer to the AFG if not otherwise stated.

1992 and rose again slightly to 5.8 million by 1994.[3] The remaining individuals were either depended on active labor market policy (ALMP) measures, were unemployed, or left the labor force.[4] In the first years after unification, the majority of people who lost employment were absorbed by ALMP. In 1993 and 1994 the shares of individuals who went into ALMP, unemployment, or left the labor force were roughly equal.[5]

Figure 1 illustrates the importance of labor market policies in East Germany in the first years after unification. In 1992 more than 30 percent of all people working in 1989 were subsidized in one way or another by the labor offices (LOs). Although this share declined, still more than 20 percent were subsidized in 1994.

Another way of measuring the importance of the ALMP in East Germany is to look at the total expenditures of the *Bundesanstalt für Arbeit* (BA).[6] In 1994 the overall budget of the BA was about DM 100 billion. A quarter of this amount was spent on ALMP in East Germany, DM 7 million for training alone. The corresponding numbers for West Germany, with a labor force nearly five times as large, are DM 10 billion for ALMP and DM 6 billion for training. In 1992, the year with the most training, the BA spent nearly DM 11 billion of its DM 89 billion budget on training in East Germany and another DM 7 billion in West Germany. Thus in 1992 the BA spent close to 5 percent of the East German GDP on training in East Germany. For all of Germany the number was just above 0.5 percent of GDP. In 1994 the expenditures on ALMP in East Germany were 7.5 percent of the East German GDP or 0.75 percent of the total German GDP. The huge number of participants, the enormous influence on the labor market, and the high expenditures demonstrate the importance of ALMP and particularly of training in East Germany in the first years after unification.

---

[3] These are individuals working without any involvement of the LO. The figures might differ from data given in other publications because often workers in a subsidized employment are included.

[4] These are macro data. Nothing is said about the individual patterns here. Seen on an individual base, 'leaving the labor force' covers regular retirement, child-bearing, net migration, and entering or leaving the labor force for other reasons. All numbers reported are 'net leavers of the East German labor force'.

[5] The corresponding figures are: 1.9 million in ALMP, 0.9 million unemployed, and 0.8 million leavers of the labor force in 1991. In 1994 these are 1.3 million, 1.1 million, and 1.4 million, respectively.

[6] For the following see BA (1995b, p. 315 Table 207).

Figure 1: Development of the East German Labor Market in the first years after Unification (in percent of 1989 labor force)

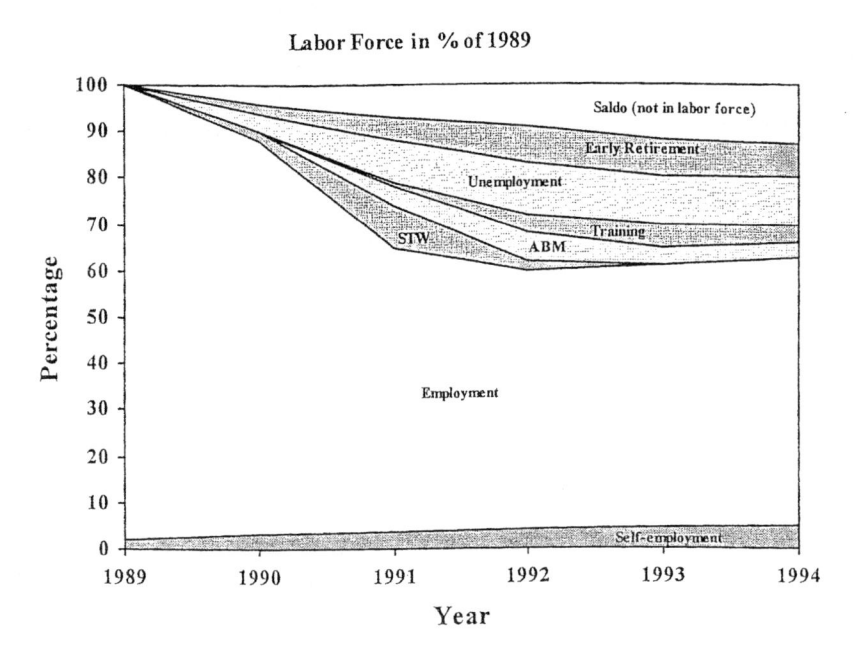

Labor Force in % of 1989

Note: 100 percent equals to 9.7 million people in the active labor force in 1989. 'Employment' is corrected for ABM and STW to avoid double counting. 'Saldo' represents net leavers of the labor force. All labor market policies and unemployment are assumed to be zero in 1989. All numbers are average participation throughout the year and full time equivalents if the LOs subsidize only a part of the (working) time, e.g. STW. Other ALMPs are excluded because of low participation. See footnote 2 for further information.

Source: IAB (1995, Table 7.2 C pp.248, Table 2.4.1 pp.42), own calculations.

2.2. "Arbeitsförderungsgesetz" (AFG) and "Bundesanstalt für Arbeit" (BA)

The legal basis for governmental labor market activities in Germany is the *Arbeitsförderungsgesetz* (AFG) from 1969. The AFG was changed frequently since 1969. In this paper we will discuss only the training part of the AFG.[7] The GDR developed an AFG as soon as spring of 1990 and put it in effect with the Economic, Monetary, and Social Union on 1 July 1990.[8] Its structure was identical to the West German AFG and the regulations were in most cases similar. The only difference, if at all, was the easier access to programs in East Germany. After unification in October 1990 the West German AFG was expanded to cover East Germany as well. Nevertheless, some of the differences in the AFG-GDR were upheld. By December 1991 most of the remaining AFG-GDR regulations were obsolete and the exceptions were either cancelled or included into the AFG.

Below the level of the AFG there were more detailed regulations, which were not passed by parliament but by the Ministry of Labor and Social Affairs or by the top level (*Verwaltungsrat*) of the BA. Most important for training is the "*Anordnung Fortbildung und Umschulung*" (AO-FuU) of the BA. This was changed corresponding to changes in the AFG and completely rewritten in 1993. There was a similar AO-FuU in the GDR, valid for East Germany until 1 May 1991.

The implementation of the AFG is administrated by an independent federal agency located in Nürnberg, the "*Bundesanstalt für Arbeit*" (BA). It is hierarchically structured into "*Landesarbeitsämter*" (labor head offices in the German *Länder*), "*Arbeitsämter*" (labor offices) and "*Außenstellen*" (local offices). In East Germany there are four *Landesarbeitsämter*, which took the responsibility from the central labor agency of the GDR between spring and fall 1991. They are regionally separated along the lines of the *Bundesländer* but in general responsible for more than one Bundesland. Two of them are 'exclusively' East German (Sachsen, Sachsen-Anhalt – Thüringen), in two cases they combine East and West German Länder (Berlin – Brandenburg, North). In the labor offices special councellors ("*Arbeitsberater*" or "*Arbeitsvermittler*") offer advice and may approve of individual-specific policy measures such as training programs.

3. AFG-Subsidized Training in East Germany

The aim of this section is to provide the necessary information on participation in AFG-subsidized training in the first years after unification. We will describe the

---

[7] Other parts are not covered, although they were to some extent important for training as well. For example the determination of former earnings which in turn determines the amount paid during training was regulated with unemployment benefits. We focus on the training participation decision which allows the limitation.

[8] To separate the two AFGs we will call this AFG-GDR while we use AFG for that of West Germany. Also we will use GDR for the time before unification, East Germany for the same territory after unification.

training possibilities and the incentive system offered by the AFG.⁹ We will also present some statistics on participation. We focus on training of individuals, which have been subsidized by the AFG: short term training to improve job search skills (also called '§41a'), continuous training in an occupation the participant is already trained in ('continuous training'), and training for a new occupation ('retraining').¹⁰

Several studies discuss ALMPs and training in particular. For example the BA (1991a, 1992a, 1993a, 1994a, and 1995a) provides extensive statistics on training participation in the first years after unification as well as a short discussion of regulatory changes. Buttler (1994a) supplies information on the financial aspects of ALMP, while Buttler (1994b) concentrates more on political aspects. Buttler/ Emmerich (1994) discuss the optimal amount and mix of ALMP instruments. Here, we combine the information in these papers with regulations in the AFG and other judicial sources, different kinds of participation statistics, information on political and financial constraints, and results of interviews in East German labor offices.¹¹

3.1. Training in General

3.1.1. Participation in AFG-Subsidized Training

Training is important to avoid or to overcome mismatch in the labor market. Thereby it should increase productivity and improve the economy's growth potential. When transforming East Germany into a market economy training was

---

⁹ In the main body of the text we will limit the discussion to the basic features. For more details see the Appendix. We used BA (1989, 1990, 1991b, 1992b, 1993b, 1994b, and 1995c) as sources for judicial texts.

¹⁰ A more detailed discussion of the training types will follow below. Some statistics include the *Einarbeitungszuschuß*, a wage subsidy paid if a new employee needed an unusually long time of introduction to a new workplace. We will not discuss it in further detail because this kind of on-the-job-training went along with an existing labor contract and was intended for a special workplace. It was quite different from the off-the-job-training we focus on here. Furthermore, we do not discuss the German apprenticeship system.

¹¹ We conducted these interviews in March 1996. They were partly questionnaire-led, partly free conversation interviews held in Berlin and Brandenburg. The aim was to get an idea of the daily handling of regulations and to get additional information on the participation process in AFG-subsidized training. However, because only three interviews on daily work with *Arbeitsberatern* and one on the general developments in the *Landesarbeitsamt* were held and because of the regional limitation these are not representative results.

thought to be especially important (BA (1991a, p.18)). An individual might gain from training, but has to bear costs as well. These costs are the hardship of study, direct monetary costs like course fees, and indirect costs like loss of income and/or leisure.

The German government considered training useful and tried to enhance it in co-operation with the BA. In the first years after unification they especially strengthened the incentives for training in East Germany. Apart from increasing human capital this was used to directly lower unemployment rates and to avoid social hardship (for example BA (1992a, p.19), Buttler/Emmerich (1994, p.64)).

The labor offices (LOs) attracted individuals to participate in training by paying an *Unterhaltsgeld* (UHG), money for one's livelihood, to replace the loss of earnings. This was slightly higher than unemployment benefits until December 1993. The LO could bear the direct costs as well. Furthermore, the LO enhanced training participation by changing the duration of benefits. The period of UHG payments was not part of the limited time during which unemployment benefits were paid. In some circumstances the duration of unemployment benefits even increased when participating in training. If someone refused to take part in training proposed by the LO, the LO could suspend the payment unemployment benefits.

These incentives for participating in training were available only if three requirements were met. First, the training had to be 'necessary'. This means it had to be necessary to bring an unemployed person back to work, to offer a qualification to someone without a completed vocational qualification, or to avoid unemployment of someone directly threatened by it. An exception was made in East Germany in that a general threat of unemployment was sufficient. Our interviews indicated different interpretations of this rule. The answers reached from 'the date of firing has to be known' to 'in East Germany everybody was threatened'. To get UHG as a subsidy, training had to be 'necessary'. If training was not 'necessary' it could still be 'useful' to reach the general goals of labor market policy e.g. to 'offer appropriate employment to everybody' and to 'avoid labor shortages'. In this case UHG was paid as a loan. Since January 1994 this was no longer possible.

Second, only people who had already contributed to the unemployment insurance (UI) for at least two years were eligible for assistance.[12] Someone receiving unemployment benefits based on less than two years of contributions gets the so-called 'small UHG' (see below). In East Germany actual contributions were not required. It was sufficient to had worked in a job before unification that would had made UI mandatory in the West German system. If non of these

---

[12] Normally, the period of contribution must have been within the last three years but there are several exceptions. Most importantly, unemployment benefits based on two or more years of contributions are sufficient.

conditions were met but if the training was 'necessary' and the participant signed a contract requiring him to work for three years after training, the LO still covered the direct costs of training.

Third, benefits were restricted to individuals with a completed vocational qualification. This means that they were either required to have a publicly approved examination of the East or West German apprenticeship system and had worked for three years, or they needed six years of work experience. After participating in training another three years of working were required before training could have been subsidized again. For 'necessary' training these requirements were reduced considerably.[13]

A special case not covered by the regulations described above was training during short time work (STW). When STW was used to avoid mass layoffs because of structural change, the employer should have provided training for workers in STW.[14] Between 1990 and 1992 STW was a very important part of ALMP in East Germany, especially the 'zero percent' STW, meaning that people were still employed but not working at all. This kind of STW was not due to a temporary shortage of labor demand, but was just disguised unemployment.

Although no offical statistics were available the interviews at East German LOs indicated that in most cases this training took place and in a majority of cases independent training institutions provided it. Training during STW appeared to be similar to other training subsidized by the LO. The AFG put the burden of providing training on the employer. Nevertheless, the interviews showed that the LOs took part in the decision on the type of training provided. In this way the LOs could impose some restrictions on the provider and the type of training. There seemed to be no further formal limitations on participation. The LO was involved in this type of training in another way as well: To attract short time workers to participate in training the LO increased STW benefits to the level of UHG during full time training, which was higher until December 1993. Furthermore, the LO could cover the direct costs of training.

Now we will turn to some statistics on training participation.[15] There was already some training sponsored by the AFG-GDR before unification. After

---

[13] For both waiting times the most important exceptions were that the time of work experience is shortened by three years for 'necessary' training and that unemployment was considered as working in most cases. Since January 1993 a one year waiting time was mandatory before entering training again even if 'necessary'.

[14] See §63(5) AFG-GDR in effect until December 1991. Since January 1992 this was possible for all of Germany according to §63(4) AFG.

[15] It has to be stressed that all data presented is on training subsidized according to the training section of the AFG. If not otherwise stated the *Einarbeitungszuschuß* is not included. Training during STW is only included if the training is subsidized in some way or another by the AFG training section. If not otherwise stated all numbers are

unification training steadily increased until it reached its peak in 1991/1992. Thereafter numbers have fallen considerably but they are still far above the level of 1990.

Let's consider these developments in more detail. Table 1 provides an overview of the data. The numbers in the upper part include only individuals receiving subsidies based on the training section of the AFG. For the last four months of 1990 the BA reports about 94,000 entries.[16] New participation in training rose sharply up to nearly 760,000 in 1991. Monthly data indicates that this was not a sudden jump but rose from 38,000 persons starting in January to 81,000 in June, stabilizing around this level for the rest of the year.[17] The much lower average of 280,000 participants partly reflects this time pattern.[18] The second fact leading to the low average participation is a high share of courses with a short duration (see section 3.1.2. below). An opposite movement is found in 1992. 774,000 entries split into high and stable numbers in the first half of the year before they started falling in the second half.[19] High numbers of entries in late 1991 and early 1992 as well as an increasing average course duration in 1992 explain the much higher average of training participants of about 490,000.[20] The contracting development in the second half of 1992 intensified in 1993 with lower entry rates.

Due to financial restrictions and institutional changes, especially the cancellation of §41a entries dropped by about one third to 263,000. The average number of individuals in training fell less dramatically to 380,000. This, as well as the high number of more than 400,000 people finishing training, again illustrates the time lag. On average the trend towards longer course duration continued as well, partly driven by deleting §41a. The situation stabilized finally in 1994 when the number of individuals entering training matched the number of those leaving training. The number of 256,000 individuals participating in training on average indicates a high average course duration.

---

entries into training. All data is taken from BA (1991a, 1992a, 1993a, 1994a, and 1995a). See tables for precise sources.

[16] Training subsidized according to the AFG-GDR before unification was continued after unification and paid for by the BA. But 80 percent of all training in 1990 started between September and December, i.e. after unification (BA (1991a, p.19)).

[17] See BA (1992a, p.20 Table B).

[18] Estimated and including the *Einarbeitungszuschuß*. Training numbers must be lower.

[19] See BA (1993a, p.13).

[20] Estimated and including the *Einarbeitungszuschuß*. Training numbers must be lower.

Table 1. Participation in AFG-Subsidized Training (in thousands)

		1990 Sept-Oct	1991 year	1992 year	1993 year	1994 year
Total training	Entries	94	760	774	263	268
	Leavers	n.a.	n.a.	473	407	312
	Average Participation	n.a.	280^a	491^a	376	256
In STW^b	Average Participation	n.a.	1,616	370	181	97
	Full time equivalents	341	898	194	85	46

Notes: (a) Estimated and including *Einarbeitungszuschuß*. (b) The numbers represent persons in STW. It is not known how many of these participate in some kind of training.

Source: BA (1995a, Table 17O p.50, Table 27 p.72, Table B p.16), BA (1991a, Table 35 p.52), IAB (1995, Table 165 p.270), BA (1995b, Table 7.2 p.248).

In the lower part of Table 1 we report data on STW. These do not refer to training during STW but to participation in STW. The first row represents average participants and the second their full time equivalents. These figures indicate the training potential during STW.

3.1.2. Characteristics of Courses

We now turn to some course characteristics. Table 2 presents some statistics. With the exception of 1990 there was a tendency towards longer courses until 1993. One reason for this tendency was that the share of courses of one to three months duration was driven by §41a-training. The sharp drop of short courses from 34 percent in 1992 to 15 percent in 1993 was due to cancelling §41a in 1993.[21] It demonstrates that this cancellation made a difference in the training structure, although this type of courses could have been offered similarly to 'normal' continuous training. The rising share of courses with durations beyond one year (until 1993) was due to the rising share of retraining. In 1994 that share as well as the share of long courses fell again.

Training courses not only had different duration but different intensities as well. The second part of Table 2 provides information on full time, part time, and at home training. At home training was nearly non existent in East Germany. Part time training with a maximum share of 15 percent in 1993 was not very important

---

[21] See section 3.2. for a detailed discussion of the types of training courses and participation statistics.

either. In West Germany full time training accounted never for more than 80 percent between 1990 and 1993. The concentration on full time training in East Germany was due to the higher share of unemployed persons in training. At the same time unemployment was the reason for the high share of 'necessary' training in East Germany. When 'useful' training was not subsidized anymore in 1994, the share of 'necessary' and of full time training rose in East and West Germany, confirming the above relationship.

Table 2: Characteristics of Training Courses (in percent of all entries)

		1990 Sep-Oct	1991 year	1992 year	1993 year	1994 year
Course[a] duration in months	1 to 3	40.7	43.7	33.9	15.0	16.0
	4 to 6	18.7	18.5	19.5	19.7	17.1
	7 to 12	23.2	20	20.2	26.4	37.0
	13 to 24	16.2	15.8	22.0	33.0	27.5
	More	1.2	1.9	4.4	5.9	2.5
Course[a] is	Full time	n.a.	n.a.	91.6	85.0	97.1
	Part time	n.a.	n.a.	8.2	14.7	2.9
	Home training	n.a.	n.a.	0.2	0.3	0.1
Training provider	Independent	52.9	39.9	55.6	75.0	89.2
	Organized by BA	42.4	45.2	31.7	14.5	4.1
	Firm (*Einarbeitung*)	4.7	14.9	12.8	10.6	6.7
Total cases (in thousands)		99	892	888	294	287

Notes: (a) Including *Einarbeitungszuschuß*. Before 1993 the *Einarbeitungszuschuß* was allowed for up to one year; since January 1993 it was limited to six months with one year in exceptional cases. This set an upper limit for its duration.

Source: BA (1991a, Table 38 p.53, Table 37 p.53), BA (1992a, Table 38 p.58, Table 37 p.57), BA (1993a, Table 20 p.46, Table 19 p.46, Table 21 p.47), BA (1994a, Table 20 p.53, Table 19 p.53, Table 21 p.54), BA (1995a, Table 20 p.53, Table 19 p.52, Table 21 p.53).

Another way of separating training courses is with respect to the responsible provider. An independent provider, either a company or a non-profit-organization, was allowed to supply the training. They were responsible for the training, with the labor office (LO) just checking the conditions. They also had to look for course participants on their own. If possible the LOs use independent providers (BA (1993a, p.22)). The other possibility for the LO was to organize training on its own and to pay a possible provider for holding a certain course with a given curriculum for persons sent by the LO.

In East Germany after unification there were only few independent providers because no market for training had existed before. Therefore, nearly half of the training starting in 1990 was directly organized by the LOs. In 1991 the supply of independently provided training increased considerably. But this was not enough to keep up with the increasing demand for training because of rising unemployment and STW. Its share fell to less than half. In the two years after 1992 the free market for training was able to provide an ever increasing share of training. In 1994 only around 5 percent of training were organized by the LOs directly.

The influence of the training provider on training results is not clear till now. On the one hand training offered by independent providers might have been of higher quality because they had to compete for participants. Further, the individual choice of a provider by the training participant might have positively influenced the motivation. On the other hand there is the argument that the LO had a better idea of the types of training which were useful in the labor market because of better access to information. Independent providers might have adapted more to what individuals like to learn or believe to be useful based on insufficient information. Still the LO were able to check this when approving courses for AFG-subsidized individuals.

Table 3. Goals of Training Courses (in percent of all entries)

Of entries in continuous training are	1990 Sep-Oct	1991 year	1992 year	1993 year	1994 year
Adaption of knowledge ...	76.7	65.3	72.6	93.0	98.0[a]
Job search skills (§41a)	15.7	29.6	21.8	--	--
Advance career	5.0	3.3	4.0	5.2	1.2
First vocational degree	0.3	0.3	0.2	0.5	0.1
Training for trainers	2.0	1.4	1.3	1.3	0.7
Total cases (in thousands)	75	630	591	182	199

Notes: (a) BA (1995a) reports 99.2. This is a printing error as easily can seen by calculating the shares from the total numbers.

Source: BA (1993a, 1994a, and 1995a, Table 18 p.45, 52, and 51 respectively); own calculations based on BA (1991a and 1992a, Table 35).

Table 3 provides information on the goals of courses. Continuous training separates in 'adaptation of knowledge and skills to technical developments', 'improving job search skills (§41a)', 'advance career', 'first vocational degree', and 'training for trainers'. The goal of retraining was always a new occupation and not further discussed.

The goal of the majority of continuous training courses was 'adaptation of knowledge.' This share increased since 1991. The jump from 70 percent up to above 90 percent of training from 1992 to 1993 was due to the cancellation of §41a. In 1994 when 'useful' training was not subsidized any more the share of 'advance career' dropped, the typical category for 'useful' training. Consequently the share of 'adaptation of knowledge' increased to 98 percent. Apart from 'adaptation' the only other category relevant in East Germany because of its size was §41a. It had been most popular in 1991 and already declined in 1992 before it was abolished in January 1993. All other categories played minor roles.

Compared to West Germany the training category 'advance career' was underrepresented in East Germany before 1994. In West Germany the share was around 25 percent, jumped up to 40 percent in 1993, and declined to 10 percent in 1994. The decline in 1994 was due to the limitation to 'necessary' training. The reasons for the differences between East and West Germany were rooted in different structures of the labor market problems.[22]

Table 4: Necessary' and 'Useful' Training (in percent of all entries)

Training is	1990 Sep-Oct	1991 year	1992 year	1993 year	1994 year
'necessary' (total)	n.a.	n.a.	742	242	265
'necessary' (in percent)	n.a.	n.a.	95.8	92.0	99.1
'useful' (total)	n.a.	n.a.	32	21	3
'useful' (in percent)	n.a.	n.a.	4.2	8.0	0.9
Total cases (in thousands)	94	760	774	263	268

Source: BA (1993a, Table 8 p.37), BA 1994a, Table 8 p.41), BA (1995a, Table 8 p.40).

Table 4 separates training into 'necessary' and 'useful'. In 1994 the share of 'necessary' training jumped up to 99 percent, reflecting the new institutional restrictions. However, even before 1994 the share of 'necessary' training was above 90 percent in East Germany. This high share was the reason why restricting subsidies to 'necessary' training in 1994 hardly changed the structure of training in

---

[22] The most obvious examples are higher unemployment rates in East Germany. The higher shares of necessary training and of participants who were unemployed before training in East Germany are closely related to this.

East Germany. In West Germany 35 percent of all 1993 entries were 'useful' and consequently the institutional changes in 1994 changed the training structure a lot.[23] The reasons for the higher share of 'necessary' training in East Germany were institutional settings with easier access to 'necessary' training.[24] Furthermore, the different structures of the labor markets influenced the necessity.

3.1.3. Payments of the Labor Office (LO)

The LO bare the direct costs of training like course fees, special clothing, travel costs, work and study materials, and child care. This was a subsidy that covered the total amount. Other possibilities were flat rates or payments up to a certain limit. They could differ for different groups of participants. The other kind of payment from the LO was *Unterhaltsgeld* (UHG), money for one's livelihood, to replace the loss of earnings. So-called 'full UHG' paid as a subsidy was 65 percent or 73 percent of former net earnings, depending on family status. Since January 1994 the rates were 60 percent or 67 percent, now set on the same level as unemployment benefits. In other circumstances the 'small UHG' was paid, with an amount equal to unemployment benefits before training. The loan that was given when training was 'useful' amounts to 58 percent of former net earnings. Until December 1993 it was mandatory for the LOs to provide UHG if the individual fulfilled the criteria. Since January 1994 it was not mandatory any more.

Table 5 provides information on the type of UHG received by the individuals entering training. More than 80 percent of all training participants did receive the 'full UHG' in 1992 and 1993, with 15 percent of all participants not receiving any kind of UHG.[25] In 1994 the number of 'full UHG' recipients rose even further and less than 2 percent of all training participants did not get 'full UHG'. This data reflects the institutional changes in January 1994 but they also reveal that the changes in the East German training structure were less dramatic.

For 1990 and 1991 no data consistent with Table 5 are available. BA (1991a, p.20) reports 18,500 people receiving UHG in December 1990. Although some of the 98,000 entries between September and December 1990 might have left training already, no more than one third of all training participants in December 1990 received UHG.[26] However, the 1990 numbers are not very informative. Short

---

[23] See BA (1995a, p.8).

[24] For example 'generally threatened by unemployment' was sufficient while in West Germany 'directly threatened' was required.

[25] These individuals only got refunds for expenses according to the training section of the AFG. Still they might have gotten continuing unemployment benefits, money for living according to another section of the AFG (like STW benefits) or from another source like the social fund of the EC.

[26] Estimated using course duration statistics.

time benefits and unemployment benefits were still paid during training because of special regulations or administrative time lags. For 1991 no data are available, but the high number of persons entering training from unemployment or STW, as well as results of our interviews made us believe that most participants either got 'full UHG' or similar benefits similar to the enlarged STW benefits.

Now we turn to the expenditures of the BA. Table 6 provides data on the total amount spent for training in East Germany. It also reports the amount for UHG, other payments including direct training costs, and "*Institutionelle Förderung*," money paid to providers to help setup courses. Again the overall numbers show the known pattern. The expenditures were relatively low in 1991 but reached a peak in 1992. In 1993 the drop in entries did not show up much in expenditures because of the time lag between institutional changes and the average number of participants in training. In 1994 the expenditures clearly reflect the institutional changes. The shift from other expenditures towards UHG is interesting. The increasing share of individuals in training receiving 'full UHG' explains that trend.

Table 5. UHG Recipients Among all Entries[a] (absolute numbers in thousands)

	1990 Sep-Oct	1991 year	1992 year	1993 year	1994 year
UHG[a]	n.a.	n.a.	671	223	263
percent of all training participants[b]	n.a.	n.a.	86.8	84.8	98.3
'Full' UHG recipients[c]	n.a.	n.a.	661	215	257
percent of all UHG receivers	n.a.	n.a.	98.4	96.1	97.9
percent of all training participants[b]	n.a.	n.a.	85.4	81.6	96.2

Notes: (a) Here *Eingliederungsgeld* and *Eingliederungshilfe* (EGG, money paid to immigrants of German culture from Eastern Europe *(Spätaussiedler)* for some time after arrival to help them integrate, e.g. through training) are included. They do not play a substantial role in East Germany. (b) The data from Table 1 is used as denominator. (c) 'Full UHG' means receiving payments according to the rates in §44. Other possibilities are UHG as a loan, UHG at the level of former unemployment benefits, UHG for part time training, or EGG.

Source: BA (1993a, 1994a, and 1995a, Table 9, p.38, 42, and 41 respectively).

Table 6. Expenditures of the BA in East Germany (in billion DM)

	1990 Sep-Oct	1991 year	1992 year	1993 year	1994 year
UHG[a]	0.039	1.578	6.010	6.562	4.620
Other expenditures for training	0.138	2.690	4.711	3.748	2.370
Sum	0.178	4.268	10.721	10.310	6.990
Subsidies for training institutions	n.a.	0.162	0.103	0.056	n.a.

Notes: (a) Including *Eingliederungsgeld* (see Table 5).

Source: BA (1991a, Table 39 p.53), BA (1995a, Table 34, p.77).

3.2. Different Types of Training

AFG-subsidized training was divided into three different types of courses: §41a, continuous training, and retraining. In the following section we will describe the special features of the different types of training and provide some participation statistics (see Table 7).

First we will take a look at the shares of the different training types in total training. STW was the most important ALMP in 1990 and 1991. It was a political decision to keep people employed since this was not a temporary employment problem as is usually necessary for STW. This opened a huge training potential, but it is not known to what extend it was used.

Ignoring STW the shares of entries into training in 1991 are 58 percent for continuous training, 24 percent for §41a, and 17 percent for retraining. In 1992 there was a shift from §41a towards retraining with shares of 60 percent, 17 percent, and 24 percent, respectively. There were no more §41a courses in 1993. Between the two remaining categories the shift towards retraining continued in 1993 with 31 percent of all entries, 69 percent remaining for continuous training. This reversed in 1994 with retraining accounting for only 25 percent of all entries.

Table 7. Participation in Different AFG-Subsidized Training Courses (in thousands)

		1990 Sept-Oct	1991 year	1992 year	1993 year	1994 year
§ 41a	Entries	12	187	129	--	--
Continuous training	Entries	63	443	462	182	199
	Leavers	n.a.	280[a]	444[a]	314	176
	Average Participation	n.a.	n.a.	n.a.	155	105
Retraining	Entries	19	130	183	81	69
	Leavers	n.a.	n.a.	29	93	136
	Average Participation	n.a.	n.a.	n.a.	222	151
Total	Entries	94	760	774	263	268
	Leavers	n.a.	n.a.	473	407	312
	Average Participation	n.a.	280[b]	491[b]	376	256
In STW[c]	Average Participation	n.a.	1,616	370	181	97
	Full time equivalents	341	898	194	85	46

Notes: (a) Including §41a training. (b) Estimated and including *Einarbeitungszuschuß*. (c) The numbers represent individuals in short time work; it is not known how many of these participate were in any type of training.

Source: BA (1995a, Table 170 p.50, Table 27 p.72, Table B p.16), BA (1991a, Table 35 p.52), BA (1995b, Table 165 p.270), IAB (1995, Table 7.2 p.248).

3.2.1. Short Training – §41a

The short courses according to §41a, in most cases between two and six weeks, provided job search skills and information about different types of work and long term training possibilities. At the same time the LO obtained information about the abilities of the participant, which was useful for future counselling. The courses could also be designed to improve the general knowledge and basic skills, which was not allowed in regular training courses, or to motivate an unemployed individual. These courses were available only for the unemployed. They did not need a completed vocational qualification or work experience as was usually required for training. §41a was abolished on 1 January 1993, but other sections of the AFG allowed somewhat similar courses. Comparable courses can also be offered as continuous training. The interviews we conducted in March 1996 indicated that cancelling §41a made some difference but not too much, because in most cases the LOs were able to provide the same type of course based on other regulations if necessary.[27] §41a-courses had been quite important, at least in terms of participation. The early peak in 1991 is a hint that help through 'orientation' courses was thought to be useful in East Germany after unification.

Data on leavers or the average number of participants is not available, but the short course duration did not allow for a huge spillover to other years. The average number of individuals in training should be around one tenth of the group entering courses. Therefore §41a did not play an important role when focusing on the direct effect of training on unemployment rates. However, if this training really helped individuals to find a job, around 270,000 individuals in East Germany received this help.

3.2.2. Continuous Training in an Old Occupation

Continuous training is training in an occupation the participant already holds. It was supposed to show, secure or strengthen the knowledge and skills or to adapt to technical developments. A special focus was on improving the labor market conditions for disadvantaged unemployed (long term unemployment, women, people above age fifty, among others). The goal of training could also be to advance the career or avoid supply shortages of labor with specific skills. The duration of courses could be between two months and two years. Since May 1993 courses were limited to one year if they did not provide a publicly approved examination. For part time training these limits were extended.

According to participation numbers this was the most important type of AFG-subsidized training. Starting from 63,000 entries in 1990, entries jumped up in 1991 and peaked a little higher at 462,000 in 1992. In 1993 the participation numbers declined but not as sharply as the training totals. Still, for 1993 they were less than half, of those for 1992. In 1994 entries rose again, but only slightly.

3.2.3. Retraining

The goal of retraining is to offer individuals appropriate job possibilities when their knowledge is useless because of personal or labor market conditions. In

---

[27] These replacements are not shown separately in the statistics. Courses offered as continuous training cannot be separated. Data for courses according to other sections of the AFG are not presented here.

normal cases the maximum course duration was two years. The courses should finish with a publicly approved examination and they should be shorter than a corresponding vocational qualification. Since May 1993 both rules were binding.

Retraining had not as high participation numbers as continuous training. Up to 1992 they increased steadily to 183,000, then they fell to 69,000 in 1994. For this type of training a longer average duration was expected. This was in accordance with the number of leavers, which indicates a time lag closer to two years than to one year as in continuous training. Another result of the longer duration is the high number of average training participants. These were 222,000 in 1993 and 151,000 in 1994. Therefore, when focusing on the direct influence on unemployment rates, retraining was the most important type of training in 1993 and 1994.

3.2.4. A Special Case: Training During Short Time Work (STW)

We already discussed the few regulations for training during STW above. Here we will present some data, although complete statistics on training during STW are not available. On average an amazing number of more than 1.6 million individuals worked short time in East Germany throughout 1991, with full time equivalents of nearly 900,000 workers. That is about ten percent of the labor force before unification. In the following years these numbers fell sharply to less than a quarter in 1992 and again halving in 1993 and 1994. In 1991, 276,000 persons received STW benefits directly before they entered training (including *Einarbeitungszuschuß*).[28] These were individuals entering training subsidized according to the training section of the AFG.[29] They made up a third of all entries. In 1990 this share was 36 percent. It is not clear whether all other individuals in STW did not receive any training.[30]

---

[28] See BA (1992a, p.20) and BA (1991a, p.20, Table B and the corresponding text p.22 and 20, respectively).

[29] All statistics on training presented here include short time workers entering AFG-subsidized training on a case – rather than a person – basis. This implies that some individuals may be counted more than once.

[30] Following these numbers only 20 percent of all individuals in STW started training in 1991. But there was a lot of emphasis put on this possibility by official statements, and interviews indicated that in most cases training took place. Possibly not all training during STW is represented in these figures.

3.3. Characteristics of Individuals in Training

3.3.1. From What Kind of Occupation to Which Kind of Occupation

Let us consider the occupation before training and the occupation people were trained for.[31] Most entries had an occupation in the service sector before training. The shares were 47 percent in 1992, 48 percent in 1993, and 53 percent in 1994. An even higher share trained for an occupation in the service sector, 59 percent, 52 percent, and 55 percent, respectively. More people have trained for service sector occupations than came out of the service sector. The 'net inflow' in service sector occupations mirrored the changing structure of the economy.

In 1992, 38 percent of the entries had an occupation in production before training and 28 percent trained for such an occupation. In the following years the flow out of production occupations continued, although not to the same extent. In 1993, the corresponding shares were 38 percent and 32 percent, in 1994, 34 percent and 33 percent. Training for technical occupations was less important. In 1992, 9 percent came from technical occupations and 6 percent trained for them. In 1993, the shares were 7 percent and 6 percent, in 1994, 8 percent and 7 percent. There was a net outflow, although very small. Again, both outflows from technical and production occupations mirrored the structural changes.

It has to be stressed that the net flows were sometimes relatively small compared to the number of individuals training for a kind of occupation they had not worked in before. Even in 1992 with relatively large net flows there was, for example, an inflow of nearly 130.000 people into service occupations while nearly 40.000 people out of service occupations trained for other kinds of occupations. In some years years the absolute flows were five times as large as the net flows. Therefore, interpreting the flows as signs of structural change should be done with some care. The flows might just have summed up individual patterns. A comparison with West Germany does not reveal substantial differences. The inflow into services in West Germany was clearly smaller in 1992, but not in 1993 and 1994. A higher share of technical occupations in training was due to the larger share of 'useful' training in West Germany because in technical occupations often the goal was to 'advance career'. Consequently, this difference vanished in 1994 when 'useful' training was not subsidized any more.

---

[31] A more detailed analysis would be interesting but is beyond the scope of this paper. The necessary information is provided in Tables 23 to 26 in BA (1993a, 1994a, and 1995a). This section is based on the above mentioned Tables and draws heavily on the corresponding description, pages 24, 27 f, and 27 f, respectively. In particular, we adapt the separation in production, services, and technical occupations.

3.3.2. Labor Market Performance Before Training

Table 8 presents an important characteristic of training participants: their labor market status directly before entering training. In 1991 half of the participants were unemployed. This share increased to 75 percent in 1992, 79 percent in 1993 and it finally reached 96 percent in 1994. In 1991 the low number is partly due to the high number of individuals in STW in that year. Throughout all years another influence is the declining number of individuals threatened by unemployment while at the same time the unemployment rate was rising until 1992. Finally, restricting subsidies to 'necessary' training in 1994 further increased the share of the unemployed.

A majority, 74 percent of all entries in 1992, 77 percent in 1993, and 96 percent in 1994, received unemployment benefits before training. Hardly any unemployed without benefits entered training. This is not surprising. After unification most people had a right to receive unemployment benefits for a long term. With unemployment not rising very much before 1991 most unemployed in East Germany still got unemployment benefits in 1994.

The next category, searching for work without being unemployed, was typical for people on STW before training as well as for individuals threatened by unemployment. The share of 20 percent in 1992 declined in the following years. This is not surprising when considering that STW declined. The same is true for the number of individuals threatened by unemployment, although no precise data is available. Training for individuals in the last category, not even searching for a job before training, was typically 'useful' training. Knowing this, it is not surprising that the share declined sharply in 1994 when 'useful' training was not subsidized any more. Turning to the length of the unemployment spell before training we observe that the share of individuals unemployed for more than twelve months before training increased significantly from 1992 to 1994, reaching about one third. Two reasons for this rise were the growing share of long term unemployed among all unemployed, and the stronger focus of ALMP on long-term unemployed persons in later years.

3.3.3. Socio-Demographic Variables

From 1991 to 1994 women accounted for approximately 60 percent of all training entries including *Einarbeitungszuschuß* (see Table 8). Their 65 percent share of all unemployed was only slightly higher. Considering the regulation of the AFG ruling that subgroups of unemployed – and especially women – should be represented in ALMP according to their share in unemployment, this seemed to be an 'appropriate' share of women in training, especially when the *Einarbeitungszuschuß* with very low female participation is excluded. Going into detail reveals a different picture. Women were overrepresented in §41a-training, especially in 1992 with 80 percent of all entries. For the years that data are available their share in continuous training was similar to their share in unemployment. The same is true for retraining in 1992. In 1993 and 1994 this share declined to 55 percent and 51 percent, respectively. This could be a hint that the training duration for women was shorter on average, but it turned out that this is not the case.[32]

Table 8. Labor Market Status and Other Socio-Demographic Variables before Entering Training

	1990 Sept-Oct	1991 year	1992 year	1993 year	1994 year
Share of unemployed before training[a]	n.a.	50.6	57.3	79.2	95.9
Thereof unemployed for ...months (in percent of all entries)					
< 1	n.a.	n.a.	13.9	8.4	4.7
1-3	n.a.	n.a.	20.7	26.9	19.8
3-6	n.a.	n.a.	24.4	19.8	15.8
6-12	n.a.	n.a.	27.7	24.8	25.7
> 12	n.a.	n.a.	13.2	20.1	34.0
Status before training (in percent of all entries)					
Unemployment with benefits	n.a.	n.a.	73.5	77.2	93.0
Unemployment without benefits	n.a.	n.a.	1.8	2.0	2.9
Searching for work, not unemployed	n.a.	n.a.	20.2	13.0	3.5
Not searching for work	n.a.	n.a.	4.5	7.9	0.6
Age (in percent of all entries)					
< 20	n.a.	n.a.	1.1	0.8	0.6
20-25	n.a.	n.a.	14.6	13.3	11.7
25-35	n.a.	n.a.	37.1	36.6	33.7
35-45	n.a.	n.a.	28.3	28.9	29.8
45-55	n.a.	n.a.	17.4	18.0	19.9
> 55	n.a.	n.a.	1.5	2.1	4.2
Women (in percent of all entries)					
All[a]	n.a.	57.1	62.0	57.2	60.9
§ 41a	n.a.	67.9	80.0	--	--
Continuous training	n.a.	56.5	62.1	62.3	67.0
New occupation	n.a.	58.9	65.4	54.8	50.6
Einarbeitungszuschuß	n.a.	42.2	36.0	33.7	34.4
Total number of cases (in 1000's)	94	760	774	263	268
Share of women of all unemployed (in percent)	n.a.	n.a.	65	65	67

Notes: (a) Including *Einarbeitungszuschuß*.

Source: BA (1993a, Table 3 p.34, Table 6 p.35, Table 7 p.36); BA (1994a, Table 3 p. 38, Table 6 p.39, Table 7 p.40); BA (1995a, Table 3 p.38, Table 6 p.39, Table 7 p.40, Table 2 p.37, Table 17O p.50 with own calculations); BA (1995b, Table 13 p.46 with own calculations).

---

[32] Table 8 does not include these data. See instead BA (1995a, p.53 Table 20).

A high and consistent share of 60 percent of individuals was aged between 25 and 45. Human capital theory would support training for individuals of this age because they remain in the labor force for a long time after training. This opens the opportunity to catch the returns on the investments made through training. In the case of older individuals the returns might not be reaped because of the few years remaining until retirement. Furthermore, individuals aged between 25 and 45 were too old as having received training through the German apprenticeship system after unification. So there was potentially a need to adapt to western technologies. The slowly decreasing share of people under 25 might be a result of the same mechanism. In 1994 a lot of people went through the apprenticeship system after unification and there was less need of adaptation.

The share of individuals above age 45 and especially of people above age 55 rose from 1992 to 1994. Training might be less efficient with only few years to catch returns, but this increasing share was a result of the focus on groups with special labor market problems.

A final comment is appropriate. The changes in the structure of individual characteristics were less important when compared to the huge changes in total participation. No particular group gained from or took an excessive burden during the up- and downsizing.

4. Empirical Evaluation

4.1. Introduction

Following the description of the rules, regulations and participants in BA-sponsored training, we now turn our attention to the question whether training participation was beneficial for the participants themselves. In addition we will contrast the results for BA-sponsored training with results for employer-provided training. For these undertakings we will use micro-data that allows us to follow a large sample of individuals from mid 1989 to early 1994.

Although a large number of evaluation results for US-training programs is available (e.g. LaLonde (1995)), there are only very few econometric evaluations of training in East Germany. The results presented in this section do not confirm previous positive findings of the effectiveness of training in East Germany (e.g. Fitzenberger and Prey (1997), Pannenberg and Helberger (1994), Pannenberg (1995)). The few studies conducted so far differ in many respects ranging from the database to the implementation of the evaluation, treatment of selection problems, and the definition of training itself. However, they share two common features that are absent from this work: They do not use an explicit causality framework, and they are based on modelling the distributions of the outcome variables or error terms given certain covariates. Here, we explicitly avoid such restrictions and put emphasis on the particular notion of causality behind the results.

This section heavily relies on results presented in Lechner (1998) for public-sector provided training, and on Lechner (1999a, 1999c) for employer-provided training. Many econometric issues are discussed in Lechner (1999b). For all details as well as an extensive description of the data and the empirical implementation of the estimation method the interested reader is referred to these sources.

4.2. Data

The sample used for the empirical analysis is drawn from the German Socio-Economic Panel (GSOEP), which is very similar to the US Panel Study of Income Dynamics. About 5,000 households are interviewed each year beginning in 1984. A sample of just under 2,000 East German households was added in 1990. The GSOEP is very rich in terms of socio-demographic information, in particular concerning current and past employment status. For an English language description of the GSOEP see Wagner et al. (1993).

Figure 2. Selected Items of the Retrospective Questions About Income in the 1993 Questionnaire (Income Calendar)

"Please indicate for each month of the previous year (1992) whether you had some income of the type or the source given on the left hand side of the following calendar:"

	Jan	Feb	Mar	Apr	...	Sep	Oct	Nov	Dec
employment as employee									
self-employment									
...									
unemployement benefits									
Unterhaltsgeld (LO)									
...									
no such income									

Note: For the complete questionnaires see Infratest Sozialforschung (1990, 1991, 1992, 1993, 1994). Own translation (summarized).

A very useful characteristic of this panel survey is the availability of monthly information between annual interviews. This covers different employment states and income categories. The information is obtained by retrospective questions about what happened in particular months of the previous year. Figure 2 shows a sketch of one type of 'calendar', the income calendar. The related employment calendar contains information on the employment status, such as full time employment, part time employment, STW, vocational training, and schooling. These calendars allow a precise observation of the individual employment states and income sources before and after training. This kind of information will figure prominently in the empirical analysis.

A balanced sample of all individuals born between 1940 and 1970 who responded in the first four waves is selected. The upper age limit is set to avoid the need of addressing early retirement issues. The population of interest is the labor force of the GDR, therefore it is required that all selected individuals work full-time just before unification. To be able to control for the entire labor market history before training (beginning in mid 1989) – which is necessary to control for the selection issues – it is required that all individuals answer the relevant survey questions in all four annual surveys. Since the fifth survey of 1994 is only used to measure post-training labor market outcome, it is not necessary to impose such a requirement.

The income and employment calendars are used to define the training measure CTRT. Individuals are considered to participate in continuous training and retraining (CTRT) if they receive *Unterhaltsgeld* (UHG) or obtain continuous vocational training during STW. It is required that the training period starts after unification but no later than March 1993. This means that all CTRT used for the empirical analysis was approved before the tightening of rules during 1993.

The mean (std.) of the duration of CTRT is about 12 (7) months. 10 percent of the CTRT spells have a duration of no more than 3 months, 25 percent of no more than 6 months, 65 percent of no more than 12 months, and 95 percent of no more than 24 months. Comparing these numbers with the duration of continuous training (CT), retraining (RT) and job-familiarization (FJ; durations are 6 to 12 months) spells as given in Table 2, it is found that a substantial part of short spells is missing from the sample. However, the comparison is not really valid because of the inclusion of FJ in the official numbers, and the following issues related to the questionnaire (calendar) need to be considered: Firstly, the fact that it is retrospective information about last year may result in participants forgetting very short training spells. Secondly, it may be that respondents do not bother to tick boxes for a particular month in case of short spells of less than a month. Thirdly, multiple spells of the same individual are added which increases duration per spell. However, by omitting these very short spells that may be related to AFG §41a the following empirical analysis is focused on longer spells that obviously absorb a much larger amount of resources. It is these longer CTRT spells that are a priori considered to be more effective. Information on employer-provided training (ET) is taken from a special part in the GSOEP in 1993.

4.3. Econometric Considerations and Some Descriptive Statistics

In typical microeconometric evaluations of training programs, outcomes measured for the sample undergoing the training are compared to outcome measures for a *comparable* group, called control group, that does not recieve the training. In most social experiments such a group consists of individuals who apply for the program, but are denied participation by randomization, for instance. Hence, such a control group should not systematically differ from the trainees. This simplifies the evaluation dramatically, because the difference of simple sample means in the trainee and the control population is an unbiased and consistent estimator for the average effect of training for the trainees. However, the huge time lag between the beginning of such an experiment and the results of the evaluations is one reason why conducting an experiment was never an option in East Germany.[33] In a study not based on experimental data the researcher should find individuals who are identical to trainees regarding all *relevant* pre-training attributes except for not having obtained the training. Since typically such individuals cannot be easily identified, additional assumptions have to be invoked to adjust for their dissimilarity to avoid potentially serious sample selection biases. Holland (1986) and Heckman/Hotz (1989) provide extensive and excellent discussions on these issues.

Various model-based procedures are suggested in the econometrics literature to avoid such biases (see for example Heckman/Hotz (1989), or Heckman/Robb (1985)).[34] However, Ashenfelter/Card (1985) and LaLonde (1986) among others conclude that the results are highly sensitive to the different stochastic assumptions made about the selection process. Both papers conclude that the econometric adjustment procedures are unreliable, and hence that social experiments are necessary to evaluate training programs. Dehejia/Wahba (1998, 1999) – using an approach very similar to the one used by Lechner (1998, 1999b, 1999c) – reevaluate the LaLonde (1986) data. By using nonparametric techniques they come to far more positive conclusions about the potential quality of inferences based on observational data than LaLonde (1986) himself.

Many problems with the statistical modelling procedures stem from the fact that the data does not provide sufficient information on all important factors that influence program participation as well as labor market outcomes. Then it is necessary to introduce unobserved 'error terms' and to model their joint distribution with the variables of the model. It is one of the major advantages of the data introduced in the previous section that it is a highly informative panel data set. Therefore, we do not need to introduce error terms and we can concentrate on controlling for observable differences of trainees and controls. Since this is done

---

[33] The state of the discussion about whether it is advantageous or not to base evaluations on social experiments can be found in Burtless (1995) and Heckman/Smith (1995).

[34] Chapter 1 in Bell et al. (1995) provides a more complete account of the development of the econometric evaluation literature.

nonparametrically by extending the methods proposed by Rubin (1979) and Rosenbaum/Rubin (1983, 1985), the results should be reasonably immune to the above criticism.

Let us very briefly give the basic idea for the estimator used for the empirical evaluations. To ease notation assume that observations in the sample are ordered such that the first N^t observations receive training, and the remaining $(N-N^t)$ observations do not. Define the differences in matched pairs in the sample that consists of independently drawn observations as

$\Delta y_n = y_n^t - y_j^c$, $\Delta b(x_n) = b(x_n^t) - b(x_j^c)$, $n = 1,\ldots,N^t$ where y_j^c and x_j^c denote values of an observation from the pool of individuals not participating in training (controls) that is matched to the treated (training) observation n.[35] The vector x contains all variables that influence participation in training as well as the evaluation targets (Y), such as employment states and earnings. The function b(x) reduces the dimension of the pairwise comparisons. It is appropriately chosen to ensure that outcomes and participation are independent conditional on b(x) when they are independent conditional on x.[36]

In this context the respective groups of the conditioning variables x are identified by the analysis in Lechner (1998) as age, expected labor market prospects, actual employment status, and other socioeconomic characteristics. The groups of variables that are used in the empirical analysis to approximate and describe the above-mentioned four broad categories of determining factors are age, sex, marital status, educational degrees as well as regional indicators. Features of the pre-unification position in the labor market are captured by many indicators including wages, occupation, job position, employer characteristics such as firm size or industrial sector, among others.[37] Individual future expectations are described by individual pre-unification predictions about what might happen in the next two years regarding job security, a change in the job position or occupation, and a subjective conjecture whether it would be easy to find a new job. Furthermore, monthly employment status information, as mentioned before, is available from July 1989 to December 1993.

Factors like motivation, ability and social contacts are approximated by the subjective desirability of selected attitudes in society in 1990, such as 'performing own duties', 'achievements at work', and 'increasing own wealth', together with the accomplishment of voluntary services in social organizations and memberships in unions and professional associations before unification, as well as schooling

---

[35] Capital letters denote random variables and small letters their realizations (or specific values).

[36] $b(x)$ is a balancing score.

[37] Pre-unification variables are assumed to be exogenous, because the total and unexpected system change invalidated all long-term plans.

degrees and professional achievements. Additionally, there are variables indicating that the individual is not enjoying the job, that high income is very important for subjective well-being, that the individual is very confused by the new circumstances, and optimistic or pessimistic regarding general future developments. Another issue is the discount rate implicitly used to calculate present values of future earnings streams. We assume that controlling for factors that have already been determined using the individual discount rate, such as schooling and professional education, will be sufficient. Other issues concern possible restrictions of the maximization problem such as a limited supply of CTRT. Supply information is available, however it is aggregated either by state or using four groups defined by the number of inhabitants of cities and villages. We conclude that, although some doubts could be raised, it seems safe to assume that these missing factors (conditional on all the other observable variables) play only a minor role. Finally, empirical papers analyzing training programs in the US point to the importance of transitory shocks before training, partly because of individual decision, partly because of the policy of the program administrators. Card/Sullivan (1988) find a decline in employment probabilities before training. Here, the monthly employment status data should take care of that problem.

Table 9 contains descriptive statistics for some characteristics of CTRT participants (column 4) and non-participants (column 2). For comparison some information is also provided on the participants in employer-provided training (typically on-the-job) (ET, column 5).[38] The table shows two features: On the one hand, CTRT participants differ substantially from the non-training population, but even more from the ET participants. On the other hand, the matching algorithm used has successfully eliminated almost all differences (column 3) between CTRT participants and the chosen control group. The evaluation figures will show that this is also true for the monthly and yearly employment status variables. The regression-type adjustment procedure takes care of the remaining differences.

Given the matched pairs, the estimate of the average causal effect of training for training participants and the respective standard error are computed as:

$$\hat{\theta}_{N^t} = \frac{1}{N^t} \sum_{n=1}^{N^t} \Delta y_n, \ \operatorname{Var}\left(\hat{\theta}_{N^t}\right) = \frac{1}{N^t}\left(S^2_{y^t} + S^2_{y^c}\right). \tag{1}$$

---

[38] The ET training information is taken from a special part of the GSOEP concerned with continuous vocational training included in the 1993 survey.

S_{yt}^2 and S_{yc}^2 denote the square of the empirical deviation of Y in the training sample and in the sample matched to the training-sample, respectively.[39] As mentioned in the previous section, when a perfect match is achieved, implying that $\Delta b(x_n) = 0, n = 1, \ldots, N^t$ these estimates are unbiased. When the sample is large enough the normal distribution can be used to perform tests and compute confidence intervals.

Table 9. Descriptive Statistics of Selected Variables of Training Participants and Control Sample (meanshares in percent)

	All Controls	Matched Controls	CTRT	ET
(1)	(2)	(3)	(4)	(5)
Gender: female	40	53	56	37
Years of schooling (highest degree in 1990				
12	18	19	28	39
10	60	67	63	51
Highest professional degree in 1990: university	13	17	19	30
Job position in 1990: highly qualified management	22	17	26	44
Job characteristics in 1990: already fired	4	10	13	1
Employer characteristics in 1990 (in industry):				
agriculture	13	13	17	6
other services[a]	13	8	8	26
Income very important for subjective well-being	56	25	15	52
Expectations for the next 2 years in 1990:				
redundancies in firm: certainly	50	57	52	25
losing the job: certainly	13	11	15	5

Note: (a) incl. nonprofit, banks, insurance, government, legal, personal services, cleaning, waste disposal, hotels, restaurants. (2) all non-CTRT-participants (N=1,063); (3) non-CTRT-participants matched to CTRT participants; (4) CTRT participants (N=103); (5) ET participants (N=222). 1990 relates to the date of the interview that for almost all cases was completed before July 1990.

---

[39] The variance estimate exploits the fact that the matching algorithm proposed in Lechner (1999b) never chooses an observation twice.

Equation (1) gives the principal estimate of the causal effect. It is refined in the following to take account of time before and after training, i.e. the panel structure of the data and the fact that training begins and ends for different individuals at different points in time. Denote by N_τ^t, $\tau \in \{\ldots, -3, -2, -1, 1, 2, 3\}$, the number of pairs observed at any distance in time to training ($\tau = 0$). Let $\iota_\tau(n) = 1$ if observation n is observed at τ. The refined estimator based on the distance as opposed to the date concept of time is defined as:

$$\hat{\theta}_{N_\tau^t} = \frac{1}{N_\tau^t} \sum_{n=1}^{N^t} \iota_\tau(n) \Delta y_n, \quad \tau \in \{-2, -1, 1, 2, 3, \ldots\} \tag{2}$$

The variances are computed appropriately. When τ is negative, then $\hat{\theta}_{N_\tau^t}$ denotes the mismatch in period τ before training, otherwise it denotes the effect of training in period τ after training. No assumption is necessary regarding whether or not the treatment effects may differ across the population of training participants.

4.4. Evaluation Results

4.4.1. Before-After Comparisons

Comparing the unemployment rates before and after CTRT should give a first impression about the dynamics involved and the selection process into CTRT. Figure 3 shows the share of CTRT participants who are unemployed in any given number of months before or after CTRT. There is a surge in unemployment 10 months prior to CTRT culminating in an unemployment ratio of about 51 percent in the month just prior to training. The respective rates for full-time employment are 24 percent and 73 percent for the combined rate of unemployment or STW. As before, the contrast to ET is particularly sharp, because pre-ET unemployment rates are very low.[40]

Considering the post-training period, it appears that many CTRT participants find jobs fairly quickly. Whether they do this fast enough to make up for the time *lost* for search during CTRT participation, which is on average twelve months, will be seen below. Although an exact comparison with official numbers is difficult, because of the different concepts of time used, they appear to lie within the ranges shown in Figure 3.[41]

---

[40] This is not surprising because employers typically train their work force, and not the unemployed. New hires do not play a significant role in this rapidly contracting economy.

[41] See Buttler/Emmerich (1994), Blaschke/Nagel (1995), and IAB (1995, p.134).

Figure 3 also shows that having monthly employment status information is quite important for any evaluation study in order to control for selection issues related to unemployment.

Figure 3. Share of Registered Unemployed Before and After CTRT for CTRT Participants (in percent)

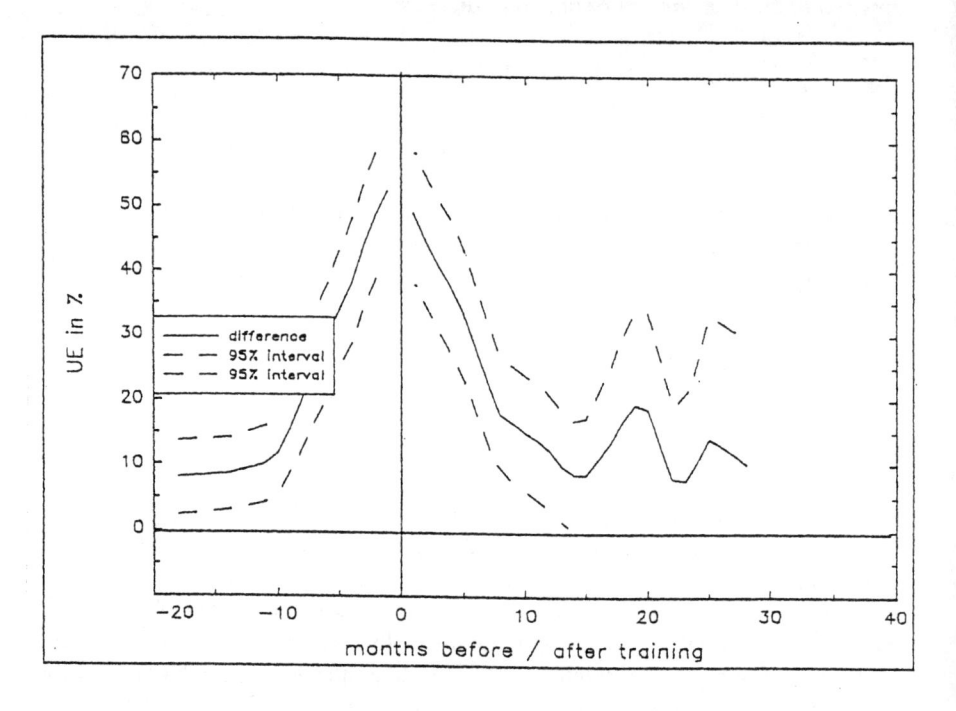

Note: Smoothed using 3 month moving averages for $|\tau| > 1$.

4.4.2. Matched Control Group Comparisons

We are particularly interested in the effects of CTRT on post-training changes in actual and anticipated labor market status and prospects. The following outcomes are measured on a monthly basis by way of the retrospective employment calendar: involuntary short-time work, registered as being unemployed, and full-time employment. In addition, the latter two variables are also available for the date of the annual interview. Another variable capturing characteristics of the actual labor market status, measured once a year, is gross monthly earnings. Labor market prospects are measured once a year as individual expectations or worries. They include expectations whether one might lose one's job in the next two years, and whether one is very worried about the security of the current job. Additionally, there is information on whether individuals expect an improvement of the current job (career) position. It is important to note for the discussion in the following subsection that, except for the earnings variable, all outcome variables are coded as binary indicators.

The results of the evaluations are given in the following Figures 4 to 6. Using equation (2) to estimate the causal effects of CTRT, they show the differences between the control and the CTRT group for specific time intervals before and after the training for the different outcome variables.[42] For variables measured by the monthly calendar the distance is expressed in months, for those measured only for the particular month of the yearly interview, the distance is expressed in years.[43] The figures cover up to 18 months or up to three 'years' before the training and up to 27 months or three 'years' after CTRT. They display the mean effect (solid line; + for the mismatch corrected estimate) and its 95 percent pointwise confidence interval based on the normal approximation (dashed line; $\nabla \Delta$ for the mismatch corrected estimates). The number of observations available to compute the respective statistics decreases the longer the distance to the incidence of CTRT. This implies increasing variances and is reflected in the widening of the confidence intervals. Additionally, a mismatch correction may be impossible or very imprecise. Hence, the results on the very right side in the following figures have to be interpreted with care.

Figure 4 presents the result of the evaluations for the monthly outcome variable unemployment.[44] The part left to the "0" vertical mark allows a judgement about the quality of the matches concerning the particular variable.

As already noted in the discussion of match quality, there is small excess unemployment just prior to the beginning of the course, that is however not at all significantly different from zero. Figure 4 shows that the immediate effect of CTRT is additional unemployment in the months following the end of CTRT. After a few months these effects disappear. At first sight this seems surprising because Figure 3 shows that the unemployment rate of CTRT participants is indeed falling rapidly during the first 12 months after CTRT. However, there is a

---

[42] The results for those outcomes that are mentioned, but do not appear here, are not qualitatively different from the ones presented.

[43] The time interval denoted as the first year is actually the time between the end of CTRT and the next interview. Therefore, this time interval may vary among individuals. The monthly data starts in July 1989 and ends in December 1993, whereas the annual data ranges from mid 1990 to early 1994.

[44] *Unemployment* here indicates that the individual has registered for unemployment. There is another monthly variable indicating the receipt of unemployment benefits. The results are almost exactly the same when using this second measurement of unemployment.

simple explanation for this effect. Remember that more than 50 percent of CTRT participants are unemployed before CTRT. For an unemployed person the immediate effect of (full-time) CTRT is that during CTRT his or her search efforts will be reduced (mean duration is 12 months!) compared to the controls. The results suggest that if there is a positive effect of CTRT it is not large enough to compensate for this initial negative outcome. These general findings are confirmed by considering either STW and unemployment together or by considering full-time employment as the respective labor market outcome. Considering only a sample of individuals who are either unemployed or on STW before CTRT sharpens these results.

Figure 4. Difference of Unemployment Rates of CTRT Participants and Matched Control Group (in percentage points)

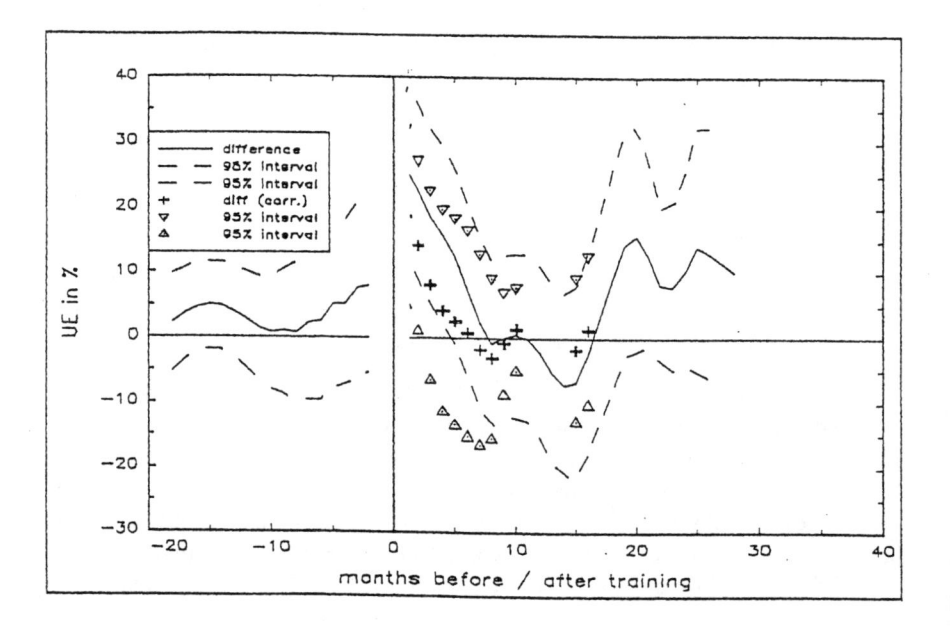

Note: $N^t_{-1} = 103.0$ Smoothed using 3 month moving averages for $|\tau| > 1$.

When performing the same evaluation for ET, there does not appear to be any effect of ET with respect to unemployment. It is obviously difficult to reduce the individual unemployment risk by means of training in a rapidly contracting economy that also adjusts to a new economic environment. This economic situation may lead to unforeseen changes in firm strategies and technologies used, leading to unexpected changes in the size and composition of the work force, so that even previous ET may only be of limited value for training participants. Obviously, if firms are changing their strategies unexpectedly, it will be difficult for the BA to predict future demand for particular skills, and, hence, to device or choose effective training programs. Figure 5 features an outcome variable that is only measured once a year, such as gross monthly earnings. There are no significant differences for the pre-training outcomes, and there does not appear to be an effect of CTRT either.

Figure 5. Difference of Gross Earnings of CTRT Participants and Matched Control Group (in 1993 DM)

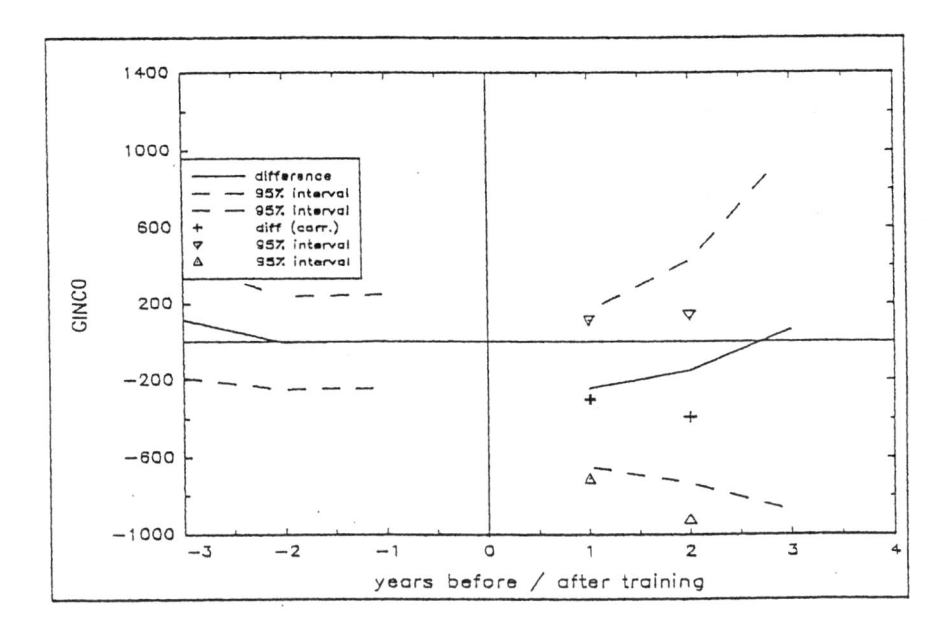

Note: $N^t_{-1} = 103.0$ when unemployed.

This is very different for the case of ET. From Figure 6 it appears that there are positive effects of about DM 350[45] from ET in the second year after completion of the last ET spell. Note that the same effect appears for the third year, but that probably the much reduced sample size leads to its insignificance. From the CTRT-ET comparison it appears that ET is more effective for participants than

---

[45] The implied average earnings increase is about 9 percent.

CTRT. Note, however, that we cannot distinguish between two possible sources of these effects: Either firms select ET participants better suited to benefit from training, or the firm-provided training itself is of higher quality. Having shown that CTRT has no positive effects in the months following CTRT, there is an indication that there might be positive effects still to come: Individuals do think that CTRT will improve their career perspective in the next two years. Since the CTRT participants expect to improve their situation even in the two years after year two, and since they have already made up the initial loss during CTRT, it might be that they will overtake the controls outside the sample period. Unfortunately, from the data at hand it is impossible to decide whether this variable really contains information about future realizations of labor market outcomes, or whether this is just wishful thinking of CTRT participants.

Finally, let us note that in a recent study Fitzenberger/Prey (1997) obtained more positive findings. They use a different data set and model the joint stochastic processes of selection, panel attrition and outcomes using joint normality. Their fully parametric approach is very much in contrast to the principally nonparametric approach used here: One way to think about these two approaches is that the nonparametric approach minimizes the bias while accepting larger variances. This is reflected in the confidence bounds. The fully parametric approach uses more assumptions and, thus, will get less variance because of less uncertainty. The price to pay there, however, is in terms of asymptotic bias if these assumptions are not correct. Whereas large variances can be detected in the outputs, biases cannot. For this and other reasons, we prefer our approach.

In conclusion, we note that no positive earnings and employment effects of CTRT in the short-run are found. Regarding the risk of unemployment there are negative effects of CTRT directly after training ends. It is an open question whether the lack of a positive effect is due to a bad signal participants send to prospective employers, or whether it is due to a lack of quality of training in a narrow sense. Nevertheless, our results for the short-run effects of CTRT suggest that it was a waste of resources, providing quantity without sufficient quality. The quality problem had been realized by the labor office, which subsequently tried to improve the quality. As has been shown in the first part of the paper, it also changed the selection process to include a higher share of individuals previously unemployed in CTRT. However, these changes are not part of our empirical investigations.

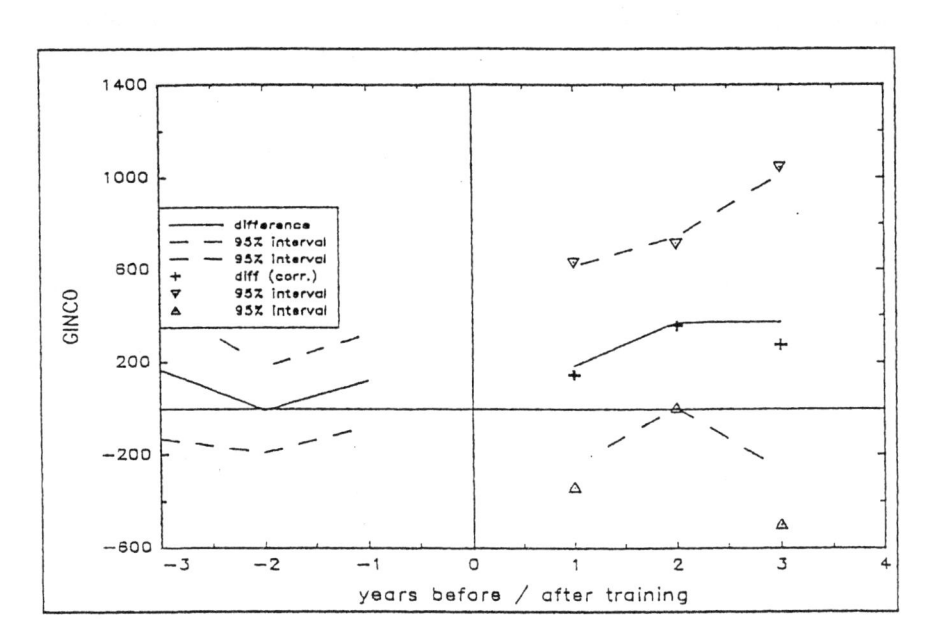

Figure 6: Monthly Gross Earnings of ET Participants and Matched Control Group
(in 1993 DM)

Note: $N^t_{-1} = 185.0$ when unemployed.

5. Conclusion

The importance of training as part of the active labor market policy in East Germany in the first years after unification was confirmed using data on participation and on expenditures for training. Especially in 1991 and 1992 training participation was very high. The institutional changes in 1993 and 1994 reduced participation and they changed the structure of the types of training and the socio-demographic structure of participants. The share of short training courses decreased, especially between 1992 and 1993. This went along with an increasing share of training participants who were unemployed directly before training. The focus of active labor market policy on persons with special labor market problems such as e.g. the long term unemployed was also illustrated by the increasing share of older workers in training. Surprisingly, no increase was seen in the participation of women who were included in the AFG-list of groups with special labor market problems. To summarize, there were two opposite effects which might have lead to different training outcomes. On the one hand, the training quality might have improved, as could be seen from the increasing course durations or changes in the training infrastructure. On the other hand, an increasing share of training participants had special labor market problems. Therefore, in future evaluations of training outcomes it would be interesting to examine whether training which started in 1991 and 1992 differs from training which started in 1994 or later.

In the evaluation part of the paper no positive earnings and employment effects of public sector sponsored continuous vocational training and retraining (CTRT) were found in the short-run. This negative picture may be an exaggeration of the real situation for several reasons: Firstly, money spent for CTRT in the first two to three years after unification might be seen as investments in the East German training infrastructure, that had to be built from scratch. In this sense, future CTRT might still yield some returns on these early investments. Secondly, the massive use of CTRT achieved a significant reduction of the official unemployment rate. This was politically desired, and hence it might be seen as an achievement per se. Thirdly, we report evidence that trainees might expect positive returns over a longer time horizon, that is beyond the sampling period used for this study. Therefore, it is still impossible to analyze empirically whether these expectations are correct or just wishful thinking. Finally, the results may improve through the efforts of the labor offices to improve the quality of CTRT supply, as well as through the introduction of a more targeted selection process. Resolving these open questions is left for future work.

Ackowledgements

Financial support from the Deutsche Forschungsgemeinschaft (DFG) is gratefully acknowledged. We thank the DIW for supplying the data of the German Socio-Economic Panel. Furthermore, we thank Klaus Kornmesser and Klaus Müller for competent research assistance. All remaining errors are our own.

Appendix: Regulations of the Arbeitsförderungsgesetz (AFG)[1]

Structure of the AFG

All German labor market policy is based on the *Arbeitsförderungsgesetz* (AFG), a federal law which was passed in 1969 and changed frequently since.[46] We will summarize parts of the section on training, more precisely §§33-39 (general regulations for training), §§41-46 (continuous training), §47 (retraining), and §§249b-249h (exceptions for East Germany). The other important source is the *"Anordnung Fortbildung und Umschulung"* (AO-FuU) passed by the *Verwaltungsrat der Bundesanstalt für Arbeit*, the top administrative level of the BA. Based on the AFG it provides much more detailed regulations. It is changed according to changes in the AFG.

The Group of Persons Getting AFG-Subsidies for Training

General Restrictions

Training must be geared to reaching the general AFG goals (§§1, 2). Especially important are

- to avoid unemployment and 'inappropriate' employment,
- to enhance occupational flexibility and to adapt to technical development, and
- to improve the labor market position of women, older or disadvantaged unemployed.

In their decisions the LOs have to take account of the course duration, curriculum, and method used, the experience of trainers, the cost efficiency, and the situation and development of the labor market (§34). The participant has to search for employment with mandatory unemployment insurance, must be 'suitable' for the training, success (finishing course, passing examinations) must be expected, and there must be a fair chance of employment in the regular labor market (§36).

Subsidizing training is not allowed if a firm has a special interest in the training (§43) or if the course is at a university (§42; §249d allows courses at universities

---

[46] In the training section the last major change was with the *"Erstes Gesetz zur Umsetzung des Spar-, Konsolidierungs- und Wachstumsprogramms"*, in effect since January 1994.

in East Germany). Training is not allowed to include basic skills and common knowledge (§1a AO-FuU, EX[47] for §41a courses). Training can be full time, part time, evening course, or at home (§34). If training was subsidized according to the AFG-GDR, the BA is further subsidizing this training after unification, regardless of all other conditions (§249d).

Restriction: Completed Vocational Qualification (§42)

A participant must have a completed vocational qualification. The requirement is met by an examination of the German apprenticeship system plus three years work experience or six years work experience.

EX: - 2 years less experience if training is less than 6 months full time (MFT) or 24 months part time (MPT) or

- 3 years less experience if training is 'necessary'.

CH since Jan. 94: Examination or 3 years of work experience are sufficient.[48]

Before participating in subsidized training again, another 3 years of work experience are required.

EX: - Minus 1 year if the earlier or the actual training is less than 6 MFT/24 MPT.

- No waiting time if earlier or the actual training is less than 3 MFT/12 MPT.

- No waiting time if the actual training is 'necessary'.

CH since Jan. 93: 3 years waiting time are necessary.

- Minus 1 year if the earlier or the actual training is less than 6 MFT/24 MPT.

- 1 year waiting time if training is 'necessary' because of unemployment or part time.

- No waiting time if actual training is 'necessary', the participant has special labor market problems, and the earlier training was less than 2 MFT/8 MPT.

CH since Jan. 94: 1 year waiting time is necessary.

---

[47] We use EX as a shortcut for 'exception', CH for 'change', and AD for 'addition'.
[48] This was not a real change, because since January 94 not 'necessary' training was not possible any more.

No waiting time is necessary if training is 'necessary', participant has special labor market problems, and the earlier training was less than 2 MFT/8 MPT.

Time of registered unemployment is equal to work experience.

EX: Before the first training at least half of the work experience must be real working.

Restriction: 'Necessary' and 'Useful' Training (§44(2), since Jan. 94: §42a)

To obtain the status of 'necessary' training, it must be necessary

- to find employment for an unemployed person,

- to avoid unemployment for somebody directly threatened by unemployment, or

- to provide qualification for somebody without a completed vocational qualification.

EX: In East Germany 'generally threatened by unemployment' is sufficient (§249d).

AD in Jan. 94: Counselling in the LO before approval of training is required. Training is 'useful' if it helps to reach the general goals of the AFG (§§1, 2) and of subsidized training (§§34, 36).

Special Case: Part Time Training (§44(2b))

Part time training is 'necessary' if

- it is necessary for full time employment of a part time employed person younger than 25

- or if an individual returning to the labor force after child care is unemployed or without vocational degree, and full time training is not possible because of the child.

AD in Jan. 91: If someone is in part time subsidized employment (ABM) and training is necessary for full time employment on the regular labor market.

CH since Jan. 94: Part time training is possible if training is 'necessary' and full time training is not possible because of child.

Restriction: Unemployment Insurance Contributions (UIC) before Training (§46)

At least two years of UIC within the last three years are required.

EX: - No three year limit if training is necessary to earn money for subsistence and not working because of a child before (for example lone parents without wealth).

- Add five years to the three year limit for every child if not working because of the child.

- Add the time of working abroad to the three year limit (maximum two years).

- No contributions are necessary if the participant got a vocational degree within the last year (add times of unemployment to the year).

- Unemployment benefits based on earlier contributions are sufficient.

In East Germany instead of actual contributions it was sufficient to have worked in a job that would have made UIC mandatory in West Germany (§249c).

Payments by the Labor Office

Unterhaltsgeld (UHG) in general requires that the participant has a vocational degree (for EX see below at §41a). The 'full' UHG is paid if training is 'necessary' and UIC are sufficient (§44). It amounts to 65 percent of former net earnings, 73 percent with a child or a dependent partner. CH since Jan. 94: The replacement rates are now 60 percent/67 percent.[49] The 'small' UHG is paid if training is 'necessary' but UIC are not sufficient (§46). It is paid at the level of unemployment benefits before training. UHG as a loan is paid if training is not 'necessary' but 'useful' and UIC are sufficient (§44). It amounts to 58 percent of former net earnings.

CH since Jan. 94: UHG is no longer paid as a loan.

Expenditures for training can be paid when UHG is paid (§45). The expenditures can be covered as well when UIC are not sufficient but training is 'necessary' and the participant commits to three years of work after training or in the case of training during STW. The payments can be in percent of actual expenditures (up to 100 percent, possibly with an upper limit) or flat rates. The amount might differ for different groups of participants. Included are course fees, travel expenses, clothing, materials, insurance, child care, and examination fees

---

[49] This is now set at the same level as unemployment benefits (*Arbeitslosengeld*). It was higher before.

among others. If the participant fulfilled the prerequisites it was mandatory for the LO until Dec. to pay UHG. Since Jan. 94 it is not mandatory anymore. It is not mandatory for the LO to reimburse for expenditures according to the AFG, but until May 1993 the AO-FuU made some refunds mandatory (for example course fees).

Types of Training

§41a

The goal of training is to improve the job search skills and the motivation of an unemployed. Also it could provide information about different types of work and training possibilities as well as in regard to the abilities of the participant. They can include training in general knowledge and basic skills. Participants do not need a vocational degree or work experience, but have to be unemployed. The duration is typically between two and six weeks.

Continuous Training (§§41, 43)

The goal is to adapt skills and knowledge to technical progress, to advance career, to avoid labor shortages, or to help women and older unemployed to return to the labor force. The duration is typically between two months and two years. Since May 1993 the upper limit is one year if the course does not finish with a publicly approved examination.

Retraining (§47)

The goal of training is to provide an 'appropriate' occupation if the old occupation is useless because of personal or labor market conditions. The duration should not exceed two years and should be shorter than a corresponding vocational qualification. The course should finish with a publicly approved examination. CH since May 93: The course must finish with a publicly approved examination and must be shorter than a vocational qualification.

References

Ashenfelter, O./Card, D. (1985), Using the Longitudinal Structure of Earnings to Estimate the Effect of Training Programs, *The Review of Economics and Statistics* 67, 648-660.

Bell, S.H. et al. (1995), Program Applicants as a Comparison Group in Evaluating Training Programs, Upjohn: Kalamazoo.

Blaschke, D./Nagel, E. (1995), Beschäftigungssituation von Teilnehmern an AFG-finanzierter beruflicher Weiterbildung, *MittAB* 2/95, 195-213.

Bundesanstalt für Arbeit (BA, 1989), *Arbeitsförderungsgesetz: Textausgabe mit angrenzenden Gesetzen, Verordnungen und BA-Regelungen: 36. Ausgabe, Stand:1. Januar 1989*, Nürnberg.

Bundesanstalt für Arbeit (BA, 1990), *Arbeitsförderungsgesetz: Textausgabe mit angrenzenden Gesetzen, Verordnungen und BA-Regelungen: 37. Ausgabe, Stand:1. Januar 1990*, Nürnberg.

Bundesanstalt für Arbeit (BA, 1991a), *Förderung der beruflichen Weiterbildung: Bericht über die Teilnahme an beruflicher Fortrbildung, Umschulung und Einarbeitung im Jahr 1990*, Nürnberg.

Bundesanstalt für Arbeit (BA, 1991b), *Arbeitsförderungsgesetz: Textausgabe mit angrenzenden Gesetzen, Verordnungen und BA-Regelungen: 38. Ausgabe, Stand:15. Januar 1991*, Nürnberg.

Bundesanstalt für Arbeit (BA, 1992a), *Förderung der beruflichen Weiterbildung: Bericht über die Teilnahme an beruflicher Fortbildung, Umschulung und Einarbeitung im Jahr 1991*, Nürnberg.

Bundesanstalt für Arbeit (BA, 1992b), *Arbeitsförderungsgesetz: Textausgabe mit angrenzenden Gesetzen, Verordnungen und BA-Regelungen: 39. Ausgabe, Stand:1. Februar 1992*, Nürnberg.

Bundesanstalt für Arbeit (BA, 1993a), *Förderung der beruflichen Weiterbildung: Bericht über die Teilnahme an beruflicher Fortbildung, Umschulung und Einarbeitung im Jahr 1992*, Nürnberg.

Bundesanstalt für Arbeit (BA, 1993b), *Arbeitsförderungsgesetz: Textausgabe mit angrenzenden Gesetzen, Verordnungen und BA-Regelungen: 40. Ausgabe, Stand:1. Februar 1993*, Nürnberg.

Bundesanstalt für Arbeit (BA, 1994a), *Berufliche Weiterbildung: Förderung beruflicher Fortbildung, Umschulung und Einarbeitung im Jahr 1993*, Nürnberg.

Bundesanstalt für Arbeit (BA, 1994b), *Arbeitsförderungsgesetz: Textausgabe mit angrenzenden Gesetzen, Verordnungen und BA-Regelungen: 41. Ausgabe, Stand:1. Februar 1994*, Nürnberg.

Bundesanstalt für Arbeit (BA, 1995a), *Berufliche Weiterbildung: Förderung beruflicher Fortrbildung, Umschulung und Einarbeitung im Jahr 1994*, Nürnberg.

Bundesanstalt für Arbeit (BA, 1995b), Arbeitsstatistik 1994 – Jahreszahlen. *Amtliche Nachrichten der Bundesanstalt für Arbeit* 43 (Sondernummer 21), July 1995, Nürnberg.

Bundesanstalt für Arbeit (BA, 1995c), *Arbeitsförderungsgesetz: Textausgabe mit angrenzenden Gesetzen, Verordnungen und BA-Regelungen: 42. Ausgabe, Stand:1. Febuar 1995*, Nürnberg.

Bundesministerium für Wirtschaft (1995), *Dokumentation, Nr. 382*.

Burtless, G. (1995), The Case for Randomized Field Trials in Economic and Policy Research, *Journal of Economic Perspectives* 9, 63-84.

Buttler, F. (1994a), Finanzierung der Arbeitsmarktpolitik, *IAB-Werkstattbericht* Nr. 8, 31.8.1994.

Buttler, F. (1994b), Berufliche Weiterbildung als öffentliche Aufgabe, *MittAB* 1/94, 33-42.

Buttler, F./Emmerich, K. (1994), Kosten und Nutzen aktiver Arbeitsmarktpolitik im ostdeutschen Transformationsprozeß, *Schriften des Vereins für Sozialpolitik* 239/4, 61-94.

Card, D./Sullivan, D. (1988), Measuring the Effect of Subsidized Training Programs on Movements in and out of Employment, *Econometrica* 56, 497-530.

Dehejia, R./Wahba, S. (1998), Propensity Score Matching Methods for Non-Experimental Causal Studies, *Columbia University, Department of Economics Discussion Paper Series, No. 9899/01*.

Dehejia, R./Wahba, S. (1999), Causal Effects in Non-Experimental Studies, *Journal of the American Statistical Association 94(448)*, 1053-1062.

Fitzenberger, B./Prey, H. (1997), Assessing the Impact of Training on Employment: The Case of East Germany, *Ifo-Studien 43(1)*, 71-116.

Heckman, J.J./Hotz, V.J. (1989), Choosing Among Alternative Nonexperimental Methods for Estimating the Impact of Social Programs: The Case of Manpower Training, *Journal of the American Statistical Association* 84, 862-880 (includes comments by Holland and Moffitt and a rejoinder by Heckman and Hotz).

Heckman, J.J./Robb, R. (1985), Alternative Methods of Evaluating the Impact of Interventions, in: Heckman, J.J./Singer, B. (eds.), *Longitudinal Analysis of Labor Market Data*, New York: Cambridge University Press, 156-245.

Heckman, J.J./Smith, J.A. (1995), Assessing the Case for Social Experiments, *Journal of Economic Perspectives* 9, 85-110.

Holland, P.W. (1986), Statistics and Causal Inference, *Journal of the American Statistical Society* 81, 945-970 (includes comments by Cox, Granger, Glymour, Rubin and a rejoinder by Holland).

Infratest Sozialforschung (1990, 1991, 1992, 1993, 1994), *Das sozio-ökonomische Panel – Ost, Welle 1, Welle 2, Welle 3, Welle 4, Welle 5*, Anlagenbände zum Methodenbericht, München.

Institut für Arbeitsmarkt- und Berufsforschung (IAB, 1995), *Zahlen-Fibel 1995* (BeitrAB 101), Nürnberg.

LaLonde, R.J. (1986), Evaluating the Econometric Evaluations of Training Programs with Experimental Data, *American Economic Review* 76, 604-620.

LaLonde, R.J. (1995), The Promise of Public Sector-Sponsored Training Programs, *Journal of Economic Perspectives* 9, 149-168.

Lechner, M. (1999a), An Evaluation of Public Sector Sponsored Continuous Vocational Training Programs in East Germany, *IZA Discussion Paper, No. 12/99*, Bonn.

Lechner, M. (1999b), Earnings and Employment Effects of Continuous Off-the-Job Training in East Germany after Unification, *Journal of Business and Economic Statistics* 17(1), 74-90.

Lechner, M. (1999c), The Effects of Enterprise-related Continuous Vocational Training in East Germany on Individual Employment and Earnings, *Annales d'economie et de statistique* 0(55-56), 97-129.

Lechner, M. (1998), T*raining the East German labor force: Microeconometric evaluations of continuous vocational training after unification*, Heidelberg.

Pannenberg, M. (1995), *Weiterbildungsaktivitäten und Erwerbsbiographie*, Campus: Frankfurt.

Pannenberg, M./Helberger, C. (1994), Kurzfristige Auswirkungen staatlicher Qualifizierungsmaßnahmen in Ostdeutschland: Das Beispiel Fortbildung und Umschulung, forthcoming in: *Schriftenreihe des Vereins für Sozialpolitik*.

Rosenbaum, P.R./Rubin, D.B. (1983), The Central Role of the Propensity Score in Observational Studies for Causal Effects, *Biometrica* 70, 41-50.

Rosenbaum, P.R./Rubin, D.B. (1985), Constructing a Control Group Using Multivariate Matched Sampling Methods That Incorporate the Propensity Score, *The American Statistician* 39, 33-38.

Rubin, D.B. (1979), Using Multivariate Matched Sampling and Regression Adjustment to Control Bias in Observational Studies, *Journal of the American Statistical Association* 74, 318-328.

Statistisches Bundesamt (1992), *Statistisches Jahrbuch für die Bundesrepublik Deutschland 1992*, Stuttgart: Metzler-Pöschel.

Statistisches Bundesamt (1995), *Statistisches Jahrbuch für die Bundesrepublik Deutschland 1995*, Stuttgart: Metzler-Pöschel.

Wagner, G.G. et al. (1993), The English Language Public Use File of the German Socio-Economic Panel, *Journal of Human Resources* 28, 429-433.

6. Active Labor Market Policies in Central Europe: First Lessons

Hartmut Lehmann, Heriot-Watt University, Edinburgh, and IZA, Bonn

1. Introduction

In the first years of their transition to a market economy the economies of Central and Eastern Europe (CEE) experienced a sharp rise in open unemployment, that reached comparable levels to the worse performing Western economies.[1] Having continuous difficulties with the fight against inflation, governments in CEE had thus far few possibilities to reflate their economies and tried early on to combat the incidence of unemployment with active labor market policies (ALMP). The rise of unemployment has, however, increasingly involved a "crowding out" of resources for ALMP in favor of unemployment benefit payments.

Nevertheless, it seems worthwhile to discuss ALMP in transition economies, even though they can only play a marginal role in the fight against unemployment. Active labor market policies are understood here in the narrow sense of policies targeted at the unemployed and at those threatened by redundancies. Clearly, sound macroeconomic policies, policies inducing large foreign direct investment, and the existence of a political and social consensus about how to distribute the cost of transition are crucial for rapid growth and thus for more employment.

There have been exhaustive surveys of the literature on ALMP in OECD countries (e.g. OECD (1993, ch.2) and Björklund et al. (1991)). Section 2 contains a brief, general discussion of the merits of transplanting the ALMP developed to fight unemployment in mature market economies to CEE.

Section 3 analyzes the mix of passive and active labor market policies and the specific ALMP instruments introduced in the Central European countries of the Czech Republic, Hungary and Poland in the first years of the transition process. These three countries have pursued the transition to a market economy most vigorously and consistently.[2] Analyzing their experiences with ALMP provides,

---

[1] The main exception to this statement is the Czech Republic where open unemployment stayed very low in the first years of the transition process.

[2] All three are now member countries of the OECD.

therefore, valuable lessons for the rest of CEE where transition to a market economy has been, at best, more hesitant. The empirical evidence on problem groups and the evaluation of ALMP in the three Central European countries in the first years of the transition process are the topic of section 4. Some results of my own work will be presented, some case studies and the major micro-econometric and macroeconometric studies in the literature will be summarized. Section 5 offers some general conclusions and policy implications.

2. The Applicability of OECD Active Labor Market Policies in Transition Economies

In mature OECD countries[3] the following program categories are considered part of ALMP:

a.) public employment services ("job brokerage") and administration;

b.) labor market training;

c.) youth measures;

d.) subsidized employment;

e.) measures for the disabled.

In most transition economies all these categories have been introduced in the first years of the transition process, with the emphasis varying from country to country. The merits of measures *a* and *e* are straightforward in both mature OECD and transition countries. What is interesting from a theoretical point of view is whether active measures in categories *b, c,* and *d* can have the same functions in transition economies as in mature capitalist economies and whether they can, consequently, be evaluated in a similar fashion.

Abstracting from counter-cyclical employment measures, ALMP in mature OECD countries like *b, c,* and *d* seek to integrate marginal social groups or to re-integrate marginalized groups into the labor market. Whilst the large majority of the labor force are continuously employed, certain groups with relatively loose labor market attachment and/or very low human capital experience great difficulties in finding permanent employment (e.g. some school leavers, older unskilled workers, minorities). By participating in a training or subsidized employment scheme, the human capital of such "marginal" persons can be increased and their labor market attachment strengthened thus boosting the

---

[3] The term mature OECD countries is used to identify that subset of OECD member countries which excludes Mexico, South-Korea, the Czech Republic, Hungary, and Poland.

probability of employment or re-employment. Integration or re-integration of "problem persons" into the labor force increases effective labor supply, *ceteris paribus* lowers equilibrium wage, and thus increases overall employment. Such an increase can also come about through the re-integration of persons who have lost their job because of structural shocks or a deep recession and who have become long-term unemployed. ALMP which successfully increase the effective labor supply, during the expansionary phase of the business cycle, can contribute to the dampening of inflationary pressures (Calmfors (1994)) and/or help in the solution of partial hysteresis of unemployment due to long-term unemployment (Layard et al. (1991)).

When evaluating measures like b, c, and d in mature OECD countries the following questions are typically asked:[4]

1. *Did the schemes target the groups identified as those having problems leaving unemployment?*

2. *Did participation in a scheme enhance individuals' productivity, expressed in higher wages?*

3. *Did the measure increase the average re-employment probability of participants?*

4. *Have distortive effects, e.g. substitution-, dead weight-, displacement of output- and fiscal substitution effects, been minimized?*

These questions are also relevant in transition countries. However, some stylized facts of labor markets in transition need to be recalled when discussing the targeting question.

Labor markets in the first years of the transition process were characterized, apart from the Czech Republic, by a low demand for labor, a stagnant unemployment pool, rising long-term unemployment, and tougher competition for jobs among the unemployed than in most mature OECD countries. Moreover, a significant component of the unemployed, and even of the long-term unemployed, had a strong labor market attachment and in some instances a large stock of accumulated human capital. Although their work profile might have been overspecialized if not obsolete, they had the potential for adapting relatively quickly to new tasks. They might, therefore, have been the typical target group for measures like further training and retraining. On the other hand, it seems inefficient to target problem groups (unskilled, low-educated, older workers, etc.) for further training and retraining as, after the completion of the scheme, they will have to compete with a large pool of unemployed who are probably better

---

[4] Evaluation is here understood in the narrow sense of establishing the effects of these measures on the overall unemployment rate by estimating their impact on the unemployed and those competing with the unemployed for jobs.

motivated and certainly in possession of more accumulated human capital. Whether problem groups could be targeted by public work programs and subsidized employment schemes will be discussed when these measures are evaluated.

When discussing the applicability of ALMP to CEE one needs to keep in mind that the net distortive effects of these policies can be larger in transition economies than in mature western economies. For example, most studies analyzing public employment programs for minorities in the US found large fiscal substitution effects. These were mitigated, though, by an increase in equity as minority persons were employed by local authorities instead of persons from the core of the employment pool. The latter found employment outside the public sector with relative ease. In transition economies, in contrast, even persons from the core of the employment pool had great problems finding re-employment once unemployed. For example, nurses who were substituted by persons on the intervention works scheme (wage subsidy scheme) in Polish municipal hospitals were in general not re-employable in the private sector. Thus, there are examples showing that fiscal substitution effects can be more detrimental in transition economies.

In mature OECD countries, measures like b, c, and d are a means of reducing mismatch by skill or region (Padoa-Schioppa (1991)). One strand of policies contributing to the solution of regional mismatch in these OECD countries focuses on helping the unemployed move to regions with better employment opportunities. Further training and retraining schemes can be an important ingredient for such policies, although more direct interventions by government, such as subsidizing public housing in high opportunity regions and government contributions to moving expenses, are more prominent components of OECD policies intent on "taking the workers to the work" (Jackman (1996)). As there were very high barriers to mobility in the CEE in the first years of transition[5] ALMP such as further training and retraining which in mature OECD countries also increase the mobility of workers might be rather ineffective when combating regional mismatch in CEE.

The second strand of regional policies of "bringing work to the workers", i.e. creating jobs in high unemployment regions, involves investment grants or subsidies to firms if they locate or undertake new capital investment in such

---

[5] Because there was a severe housing constraint inherited from the old regime and in the first years of the transition process no housing policy exists, which could help promote the movement of workers to high opportunity regions, transition economies were characterized by high barriers to mobility (cf. Boeri/Scarpetta (1995)). The available empirical evidence from the supplement to the August 1994 wave of the Polish Labor Force Survey (LFS) (Góra/Sztanderska (1996)) showed virtually no inter-voivodship mobility while, for the Czech Republic, Erbenova (1995) found that people commuted but did not move to high opportunity regions.

regions. As nearly all governments in transition economies had severe budgetary problems and these traditional regional policies are very expensive, it is inconceivable that such policies would have reduced regional mismatch in transition economies. What might have been relatively useful in this context, though, is the targeting of subsidized public employment in high unemployment regions.

Further training and retraining is in principle an important tool to combat skill mismatch in transition economies. However, as already alluded to, in the light of the above stylized facts of labor markets in transition, targeting these measures at identified problem groups seems arguably inefficient.

3. Labor Market Policies in the Czech Republic, Hungary and Poland

3.1. Expenditures on Labor Market Policies in the Three Countries

Tables 1, 2, 3 and 4 show public expenditure on all labor market policies and participant inflows into ALMP for Hungary, the Czech Republic, and Poland in the first of the transition process. In these tables the OECD classification is used when describing labor market policy measures. When inspecting these tables one should keep in mind the large differences in the unemployment rates of Hungary and Poland on the one hand and of the Czech Republic on the other, that rose to the lower teens in the case of Hungary and Poland, while remaining at between three and four percent in the Czech Republic.

The evolution of expenditures on unemployment compensation points to a tightening of eligibility criteria and a shortening of entitlement periods in all three countries in this period. In Hungary and the Czech Republic these expenditures fell sharply against a stable stock of unemployment while they slightly rose in Poland against a rapid rise in the number of unemployed. Also noteworthy is the fact that both Hungary and Poland spent the bulk of their expenditures on unemployment compensation while the Czech Republic has a strong focus on ALMP.

Looking at the expenditure patterns of mature OECD countries (cf. OECD (1995), Table 2.B.1 and Chart 2.1) some interesting comparisons can be made regarding the labor market policy stance of the three transition countries.

Table 1. Public Expenditure and Participant Inflows in Labor Market Programs in Hungary

Program categories	Total expenditures (in percent of GDP)			Participant inflow (in percent of labor force)		
	1992	1993	1994	1992	1993	1994
1. Public employment services and administration	0.15	0.16	0.15	-	-	-
2. Labor market training	0.15	0.24	0.20	0.9	1.4	1.3
a) Training for unemployed adults and those at risk	0.15	0.24	0.20	0.9	1.4	1.3
b) Training for employed adults	-	-	-	-	-	-
3. Youth measures	-	-	-	-	-	-
4. Subsidized employment	0.33	0.30	0.28	2.9	2.6	3.0
a) Subsidies to regular employment in private sector	0.15	0.11	0.12	1.9	0.9	1.6
b) Support of unemployed persons starting enterprises	0.08	0.05	0.02	0.6	0.7	0.2
c) Direct job creation (public or non-profit)	0.10	0.14	0.14	0.4	1.0	1.2
5. Measures for the disabled	-	-	-	-	-	-
6. Unemployment compensation	2.26	2.14	1.08	-	-	-
7. Early retirement for labor market reasons	0.06	0.11	0.15	-	-	-
TOTAL	2.95	2.96	1.85	-	-	-
-Active measures (1-5)	0.64	0.70	0.63	3.83	4.06	4.3
-Passive measures (6-7)	2.32	2.26	1.23	-	-	-

Source: Labor Ministry, Budapest, Hungary.

Table 2. Public Expenditure and Participant Inflows in Labor Market Programs in the Czech Republic

Program categories	Total expenditures (in percent of GDP)			Participant inflow (in percent of labor force)		
	1991	1992	1993	1991	1992	1993
1. Public employment services and administration	0.08	0.10	0.11	-	-	-
2. Labor market training	0.01	0.01	0.01	0.10	0.34	0.20
3. Work experience for school leavers	0.01	0.05	0.03	0.27	0.42	0.14
4. Subsidized employment	0.08	0.16	0.05	0.89	2.27	0.47
a) Subsidies to regular employment in private sector	0.05	0.10	0.02	0.40	1.22	0.16
b) Support of unemployed persons starting enterprises	0.02	0.03	0.01	0.22	0.50	0.08
c) Direct job creation (public or non-profit)	0.01	0.03	0.02	0.27	0.55	0.23
5. Supported work for the disabled	-	0.01	0.01	-	0.03	0.02
6. Unemployment compensation	0.23	0.20	0.16	-	-	-
TOTAL	0.41	0.53	0.36	1.26	3.05	0.83

Source: OECD-CCET data base.

For the reported period, with the exception of Sweden all countries with a substantial un-employment rate spend more on passive than on active policies. Given these facts expenditures were higher the higher the unemployment rate was. It, therefore, comes as no surprise that Hungary with its relatively high unemployment rate had expenditures on labor market policies, which were (in terms of percent of GDP) comparable to many mature OECD countries. Among those countries which in 1992 had similar unemployment rates as Hungary only Belgium spent decisively more on labor market programs in general and on ALMP in particular. Britain, on the other hand, which had an average unemployment rate of 10 percent in that year spent somewhat less on total labor market policies and a lot less on ALMP than Hungary (!), while Canada spent exactly the same percentage of GDP. This international comparison certainly leads to the conclusion that as far as labor market expenditures are concerned Hungary did not perform worse than most mature OECD countries.

Table 3. Public Expenditure on Labor Market Programs in Poland

Program categories	1990	1991	1992	1993	1994
1. Public employment services and administration	0.02	0.03	0.02	0.02	0.01
2. Labor market training	<0.01	0.01	0.02	0.03	0.03
3. Work experience for school leavers	-	-	-	-	-
4. Subsidized employment	0.21	0.11	0.08	0.20	0.25
a) Subsidies to regular employment in private sector	0.04	0.06	0.04	0.09	0.12
b) Support of unemployed persons starting enterprises	0.17	0.05	0.02	0.03	0.03
c) Direct job creation (public or non-profit)	<0.01	<0.01	0.02	0.08	0.10
5. Supported work for the disabled	-	-	-	-	-
6. Unemployment compensation	0.34	1.34	1.71	1.72	1.79
TOTAL	0.57	1.53	1.83	1.97	2.08
Total expenditures on ALMP	0.23	0.15	0.12	0.25	0.29

Source: Polish Ministry of Labor and Social Policy.

The Czech Republic, on the other hand, spent for the reported period less on labor market policies than virtually all mature OECD countries by the GDP measure.[6] Only Japan with on average around 0.35 percent of GDP for the period 1990-94 spent less spent on labor market policies. The other "low spender" among the mature OECD countries, the United States, averaged 0.80 percent of GDP between the years 1990 and 1994.

---

[6] However, if one normalizes by the stock of unemployment, then expenditure on labor market policies is quite high.

Table 4. Participant Inflows into Active Labor Market Programs in Poland

Program categories	1990	1991	1992	1993	1994
2. Labor market training	0.06	0.39	0.40	0.43	0.50
4. Subsidized employment	0.96	0.33	0.83	1.26	1.80
a) Subsidies to regular employment in private sector	0.61	0.21	0.59	0.76	1.11
b) Support of unemployed persons starting enterprises	0.35	0.12	0.04	0.07	0.06
c) Direct job creation (public or non-profit)	-	-	0.20	0.43	0.63
TOTAL	1.02	0.72	1.23	1.69	2.3

Source: Polish Ministry of Labor and Social Policy.

Comparing Czech expenditures on ALMP with the expenditure patterns on such policies in mature OECD leaves one to conclude that ALMP was not the main cause of the low unemployment rate in the Czech Republic relative to other CE economies. While it is true that the Czech Republic was the only country among the Visegrad states which had a high proportion of expenditures on ALMP throughout the reported period and which spent more than 50 percent of total expenditures on ALMP in 1992 and 1993, if ALMP were mainly responsible for the low unemployment, the Czech government would have had to spend for active measures on a level at least comparable to that of Sweden. In 1990-92, when the Swedish unemployment rate was still similar to the unemployment rate of the Czech Republic and to a great extent driven by a focus on ALMP, Sweden spent about 2 percent of GDP on ALMP, while the highest level of Czech expenditures was reached in 1992 with 0.33 percent of GDP.

When the unemployment rate is within low bands as it was the case in the Czech Republic, ALMP can, however, have a noticeable effect on the unemployment rate. The changing expenditure patterns for 1991-1993 makes this point. With de-registration of employment scheme participants the big jump in expenditure for such schemes from 1991 to 1992 resulted in a fall of the unemployment rate caused entirely by increased outflows from unemployment. According to back-of-the-envelope calculations, in the absence of these schemes and assuming no substitution effects or dead weight losses, the unemployment rate for 1992 would have been 5.1 percent instead of 2.6 percent. In 1993 when expenditures on ALMP fell back to 0.20 percent the unemployment rate rose to 3.5 percent. So, given low levels of unemployment ALMP could be used by the Czech government to reduce the overall unemployment rate. These unemployment levels which were low relative to other transition economies but also relative to most mature OECD countries cannot, however, be explained by ALMP. The decisive determinants of low Czech unemployment within the reported period have to be sought elsewhere (see e.g. the discussion in Svejnar et al. (1995) and in Lehmann (1995)).

Hungary had a high proportion of expenditure on public employment services and administration, roughly comparable with the "high spenders" on this item in the mature OECD group, while the Czech Republic had an average value for this category of active policy. Poland, on the other hand, spent very little on this item. These figures reflect the relative performance of labor offices in these countries, while Hungary and the Czech Republic had relatively well functioning and Poland very poorly functioning labor offices (Góra et al. (1996)).

Also interesting is the fact that the Czech Republic spent only negligible amounts on labor market training and the vast bulk of its funds was designated for active measures on subsidized employment and work experience for school leavers. Hungary seems to have a more balanced approach with expenditure on labor market training being of growing importance. One should add that although Hungarian employment offices also had to provide further training for youngsters who had only eight years of elementary schooling, these expenditures are not included in Table 1. The Polish figures show, in contrast, a shifting composition of expenditures on ALMP. Excluding expenditures on public employment services and administration, one observes two relevant developments: The expenditure share on start-up loans fell from 81 percent in 1990 to approximately 10 percent in 1994 while the share of subsidized employment rose from 18 percent in 1990 to around 80 percent in 1994. Finally, apart from 1990, training measures had a relatively constant share between 10 percent and 17 percent. In the opinion of Góra et al. (1996) this shifting composition can be explained by a combination of political reasons and learning effects by central authorities and regional labor offices.

The ratio of participant inflows (as a percentage of the labor force) over expenditures (as a percentage of GDP) can be used as a rough measure of the average quality of labor market training. A high value implies that on average many participants were put through training and/or the average value added of such courses was low. Among the countries in the mature OECD group where this measure can be calculated not many had a value below Hungary's. Only Sweden has with 4.6 in 1992 a clearly lower value, while countries like Germany and the United Kingdom had values that are low relative to many other mature OECD countries but comparable to the 6.3 and 5.9 Hungary has in 1992 and 1993. As Germany had relatively lengthy training courses with on average substantial value added this could only mean that Hungarian labor market training was of relatively high quality. The Czech values of this measure varied between 10 and 34 and the Polish values between 14 and 33, pointing in both cases to larger throughput and/or lower human capital enhancing content than in the Hungarian case.

The most important ALMP measures of the three countries, as they appear in employment legislation in the first years of the transition process, will now be described.

3.2. ALMP Measures in the Three Countries – a Brief Summary

3.2.1. Czech ALMP[7]

Socially Purposeful Jobs (SPJ)

The SPJ scheme consisted of two different types of programs: assistance to new entrepreneurs and the creation of jobs with already existing enterprises (both private and state sector). In both cases, assistance was only given to unemployed people. All proposals for SPJ had to be for newly created jobs that have a reasonable chance to be viable in the long run. Czech law stated that a SPJ should last for at least two years. There was a penalty for not maintaining a SPJ for that period, but it is not clear how well this was monitored. The program was administered through the district employment offices. The offices were responsible for distributing, funding and monitoring these jobs. Funding was provided in the following three ways:

– *subsidy*

– *interest free loan and/or*

– *payment of interest on loans taken by employer*

A combination of these payments was also possible, but the maximum reimbursement per job was 12 times the average monthly rate of unemployment benefit in the district. Although the offices' contribution to the cost of creating a new job was considered marginal, it still acted as an incentive, especially for people starting new businesses who lack capital.

Publicly Useful Jobs (PUJs)

PUJs offered temporary employment for unemployed people for a period of up to six months in order to provide work experience to the unemployed. PUJs were essentially public works jobs that were considered beneficial to the local community. The district employment office was in charge of the administration of the PUJs. These jobs were mostly supplied by local authorities and require unskilled or semi-skilled individuals. A large portion of these jobs was of the menial type (e.g. street cleaning). Benefits could be withdrawn for refusing a PUJ,

---

[7] Source used are Terrell/Munich (1996) and Lehmann (1995).

as long as the work refused was of a suitable professional level and appropriate to the general circumstances of the individual benefit recipient.

PUJs were especially used for difficult groups and workers to whom an offer on the scheme counted as an offer of suitable work. Many employment offices used PUJ as an instrument to test willingness to work. PUJs were generally seen as short-term and a very small percentage of workers on this scheme stayed with their employers after completion of the PUJ.

Practice for School Leavers

Under this scheme the district employment offices paid subsidies to employers who provided working positions for school leavers and graduates. In addition, there might have been a modest tax relief for these employers. The aim was to help young labor market entrants to get their first job in order to acquire practical experience. Jobs provided should have been newly created working positions. The work contract between employer and school leaver or graduate was to be of unlimited duration. The program generally last one year during which the employed had to spend at least six months of specialist practice corresponding to the individual's qualifications.

Retraining

Retraining necessary for getting a job was an aspect of the right to employment created by the Employment Act. However, individuals had no specific entitlement to retraining. District employment offices were responsible for arranging retraining for registered unemployed people where it was an essential prerequisite for their finding a job. District employment offices had to take into account the current need for specific professions in the labor market as well as the structure of the newly emerging vacancies. Duration and achievement of a retraining program were not defined by law. There were two types of retraining courses: training in job-specific skills and training in general skills not linked to a particular kind of job. Under certain circumstances retraining of employees was undertaken to avoid redundancies.

3.2.2. Hungarian ALMP[8]

The Hungarian authorities applied a full menu of ALMP in order to combat unemployment. Here only the two largest schemes (in terms of participants) are discussed.

---

[8] Sources used are O'Leary (1997) and Szemlér (1997).

Further Training and Retraining

Unemployed persons interested in further training and retraining were normally informed about the availability of courses at the local employment center. Anyone who was unemployed could apply for retraining. In fact, according to the law, the unemployed might have been obliged to enter retraining, but this was not in general applied in practice. As will be discussed below, strong "creaming effects" seemed to be at work as counselors tried to place those with the highest aptitude into these training courses. Instead of unemployment compensation participants received a slightly higher training subsidy from their local employment center.

Public Service Employment (PSE)

This measure is comparable to the British Community Program or the German *Arbeitsbeschaffungsmaßnahmen (ABM)* program. Local employment centers financed work places that have been established by firms or public organizations at the local level, which were engaged in production of goods useful to the community. The unemployed was obliged to take the offered place as long as it was commensurate with his/her educational and professional background which implied, given that in most cases the nature of the performed jobs was of a low level, a selection of participants with characteristics less favorable than those of the average unemployed. To avoid displacement of output effects the stipulation applied that only goods should have been produced which without subsidy would not have been produced by the private sector. As there were not many private firms which were yet able to fulfill the legal requirements the large majority of these work places was created by local government.

3.2.3. Polish ALMP[9]

Public Works

Local authorities employed those with uninterrupted unemployment spells of more than six months on public projects. Most projects were intended to expand or maintain the public infrastructure. Some workers found employment on projects of environmental protection or amelioration. The duration of these jobs could not exceed six months and it was the expressed intention of the government to rotate them among the long-term unemployed. It is important to note that the nature of public works was different from that of pre-World-War-Two public works, which were organized in a quasi-military fashion. public works in the reported period were strongly decentralized and local authorities were encouraged to suggest worthwhile projects. There are no nation-wide data on average remuneration, but

---

[9] Sources are Lehmann (1996) and Polish Ministry of Labor and Social Policy (1994).

there is some casual evidence from Ministry of Labor officials that people employed on public works might have received wages that were above the minimum wage.

Intervention Works (Wage Subsidies)

This term is somewhat misleading. Firms (private or state-owned) could have approached the local employment council (Polish: *Rada Zatrudnienia*) and have asked for subsidized additional work places. In order to qualify for this scheme the firm needed to have more than 10 employees and was not allowed to have released more than 10 percent of its workforce in the last six months. Again, subsidized employment was not to exceed six months. The state paid a wage subsidy to the firm equal to the level of benefits and often firms or local employment councils paid additional wages to these workers.

Further Training and Retraining

Private and public agencies are paid a fee to train some of the unemployed who in turn are paid an allowance (115 percent of benefits) while on the course. Many of these courses are of short duration[10] and casual evidence tells us that the human capital enhancing content of the majority of such courses might be dubious.

Start-up Loans

This scheme is comparable to e.g. the British Enterprise Allowance Scheme where the unemployed were subsidized by employment offices to start-up their own businesses. In the Polish case, credits were granted to unemployed people which were not allowed to exceed 20 times the average remuneration. While these grants were also given to engage in economic activity in the agricultural sector, the use of these funds for the purchase of land was precluded. If after 24 months of founding a business it was still operative, 50 percent of the loan would have been written off. Employment offices seemed to examine applicants well as many of the started businesses presumably survived for more than two years. Most of the started businesses were in the services sector which was underdeveloped in Poland. Displacement of output effects which, in the case of the British Enterprise Allowance Scheme, were estimated to be approximately 50 percent (cf. Stern (1988)) should, therefore, have been negligible.

---

[10] Steady state calculations using administrative data show that in 1992 the average duration of a training course was 1.58 months for women, and 1.75 months for men (Lehmann (1996)). The micro data of the Labor Market Policy Supplement, discussed in the main text, indicate a mean duration of 10.5 weeks. The law, on the other hand, stipulated that training courses for the unemployed should under normal circumstances not exceed 6 months, they could in principle last 12 months, though.

4. Evaluation of Active Labor Market Policies in the Czech Republic, Hungary and Poland

First, some techniques of ALMP evaluation will be discussed as they underlie parts of the country analysis that follows.

4.1. Evaluation of ALMP in Transition Economies: Methodological Considerations

The effectiveness of ALMP schemes can, according to mainstream opinion, be assessed answering the four questions which have been posed in section II and which are repeated here for convenience:

– *Did the schemes target the groups identified as those having problems leaving unemployment?*

– *Did participation in a scheme enhance individuals' productivity, expressed in higher wages?*

– *Did the measure increase the average re-employment probability of participants?*

– *Have distortive effects, e.g. substitution-, dead weight-, displacement- of-output- and fiscal substitution effects, been minimized?*

To answer the last question solidly one would need a general equilibrium model of transition economies which goes beyond the task of this paper. However, some of the distortive effects (substitution and dead weight) can in principle be analyzed with some of the methods discussed here.

The non-experimental evaluation of ALMP, addressing questions two and three, and taking place in a partial equilibrium framework is dominated by two approaches.

The first approach looks at earnings and re-employment probabilities of persons who have been on a ALMP scheme and compares them with the earnings/re-employment probabilities of a "control group." For example, training measures intended to raise the productivity of participants should be mirrored, ceteris paribus, in higher wages relative to persons with similar characteristics who have not been given training. This approach uses micro data and tries to ensure that unobservable individual-specific determinants of earnings are controlled for (cf. e.g. Ashenfelter/Card (1985)). Participation in any ALMP measure, meant to enhance human capital relative to non-participants, should also express itself, ceteris paribus, in increased re-employment probabilities. These re-employment probabilities are estimated using hazard rate models or binomial/multinomial probit and logit models. The former estimate instantaneous outflow rates from unemployment conditional on having been unemployed up to the time of exit, while the latter estimate transition probabilities from unemployment into other labor market states. Dummy variables accounting for participation in specific ALMP schemes are added to the usual set of regressors and tests are performed that try to see whether there is a positive correlation between being an ALMP participant and the re-employment probability of this person. Both types of models can also be used to analyze the targeting issue addressed in the first question. In the European context, the main drawback of this approach is the lack of readily available micro-datasets that include a large enough number of ALMP participants.

The second approach does not suffer from this problem as it undertakes flow analyzes of administrative macro data to establish the overall effect of a measure on outflows from unemployment to employment. The idea behind this approach, formulated by Haskel/Jackman (1988) and Lehmann (1993) among others, is that a measure which is administered on a large scale can only be considered effective if there is a statistically significant positive correlation between such a measure and outflows from unemployment to employment. One of the strong points of such an approach is the ability to take account of dead weight loss and substitution effects. For example, if we model the determination of overall outflows from unemployment to employment, a positive impact of a measure can be considered its net effect, after all distortions have been accounted for.

A very simple and general model of an outflow function might be presented to heuristically demonstrate how ALMP can be evaluated in this framework.

Let $O = f(x_1; x_2)$, $f_1 > 0$, $f_2 \leq 0$ or $f_2 \geq 0$.

Outflows from unemployment (O) are determined by a vector of labor market variables (x_1) and possibly by some or all elements of a vector of ALMP (x_2), where f is a general function. An econometric test of the effectiveness of ALMP consists then in establishing whether elements in vector x_2 have some predictive power. Such a test is especially sensible if the application of an ALMP scheme does not entail automatic de-registration of the unemployed participants.[11] For example, participation in the Restart program in Britain, which invites persons with unemployment spells lasting more than six months to an interview in the local labor office, does not imply automatic exit from the register. Also, while participating in training programs the Polish unemployed remain registered as such. A positive correlation between e.g. these measure and outflows from unemployment to employment is taken as strong evidence that the programs have improved the search effectiveness of some of the unemployed.

---

[11] For a critique of applying augmented matching functions even when ALMP participation implies de-registration see Calmfors (1994).

The "working horse" giving economic content to models of outflows from unemployment to employment is the matching (hiring) function where in its simplest form unemployed job searchers are matched with vacant jobs. In this context ALMP can be thought of as measures which facilitate this matching process. When ALMP are added to the stock of unemployment and vacancies as factors potentially determining job matching we speak of an "augmented" matching function. The following briefly motivates one theoretical derivation of an estimable "augmented" matching function.

Let c be an index of the search effectiveness of the unemployed in the absence of search enhancing labor market schemes which takes a value between 0 and 1 and let

$$\tau = c(1 + \alpha M),$$

with $M = \sum_{i=1}^{i=n} \beta_i E_i$, and $\sum_i \beta_i = 1$. \hfill (1)

M is here the weighted sum of search enhancing employment measures E_i (i=1,....,n), while τ is the search effectiveness index which is impacted by such labor market measures. Enhancing the search effectiveness of some of the unemployed and having a substitution effect which is less than 100 percent would imply a positive α. Let H be the number of unemployed being hired in regular, non-subsidized jobs, measured during a certain period, U and V the stock of registered unemployed and of notified vacancies, respectively, both measured at the beginning of the period as are the search enhancing employment measures E_i. Then τU is the search effective stock of the unemployed[12] and the augmented hiring function can be written as follows:

$$H = f(V, \tau U), \quad f_1, f_2 > 0. \hfill (2)$$

A general Cobb-Douglas functional form is assumed as we do not want to impose any priors about the returns to scale properties of hiring functions in transition economies even though most of the evidence hints at decreasing returns to scale (cf. Boeri (1994)). Log-linearizing this last equation and adding a constant term we get

$$\ln H = \ln \gamma_0 + \gamma_1 + \ln V + \gamma_2 \ln(\tau U). \hfill (3)$$

For small values of αM the equation becomes[13]

$$\ln H \approx \delta_0 + \delta_1 \ln V + \delta_2 (\ln U + \ln c) + \delta_3 M, \text{ where } \delta_3 = \alpha \gamma_2. \hfill (4)$$

---

[12] A detailed discussion of the concept of search effective unemployment can be found in Layard et al. (1991). In order to be a meaningful concept, τ must also take values between 0 and 1.

[13] Note that $\ln(\tau U) = \ln U + \ln \tau$. But $\ln \tau = \ln[c(1 + \alpha M)]$. As for small x we have the rule $\ln(1 + x) \approx x$, $\ln[c(1 + \alpha M)] \approx \ln c + \alpha M$.

Econometric estimations of this "augmented" matching function when applied to transition economies use regional macro "panel" data rather than time series at the national level as is done in a Western context (cf. Haskel/Jackman (1988) and Lehmann (1993)). With such data ALMP variables often need to be instrumented to avoid endogeneity problems: A high (low) level of spending on ALMP in a region might be triggered by a low (high) outflow rate from unemployment. Estimation of "augmented" matching functions for transition countries is sometimes criticized on the ground that vacancy data are extremely poor in these countries as vacancies notified to labor offices supposedly make up only a very small fraction of all vacancies available. Casual evidence from labor offices in many transition countries tells us, however, that the registered unemployed do not have access to many of the non-notified vacancies. So, if hired, most of the registered unemployed are matched with a notified vacancy. Therefore using the available stock data for unemployment and vacancies seems appropriate for our matching framework. Most econometric specifications model the search effectiveness of the unemployed by looking at the composition of the stock of unemployment by duration. In its simplest variant, the stock of unemployment is divided into the stocks of short-term and long-term unemployment where the latter stock is assumed to have a lower elasticity with respect to hirings than the short-term unemployment stock. As the share of long-term unemployment rises (falls) over time the search effectiveness of the unemployment stock falls (rises) over time.

Finally, one method to identify problem groups in the labor force is Markovian analysis of flows between the labor market states employment (E), unemployment (U) and not-in-the-labor-force (N).[14] On the basis of the Labor Force Survey (LFS) data transition probability matrices (P) of the following type can be estimated for specific groups of the labor force:

$$P = \begin{bmatrix} P_{EE} & P_{EU} & P_{EN} \\ P_{UE} & P_{UU} & P_{UN} \\ P_{NE} & P_{NU} & P_{NN} \end{bmatrix}$$

where e.g. P_{EU} denotes the transition probability of an individual who has been employed at the beginning of period t-1 and who is unemployed at the beginning

---

[14] The assumption that movements between labor market states are governed by a Markov process implies that the transition probabilities depend only on the state currently occupied. Applications of Markovian flow analysis to Western labor markets are Marston (1976), Toikka (1976) and Clark/Summers (1979,1982a,1982b), among others, while applications to a labor market in transition are Abraham/Vodopivec (1993), Bellmann et al. (1995), Góra/Lehmann (1995) and Steiner/Kwiatkowski (1995). The Markovian assumption can be considered appropriate for a transition economy subject to a sudden structural shock, where individual work histories will be of lesser importance.

of period t. Such matrices give a richer picture of the labor market situation of specific groups than the unemployment stocks, the inflow rate into and outflow rate from unemployment computed from register data (these rates correspond to the sums P_{EU} + P_{NU} and P_{UE} + P_{UN} respectively). A large outflow rate from unemployment can come about because of very different scenarios: for example, because of a large P_{UE}, i.e. this group of unemployed has very favorable reemployment prospects, or because of a large P_{UN}, i.e. among this group of unemployed there are many discouraged workers.

4.2. Evaluation of Hungarian ALMP

4.2.1. Characterization of the Unemployed and Identification of Problem Groups

One of the best analyzes of the insured unemployed in Hungary can be found in Micklewright/Nagy (1996, 1999). The following section is mainly based on their papers but also uses some information from Szemlér (1994) and from the survey of benefit exhaustees performed by Lázár/Székely (1994).

The analysis provided by Micklewright and Nagy is based on the cohort of people flowing *from employment* into unemployment insurance (UI) receipt in March 1992, giving approximately 40.000 spells. Only 40 percent of the stock of unemployed is covered by insurance as of August 1994. However, the results of their analysis are extremely interesting insofar as even the most privileged unemployed in Hungary, i.e. those who receive benefits, have on average a poor labor market experience expressing itself in very low outflow rates from unemployment relative to OECD levels (see also Boeri (1994)).

Micklewright and Nagy (1996, 1999) essentially document inflow into and outflow rates from insured unemployed disaggregated by the following set of characteristics: sex, age, education, occupation (manual or non-manual), region.

Inflow Rates into Insured Unemployment

The monthly inflow rates estimated by Micklewright and Nagy (1996, 1999) are roughly comparable to those of most European mature OECD countries during recession and definitely not high by OECD standards. More interesting than this result are the presented relative magnitudes of the inflow rates calculated for the above mentioned characteristics. Hungary was an exception in transition economies insofar as the female unemployment rate as lower than the rate for males. This was entirely due to a lower inflow rate into unemployment (0.80 percent versus 1.14 percent). This lower inflow rate could in turn be explained to a great degree by the different occupational structure of male and female employment, with half of all females and only a quarter of all males in non-manual jobs. As manual workers had on average an inflow rate which was about 3.5 times larger than that for non-manual workers, more non-manual jobs for women implied a lower female inflow rate into unemployment.[15]

The inflow rates disaggregated by age and education show expected patterns. Younger groups tended to have higher inflow rates than older ones, a finding observed in Western economies as well as in transition economies.[16] For women the variation by age was, however, not as strong as for men. Educational attainment and inflow rates into unemployment were inversely related, where persons with a vocational training had the same high inflow rate as persons with only primary education. Vocational training before the regime switch seemed to have led to skills which are required less than other skill groups, as the implied higher separation rate indicates.

Outflow and Hazard Rates from Insured Unemployment

Micklewright and Nagy (1996, 1999) first reported the exit states for spells of unemployment insurance (UI) starting in March 1992. Most importantly the largest fraction of exits from UI occured because of exhaustion of benefits (41.9 percent and 46 percent for men and women, respectively). This hinted at the large share of long-term unemployed among the unemployed as maximum entitlement periods for benefits are 18 or 24 months for this cohort. Those who quitted voluntarily had a larger fraction of exhaustees than those who had been laid off (52.9 percent versus 42.6 percent). The second largest fraction of exits was into regular employment (37 percent and 28.8 percent for men and women, respectively) while only 5.5 percent of the male cohort and 5.2 percent of the female cohort exited into one of the ALMP measures. The largest measure was training, with proportionately more women participating than men (2.8 percent of all exits versus 2 percent of all exits).[17]

The survivor functions for females and males, plotted by Micklewright and Nagy (1996, 1999), had the same slope for most spell lengths; only for very long spells does the survivor function for females became flatter than that for males. For all spell lengths the former function lied slightly above the latter thus pointing to somewhat lower outflow rates from insured unemployment for women. As these differences were small the much lower inflow rates into unemployment

---

[15] When controlling for occupational status the differences by sex nearly disappeared; for manual female workers we observed a monthly inflow rate of 1.24 percent (men 1.41 percent) and for non-manual female workers a monthly inflow rate of 0.36 percent (men 0.38 percent).

[16] The same pattern was observed for eastern Germany in the period 1990-1991 by Bellmann et al. (1995) and for Poland in the period 1992-1994 by Góra/Lehmann (1995).

[17] The remaining categories of exit are disqualification and normal or early retirement.

caused a smaller stock of female unemployment. However, once unemployed, the experience of Hungarian women was not very different from the experience of women in most other transition economies; they had a lower re-employment probability than men, stayed longer in unemployment and had a larger share of long-term unemployment (cf. Szémlér (1994)).

Using a "competing risks" model Micklewright and Nagy (1996, 1999) estimate the hazard rate into each state separately.[18] Here, only the estimated of three hazards, to go to regular employment, to going to training and to public works (the two most important ALMP measures), are discussed.

For both men and women the probability of a transition to regular employment increased monotonically with education. With the default category being primary education, males with vocational education had a 36 percent higher hazard than the base hazard, while males with university education had a hazard which is 89 percent higher. For women we found a similar relationship between the hazards (an increase of 16 percent for vocational, an increase of 59 percent for university education over the base hazard). Higher age meant roughly a lower probability of flowing into regular employment. With a base group of those 21-25 years of age, all older groups had a lower re-employment probability. The age groups awaiting retirement (over 56 years for men and between 51 and 55 years for women) had only approximately one tenth of the re-employment probability of the base group. Not only for insured unemployed but also for exhaustees age and educational attainment were powerful predictors of flowing into employment (cf. Lázár/Székely (1994)).

The estimated hazards of going to training for men and women seemed to indicate a wrong targeting of this ALMP measure. Those people who had a higher probability of flowing into regular employment, i.e. the young and the well educated, also had a higher probability of being taken onto a training scheme. In other words, those unemployed who seemingly had the least difficulty finding re-employment on their own are above all targeted for training measures. That Hungarian employment offices engaged consciously in "creaming" when targeting training measures will be discussed below. The estimated hazards of going to public works showed for men an inverse relationship between education and the probability of entering the scheme. This might have been a reflection of the type of work performed by men in this scheme or a reflection of targeting the underprivileged among the unemployed. Age was not a significant determinant in this instance. For women who were much less likely to exit into public works education was not a significant predictor of this hazard rate, while non-manual

---

[18] "The hazards of exit to different states were assumed to be independent and we estimated this 'competing risks' model by successively maximising the likelihood with respect to the parameters of the hazard of each state j while treating as censored all exits to states other than j." (Micklewright/Nagy (1999))

occupation was. That this latter co-variate has predictive power points to the often heard fact that municipal administrations used unemployed women in clerical and health care related jobs and that fiscal substitution effects were present in the application of public works.

4.2.2. Evaluation of Active Labor Market Policies

Hungary was the only transition economy where micro data were used to evaluate the retraining and public works measures (O'Leary (1997)). In these papers, the sample to be evaluated consists of three sub-samples: registered unemployed who did not participate in ALMP, those who participated in retraining in the second half of 1991 and those who participated in public service employment (PSE) in September 1991. This sample was interviewed in November 1993. The impact analysis of ALMP looks above all at differences in the re-employment probabilities and earnings of the three sub-samples. O'Leary used various methods to control for differences in observable characteristics of the three subsamples. With respect to differences in observable characteristics O'Leary (1997) stated the following: "Compared to the sample of registered unemployed those in the retraining sample are significantly younger, more likely to be female, more educated, more specialized in professional and technical skills, much more likely to have worked in white collar jobs, less likely to have received UI since June 1991, less likely to have special problems in finding a job, and less likely to be unskilled. [.....] Relative to the registered unemployed PSE workers tend to be somewhat younger, more likely to be male, less educated, less specialized in either manual or technical skills, much less likely to have worked in white collar jobs, much less likely to have received UI since June 1991, more likely to have special problems in finding a job, and much more likely to be unskilled." This confirmed the results of the hazard rate analysis undertaken by Micklewright and Nagy (1996, 1999); participants of the retraining measure were on average much "better" than registered unemployed who did not participate in an ALMP measure, while PSE participants were a lot "worse".

There seemed to be a conscious policy by the authorities to "cream off" the best candidates among the unemployed for retraining courses as the following quote from an administrator of a retraining center shows. "Applicants undergo an aptitude test and a health examination [...]. With courses where there are too many applicants, there is a kind of ranking based on the psychology test results. [...] Recently an attempt was made to encourage training institutions to use specialists *to do deeper examinations to reduce dropouts among retraining participants.* In this field *we are extremely happy about the methods used by the regional retraining center.*" (O'Leary (1997), emphasis added). While consciously targeting those individuals with a comparative advantage with retraining might have been a very questionable practice,[19] even if one accepted such targeting as appropriate the success of the retraining program still needs to be investigated. Those individuals with the more favorable characteristics of the retraining participants might have far higher re-employment probabilities in a regular job than the average unemployed even in the absence of the retraining program.

The simplest way to compare labor market outcomes, in our case consisting of re-employment probabilities and earnings, is to look at the unadjusted mean outcomes of the treated group (i.e. the retraining participants) and the control group (i.e. the unemployed who never participated in an ALMP measure). If the selection of both groups were entirely random, this would be the appropriate method to evaluate the retraining measure. O'Leary computed a re-employment probability of retrainees which is 19.2 percentage points higher than the one for the unemployed without an ALMP measure, with the difference being statistically significant at the 95 percent level. The also computed difference in earnings (1.500 Forints) was not significant at conventional levels. Once he controlled for the difference in observable characteristics of retrainees and the unemployed without participation in ALMP, much of the higher mean re-employment probability of the retrainees disappears. Using a synthetic comparison group[20] the difference in the re-employment rate fell to 1.2 percent which was not significant. Average monthly earnings of the synthetic group were, however, lower by 2.052 Forint pointing to the fact that the most productive among the registered unemployed were chosen for the training measures. Using regression adjusted impact estimates for retraining the difference in the re-employment probability fell to 6.4 percent with average higher earnings of those retrainees in regular jobs of 500 Forint. The latter difference was however not statistically significant.

Whatever the method used to adjust for observable characteristics the Hungarian retraining program produced larger re-employment probabilities and higher earnings for the retrainees than for the unemployed not participating in an ALMP because of the observable "better quality" of the former. This result should be treated with caution, though, as unobservable characteristics of retraining program participants were not controlled for.

---

[19] Conventional wisdom, as e.g. expressed by Micklewrigh/Nagy (1994, p. 17), clearly says that targeting the "best" among the unemployed for retraining courses is a failed policy as these individuals have the highest chances of regaining employment anyway. Given the very weak labor demand in most transformation economies within the reported period it is not obvious that targeting "problem groups" among the unemployed for training would in fact have increased the chances of such groups for regular employment at all. Therefore, targeting such groups might have been highly inefficient.

[20] It was constructed by choosing *with replacement* for each retrainee that person of the comparison group which had the closest observable characteristics.

Sub-group analysis of retraining performed by O'Leary showed that "groups considered to be the most difficult to re-employ appear to have gained the greatest help in getting a normal job by retraining, these groups are: older workers, those with less education , and those without a manual trade." (O'Leary (1997)). One could imply from this result that targeting those with comparative disadvantages in the labor market will generate the largest gains. As this sub-group analysis also cannot take account of selection bias a plausible explanation of the quoted result could be that given the selection process only the most motivated among the older and less educated workers were chosen and that in these age and educational groups motivation was a much more important determinant of gaining re-employment than among younger and more educated workers.

Summarizing this section on the evaluation of Hungarian retraining measures, the "best" among the unemployed were targeted for this measure. Once controlling for observable characteristics the greater chances of re-employment of those who had completed a retraining course compared to the unemployed who did not participate in an ALMP diminish dramatically. Members of problem groups among the unemployed *if taken on the retraining scheme* had the highest re-employment probabilities. This result was achieved without controlling for selection bias. A possible inference from this result could be that "problem groups" among the unemployed should be targeted *and* members of these groups carefully selected based on motivation, flexibility and intrinsic ability. This combination of targeting and selection might give the "biggest bang" for the expenditure on retraining.

The evaluation of the Public Service Employment (PSE) scheme tried to correct for the mentioned sample selection, i.e. tried to correct the fact that the "worst" among the unemployed were selected. Unadjusted impact estimates gave a lower re-employment probability for PSE participants of 16.4 percentage points compared to the unemployed who did not participate in an ALMP. Once controls for observables were included in the analysis, this value was only slightly lowered; depending on the adjustment method the value ranges between 13.3 and 16 percentage points. This re-employment probability which was robust to using controls can, in my opinion, be obtained because the duration of unemployment was not a characteristic controlled for by O'Leary, and many of the PSE participants were from the pool of the long-term unemployed. In the absence of an ALMP they might have lower re-employment probabilities because of loss of human capital, lower search efforts or outright discrimination by employers. Clearly, participating in PSE seemed to be ineffective insofar as it did not rebuild human capital, boost search efforts or improve the image of the long-term unemployed individual. A second explanation for the virtually constant re-employment probability across the different methods of impact analysis could be that participation in the scheme is viewed to be a negative signal to the employer. From OECD countries' experiences we know that negative signaling problems arise from the participation in certain schemes.

Finally some results of the study by Frey (1993) are presented in order to above all discuss possible distortive effects of PSE. The main, very limited data base for this study was generated by a survey of PSE contract employers in two counties (Jász-Nagykun-Szolnok and Tolna).

One major problem of the implementation of PSE was the conflict of interest between the labor offices and prospective employers many of which were municipal authorities. The latter would have liked to employ capable and reliable workers chosen by themselves for long periods of time while the labor offices were mainly interested in placing temporarily as many people as possible into these jobs who without assistance would have had great difficulties in finding any job.

Some of the local authorities clearly saw PSE as a tool to provide certain services to their community at lower costs or to provide services which they otherwise would not have provided at all. In both cases certain distortive effects which are well known in OECD countries when analyzing public employment might exist. From the above mentioned survey of PSE contractors the following emerged:

– *dead weight loss was a minor problem; only 2.5 percent of PSE workers performed jobs which were actually permanent jobs but had been renamed as PSE jobs.*

– *Among the contractors 12 percent substituted PSE workers for their own municipal workers.*

– *Fiscal substitution was a slightly larger problem, 15 percent of PSE contractors increased their numbers of PSE workers while decreasing the number of their own employees.*

– *Displacement of output effects seemed to be quite strong as local governments often wanted certain work done by their subsidized PSE employees which previously had been given to outside private entrepreneurs. From the result of the survey one can infer that this effect has an upper bound of 24 percent of work done by private entrepreneurs in the absence of the PSE program.*

Given that many of the participants in the PSE program belonged to problem groups among the unemployed it was not surprising that substitution and dead weight loss effects were quite small. That they existed at all plus the magnitude of the other distortive effects point to a poor design of this program.

4.3. Evaluation of Polish ALMP

4.3.1. Problem groups and targeting of ALMP

A detailed discussion of problem groups in the Polish labor market in the first years of the transition process can be found in Lehmann (1995), Puhani (1998), and Puhani/Steiner (1997). Table 5 roughly contrasts the main problem groups with the actual targeting of ALMP by demographic characteristics. The table was constructed using information from Lehmann (1995), Steiner/Kwiatkowski (1995) and Sztanderska (1996).

Problem groups were determined on the basis of the transition probabilities which were discussed above. In particular, relative job accession rates from unemployment (P_{UE}) were used as the main criterion in determining whether a demographic group experiences special problems in the labor market. In Poland, women, persons older than 45, those with little education, and the long-term unemployed seemed to have particular difficulty leaving unemployment for employment. Interactions of the characteristics were not explicitly considered in the table. It is clear, however, that an older long-term unemployed female with little education would have had extremely low chances of finding re-employment compared to a middle aged short-term unemployed male with university education.

Table 5. Problem Groups Among the Unemployed and Actual Targeting of ALMP

Demo-graphic charac-teristic	Problem Group	Actual Targeting – main groups [a]			
		Training	IW	PW	Loans
Gender	female	male	female	male	male
Age	>44 years	<25 years	between 25 and 44 years	between 25 and 44 years	between 25 and 44 years
Education	Primary education and incomplete education	Secondary General education	Primary education	Primary education	Secondary General education
Duration of unemployment	>12 months (long-term unemployed)	short-term unemployed	long-term unemployed	long-term unemployed	short-term unemployed

Notes: (a) These characterizations are based on Puhani/Steiner (1997) and Sztanderska (1996) which has surveyed officials from local labor offices; these characterizations can differ from the distributions of participant stocks across the various categories.

As our problem groups with respect to age and to education were essentially based on job accession rates out of unemployment and not on unemployment incidence, they differed from the problem groups usually provided. People with vocational education, while having a higher incidence of unemployment than persons with elementary education, had a statistically significantly higher transition probability out of unemployment than the latter group (Steiner/Kwiatkowski (1995) and Lehmann (1995)). Similarly, persons less than 25 years of age while having a much higher unemployment incidence than the middle-aged (between 25 and 44 years of age) did not seem to have lower job accession rates than this latter group.[21]

Women having a worse experience in the labor market than men were less targeted than the latter in three out of four programs. While it was in the nature of public works (mainly construction) that men were frequently more observed, it is not clear why this should be the same with training measures. As far as age was concerned, the main problem group (those above 44 years of age) was never targeted while intervention and public works did target the indicated educational problem group. Finally the long-term unemployed were the main target group of the two big ALMP measures (intervention and public works).

What is apparent from inspection of the table is the fact that the two more effective programs – training and loans – (see below) never targeted any of the indicated problem groups.

Table 5 in its simplicity does not reflect the complex reality under which local labor office workers came to decisions when selecting ALMP participants from the pool of unemployed. For example, in the public works program the type of project determined the selection of participants. Often construction workers and brick layers who with relative ease find employment without help were selected for public works projects.

"Creaming effects" are frequent in the selection process. Local labor office workers were judged by the rate at which participation in an ALMP scheme translated into regular employment. Especially when selecting for training and the wage subsidy measures they, therefore, chose candidates considered to have the best chance of entering regular employment after having participated in a scheme. Targeting of certain groups among the unemployed could have also caused "churning" of parts of the unemployment pool: Some of the long-term unemployed were taken on public works so that they qualified again for unemployment

---

[21] Schmidt (1996) argues that the high unemployment figures for the young were based on low participation rates compared to Western countries and reflect false reporting of not being in the labor force and actual work in the large Polish shadow economy where particularly the young have opportunities. When participation rates of the young are assumed to be similar to those e.g. in Sweden and Germany, the unemployment rate would have fallen to the average.

benefit. This and other interactions of ALMP and PLMP in the Polish context is discussed thoroughly in Góra et al. (1996).

Apart from these distortive effects arising from the targeting practices of local labor office workers, the main lesson from this section has to be that problem groups were targeted for intervention and public works but not for start-up loans and training. In the next two sections it is shown that the former measures are particularly ineffective in raising the probability that participants enter regular employment. Especially public works appeared to be an employment measure of the last resort undertaken above all for equity reasons in Poland.

4.3.2. Supplement to the August 1994 PLFS on Labor Market Policies: Analysis of Raw Data

The supplement on labor market policies added to the PLFS in August 1994 produced the first data set in Poland as far as active labor market policies participants are concerned. Puhani/Steiner (1997) used this data set to econometrically evaluate Polish ALMP. Their results will be presented in the next section. In this section, we just look at some outcomes and the frequency distributions of the given answers to get an intuitive feeling about the effectiveness of the various ALMP measures. We also look at how scheme participants themselves evaluated these measures. Besides loans to start a business, intervention works (wage subsidies), public works and training measures for the unemployed, the job brokerage function of labor offices is discussed.[22] To generate the largest possible numbers of ALMP participants individuals who were registered as unemployed in a labor office at least once between January 1990 and August 1994 were asked whether they *at any time* after January 1990 had been or were involved in a scheme. In some instances this made inferences more difficult.

Loans to start a business

Of those individuals who identified themselves as being registered at a labor office at least once between January 1990 and August 1994, 3.3 percent asked at any time after January 1990 for a start-up loan. Successful with their application were in turn 24.2 percent. Roughly 60 percent of those acquiring the loan had created a work place for themselves which still existed during the survey week, 31 percent had created such a work place, but it no longer existed while only 10 percent were unable to use the money for establishing work for themselves. Given the data, one evaluation criterion that can be used is the duration of a thus created work place. The mean duration of the observed *completed* spells of scheme participants was 20 months. The government set 24 months as the lower limit beyond which only 50

---

[22] This section is based on Lehmann (1995).

percent of the loan had to be repaid. The average duration of *all* spells in the sample should have been longer than 20 months and could be a lot longer as the sub-sample of the completed spells gave the sub-sample of all those who have "failed" in their business activities.[23] Labor offices seemed, therefore, to be successful in their examination of loan applications. Since there were probably only small displacement effects of output the quite impressive duration figures seemed to indicate that start-up loans were a relatively efficient ALMP measure in Poland and maybe should have been extended. One question which certainly still needs to be investigated is whether dead weight losses occurred with the application of this measure.

The often heard criticism that these loans entailed amounts not sufficient to set up a business (e.g. Lehmann (1992)) did not seem to be borne out by the data and was, furthermore, only voiced by 11 percent of those unemployed who did not apply for a loan. A majority of those not applying for a loan said that they were not able to run their own business (39 percent) or that they did not know about the existence of the scheme (20 percent).

In summary, only a small minority of the unemployed applied for a start-up loan, the loan applications seemed to have been allocated well as the average duration of a thus created business most likely was in excess of two years.

Intervention Works (Wage Subsidies)

Approximately nine percent of those having registered at a labor office at some point in time were offered a slot on the intervention works scheme. Nearly one third (32 percent) of the then unemployed to whom these offers were made rejected them. To shed some light on this relatively large number one would need to link this outcome with the characteristics of the person (demographic and educational characteristics, duration of unemployment, benefit status). Here, one can just look at the reasons for the end of the work on the scheme. Of those who entered the scheme but are no longer working in the scheme 12.2 percent found regular employment in the same firm which is certainly not a negligible portion of participants. The vast majority of those not kept on (85 percent) left the firm because the foreseen period of their intervention works job had ended. Most firms clearly took the subsidy and release subsidized labor once the subsidy ended. The timely ending of most intervention works jobs indicates, on the other hand, that dead weight loss was not a major problem.

---

[23] In our sample 18 out of 57 self-employed work places have been terminated. With 18 loans granted in 1990 in our sample, and assuming that some of the failures have occurred in subsequent years, this must mean that some of the in 1990 created businesses still existed in August 1994.

Of course, from the given data we do not know how many found employment in regular jobs in other firms after the period of the wage subsidy ended. However, the majority (60 percent) of those not staying on in the same firm did not believe that participating in intervention works will have increased their re-employment probabilities in the regular labor market. This can be taken as evidence that for most workers on the scheme participation did not enhance their human capital and that they had difficulties finding regular employment.

Public Works

Since public works only started in 1992 the number of unemployed in the August sample who had been offered a public works slot was very small, namely two percent. Most of these slots were in the state sector at the municipal level. 44 percent rejected this offer; of those who accepted and already finished their work within the scheme, 8.5 percent stayed on in the same firm in another capacity. Most people, however, left the firm when the public works they were assigned to were finished. Nearly 65 percent of these people thought that participation in public works did not increase their re-employment probabilities (65 percent), while 24 percent did not know. The public works scheme probably prepared the unemployed the least for regular employment. This does not mean, of course, that the benefits of this measure did not outweigh the costs. One can think of this measure as improving equity as some of the long-term unemployed gained access to employment which increased their income at least temporarily. Even when the long-term unemployed, who did not receive unemployment benefits any longer were put on the scheme, as long as the value added of public works production exceeded the difference of the wage and the income support which had to be paid to the long-term unemployed this measure was also more efficient than paying only income support. When public works concentrate on enlarging and improving the infrastructure the social value added might in fact have been quite large.

Further Training and Retraining Measures

Inspection of the raw data allows only a very limited evaluation of the training measures that were offered to the unemployed in Poland. One statistic to be looked at is the mean duration of such measures. By comparing it to the mean duration of training of the full sample one might get a hunch about the quality of training measures for the unemployed.

Approximately six percent of those having registered at a labor office had at any time been offered a training course by their labor office. The fraction of those rejecting this offer is large (45 percent). Most of the training courses were paid for by the labor offices (92 percent). The mean duration of the completed courses is 10.5 weeks, compared to 16.5 for those persons who took part in further training and retraining courses. If length was an indicator of quality, on average training courses for the unemployed seemed to be of a lesser quality. Unemployed participants in such courses evaluated them, however, rather positively as 51 percent of them believed that their re-employment probabilities had a little bit improved and 13 percent of them believe that these probabilities were improved a lot. So, at least as far as the unemployed participants themselves are concerned, training measures were valued much higher than the previously discussed measures of direct job creation.

Job Brokerage

The raw data of the supplement also allows us to say something about the placement activities of labor offices. Of those in the August 1994 sample who entered into a new relationship with an employer 6.6 percent found their last job through a labor office. The majority found a job through personal contacts – i.e. through family and friends – (30.7 percent), through professional contacts (8.5 percent), through a direct application to the firm (18 percent) or through an announcement of an employer (8 percent). Thus, labor offices seemed to be a marginal contributor to job brokerage in Poland as far as the national average was concerned. With respect to the unemployed, only eight percent were ever offered a job placement in the regular labor market. Of the offered job slots 47 percent were not taken up by the unemployed. That there were serious problems with the brokerage function of labor offices could be seen from the reasons given for not having taken up the offered job: More than a quarter of the job offers were already filled when the applicants arrived at the firm (26 percent). In 14 percent of the cases the employer asked for qualifications which the applicant did not have, while in 13 percent of the cases the employer did not want to hire the applicant outright. The probably low quality of many of these job offers might be inferred from the fact that among those who took up the offered job but at the time of the interview already terminated this work, 33 percent quit voluntarily.

4.3.3. Supplement to August 1994 PLFS on Labor Market Policies: An Econometric Analysis

Puhani/Steiner (1997) used the August 1994 supplement in an attempt to evaluate the effectiveness of the major Polish ALMP econometrically. They estimated a multiinomial logit model with the records of all those who in the reference week in August 1994 were not involved in an ALMP or private training scheme and who were unemployed between 1990 and August 1994 at least once. Because of data limitations, the authors aggregated intervention and public works to a new variable "works." By adding a dummy variable to the usual covariates in their regression, they then looked at the effect of having participated in works at any time on labor market status in the reference week of August 1994. They also looked at similar effects of three types of training: public training, self-financed, and employer-financed training. The aggregation of intervention works and public works striked me as somewhat problematic. Intervention works were actually wage subsidies paid to municipal or private firms while public works were mainly a government employment measure of last resort. Also, it was not clear to me why self-financed and employer-financed training courses were considered ALMP measures by the authors. The data did not tell us whether somebody who was unemployed at any time between 1990 and 1994 and took a self-financed or employer-financed training course was actually unemployed when he/she participated in the training course. Only public training referring to a training measure for the registered unemployed could unequivocally be considered an ALMP measure.

A second major problem with Puhani's and Steiner's econometric work is the specification of their multinomial logit model. They looked at all persons who at any time were unemployed for any length of time between 1990 and 1994 and then check the labor market status in the reference week of ALMP participants against those who never participated in an ALMP measure. The origin state was poorly defined, as people, while going on record of being unemployed at least once, could have changed their labor market status many times between 1990 and 1994.

Keeping these drawbacks in mind, Puhani/Steiner (1997) showed that "after controlling for various demographic and socio-economic characteristics, having participated in a works program increases the probability of being unemployed almost sixfold, but has no effects on non-participation. No significant effects are found for public training or self-financed training". As Puhani and Steiner readily admitted, these results did not necessarily imply a causal relationship going from ALMP measure to labor market status. For example, it is possible that those who were strongly represented in the unemployment pool were favored by local labor office workers to be taken on works programs. Another interpretation of the positive correlation between participation in works and unemployment is that the targeting practices generated substantial "churning" among the long-term unemployed (see above). The overall noteworthy result is, though, that no ALMP measure seemed to raise the relative re-employment probabilities of participants.

4.4. Evaluation of Czech ALMP

Most of the analysis employing econometric techniques was confined to the estimation of augmented matching functions which is the topic of the next section. Here some results on the "raw" impact of Czech ALMP flows on outflows from unemployment that are presented in Terrell/Munich (1996), are briefly summarized.

Terrell and Munich looked at quarterly data of inflows into ALMP measures and compared these to quarterly outflows from unemployment into a job.[24] In 1992 when expenditures on ALMP were highest in absolute and relative terms inflows into SPJs accounted for nearly one quarter of all outflows from unemployment into a job, in the same year inflows into PUJs made up between six and eleven percent of all outflows. For both schemes this "raw" impact reduced to between 3 and 4 percent in the following years. Of course, these back-of-the-envelope calculations did not take into account dead weight, substitution, worker, and output displacement effects and said, therefore, little about the net impact of these programs on the unemployment rate.

As stated elsewhere (Lehmann (1995)) SPJs as implemented in the Czech Republic could have had distortive and positive effects. On the one hand, there was a risk of dead weight loss, as SPJs tended to be given to individuals, who were well qualified. Possibly they might have found a job anyhow, and the subsidized job would have been created even without the subsidy. On the other hand, in a transforming economy with capital markets only emerging and an initial lack of entrepreneurial skill, subsidizing job creation for well qualified individuals might have helped in enterprise formation; for instance, such subsidization might have allowed a new firm to access the capital market with the guarantee of the employment office. If subsidized jobs supported the development of the private sector that would not have taken place otherwise due to market imperfections, a SPJ, but also a retraining scheme or trainee program might have triggered further job creations and thus could have led to more than just the direct effect of keeping an unemployed "off the dole" for a certain period of time.

4.5. Augmented Matching Functions: the Czech Republic and Poland

Much of the work with augmented matching functions deals with the Czech Lands (and Slovakia). The results of the most important papers related to the Czech Republic will be presented in turn without discussing the technical details of the econometric models.

Burda/Lubyova (1995) estimated augmented matching functions for the Czech and Slovak Republics using monthly district level data. For the Czech Republic, their variables capturing regional ALMP activity were potential stocks of PUJ and SPJ or total district expenditures on ALMP. The available data on ALMP participants were in the form of "agreements" concluded with municipalities or private employers and were, therefore, clearly an upper bound of the actual stocks.

---

[24] As of now, persons taken on the Socially Purposeful Job (SPJ) and Publicly Useful Job (PUJ) schemes are taken off the register and counted as flows into employment. In the first years of transition participation in the PUJ scheme did not imply de-registration.

According to their results, in the Czech regressions ALMP participation stocks were not statistically significant predictors of outflows from unemployment into employment while total district spending on ALMP were statistically significant in all specifications. The imputed long-run elasticity of spending with respect to outflows, 0.068, means that if in the Czech Republic spending would not have fallen from 1992 to 1993 by 56 percent, outflows from unemployment would have been raised by 12.4 percent implying a decrease in the steady state rate of unemployment from 3.3 percent to 3 percent. Their econometric evidence confirmed the previous supposition about the marginal influence of ALMPs on the Czech labor market as it points to a discernible but small effect of ALMPs on the Czech unemployment rate.

Boeri/Burda (1996) estimated an augmented matching function for the Czech Republic using quarterly observations on 76 district labor offices over the period 1991:I to 1994:II. They employed three different measures for the SPJ and PUJ schemes whose impact on the outflows from unemployment to jobs they wish to analyze: expenditures, i.e. spending on these programs at the district level, excluding staff and overhead costs, inflows of positions created by or with the assistance of the district labor offices and, finally, inflows of persons into the schemes, i.e. actual placements. Their most interesting result was that their instrumental variables estimates implied that each quarterly position created (each placement) in a SPJ or PUJ scheme, on average, generated 1.1 (1.4) additional outflows into jobs in the long run. This small positive net effect of ALMP over and above the one-to-one outflow from the register in connection with participation in the scheme could, according to the authors, be explained by increased staff time for counseling of those remaining in the register. Their instrumental variables estimate using ALMP expenditures generated a long-run expenditure elasticity of around one tenth.

Svejnar et al. (1995) estimated seemingly unrelated regressions explaining average monthly outflows from unemployment at the level of individual districts in the Czech Lands and Slovakia in 1992 and 1993. Regressing average monthly outflows in each district in each year on district-level stocks of vacancies and unemployment, demographic characteristics of the district, district demand variables, structural variables, and the level of per capita expenditures on ALMP they found that a 1 percent increase in per capita expenditures on ALMPs increased outflows by 0.17 percent in the Czech Republic.

Finally, Lehmann (1995) estimated an augmented matching function to evaluate Polish training programs using quarterly voivodship-level data for the period covering 1993:I to 1994:II. As participation in training did not imply de-registration, these estimates could detect the net impact on hirings in regular jobs. Regressing outflows into regular jobs on the stock of training participants, lagged appropriately[25], allowed the evaluation of the question whether an increase in the stock of training participants had a positive net effect on the hirings of the unemployed. A positive net effect would have meant that some of the unemployed through their participation in a training scheme became more effective in their search for a regular job and that substitution of non-participants by participants in the hiring process was not at 100 percent.

The regression results showed no statistically significant impact of (lagged) training on regular hirings of the unemployed. This result could be interpreted that after having ended a training course an unemployed person did not increase his/her effectiveness in search of a job, it could, however, also be interpreted that training participants among the unemployed had increased their search effectiveness but had, in the hiring process, then "crowded out" non-participants among the unemployed. While the results of this regression did not allow to discriminate between the two scenarios they seemed to imply that an increase in the (lagged) stock of training participants did not push up the flow from unemployment into regular employment. This result is in line with the findings of the ineffectiveness of public training by Puhani/Steiner (1997) cited above.

5. Conclusions

Transition economies introduced a wide range of OECD ALMP to combat unemployment in the first years of the transition process. Many of these measures were, however, not employed in any substantial way in practice since with the rise of the stock of unemployment in most transition economies to levels comparable to OECD countries, passive measures crowded out ALMP. Where this was not the case, as in the Czech Republic, ALMP contributed marginally to the lowering of the unemployment rate. To remove public misperceptions, one important task of policy makers in CEE would have been – and maybe still is – to bring across the message that even under the best circumstances ALMP can only play a marginal role in reducing the unemployment rate.

Despite their marginal role, ALMP can be useful also in transition economies. Since the situation in CEE labor markets is different from that in mature OECD countries this prohibits a mechanical transposing of OECD ALMP to these labor markets. Because of severe and persistent shortages in capital and managerial

---

[25] The analysis of the raw data of the August 1994 LFS supplement showed the average length of a public training program to be around 3 months. The stocks of training participants are, therefore, lagged one quarter in the regression. It is also worth noting that while stocks of training participants are very small relative to the stock of total unemployment, they are rather large relative to outflows into regular jobs (a ratio of 0.2 on average).

ability, labor demand was weak while labor supply, among others for demographic reasons, was abundant. Consequently, labor shed in those enterprises which have been restructured or liquidated could not be absorbed in its entirety by the expanding private sector. This led to unemployment also affecting core groups of employment and to more competition among the unemployed than exists in mature OECD countries. Certain problem groups, which were identified in the Hungarian and Polish cases as those who were older and less educated, seemed to have very poor prospects for future employment. In these two countries, also women had lower probabilities of regaining employment than men.

Because problem groups had to compete for jobs in the expanding private sector with many unemployed from core groups of employment and with persons who were still employed in the state sector in the first years of the transition process, the usual rationale for targeting retraining and public employment measures at problem groups, i.e. to integrate them into the effective labor supply, had to be questioned in the case of transition economies. If e.g. one would have targeted retraining measures at those with vocational training who had both in Hungary and Poland a high incidence of unemployment it is unclear whether this would have on average increased their re-employment probabilities as they would have had to compete with many individuals with much better educational backgrounds who were in addition probably perceived as more productive by prospective employers. As an alternative to targeting retraining measures at all members of problem groups one could have carefully examined these groups for flexibility, intrinsic ability, and drive and choose only people with these characteristics for such measures. O'Leary's (1997) results for Hungary seem to suggest that members of problem groups with these characteristics would have benefited most from being taken on a retraining program. Given the very low staff/client ratios in most CEE countries the large scale realization of this alternative seems, however, to have been not feasible. Because of the scarce resources for ALMP it might have been more sensible to use the funds for retraining in order to solve various skill bottlenecks by targeting the most able among the unemployed.

Public employment programs should above all be targeted at problem groups and the long-term unemployed.[26] This should be done mainly for equity rather than efficiency reasons. Since participation in a public works scheme does on average not improve or might even reduce re-employment probabilities because of signalling problems, and because the value added from public employment programs is in most cases small, efficiency gains cannot be great. Nevertheless, it is certainly more equitable to temporarily allow groups access to relatively high

---

[26] Assuming some heterogeneity among the unemployed and efficient sorting, many of the long-term unemployed belong to one of the problem groups. With very low outflow rates from unemployment, many of the long-term unemployed do not belong to a problem group, but are just unlucky.

income who have suffered disproportionately from income losses. The main point is to have a clear idea whether both efficiency and equity aims *can* be pursued and if efficiency gains are unrealistic, whether equity considerations are politically indispensable.

One program of ALMP which was used only rarely promotes self-employment. Given embryonic financial structures risk assessment could not have been –and still can't be – performed extensively by the private banking sector. Therefore those among the unemployed who wanted to create their own businesses experienced severe credit rationing. Employment offices could have contributed to the removal of this distortion arising from credit rationing – and still have the possibility – by granting start-up loans. The empirical evidence cited from the Czech Republic and from Poland hinted at the effectiveness of such programs. As services in the untradables sector were underdeveloped in most transition economies, displacement of output effects which are prominent in OECD countries with self-employment schemes should be small.

Employment Offices in Hungary and Poland had a very poor record as far as job brokerage was concerned. Empirical evidence in Poland, that can be generalized to other East European countries, pointed also to large information deficits among the unemployed. One aim that should have been pursued vigorously before a wide menu of ALMP was implemented would have been the improvement of counseling services for the unemployed. In this context increasing the counseling efforts for problem groups would have been especially worthy. The longer-term unemployed[27] should have been interviewed and given advice about possible job openings and eligibility criteria for state funded employment activities (e.g. along the lines of a program like Restart in the United Kingdom). Putting counseling programs at the center of ALMP rather than falling into some "wild activism" which tried to apply a wide menu of OECD ALMP would have been a more modest but also a more realistic aim.

Acknowledgements

Financial support for this research from the Volkswagen Foundation within the project "Labor Market Policies in Transition Countries: Monitoring and Evaluation" is gratefully acknowledged.

---

[27] Since unemployment benefits are in most transition economies cut off after 12 months and many persons are deregistered after the cut off point it seems sensible to invite the unemployed to an interview after six months of unemployment as it is done in Britain (see Lehmann (1993)).

References

Abraham, K./Vodopivec, M. (1993), Slovenia: A Study of Labor Market Transitions, Washington, *mimeo*.

Ashenfelter, O./Card, D. (1985), Using the Longitudinal Structure of Earnings to Estimate the Effects of Training Programs, *Review of Economics and Statistics* 67, 648-80.

Bellmann, L. et al. (1995), The Eastern German Labor Market in Transition: Gross Flow Estimates from Panel Data, *Journal of Comparative Economics* 20 (2), 139-170.

Björklund, A. et al. (1991), *Labor Market Policy and Unemployment Insurance*, Oxford.

Boeri, T. (1994), Labor Market Flows and the Persistence of Unemployment in Central and Eastern Europe, in: Boeri, T. (ed.), *Unemployment in Transition Countries: Transient or Persistent?*, OECD, Paris, 13-56.

Boeri, T./Burda, M.C. (1996), Active Labor Market Policies, Job Matching and the Czech Miracle, *European Economic Review* 40, 805-817.

Boeri, T./Scarpetta, S. (1995), Convergence and Divergence of Regional Labor Market Dynamics in Central and Eastern Europe, in: Scarpetta, S./Wörgötter, A. (eds.), *The Regional Dimension of Unemployment in Transition Countries*, OECD, Paris.

Burda, M./Lubyova, M. (1995), The Impact of Active Labor Market Policies: A Closer Look at the Czech and Slovak Republics, in: Newberry, D. (ed), *Tax and benefit reform in Central and Eastern Europe*, London, 173-205.

Calmfors, L. (1994), Active Labor Market Policies and Unemployment. A Framework for the Analysis of Crucial Design Features, *OECD Economic Studies* 22, 7-47.

Clark, K./Summers, L.H. (1979), Labor Market Dynamics and Unemployment: A Reconsideration, *Brookings Paper on Economic Activity* 1, 13-60.

Clark, K./Summers, L.H. (1982a), Unemployment Insurance and Labor Market Transitions, in: Baily, M.N. (ed.), *Workers, Jobs and Inflation*, Washington DC: Brookings, 274-318.

Clark, K./Summers, L.H. (1982b), The Dynamics of Youth Unemployment, in: Freeman R./Wise D. (eds.), *The Youth Labor Market Problem*, University of Chicago Press, 199-234.

Erbenova, M. (1995), Regional Unemployment and Geographical Labor Mobility: A Case-Study of the Czech Republic, in: Scarpetta, S./Wörgötter, A. (eds.), *The Regional Dimension of Unemployment in Transition Economies*, OECD, Paris.

Frey, M. (1993), An Evaluation of the Public Service Employment Program in Hungary, Budapest, *mimeo*.

Góra, M./Lehmann, H. (1995), How Divergent is Regional Labor Market Adjustment in Poland?, in: Scarpetta, S./Wörgötter, A. (eds.), *The Regional Dimension of Unemployment in Transition Economies*, OECD, Paris.

Góra, M. et al. (1996), Labor Market Policies in Poland, in: Boeri, T. et al. (eds.), *Lessons from Labor Market Policies in the Transition Countries*, OECD, Paris, 201-222.

Góra, M./Sztanderska, U. (1996), Evaluation of Labor Market Policies: Supplementary Labor Force Survey Questionnaire, in: Lehmann, H./Wadsworth, J. (eds.), *Labor Markets by Design? Labor Market Policies and Creative Use of Household Surveys in Transition Economies*, Ifo Studies on Eastern Europe and the Economics of Transition, No. 21, Munich, 195-210.

Haskel, J.E./Jackman, R. (1988), Long-term Unemployment and the Effects of the Community Program, *Oxford Bulletin of Economics and Statistics* 50, 379-408.

Jackman, R. (1996), Regional Labor Market Policies in OECD Countries, in: Lehmann, H./Wadsworth, J. (eds.), *Labor Markets by Design? Labor Market Policies and Creative Use of Household Surveys in Transition Economies*, Ifo Studies on Eastern Europe and the Economics of Transition, No. 21, Munich, 112-125.

Layard, R. et al. (1991), *Unemployment, Macroeconomic Performance and the Labor Market*, Oxford University Press.

Lázar, G./Szekely, J. (1994), An Analysis of the Labor Market Position of Those Who Exhausted their Eligibility for Unemployment Benefit, Budapest, *mimeo*.

Lehmann, H. (1992), Labor Market Policies in Poland: Some Critical Remarks in the Light of Western Experience, Warsaw University, *Polish Policy Research Group Discussion Paper* No. 17, Warsaw.

Lehmann, H. (1993), The Effectiveness of the Restart Program and the Enterprise Allowance Scheme, London School of Economics-Center for Economic Performance, *Discussion Paper* No. 139.

Lehmann, H. (1995), Active Labor Market Policies in the OECD and in Selected Transition Countries, *Economic Policy Working Paper* No. 1502, The World Bank, Washington.

Lehmann, H. (1996), Labor Market Flows and the Evaluation of Labor Market Policies in Poland – 1990-92, in: Lehmann, H./Wadsworth, J. (eds.), *Labor Markets by Design? Labor Market Policies and Creative Use of Household Surveys in Transition Economies*, Ifo Studies on Eastern Europe and the Economics of Transition, No. 21, Munich, 46-92.

Marston, S. (1976), Employment Instability and High Unemployment Rates, *Brookings Papers on Economic Activity* 1, 169-219.

Micklewright, J./Nagy, G. (1996), Evaluating Labor Market Policy in Hungary, in: Boeri, T. et al. (eds.), *Lessons from Labor Market Policies in the Transition Countries*, OECD, Paris.

Micklewright, J./Nagy, G. (1999), Living Standards and Incentives in Transition: The Implication of UI Exhaustion in Hungary, *Journal of Public Economics 73(3)*, 297-319.

OECD (1993), *Employment Outlook*, Paris.

OECD (1995), *Employment Outlook*, Paris.

O'Leary, C. (1997), A Net Impact Analysis of Active Labor Programs in Hungary, *Economics of Transitions 5(2)*, 453-484.

Padoa-Schioppa, F. (1991), *Mismatch and Labor Mobility*, Cambridge, Cambridge University Press.

Polish Ministry of Labor and Social Policy, Project on Employment Legislation, Warsaw, *mimeo*.

Puhani, P. A./Steiner V. (1997), The Effectiveness and Efficiency of Active Labor Market Policies in Poland, *Empirica 24(3)*, 209-231.

Puhani, P. A. (1998), What Works? An Evaluation of Active Labor Market Policies in Poland during Tranisition, München.

Schmidt, C.M. (1996), Cohort Sizes and Unemployment: Lessons for Poland, in: Lehmann, H./Wadsworth, J. (eds.), *Labor Markets by Design? Labor Market Policies and Creative Use of Household Surveys in Transition Economies*, Ifo Studies on Eastern Europe and the Economics of Transition, No. 21, Munich, 126-154.

Steiner, V./Kwiatkowski, E. (1995), The Polish Labor Market in Transition, *ZEW Discussion Paper* No. 95-03, Mannheim.

Stern, J. (1988), Methods of Analysis of Public Expenditure Programs with Employment Objectives, *HM Treasury Working Paper* No. 53.

Svejnar, J. et al. (1995), Unemployment in the Czech and Slovak Republics, in: Svejnar J. (ed.), *The Czech Republic and Economic Transition in Eastern Europe*, San Diego, 285-316.

Szemlér, T. (1994), *Arbeitslosigkeit und Arbeitsmarktprogram in Ungarn, Integration, Strukturwandel und konjunkturelle Aussichten in Ost- und Westeuropa*, Ifo Studien zur Ostforschung No. 18, Munich.

Sztanderska, U. (1996), Aktywne polityki rynku pracy w opinii rejonowych urzedów pracy. Wyniki badania ankietowego, in: Bednarski, M. (ed.), *Efektywnosc polityk rynku pracy*.

Terrell, K./Munich, D. (1996), Labor Market Policies in the Czech Republic, in: Boeri, T. et al. (eds.), *Lessons from Labor Market Policies in the Transition Countries*, OECD, Paris.

Toikka, R. (1976), A Markovian Model of Labor Market Decisions by Workers, *American Economic Review* 66 (5), 821-34.

Indices

1. Authors Index

Abel, A. B. 41, 54

Abraham, K. *278; 298*

Arbeitsgemeinschaft zur Förderung der Partnerschaft in der Wirtschaft (AGP) *214*

Akerlof, G. *12; 31; 40; 54; 63; 64; 66; 69; 70; 77; 85; 156; 169; 176; 179; 188; 159; 198*

Albach, H. *110; 129*

Andreß, H.-J. *130*

Arbeitsamt Leipzig *115; 129*

Arbeitsmarktmonitor Ost *20; 21*

Ashenfelter, O. *86; 240; 257; 275; 298*

Atkinson, A. B. *33*

Bannasch, H.-G. *109; 129*

Barro, R. *44; 54; 83; 85*

Bauer, T. *31*

Becker, G. S. *111; 129*

Begg, D. *8; 147; 154; 188; 159; 198*

Behringer, F. *145*

Bell, S. H. *240; 257*

Bellmann, L. *33; 278; 298*

Berney, R.E. *110; 129*

Birch, D. *110; 111; 129*

Bird, E. J. *129; 132; 144*

Björklund, A. *261; 298*

Blaschke, D. *244; 257*

Bodie, Z. *107*

Boeri, T. *129; 264; 277; 279; 294; 298*

Boje, J. *32*

Bolton, R. *149; 159*

Börsch-Supan, A. H. *8; 92; 95; 99; 100; 104; 107*

Bös, D. *132; 144*

Brandt, M. *111; 129*

Brenke, K. *13; 32*

Brezinski, H. *130*

Brinkmann, C. *17; 32*

Brüderl, J. *110; 111; 129*

Büchel, F. *144; 145*

Bühler, C. *110; 129*

Bundesanstalt für Arbeit *13; 15; 16; 17; 22; 162; 176 217; 220; 223; 224; 225; 226; 227; 228; 229; 230; 231; 233; 234; 236; 257; 258*

Bundesministerium für Wirtschaft *109; 129; 258*

Burda, M. C. *35; 39; 50; 54; 62; 67; 68; 69; 70; 79; 83; 84; 85; 86; 87; 153; 156; 159; 293; 294; 298*

Burkhauser, R. *145*

Burtless, G. *258*

Buttler, F. *220; 221; 244; 258*

Calmfors, L. *263; 276; 298*

Card, D. *240; 242; 257; 258; 275; 298*

Carlin, W. *149; 160*

Carter, J. R. *174; 177*

Chadha, B. *53; 54; 84; 86*

Clark, K. *278; 298*

Crafts, N. *149; 160*

Cramer, U. *110; 129*

De La Dehesa, G. *177*

Dehejia, R. *240; 258*

Demougin, D. *202; 214*

Deutsche Bundesbank *168; 177*

DGB *49*

Diewald, M. *130*

DIW *15; 21; 22; 24; 30; 32; 49; 50; 54; 58; 60; 62; 65; 86; 130; 132; 133; 145*

Djajic, S. *53; 54*

Donges, J. *81; 86*

Dornbusch, R. *158; 160*

Dyck, A. *132; 145*

Eckart, W. *110; 130*

Eichler, M. *9; 21*

Emmerich, K. *220; 221; 244; 258*

Erbenova, M. *264; 298*

Farber, H. *69; 86*

Federal Labour Office
 → *Bundesanstalt für Arbeit*

Fink, U. *86; 199; 214*

Fischer, B. *84; 86*

Fitzenberger, B. *21; 32; 237; 249; 258*

Fitzroy, F. *53; 55*

Flassbeck, H. *131; 132; 145*

Flemming, J. *158; 160*

Franz, W. *148; 160; 163; 177; 181; 198*

Freeman, J. *110; 130*

Frey, B. S. *174; 177*

Frey, M. *298*

Fritsch, M. *130*

Funke, M. *35; 37; 50; 53; 54; 55; 62; 67; 68; 69; 70; 83; 84; 85; 86; 153; 159*

German Federal Statistical Office
 → *Statistisches Bundesamt*

Ghaussy, A. *33*

Giersch, H. *63; 86*

Gladisch, D. *27; 32*

Glatzer, W. *145*

Góra, M. *264; 270; 278; 280; 288; 299*

Gorter, C. *31*

Görzig, B. *51; 52; 55*

Gottsleben, V. *17; 32*

Grabka, M. M. *144; 145*

Grossman, S. *207; 214*

Gruhler, W. *20; 32; 111; 130*

Grünert, H. *17; 32*

GSOEP *21; 89; 90; 94; 95; 96; 97; 100; 135; 136; 137; 138; 140; 141; 142; 238; 239; 242; 259*

Hannan, M. T. *110; 130*

Harris, M. *206; 214*

Hart, O. *207; 214*

Haskel, J. E. *276; 278; 299*

Hauser, R. *131; 145*

Hayashi, F. *41; 55*

Heckman, J. J. *240; 258*

Helberger, C. *21; 32; 237; 259*

Hemmer, H. *76; 86*

Herrmann, B. *129*

Hinz, T. *8; 110; 113; 114; 128; 130*

Holland, P. W. *240; 259*

Horn G. A. *131; 132; 145*

Hotz, V. J. *240; 258*

Hübler, O. *21; 32*

Hull, Ch. *130*

Institut für Arbeitsmarkt- und Berufsforschung (IAB) *165; 177; 218; 244; 259*

Irons, M. D. *174; 177*

Jackman, R. *264; 276; 278; 299*

Johnson, C. *107*

Kamien, M. I. *41; 55*

Keil, M. *32*

Kiel Institute of World Economics *32*

Kleinhenz, G. *37; 49; 55; 107; 145*

Klodt, H. *8; 55; 169; 171; 177; 181; 198*

König, H. *33*

Kraus, F. *21; 32; 33*

Kreps, D. *214*

Kwiatkowski, E. *278; 286; 287; 300*

Labor Ministry Budapest *266*

LaLonde, R. J. *237; 240; 259*

Lange, T. *22; 27; 32; 63; 86*

Lawrence, C. *55; 70; 86*

Lawrence, R. Z. *55; 70; 86*

Layard, R. *86; 263; 299*

Lázar, G. *279; 281; 299*

Lazear, E. P. *97; 107*

Lechner, M. *9; 21; 33; 238; 240; 241; 243; 259*

Lehmann, H. *9; 270; 271; 273; 274; 276; 278; 280; 286; 287; 288; 289; 293; 294; 297; 299*

Lehmbruch, G. *111; 130*

Leipzig founder study
→ *Leipziger Gründerstudie*

Leipziger Gründerstudie *112; 114; 115; 116; 117; 118; 119; 120; 121; 122; 124; 126; 127*

Lewis, G. *73; 86*

Link, F. *23; 33*

Lubyova, M. *293; 298*

Lucas, R. E. *44; 55; 83; 86*

Lumbsdaine, R. L. *99; 107*

Lutz, B. *17; 32*
Maaß, C. *30; 33*
Marston, S. *278; 299*
Mayer, C. *149; 159; 160*
Mayer, K. *130*
Meade, J. *209; 214*
Meckl, J. *68; 86*
Meghir, C. *99; 107*
Micklewright, J. *279; 280; 281; 282; 300*
Ministry of Labor and Social Affairs *28*
Moore, R. *97; 107*
Morgenson, G. V. *33*
Munich, D. *271; 292; 293; 300*
Nagel, E. *244; 257*
Nagy, G. *279; 280; 281; 282; 300*
Neu, A. *161; 177*
Neumann, M. J. *148; 160*
Newell, A. *32; 132; 145*
Nijkamp, C. P. *31*
Noack, G. *51; 52; 55*
OECD *261; 267; 300*
Offe, C. *130*
Okun, A. M. *175; 177*
O'Leary, C. *272; 282; 283; 284; 296; 300*
Oppenländer, K. *33; 55*
Padoa-Schioppa, F. *264; 300*
Pagh, G. *22; 27; 32; 63; 86*
Pannenberg, M. *21; 32; 237; 259*

Paqué, K.-H. *8; 63; 73; 78; 87; 163; 172; 177*
Parmentier, K. *177*
Phelps, E. S. *172; 177*
Phillips, B. D. *110; 129*
Pischke, J.-S. *33*
Pohjola, M. *201; 214*
Pohl, R. *32; 50; 55*
Polish Ministry of Labor and Social Policy *269; 273; 300*
Pommerehne, W. W. *174; 177*
Poot, J. *31*
Portes, R. *147; 154; 159; 188; 198*
Porteus, E. *214*
Preisendörfer, P. *111; 114; 129; 130*
Prey, H. *21; 32; 237; 249; 258*
Puhani, P. A. *286; 288; 292; 295; 300*
Purvis, D. *53; 54*
Raviv, A. *206; 214*
Rawls, J. *76; 87*
Reilly, B. *132; 145*
Rendtel, U. *145*
Riphahn, R. T. *3; 86; 106; 107; 159; 177; 198; 214*
Robb, R. *258*
Roland G. *149; 159*
Rosenbaum, P. R. *241; 259*
Rubin, D. B. *241; 259*
Sabathil, M. *129*
Sachverständigenrat *25; 33; 35; 53, 55; 59; 60; 61; 63; 79; 87; 168; 177*

Sala-i-Martin, X. *44; 54; 83; 85*

Sander, B. *24; 33*

Scarpetta, S. *264; 298; 299*

Scheremet, W. *39; 55*

Scheuer, M. *111; 130*

Schmähl, W. *93; 94; 107; 108*

Schmidt, C. M. *287; 300*

Schmidt, K.-D. *8; 13; 32; 33*

Schmidt, P. *106; 107; 108*

Schmieding, H. *169; 178*

Schmitz, K. *76; 86*

Schneider, H. *32; 33; 99; 108*

Schultz, B. *22; 33*

Schwartz, N. L. *41; 55*

Schwarze, J. *8; 129; 133; 134; 144; 145*

Selten, R. *174*

Siebert, B. *158; 160*

Siebert, H. *22; 33; 35; 63; 85; 87; 171; 178; 181; 198*

Sievert, O. *199; 201; 214*

Singer, B. *258*

Sinn H.-W. *22; 33; 35; 37; 49; 53; 55; 63; 87; 148; 160; 169; 178; 202; 214*

Sinn, G. *214; 22; 33; 35; 37; 49; 53; 55; 63; 87*

Smith, J. A. *240; 258*

Snower, D. J. *3; 86; 159; 172; 177; 198; 199; 214*

Sozio-ökonomisches Panel
→ GSOEP

Spinanger, D. *84; 86*

Staat, M. *21; 33*

Stahl, K. *130*

Statistisches Bundesamt *19; 38, 49; 75; 145; 166; 259; 260*

Steiner V. *21; 33*; *278; 286; 287; 288; 292; 295; 300*

Stern, J. *274; 300*

Stiglitz J. *204; 206; 214*

Stock, J. H. *97; 99; 107; 108*

Storey, D. J. *110; 130*

Sueyoshi, G. T. *99; 108*

Suhr, W. *84; 87*

Sullivan, D. *242; 258*

Summers, L. H. *278; 298*

Svejnar, J. *270; 294; 300*

Szekely, J. *279; 281; 299*

Szemlér, T. *272; 279; 281; 300*

Sztanderska, U. *264; 286; 299; 300*

Terrell, K. *271; 292; 293; 300*

Thimann, C. *33*

Thomson, D. *107*

Timmermann, D. *32*

Tisch, H. *37*

Toikka, R *278; 300*

Tomann, H. *201; 214*

Tooze, M. J. *39; 55*

Trabert, L. *27; 32*

Treuhandanstalt *16; 17; 36; 39; 40*

v. Einem, E. *130*

van der Ploeg, R. *50; 55*

Vives, X. *159*

Vodopivec, M. *278; 298*

Vogler-Ludwig, K. *22; 33; 49; 55*

Wadsworth, J. *299*

Wagner G. G. *8; 14; 110; 129; 130; 131; 135; 144; 145; 238; 260*

Wahba, S. *240; 258*

Weiss, A. *204; 206; 214*

Weitzman, M. *200; 214*

Welfens, P. *160*

Whitehouse, E. *99; 107*

Wiedemann, E. *32*

Wise, D. A. *97; 99; 107; 108*

Wörgötter, A. *298; 299*

Wyplosz, C. *67; 79; 85; 87; 156; 160*

Ziegler, R. *8; 110; 111; 114; 129; 130*

Zimmermann, K. F. *3; 22; 31; 33; 86; 159; 177; 198; 214*

2. Subject Index

Active labor market policies *12; 20-23; 167; 171f.; 215ff.; 250; 261f.; 275; 282; 288*

Allocation *80; 111; 174; 201; 207; 210*

Arbeitsbeschaffungsmaßnahmen *16; 273*

Arbeitsförderungsgesetz *218; 252*

Asymmetric information *200; 201ff.; 204; 208f.*

Bargaining *23f.; 31; 35ff.; 48ff.; 53f.; 57; 62; 75-71; 74; 135; 158; 182-185; 189; 192f.; 197; 201; 121; 263*

Bundesanstalt für Arbeit *162; 177; 216ff.; 252*

Business cycle *15; 162ff.; 166*

Capital

– Capital markets *150; 155f.; 169; 199; 201ff.; 209*

– Capital stock *11f.; 25f.; 29; 40; 42f.; 46; 48; 63; 70; 79f.; 82; 122; 144; 151; 181; 199; 203*

Collective agreements *23; 49; 60; 62; 66; 71; 77*

Command economy *11f.; 30; 57*

Control group *125; 240; 242; 245; 247f.; 250; 275; 283*

Costs *12; 16; 24; 29; 31; 36-42; 51ff.; 62f.; 65f.; 79f.; 83; 147; 150-159; 165; 170; 172; 187-191; 194-197; 204ff.; 210ff.; 221f.; 228f.; 252; 261; 271; 285; 290; 294*

Czech Republic *85; 148; 150; 261; 263; 265; 267-270; 275; 293ff.; 297*

Earnings *61f.; 64; 73; 75; 93; 131; 133; 135-138; 143; 149; 161; 167f.; 173; 182; 202f.; 205; 215; 221; 228; 241f.; 245f.; 245f.; 248-251; 275; 282f.*

Economic activity *11; 80; 165; 274*

Economic integration *15; 29f.; 30; 53*

Efficiency *36; 47; 80f.; 133; 143; 152; 161; 173-176; 188; 199ff.; 205; 252; 296f.*

Europe *79; 131; 149; 154; 199; 201ff.; 210ff.; 229; 261f.*

Evaluation *21; 114; 154; 215f.; 237; 240ff.; 244-247; 251; 262; 275; 279; 282; 284; 286; 288; 290; 292; 295; 297*

Exports *11; 140; 154; 180; 197*

Fiscal burden *169; 173*

Gross domestic product (GDP) *11; 181; 216f.; 266ff.*

Human capital *36; 44-48; 50; 53; 57; 63; 73; 78f.; 98; 100; 104; 111; 113; 123f.; 128; 131-134; 137; 144; 150; 155f.; 167; 201; 221; 237; 262; 263f.; 270; 274; 284; 290*

Hungary *148; 179; 261; 265; 268; 270; 275; 279; 282; 296f.*

Investment wages *199-205; 207-213*

Investments *35-48; 50; 53; 70f.; 74; 76ff.; 80; 83; 111; 121; 128; 132f.;*

156; 151-156; 158; 168-171; 180; 197; 199-213; 237; 251; 261; 264

Job creation *16f.; 20ff.; 109; 111; 113f.; 116; 162; 164; 190; 266ff.*

Labor

– Labor demand *23; 36; 39; 41; 44; 46ff.; 53; 68ff.; 83; 162-165; 170; 184; 222; 296*

– Labor supply *15; 26f.; 29; 59; 67f.; 106f.; 111; 163; 165; 187; 195; 263; 296*

Market failure *147; 149-154; 158f.; 159; 204*

Matching *242; 277f.; 292ff.*

Migration *14f.; 23; 37; 39f.; 65; 67f.; 78-82; 85; 148; 151f.; 157ff.; 182; 217*

Misallocation *131; 133f.; 138; 181; 200*

Mismatch *163ff.; 166; 220; 244; 246; 264f.*

Modernization *12; 19; 29; 31; 144; 180*

Pension system *90-93; 96f.; 99; 105f.*

Poland *148; 179; 261f.; 265; 268ff.; 274f.; 286; 288ff.; 291; 293; 296f.*

Privatization *11; 16; 109ff.; 149; 180f.; 196; 213*

Production function *40; 169f.*

Productivity *11f.; 24ff.; 29; 44; 47; 50; 63f.; 67; 73; 78-83; 111; 116; 123; 128; 131f.; 148; 150-155; 159; 166f.; 169; 180; 181f.; 185; 216; 220; 263; 275*

Profit-sharing *179; 191; 196f.; 200f.*

Public

– Public expenditure *265ff.; 268*

– Public sector *18; 91; 143; 215; 251; 264*

– Public work *17; 21; 264; 271; 273; 281; 287f.; 290ff.; 296*

Qualification

– Qualification programs *20ff.*

– Qualification vouchers *171f.*

Retirement *15; 39; 58f.; 89-107; 163; 180; 237; 239; 266; 281*

Retraining *16; 21f.; 27; 36; 39; 47; 84; 132; 144; 180; 220; 224; 227; 230-233; 236; 239; 251f.; 256; 263ff.; 272ff.; 282ff.; 290f.; 293; 296*

Risk aversion *209f.*

Social acceptance *162; 173; 175f.*

Structural adjustment *35; 54; 165; 172*

Structural changes *35f.; 39f.; 50; 53; 57; 78f.; 82; 85; 162; 164; 167; 176; 222; 234*

Subsidies

– Government subsidies *139; 149; 191; 194; 213*

– Wage subsidies *17; 53; 83; 147; 154-159; 161; 172; 179; 180; 186ff.; 190f.; 195ff.; 213; 246; 220; 264; 274; 287ff.; 290; 292*

Subsidization

– Wage subsidization *161; 167-172; 176*

Training *14; 16f.; 20f.; 23; 31; 44; 47; 83f.; 100ff.; 104; 122; 124; 134; 136; 139; 163; 165; 171; 173; 180;*

183; 190f.; 215-256; 262-277; 280f.; 286-296

Transformation *11; 13; 15; 17; 19f.; 23; 25ff.; 29ff.; 123;125; 128; 131; 137; 144; 154f.; 162f.; 168f.; 171; 175; 176; 179; 197; 199; 283*

Transition economies *261f.; 264f.; 269; 275; 277-281; 295ff.*

Treuhandanstalt *16; 36; 39f.; 69; 132; 149f.; 152; 155; 158; 180; 213*

Unemployment *11-18; 20; 22f.; 25; 27ff.; 31; 35f.; 39; 44; 47-50; 53; 57ff.; 63; 65; 67f.; 71f.; 78; 82ff.; 90f.; 93f.; 100; 104; 106; 115; 123f.; 148ff.; 155; 157; 161-168; 172f.; 176; 181f.; 184f.; 187; 199; 204; 210ff.; 215; 217f.; 221f.; 225f.; 228f.; 232f.; 235f.; 244-247; 249; 251-255; 261; 263-273; 275-281; 284; 286f.; 289f.; 292-296*

Unions *11f.; 23ff.; 28; 31; 35-39; 44; 46-49; 53; 55; 62; 65f.; 68-74; 76f.; 148f.; 152; 158; 176; 181f.; 187; 212*

Unit labor costs *39; 50; 51ff.*

Wages

– Wages *17; 23-26; 29; 47f.; 35-44; 47-54; 61ff.; 65ff.; 69-73; 81;84; 131; 134; 143f.; 148-153; 156ff.; 166f.; 169f.; 170; 172; 182ff.; 188; 196f.; 216; 241; 263; 274f.;*

– Wage explosion *35ff.; 40; 48; 53*

– Wage rigidity *57*

Work creation *13; 17; 21; 58; 59; 60*

Working hours *16, 24, 28f., 216*